HISTORY OF THE ARTS OF DESIGN

End papers: George Town and Federal City, or City of Washington, drawn by G. Beck, engraved by T. Cartwright.

Robert Gilmor, Jr. by Thomas Sully.

HISTORY

OF THE RISE AND PROGRESS OF

THE ARTS OF DESIGN

IN THE UNITED STATES

BY

WILLIAM DUNLAP

Introduction by William P. Campbell

Assistant Chief Curator, National Gallery of Art

Newly edited by Alexander Wyckoff
incorporating the notes and additions
compiled by
Frank W. Bayley and Charles Goodspeed

Vol. II

Benjamin Blom

First published New York, 1834

Reissued in a revised and enlarged edition, edited by
Frank W. Bayley and Charles E. Goodspeed, Boston, 1918

New edition, revised, enlarged and
edited by Alexander Wyckoff
with preface by William P. Campbell
Published 1965 by Benjamin Blom, Inc., N.Y.C. 10452

Printed in U.S.A. by
NOBLE OFFSET PRINTERS, INC.
NEW YORK 3, N. Y.

CONTENTS OF VOLUME II

Page

CHAPTER I

Architecture — L'Enfant 1

CHAPTER II

John Trumbull 13

CHAPTER III

Trumbull (*Continued*) 28

CHAPTER IV

Trumbull (*Continued*) 41

CHAPTER V

Trumbull (*Concluded*) 55

CHAPTER VI

Winstanley — S. King —Archibald Robertson— Ceracchi —
Trott — Paul 77

CHAPTER VII

The School for the Fine Arts — The Columbianum — The
New York Academy of the Fine Arts — Pennsylvania
Academy of Fine Arts — Society of Artists of the United
States 104

CHAPTER VIII

Alexander Robertson — Cantir — Belzons — James Earl —
Roberts — Edward Trenchard — Walter Robertson —
Field — Wertmüller — William Birch — Vallance —
Thackara — Lawson — Jennings 112

CHAPTER IX   *Page*
Anderson — History of Wood Engraving   126

CHAPTER X
Malbone — Tiebout   137

CHAPTER XI
John Vanderlyn   157

CHAPTER XII
Barralet — Tisdale — Clark — Fox — Tanner — Martin —
Reed — Marten — Groomrich — Fairman   .   .   .   170

CHAPTER XIII
Rembrandt Peale — Sargent — Woolley — Weaver — Holland — Pigalle — Edwin — Sharples   180

CHAPTER XIV
John Wesley Jarvis   208

CHAPTER XV
Wood — B. H. Latrobe — Sully   229

CHAPTER XVI
Sully (*Continued*)   252

CHAPTER XVII
Sully (*Concluded*) — House   270

CHAPTER XVIII
Simond — Maras — Gallagher — Miles — Murray — Raphael
West — Eckstein — Guy — Tuthill — Fraser — Stewart
— Hutchins   283

CHAPTER XIX
Washington Allston   296

CONTENTS OF VOLUME II

CHAPTER XX

Page

Allston (*Continued*) 312

CHAPTER XXI

Allston (*Concluded*) 324

CHAPTER XXII

Alexander Wilson 336

CHAPTER XXIII

Paradise — Waldo — Catton — [Kearny — Frothingham —
Dickinson — Peter Maverick 354

CHAPTER XXIV

Cogdell — Hovey — Fürst — Mills 371

CHAPTER XXV

Beck — Dearborn — Bourdon — West — Leney — Otis —
Mason — Eicholtz — Metcalf — Crawley —Thompson —
Krimmel — Tilyard 382

Appendix 398

Postliminy 404

HISTORY OF THE RISE AND PROGRESS OF THE ARTS OF DESIGN IN THE UNITED STATES

CHAPTER I.

ARCHITECTURE — L'ENFANT.

A HISTORY of architecture in a work like this must necessarily be exceedingly brief, my object being the progress of the art in our own country; but a rapid view of its rise and progress in other countries, until Europeans colonized America, appears desirable, as an introduction to what I can record comformably to my general plan.

To Mr. A. J. Davis, and to the splendid library of Mr. J. Town,[1] I am indebted for information and opportunities which might have led to more valuable results.

I adopt the opinion which gives the highest antiquity to the architecture of Egypt. That country of wonders furnished the leading principles of that style which has been diffused throughout the world, and is now acknowledged the standard of the art — *the three orders of Greece.*

The Egyptian style is colossal. It is simple, solid, and gigantically sublime. In its decorations the vegetable products of their country were imitated with truth and taste. The early people of Egypt appear to have been assiduous cultivators of science and art. The wonders of their temples and other buildings have been, until of late, unknown; and the work of discovery begun by Pocock and Norden, continued by the French *savants*, and yet in progress, fills the mind with astonishment and ardent anticipation.

The excavated temples and other stupendous monuments of Indian and Persian architecture, are immediately derived from Egypt. The conquests of Osiris and Sesostris carried the arts and religion of Egypt to Hindoostan. The ruins of

1

1   For J. Town read I. Town

Persepolis may be traced to the same original. In all, the huge block, the heavy column, the colossal statue, the enormous animals supporting immense piles of stone, the extent of the buildings, and their suitableness to resist time, mark the genius of the same people. Everywhere are seen hieroglyphics, zodiacs, celestial planispheres, sphynxes, lions, and other animals, with beautifully executed bas-reliefs, all replete with knowledge, which time has locked up from modern research, but with a key that will be discovered, and reward the phil-osophers of a day close at hand. We may hope that what has for ages been viewed with stupid wonder by the barbarian, or with delight by the man of taste, as beautiful decoration, will unfold hereafter sublimer views of the attributes of the Creator of the universe, than have generally been supposed to have existed among that great people, and precepts for the govern-ment of his creatures, mingled with the records of a nation, from which the successive generations of mankind have received the genius of science, yet slowly unfolding.

To Denon, Belzoni, and Champollion, we are indebted for much of what we know of the pyramids, the obelisks, the temples, statues, bas-reliefs, and hieroglyphics of Egypt. I proceed to trace the elegance and proportions of Grecian architecture to their originals in the country of the Pharaohs.

The Egyptian column, always heavy, sometimes repre-sented the trunk of a tree — sometimes bundles of reeds — or the whole plant of the papyrus — bound together at different distances, and ornamented at the base with palm leaves. Hence the flutings and the astragals of the Greeks. Both capitals and shafts of the Grecian columns may be traced to the Egyptians. The Ionic *volute* is to be seen. The peristyles supported by human figures, as in the Parian and Persian peristyles of the Athenians, are of Egyptian invention, as well as many other ornamental or fundamental portions of the art.

But *that* susceptibility to the beauty of form which charac-terized ancient Greece, gave elegance, simplicity and propor-tion to its architecture which more than compensate for the enormous masses of the Egyptian, and by its sculpture added decorations, which are the wonder of mankind to this day. Greece borrowed science and art from Egypt, and brought the latter to a state of perfection from which men have only wandered to return with renewed admiration.

It must be borne in mind, that it is principally to the Asiatic Greeks, or the colonies from *Grecia* proper, that we owe the arts borrowed from Egypt, and the improvement on them. The names of Doric and Ionian show from whence these improvements in architecture came, and the improvements borrowed by the colonists from their African neighbors, stimulated the artists of the mother country, until, under Pericles and Phidias, the acme of Grecian skill and architectural greatness was established.

The Doric, Ionic, and Corinthian are acknowledged the universal standard of taste in the art.

P

The Doric is the oldest of the three great orders, and was invented by the Asiatic Dorians, borrowing from Egypt in part. Prior to the days of Alexander, it prevailed throughout Greece. Its characteristics are the short thick column, fluted, as seen in the ruins of Pæstum and elsewhere. The capital is composed of the abacus, or square flat slab; and the ovolo, the lower member, resting on the capital. The whole column is five and a half or six modules in height; the capital being half a module. The entablature is one-fourth of the whole column in height, and divided into twenty-four parts; six are given to the cornice, eight to the frieze, and ten to the architrave. The cornice is the most simple of the three orders, a thick heavy corona, under which are placed carved mutules, in imitation of roofing rafters.

The spiral volute particularly distinguishes the Ionic order, the invention of the Ionians of Asia Minor. This ornament is borrowed from Egypt. The Ionic is a medium between the massy Doric and the slender Corinthian. The order is distinguished by a lighter and more ornamental entablature than the Doric, a more slender column with the spiral volute, the abacus of the capital is scooped, the whole is supported by an echinus, cut into eggs, and bordered by a beaded astragal.

The column of this order has a base supported on a square plinth.

The proportions of the Ionic column are, a height of eight modules, of which the base occupies thirty lines; the capital twenty, and the shaft seven and a half modules. The best specimens of the Ionic are the temples of Minerva Polias, at Priene and Athens, and of Jupiter Erectheus at Athens.

The Corinthian order, more ornamented and in greater favor with the Roman conquerors of Greece, did not supersede the Ionic in Grecian estimation. Its bell-shaped capital is borrowed from Egypt, and decorated with the leaves of the acanthus. The ruins of Balbec and Palmyra, remains of Roman grandeur, give specimens of the Corinthian temple. The column is nine and three-quarter modules, of which the capital occupies one, the base twenty lines, and the shaft eight modules. The entablature is one-fifth of the height of the whole column, and is divided into an architrave of thirty-six lines, a frieze of thirty-three lines, and a cornice of thirty-nine.

When two or three orders are employed in one edifice, the heaviest should form the base, and the lighter surmount it.

Another style of architecture adopted by the Greeks is composed of male and female figures, occupying the place of columns, and made to support a heavy Doric entablature. The male figures represent Persians, and commemorate conquests over them, and the female Careans — the latter are called Caryatides. The invention is founded on a barbarous system of moral feeling, and we are happy to say that even among the ancients it did not much prevail. Specimens are found in the Pandroseam at Athens. The artists of modern Italy, in many instances, adopted them.

The Grecian temples and theatres gave scope for the exercise of the exalted taste displayed by the nation in architecture and sculpture. I have said enough to lead the reader on for our purpose, and I hope enough to stimulate him to the study of those who will satisfy the thirst I wish to create.

The Roman architecture is built on that of Etruria, and

finished after the models of the Greek. The arch, unknown to the Egyptians, may have originated with the Etruscans, but the Romans brought it to perfection, and bestowed on architecture an inestimable gift.

In other respects Roman architecture only combined the Grecian orders with variations, which are now justly rejected. Rome, however, invented what are called the Tuscan and Composite orders. The first is the simplest of all the orders, and most solid. Its column is only five modules in height — the shaft is four: the base thirty lines, and the capital the same. This order may support even the Doric.

The great architectural remains of the Romans, peculiarly their own, are the cloacæ, circuses, acqueducts, columns, amphitheatres, and baths.

With the overthrow of the Roman empire, architecture, as a fine art, vanished; and it is only in more extensive works that its decline and revival can be recorded. The Goths robbed the beautiful specimens of art to form castles and strongholds — the Lombards followed, even more rude than their predecessors — Christianity raised churches, and, even in the dark ages, infused some life into architectural science. Then followed the Arabian, Saracenic, and Moorish architecture. And the Arabians, imbibing science and taste from the nations they subdued, produced a fanciful style of architecture, combined with great skill, taste, and science, from the models of antiquity; and kept distinct from the temples of Pagan or Christian, equally abominations in their eyes. They adopted the Roman arch. They invented the pointed arch, and the sacred or horseshoe arch. The Turks are the only Mohammedans who have adopted Christian architecture, which is attributable to their conquest of Constantinople.

Specimens of Mohammedan architecture are to be seen in many parts of the world, but the most worthy of admiration are the mosques of Benares and Lucknow.

For the Norman architecture we must refer to others; only remarking that they adopted the cross for the form of their churches, and the tower or steeple as an ornament: but the

Gothic, into which it passed in the eleventh and twelfth centuries, as it is still imitated, we must pause upon.

The Gothic style differs from all others. By whom invented is yet in dispute. A plausible conjecture is, that it arose in Spain during the struggles of the Goths and Moors. In the twelfth century it was adopted in France. The doors, like the Norman, were deeply recessed, and three were adopted as typical of the Trinity. The windows were narrow, and terminated with the sharp arch — columns were clustered pillars encircled with fasces — the capitals formed of flowers or delicate foliage — projecting buttresses and the spire were introduced. — Little turrets and parapets were adopted from the castles.

By degrees this style improved in magnificence, with the rule of the clergy. The doors were enlarged, and surmounted with triangular pediments, and ornamented with sculptures. The windows were enlarged and ornamented with pillars, whose tracery imitated the most beautiful flowers. The columns became more delicate and elevated. The crocket or *crochet* was introduced at the angles of spires, tabernacles, canopies, and turrets. Buttresses were made more projecting and ornamented with tablets and niches. The 14th century increased this gorgeous style, and statues evince the improvement of sculpture. The vaulting of the naves and aisles became more complex and rich in ornament. The specimens of this best style are the Church of St. Owen, that of St. Sepulchre, and St. Stephen at Rouen, Paris and Caen.

To this succeeded the florid style, and this is the period of decline. This style, in the 15th century, degenerated into false taste and fantastic refinement. By degrees every species of architecture was combined with the *Gothic*, and finally the Gothic gave way to a pure taste in the revival of the antique or Grecian style. As in sculpture so in architecture, the Greeks are our models and our masters.

We have not at all times (when speaking of Greece) been sensible of the obligations which Greece proper owed other colonies. Not only the two most perfect orders of architecture, the Doric and Ionic, were invented by the colonists, but the history of Herodotus, and the poems of Homer, were bestowed by the colonies on the mother country and the world.

English writers tell us that in the land of our forefathers architecture has declined since the days of Inigo Jones and Sir Christopher Wren, and they complain of the want of invention and taste, and even common sense in their late architects. They complain of abortive attempts at Roman, Grecian and Gothic architecture — of ornaments so misapplied as to become ludicrous, and of monuments which are only monuments of absurdity.

Let us now come home, hoping that our brief sketch may elucidate the rise and progress of this inestimable art in our own country. Public architecture seems principally connected with our subject, but the effect of domestic architecture upon the moral feelings and character of mankind, renders it a subject not to be disregarded by us. This is beautifully illustrated by T. Dwight, D.D., president of Yale College, in the 2d volume of his travels through the eastern and middle States.

The learned and amiable president has enforced the utility of the fine arts, and shown how intimately utility and the most refined and ennobling pleasure are connected. Roscoe has beautifully said, "Utility and pleasure are bound together in an indissoluble chain. And what the Author of nature has joined let no man put asunder." These reflections are applicable to other fine arts as well as architecture. Dugald Stewart has said, "A man of benevolence, whose mind is tinctured with philosophy, will view all the different improvements in arts, in commerce, and in science, as co-operating to promote the union, the happiness, and the virtue of mankind."

Before speaking of such architects as have imprinted their names on our public works, in hopes of a *short-lived immortality*, I will republish a "few remarks respecting the city of Washington, the capitol, and those who have contributed, by their talents, wealth, or industry, to raise" the metropolis of the United States.

"The design for the capitol was made by Dr. Thornton,

who received the premium for the same. He was a scholar and a gentleman — full of talent and eccentricity — a Quaker by profession, a painter, a poet, and a horse racer — well acquainted with the mechanic arts — at the head of the patent office, and was one of the original projectors (with John Fitch) of steamboats, and the author of an excellent treatise on language, called 'Cadmus.' He was 'a man of infinite humor' — humane and generous, yet fond of field sports — his company was a complete antidote to dullness.

"The north wing of the capitol was chiefly built by Mr. George Hadfield. He was a man of uncommon talents, and was selected by Colonel Trumbull, in London, under the authority of the commissioners for laying out the city, to superintend the building of the capitol; but, unfortunately, a dispute arose between him and them, which ended in his leaving the public employment, by which we were deprived of his eminent talents. He gave the plan of the public offices, the City Hall, Custis's Mansion, Commodore Porter's, Gadsby's Hotel (when Weightman's buildings), Fuller's Hotel, the United States Bank, Van Ness' Mausoleum, etc. He died 1826.

"Mr. Latrobe built the south wing, and gave the final plan for finishing the capitol. He also was a man of brilliant talents. He died some years ago in New Orleans. Mr. Charles Bulfinch erected the rotunda, improved the design of the eastern front, and finished the building.

"Mr. G. Blagden was the chief builder — a worthy man and an excellent workman. He was killed three or four years ago by the falling in of some earth at the capitol.

"Mr. Lenthall, the clerk of the works, was killed by the falling of an arch over the room of the Supreme Court some years before Mr. B.

"Mr. Lenox was the chief carpenter, and the late Mr. Andre the chief sculptor. They were both distinguished men, and the public spirit of the former (lately deceased) has contributed much to the embellishment of the city by good buildings.

"The trees and shrubs around the capitol, and other public places, were chiefly planted by our friend, Mr. John Foy. In this business he has shown much skill, and his labors have been attended with complete success. In after ages, when the old and the young shall take shelter from the heat under their shade, they will bless the memory of the honest Irishman who planted them.

"The great Chesapeake and Ohio Canal owes its first suggestion to the sagacious mind of Washington; but it received its impetus and beginning, its noble dimensions, and admirable execution, from the enlightened and indefatigable Mercer.

"The *conveying of the pure water* from the source of Tiber Creek to the capitol, in pipes, is the suggestion of the Columbian Institute, a committee of which took the levels for that purpose about four years ago, by which it was ascertained that the source of the water was about thirty feet above the base of the capitol; that sixty-five gallons of pure spring water per minute could be delivered; and recommended, in a petition to Congress, that the water be brought into a reservoir in the capitol square, and afterwards thrown up in a *jet* in the Botanic garden. This work is in a state of forwardness, but the main reservoir, it is feared (as mentioned by Mr. F.), is in too low a situation, and is too near the capitol. By placing it in the east or upper side of the square, all the grounds might have been irrigated, which would have given them a green and beautiful appearance in the heat of summer.

"As to the *enlargement* of the grounds around the capitol, as suggested by Mr. F. and others, my opposition is founded on preserving the original plan of the city entire — a plan beautifully consistent in all its parts. And a serious question may one day arise, whether the plan of the city can be altered to the injury of private property.

"During the administrations of Presidents Washington and Adams, the plan of the city was laid out, and the capitol, president's house, two of the executive offices, and navy yard were commenced, and carried on to a considerable extent.

"Mr. Jefferson adopted Mr. Latrobe's plan of the hall of representatives and senate chamber, and caused Pennsylvania avenue to be opened and planted with trees. Owing to the

restrictions on commerce and the late war, little was done in
Mr. Madison's administration for the benefit of the city, except
by friendly feelings, etc. In Mr. Monroe's administration two
new executive offices were built, the president's house nearly
finished, the north entrance of the square in which it stands
ornamented with a handsome gateway and iron railing, both
wings of the capitol restored, the center building commenced,
and the capitol nearly completed; the square surrounded with
an iron railing, and trees and shrubs planted.

"During the administration of Mr. J. Q. Adams, the east
front and the rotunda of the capitol were finished, the west
partially altered, a penitentiary erected, the general post office
enlarged, and a new patent office and city post office erected.

"The present aspect and future prospects of the city are
encouraging; and it is hoped that the present administration of
General Jackson will leave further marks of its munificence to
the metropolis."

MAJOR L'ENFANT.[0]

This gentleman was a native of France, and the first I
know of him is his being employed to rebuild, after a design
of his own, the old New York City Hall in Wall Street, front-
ing Broad Street; making therefrom the Federal Hall of that
day. The new building was for the accommodation of Congress; and in the balcony, upon which the senate chamber
opened, the first president of the United States was inaugu-
rated. A ceremony which I witnessed, and which for its simplicity, the persons concerned in it, the effect produced upon
my country and the world, in giving stability to the federal
constitution, by calling George Washington to administer its
blessings, remains on my mind unrivalled by any scene witnessed, through a long life, either in Europe or America.

This building gave way, as perhaps it ought, to utility and
the convenience of the citizen. It projected into Wall Street,
and the foot passage was under the balcony made sacred by
the above-mentioned inauguration. It likewise projected into
Nassau Street. The late custom house was upon a part of the

0   Major L'Enfant died on June 14, 1825.

site of Federal Hall, as Major L'Enfant's building was called; and the great custom house now erecting has likewise its foundation on a small part of the same building.

When Congress removed to Philadelphia, Major L'Enfant accompanied them. Whether any public building in that city was designed by him, I know not; but many will remember the enormous house begun by him for Robert Morris, the great financier of the Revolution, the foundation of which exhausted a fortune, and which, being discontinued, is now the site of a large square, or block of elegant houses, accommodating numerous families of wealthy citizens.

The name of L'Enfant is not only associated with the inauguration of our first president, but with a permanent monument to his name in the city of Washington. It is well known that Washington himself fixed upon the site of this city as the seat of government of the United States, and Major L'Enfant had the honor of designing the plan.

I republish from an anonymous writer the following: —

"When the present generation shall have passed away, and mixed with those beyond the flood; when party strife shall have ceased and be forgotten, it is to be hoped that the future historian of our city will do justice to the memory of *all* those who have struggled through so many difficulties to make what was lately a morass and forest, the abode of reptiles, wild beasts, and savages, a suitable habitation for legislators, ambassadors, presidents, ministers, and strangers of distinction. In that day, when *our* eyes shall be closed, and others shall look with delight on the majestic Potomac's placid stream, covered with the riches of the east and the west, the beautiful surrounding heights (now covered with woods) studded with elegant villas; the grand canal pouring into the city the produce of the west; when all private jealousies shall have entirely ceased, and the character of every man who has contributed to the rise and progress of our city shall be estimated by the good he has done — the names of Washington, John Adams, Jefferson, Madison, Monroe, J. Q. Adams, and Jackson, etc. will be recorded as the great patrons of the city; those of

Carroll, Burns, Young, etc., the liberal donors; Major L'Enfant, for his genius in planning the city; Ellicott, Roberdeau, and the Kings, in laying it out; Thornton, Hadfield, Hallett, Latrobe, and Hoban, for their ingenious and chaste designs; and Blagden, Brown, Lenox, and Andre, for their good execution. To the enlightened efforts of Judge Thompson, of Pennsylvania (now no more), when he was in Congress, we owe the erection of the penitentiary, and the consequent humane code of criminal laws, which was afterward carried through by the profound jurisconsult, the lamented Doddridge, and his liberal coadjutors. To Major Eaton, also, when he was in the Senate, the city is indebted for his steady friendship; and to General Chambers, for his successful exertions in effecting various valuable appropriations for its benefit. There are others of both houses of Congress who might be mentioned with gratitude; and among the patriots who have contributed to the useful institutions of the city, may be ranked a number now living, of our own citizens, whose names may hereafter be recorded as its benefactors.

"The plan of the city was made by Major L'Enfant, a French officer of great talents and of singular habits; who was too proud to receive such a compensation for his services as his friends and President Monroe thought just (because less than what he claimed), yet accepted an eleemosynary support from Mr. Digges and others, till his death. The site of the capitol, as well as that of the city, was selected by General Washington himself."

Major L'Enfant was of ordinary appearance, except that he had an abstracted manner and carriage in public. It appears that he had the irritability belonging to ambition, but which is falsely made appropriate to genius; and that he thought himself wronged. That he died poor is too certain.

CHAPTER II.

JOHN TRUMBULL.

IT will be seen, by the following pages, that this gentleman made his first effort at historical composition in the year 1774, and at the age of eighteen. But as I take the time of each artist's *professional* exertions, *in this country,* as the period for introducing his biography in my work, I must date that of Mr. Trumbull from 1789, the time at which he returned from his second visit to Europe, and appeared professionally in America. This painter was emphatically well born; and we shall see that he reaped, as is generally the case, through life, the advantages resulting from the accident.

The many biographical sketches which have been given to the world of Mr. Trumbull afford me ample materials for my work, when combined with my own personal knowledge and the printed documents published with his name as author. — But I shall principally rely upon a narrative communicated by Mr. Trumbull to Mr. James Herring, secretary of the American Academy of Fine Arts, of which Mr. Trumbull is president, for the purpose of publication. This narrative I shall accompany with such remarks as may be suggested by it, and facts within my own knowledge.

The narrative says of the painter's ancestors: — "Two brothers first settled in Massachusetts about 1630. One or both of them removed to what is now Enfield, Connecticut. John Trumbull (the subject of the narrative) was born in Lebanon, Connecticut, on the 6th of June, 1756.[0] He was the son of Jonathan Trumbull, first governor of the *State* of Connecticut of that name." I presume this alludes to the painter's brother Jonathan, who was afterwards governor of the State: his father was first governor of Connecticut as an independent State, and had the additional honor of guiding her through the storms of the Revolution.

13

0   Trumbull died on November 10, 1843.

The narrative proceeds: — "His mother's name was Faith Robinson, the fifth in descent from the famous John Robinson, often called the father of the Pilgrims, who died in Holland, but whose son came into this country in the spring of 1621. The painter's ancestors resided in the county of Springfield, Massachusetts, until 1690, when his grandfather removed to Lebanon. The little boy had a feeble infancy, but recovered when about three years old."

In the National Portrait Gallery Mr. Herring says, "The carelessness or ignorance of the family physician had nearly consigned our infant genius to a life of idiocy or an early grave. After being afflicted with convulsions nine months, it was discovered that the bones of his skull had been allowed to remain lapped over each other from his birth: but by skilful applications and maternal care they were adjusted; and, as we have heard him express it with filial veneration, 'he owed his life a second time to his mother.'

"At Lebanon he went to school to Nathan Tisdale, who kept one of the best schools of that or any other period, and whose reputation brought to his school, youth from the southern colonies and from the West Indies. He received, under the tuition of this gentleman, an excellent education, and entered the junior class at Harvard in January, 1771 or 2, and graduated in 1773, at the age of seventeen. This early entrance at college was, as he considers, one of the misfortunes of his life; he found himself a better scholar than those with whom he was associated, and he became idle; but, by way of amusement, he frequently visited a French family in the neighborhood which had been banished from Acadie, a respectable family in humble life, from whom he obtained a sufficient knowledge of the French language to read and write it. He ransacked the college library for books on the arts: among others he found Brook Taylor's 'Jesuit's Perspective Made Easy.' This work he studied thoroughly, and copied all the diagrams: he also copied a picture which the college possessed of an eruption of

Mount Vesuvius, painted by some Italian; and copied a copy of Van Dyck, the head of Cardinal Bentivoglio, and Nicholas Coypel's 'Rebecca at the Well.' — He copied them in oil. He got his colors from a house painter."

The advantages flowing from being well born gave to young Trumbull one of the best educations the country could furnish. These advantages are no trifles, however they may be sneered at by those who become leaders in the world's affairs by their own energies, unassisted by wealth or ancestry. In the year 1773, and at the early age of seventeen, he had graduated at college, and had received instruction from the works of Smibert and Copley in that career he wished to pursue. The head of Cardinal Bentivoglio, here mentioned, is the same which Allston says first gave him an idea of coloring. The amanuensis proceeds: —

"He got, before he went to college, a book called the ' Handmaid to the Arts.' He had somewhere picked up the title page, and requested his brother-in-law to send to London for the book. Copley was then in Boston, and young Trumbull's first visit to that distinguished artist happened to be made at a time when he was entertaining his friends, shortly after his marriage. He was dressed on the occasion in a suit of crimson velvet and gold buttons; and the elegance of his style and his high repute, impressed the future artist with grand ideas of the life of a painter."

The works of Smibert, Blackburn and Copley, at Boston, so immediately under the eye of the young man, doubtless strengthened his desire to become a painter; and on his return to Lebanon he made his first attempt at composition. — The narrative proceeds thus: —

"After leaving college he painted the Battle of Cannæ, which shows the bent of his mind, being particularly struck with the character of Paulus Emilius. This picture is now at Yale College. He painted several other pictures; among them one of Brutus condemning his sons. What has become of that is unknown. Very soon after, all other subjects were absorbed in the stirring incidents of the times.

"His father wished him to be a clergyman; he did not like it — his object was to be a painter. He hoped, that by being active in the political commotion of the time he should get clear of being a clergyman. He obtained a book on military tactics; he was made an adjutant of militia before he had ever seen a regimental line formed; and a few days before the review was to take place, the battle of Lexington took place; and his mock adjutancy became a real one of the first Connecticut regiment which was stationed at Roxbury, under General Spencer."

Boston and its environs had become the seat of warfare, and the good old Governor Jonathan Trumbull was not backward in forwarding troops to the scene of conflict, in support of his country's rights. Thus we see that the young painter, glad to escape from the threatened prospect of a pulpit, at the age of nineteen was enrolled as an adjutant, and marched to join the undisciplined forces which were assembling round the headquarters of General Gage.

On the 17th of June, 1775, was fought the memorable battle of Breed's Hill (commonly called Bunker's Hill), at which time the young adjutant was stationed with his regiment at Roxbury. In the catalogue of his paintings, which he published in 1831, after describing his beautiful small picture called "The Battle of Bunker's Hill," he says, "The artist was on that day, adjutant of the first regiment of the Connecticut troops, stationed at Roxbury, and saw the action from that point." This he repeats in 1832 in the catalogue written for Yale College, where the picture is deposited.

A foreigner, or a person not intimately acquainted with the topography of the town of Boston, and the neighboring villages, might suppose that the painter meant to say, that he saw the battle he shows us in his admirable picture. This he could not mean. Roxbury is to the south of Boston, and the scene of action on the north. From Roxbury to Breed's Hill is three, or perhaps four miles; the town of Boston (the tri-mountain town), with its three hills, then towering undiminished, is midway between. Boston Neck is on the south, and part of the waters of the bay on the north of the elevated ground on which the town stands. The British ships of war added the smoke of their guns to that of the combatants, and of the burning village of Charlestown. And all these intervened between the painter and the battle. The inhabitants of the *north* side of Boston might see the landing of the British troops, and some of the movements on the hill, but a person at Roxbury, or at any point south of Boston Neck, could only know that a battle was being fought, by the noise of guns, and the clouds of smoke proceeding from the combatants, the ships, the floating batteries, and the conflagration of Charlestown.

In July, General Washington arrived at Cambridge, and took command of the troops which were beleaguering Boston. Mr. Herring thus continues his narrative as dictated by Mr. Trumbull: —

"There" (that is with the army), "his drawing became first of use to him. General Washington was desirous to obtain a draft of the enemy's works, and hearing that Trumbull could draw, he was requested to draw a plan of their works, but before he had proceeded far, a deserter came — the man could draw a little himself, and he completed a rude plan which confirmed Trumbull so far as he had gone, but rendered another unnecessary (whose information assisted him to complete the plan to the satisfaction of the commander-in-chief, and probably led to his appointment of aid to him) — but it showed the correctness of his drawing — he had gone near enough to count every gun and ascertain their situation exactly."

Previously to having seen this (rather confused) account of the immediate causes which transferred the young adjutant to the family of the general, we had supposed that it was a compliment paid by Washington, to Governor Trumbull, but it seems not.

"In August 1775," continues the narrative, "he was appointed aid to the commander-in-chief, and after serving in that capacity some two or three months, he was appointed major of brigade, and in that situation he became more particularly known to the Adjutant-General Gates, whose observation of the accuracy of the returns rendered by Trumbull, induced him the year following to offer him the office of adjutant-general of the Northern Department under his command, and which he accepted." *

It might have been supposed that the amanuensis misunderstood Mr. Trumbull as to the appointment of adjutant-general, *only* that Mr. Trumbull, in a letter published January 7th, 1830, in the New York *American*, addressed to the Hon. M. Wilde, says the same thing in the following words: "In July 1776, I was appointed adjutant-general of the Northern Department with the rank of colonel, under the command of General Gates." Now, General Schuyler was the commander of the Northern Department until August 1777, which was four months after Mr. Trumbull had resigned his commission of deputy-adjutant-general, as we shall see hereafter, and retired from military life.†

The narrative proceeds thus: "He then went with the army to New York, stopping a day or two with his father, which was the only leave of absence he had while in the service. Left New York on the 20th of June 1776, with General Gates, at which date his rank of colonel and adjutant-general was presumed to have commenced. He was ten days getting to

* Gates was appointed a major-general in May 1776, and in June following, to the command of the *army in Canada.* He never was appointed to command the army of the north. For the aids of the commander-in-chief at this time, see Washington's letters.

† For the time of Mr. Trumbull's resignation, and at which Congress accepted his commission of deputy-adjutant-general, the reader may see the minutes of Congress, March 1777. For the time during which General Schuyler held the command of the Northern Department, see Chancellor Kent's discourse before the Historical Society, 1826. General Schuyler held the command of the Northern Department when Burgoyne's advance induced Sinclair to evacuate Ticonderoga, and Schuyler met that news on the upper Hudson, while using the utmost diligence and judgment to oppose the enemy; likewise see Marshall's " Washington," Vol. III. p. 247. It will be seen hereafter that Mr. Trumbull had acted in the adjutant-general's department without a commission, and that on receiving it he enclosed it in a letter, the receipt of which is acknowledged on the minutes of Congress, of March 1777, as a letter enclosing the commission of John Trumbull, deputy-adjutant-general, which commission, we shall see, was sent back by him, not because it was deficient in rank, but because it was dated in September, 1776, whereas he thought it ought to have been dated in June. I further remark that the British were driven from Boston in March 1776, and took possession of New York in September, and that Mr. Trumbull tells Mr. Wilde that he was appointed adjutant-general of the *Northern Department* with the rank of colonel, in July 1776.

Albany in a sloop. Gates was at this time expected to have proceeded to Canada, but he met the army driven out, and thus caused some confusion in the command."

There is an interlineation after the word Canada of these words, "At that time probably the Northern Department." Not so. Gates, who was a presuming and assuming man, and the enemy of Washington and Schuyler, showed his disposition so plainly on his appointment to command in Canada, that Congress passed a resolution "that they had no design to invest him with a superior command to Schuyler, while the troops were within the bounds of the States." Mr. Sparks says, "the instructions of General Gates were too explicit to raise a doubt in any other mind than his own." Though Congress decided against his pretensions, there was a New England party in that body and elsewhere, who encouraged him in his intrigues to overthrow Schuyler and Washington.

General Philip Schuyler was commander of the Northern Department from July 1775 to August 1777, four or five months after Mr. Trumbull retired to private life. General Schuyler did at one moment tender his resignation to Congress, but it was several months after the date of Mr. Trumbull's voyage to Albany with Gates. Congress "declared that they would not dispense with his services during the then situation of affairs, and they directed the president to request him to continue in his command." (See Kent and Marshall.) Schuyler had been treated unceremoniously according to military etiquette; but his object was to serve his country, not himself alone: he made allowances for the confusion caused by the public danger, and continued in his command. As early as September 1775, he had proceeded as far as *Isle au Noix* with intent to enter Canada, but was obliged, by severe illness, to leave the expedition to Montgomery. While that officer was employed in Canada, Schuyler was called to oppose the Tories under Johnson; and in January 1776, he was ordered, by Congress, to have the St. Lawrence explored and to fortify Ticonderoga. In February he was ordered to repair to New York, and in March to establish his headquarters in Albany

and superintend the supplies for Canada; and these orders
were renewed April and May 1776. (See Journals of Congress,
vols. I. and II.) "He gave life and vigor to every branch of
the service." (See Kent.) On the 17th of June, he was ordered
to clear Wood Creek, and to build armed vessels for the mastery
of the lakes. "There can be no doubt," says Kent, "that the
northern frontier, in the campaign of 1776, was indebted for
its extraordinary quiet and security, to the ceaseless activity
of General Schuyler. General Sullivan had the command of
the Northern or Canadian army, and on the 18th of June
1776, received orders from General Schuyler to embark on
Lake Champlain for Crown Point. General Gates at this time
was ordered to take command of the Northern or Canadian
army (see Marshall), that is, of the forces that had been commanded by Sullivan under the orders of Schuyler. At the close
of that year Schuyler was further instructed to build a floating
battery on the lake, and a fort on Mount Independence, and
also to strengthen the works at Fort Stanwix." In the campaign of 1777, Schuyler made all the dispositions to receive
Burgoyne, and was only superseded in consequence of Sinclair's
evacuation of Ticonderoga, and that senseless, popular clamor
which induced the appointment of Gates, in August 1777, long
after Mr. Trumbull's retirement from military life. When
superseded by Gates and robbed of his well-earned laurels,
General Schuyler still continued to serve his country. The
Baroness Reidesel's account of his behavior, at the capture of
Burgoyne, is one of the most beautiful passages of history.
There may be readers who will think I "travel out of the
record" in this brief sketch of the services of Philip Schuyler;
but I am perfectly satisfied that I could not have given Mr.
Trumbull's narrative without this explanatory comment, and
left the fair fame of a distinguished patriot unsullied by doubts,
as far as that narrative concerns the affairs of the Northern
department.

The amanuensis of Mr. Trumbull proceeds: — "He" (that
is, Mr. Trumbull), "proceeded to Ticonderoga. He was the
first person who reconnoitered Mount Independence": a post

which, as we have seen, Congress had ordered, near the close of this year, General Schuyler to fortify; "which he," Trumbull, "soon after explored, with General Wayne, which led to its occupation. While there he was impressed with the belief that the whole position of the army, both at Ticonderoga and Mount Independence, was commanded by a height situated nearly at an equal distance from both those points, being elevated about 500 feet higher than either of them, and at the distance of about a mile, well known as Mount Defiance. He mentioned his observation at the dinner table. He ventured to advance an opinion, that their entire position was commanded by that hill; but they universally laughed at the idea: the general opinion was, that it was too distant, even if an enemy were there. Finding argument useless, he proposed settling the question by experiment. As the commanding officer of artillery was proving guns at the most remote part of Mount Independence, he, the next morning, caused the experiment to be made with a double-shotted gun. The shot reached near the summit of the hill, which of course confirmed his opinion. In the afternoon the experiment was repeated, in the presence of the officers, with a six-pounder, from the glacis of the old French fort: the shot reached nearly to the summit. Several of the officers afterwards ascended the hill, and, when there, it was the unanimous opinion, that there would be no difficulty in ascending with a yoke of oxen, and, of course, getting cannon to the summit. Two memoirs were drawn up: one setting forth the expense and force necessary to maintain the post as then occupied; for which it was shown ten thousand men and one hundred pieces of cannon were necessary: the other was grounded on the proposition to abandon the whole, and establish another post on the summit of Mt. Defiance, with a force of five hundred men.

This suggestion of the *adjutant-general* was not acted upon; and the consequence was, that the next campaign Gen. St. Clair was left to defend the original lines with 3000 men, and the first movement of the British force was to take possession of Mount Defiance; from which, according to their account, they could observe every movement of the Americans within their lines. The abandonment of the entire position became immediately necessary; and St. Clair deserved great praise for his well-conducted retreat, by which the army was saved from capture, and became the nucleus of that force which afterwards prostrated the British power in the Northern Department."

As St. Clair's retreat, and all the events last mentioned took place after Mr. Trumbull had resigned, gone home, and was pursuing his studies in Boston, we are as well qualified to speak of them as far as facts are concerned, as he can be if we use an equal degree of industry in the investigation.

The people of the United States have been habituated to surround with a halo every head presented to their view as that of a soldier of the Revolution. The feeling is natural, and has its origin in our *better* nature. But it appears to me high time to pass the grain through the sieve and separate it from the chaff which has heretofore claimed equal weight. It is time and high time that we should discriminate, and teach our children to discriminate, between the mercenary and selfish, who took up arms to serve themselves, and the real patriotic soldier of the Revolution. There are people who cry "Huzza for the Revolutionary soldier!" when the name of Gates is mentioned, with as much well-meant good will as when that of Schuyler or Washington meets their ears (the men whom he endeavored to undermine and disgrace) or that of Green, who saved the South from the effects of his imbecility.

Washington, speaking of his army at Cambridge, says, — "Such a dearth of public spirit, and such a want of virtue! such stock-jobbing, and felicity at all the low arts to obtain advantages in this great change of military arrangement, I never saw before, and pray God's mercy that I may never see again." And again "such a mercenary spirit pervades the whole, that I should not be surprised at any disaster that might happen." Yet these blasted and worthless shoots are bound up in the same sheaf with the wholesome ears from which we derive our bread. Men who only thought of their own promotion and emolument are confounded with the gallant Prescott and his companions at Breed's Hill — with a Whitcomb, who, having a regiment, and being omitted in the new modelling of the army, encouraged his men to enlist anew, by offering to join the ranks with them — with Brewer, who, being appointed to Whitcomb's command, insisted upon resigning it to him and taking an inferior station — with the many glorious names who served for honor and their country's good.

It may be my task, in these pages, to state facts which will militate against the preconceived opinions formed of individuals; but I shall do it conscientiously, that the self-exalter may not occupy the ground which should be kept clear for the man of real worth.

The judgment which pointed out the importance of Mount Defiance is highly creditable to the young officer; but there appears to be no cause for censuring General Schuyler. It appears, that long after the memorials Mr. Trumbull mentions, General Schuyler was acting under the immediate orders of Congress, in strengthening Mount Independence, a part of the position which was thought untenable. I do not know by whom these memorials were drawn up or signed, or to whom transmitted. I know that if Burgoyne had been stopped on Lake Champlain, as Prevost was in 1814, he could have saved his army by retreat, and that the surrender at Saratoga would not have taken place. And I am perfectly convinced (in the year 1834), that if Philip Schuyler had not been superseded, Burgoyne must have surrendered to him, and that without any convention. I now return to Mr. Trumbull's narrative, and to the summer of 1776, one year or more before Schuyler was superseded by Gates.

"In the meantime the adjutant-general," meaning Mr. Trumbull, "had remained without a commission. This rendered his situation peculiarly painful; and what rendered it more so was, that other and inferior officers did receive commissions, giving them rank equal to his own."

Here there is a break in the ms. with a memorandum re-

ferring Mr. Herring to one of the catalogues published by Mr.
Trumbull. This points to a passage respecting Gates' command of the Northern Department, which we have already
commented upon; and goes on to the defeat of the American
flotilla, which, as we have seen, was constructed by Schuyler,
under the immediate orders of Congress, and which was entrusted to the command of Arnold. The British, commanded
by Carleton, broke through this impediment, and having reconnoitered Ticonderoga, in October, 1776, retired to winter
quarters.

"Thus," says Mr. Trumbull, "terminated that campaign,
and the principal part of the disposable force moved down to
Albany, about the 20th of November"; where, as we have
seen, General Schuyler had been ordered by Congress to establish his headquarters, as commander of the Northern Department. "General Gates received orders from the commander-
in-chief to join him with all his disposable force behind the
Delaware. He moved of course by the route of Esopus, Hurley,
the Minisink, Sussex Court House, Easton, Bethlehem, and
joined Washington at Newtown, Pennsylvania, a few days
before the battle of Trenton. News was at that time received
that the British had landed at Newport, Rhode Island, with a
considerable force. General Arnold was ordered to proceed
to Rhode Island to assume the command of the militia to oppose them; and Trumbull was ordered to proceed with him as
adjutant-general. The headquarters were established at Providence for the winter; and there, in the month of March, Colonel
Trumbull received his commission, as adjutant-general, with
the rank of Colonel; but dated in the month of September
instead of the month of June."

I have already shown that this commission was that of
deputy-adjutant-general by reference to the journals of Congress. In a manuscript memoir in Mr. Trumbull's handwriting,
given for publication in 1817, and now in possession of Robert
Gilmor, Esq., he speaks of himself as in the inferior capacity.
In his letter to Mr. Wilde, he calls himself adjutant-general, and
the next year, in a memoir appended to a catalogue of his

pictures, published in 1831, he says his appointment was deputy-adjutant-general, yet in 1833, when dictating to Mr. Herring, he claims the full rank. I have quoted the passage from the minutes of Congress, which settles this point. After mentioning the receipt of the commission, the narrative proceeds:

"By whatever accident or cause is unknown, but this added to the chagrin and vexation of the officer commissioned, and within an hour he returned it under cover to the president of Congress, accompanied with a letter, perhaps too concise and laconic, stating the impossibility of serving, unless the date was altered, to correspond with the date of his actual service. A correspondence of some length ensued, which terminated after some weeks, in the acceptance of the resignation, and thus his military career terminated."

As the commission was received in Rhode Island during March, and the resignation accepted in the same month, the above-mentioned correspondence could not have been of much length or duration. Although to this abandonment of military life, we are indebted for one of our most distinguished artists, I cannot but think that the young gentleman made a great mistake even upon the narrow calculation of self-interest. Before the age of twenty-one he had been advanced from the grade of adjutant of a regiment, to that of deputy-adjutant-general, and appears to have been doing the duty as principal at the post to which he was assigned, yet for a difference of dates from June or July 20th (for he has stated both as the date of appointment), and some day in September, he abandoned the cause of his country, at the time that "tried men's souls," and gave up prospects, as fair as any young man of the period could have, of being an honorable agent in the great events which followed.

"He then," continues his amanuensis, "returned to Lebanon (to the object of his first love, he said), and afterward went to Boston to profit by studying the works of Copley and others, where he remained until 1779, occupying the room which had been built by Smibert, in which remained many of

ₚ his works. He there became acquainted with Mr. John Temple,
afterwards first consul-general of Great Britain to the United
States, who was connected with the families of Grenville and
Temple, and by marriage with the family of Governor Bowdoin
in the United States; through him he ascertained the possibility of his going in safety to London, to study his profession
under Mr. West. In May 1780, he embarked for France, and
after a short stay at Paris he found his way to London, in
August, by the way of Ostend. He was kindly received by
Mr. West, to whom he had a letter of introduction from
Doctor Franklin, and from whom he received the most liberal
instruction.

"Mr. West asked Trumbull if he brought any specimen of
his work, and being answered in the negative, told him to copy
some one of his pictures and bring it to him. 'Go into that
room, where you will find Mr. Stuart painting, and choose
something to copy.' Trumbull selected one (by an old master),
the copy of which is with him still. West asked him if he knew
what he had chosen, he said, 'No.' West told him, adding, 'You
have made a good choice; if you can copy that, I shall think
well of you.'" The picture was Raphael's "Madonna della
seida." This anecdote is given from Mr. Herring, but is not
in the ms. narrative, which proceeds thus: — "There he
pursued his studies uninterruptedly for about three months,
to the middle of November. At that time the news of the
death of Major André was received, and occasioned a violent
irritation in the public mind. It was his misfortune to lodge
in the same house with another American gentleman, who had
been an officer, against whom a warrant had been issued to
apprehend him for high treason. Instructions had been given
to the officer who was to execute the warrant, to arrest, *ad
interim*, the painter, and secure his papers, in expectation of
finding something of importance. The following day he was
examined before the principal magistrates of the police, and
in the course of the examination something occurred which
wounded his military pride, and called forth an address to
this effect: — 'Gentlemen, you are rude. You appear to be

more in the habit of examining pickpockets and highwaymen than gentlemen. I will cut this examination short, gentlemen, by telling you who I am, and what I am. I am the son of him you call the rebel governor of Connecticut, and I have been aid-de-camp to him you call the rebel General Washington. I know that in saying this I put my life in your hands. You will treat me as you please — remembering, that as you treat me, so will those gentlemen whom I have named treat your countrymen who are their prisoners, and in their power.' "

Mr. Trumbull ought to have known, that if his life was in danger, it was not as a prisoner of war, but as a spy; and that the circumstance of his being the son of Governor Trumbull, and having been in the army, could not be kept from the knowledge of those who had arrested him: so that what he avowed did not put his *life in the hands* of the police magistrates; and his threat was utterly ineffective and irrelevant. The narration proceeds: — "This, perhaps imprudent, declaration had, however, a good effect. He was treated with greater civility. He was, however, confined, and remained in confinement until the month of June following, more than eight months."

CHAPTER III.

TRUMBULL — *Continued.*

MR. TRUMBULL was arrested on the 19th of November, and released the June following. Some other particulars, connected with the arrest and examination, were communicated to Mr. Herring, which are not noticed in the manuscript. Difficulties occurred at the police respecting a place of confinement, the prisons of London having been destroyed by the rioters in June 1780, and a message being sent to the secretary of state's office, Trumbull had the choice of the place left to himself.

However much Mr. Trumbull may have regretted the resignation of his commission of deputy-adjutant-general, he probably now regretted still more that he had taken up his abode in the capital of Great Britain, while those with whom he had been engaged were struggling for life and liberty against that mighty power. I remember distinctly all the circumstances of this incident, as detailed to several listeners by Mr. Trumbull many years ago. He then attributed his arrest to Thompson, afterward Count Rumford, saying that this man had applied for a commission in the rebel army before Boston, and had been refused — that afterward he joined the English, and was, at the time of Trumbull's arrest, in the secretary of state's office. He gave formal notice to the secretary of state, that John Trumbull, son to the governor of Connecticut, and known to have served in the rebel army, was in London. It is well known that Thompson was afterward under-secretary of state; that he procured an appointment for himself as colonel of a regiment of horse to be raised in America; and that he came to this country, and staid long enough to secure the emoluments appertaining to his appointment, serving with his regiment in the South. Although Mr. Trumbull had received assurances previous to leaving Boston that he would not be molested, this formal information could not be passed over, and he was arrested. This was in November, 1780; and Mr. Trumbull stated that the irritation caused in England by the recent execution of the spy, Major André, and the circumstance that the young painter had served in the adjutant-general's department of the rebel army, caused alarm to his friends; and caused Mr. West, immediately on hearing of the arrest, to wait upon the king, and represent the facts of his pupil's former and present situation; the long time which had intervened between his quitting the rebel army and his coming to England; and his present entire devotedness to the study of the fine arts. Finally, by pledging himself for the young man's good disposition, the benevolent Benjamin obtained the king's assurance that no further interruption to the studies of the young painter should take place than what the forms of office required, and that at all events his personal safety should be fully attended to; and at the worst — his life be perfectly safe. I give this from memory — but in the anecdote told of Thompson, and the statement of his agency in the arrest, I cannot be mistaken. I might have forgotten it — I could not have invented it; and I am certain that West's application to George the Third was not attributed to selfish motives at the time I first heard of it.

Another account of this affair may be found in Stuart's "Three Years' Residence in America," where, after stating that the painter "was apprehended and *sent to the tower*, on the ground that he was a spy," the author gives the following in the words of Trumbull:

"I was arrested at twelve o'clock at night of the 19th of November, in London, on suspicion of high treason. I was then principally occupied in studying the art of painting under Mr. West. Mr. West well knew that his attachment to his native country gave offence to some individuals who were about the king's person. He therefore went the next morning early to Buckingham House, and requested an audience of the king. It was granted; and he proceeded to state the origin

and nature of his acquaintance with me, concluding that,
whatever might have been my conduct in America, he could
conscientiously state to his majesty, that since my arrival in
London the principal part of almost every day had been passed
under his eye, in the assiduous study of his profession, leaving
little or no time for any pursuit hostile to the interests of
Great Britain. The king, after a moment's hesitation, made
this answer: 'Mr. West, I have known you long — I have
confided in you — I have never known you to mislead me — I
therefore repose implicit confidence in the representation.
This young gentleman must in the meantime suffer great
anxiety. He is in the power of the laws, and I cannot at present
interfere. But go to him, and assure him from me, that in the
worst possible legal result, he has my royal word that his life
is safe.' Mr. West came to me with this message immediately;
and you may well believe that it softened essentially the rigor
of an imprisonment of eight months."

Here the motive ascribed to Mr. West's prompt interference
is *self*. To screen himself from any injury that might be done
him by the "individuals about the king's person." I had
hoped that this might have been a mistake of Mr. Stuart's,
but the narrative as given to Mr. Herring for publication confirms the suggestion: — "On hearing this adventure the ap-
prehensions of Mr. West were aroused; for he well knew that
he had enemies about the person of the king, and therefore
hastened to the palace and asked an audience, which was
granted. He proceeded to state to the king his personal
knowledge of the conduct of Trumbull while in London. —
After listening to him patiently, the king replied, 'West, I
have known you long, and I don't know that I have received
any incorrect information from you on any subject; I therefore fully believe all that you have said to me on the present
occasion. I sincerely regret the situation of the young man;
but I cannot do anything to assist him. He is in the power of
the law, and I cannot interfere. Are his parents living?'
To which Mr. West answered that his father was. 'Then I
most sincerely pity him,' said the king. After a moment's

pause, he continued, 'Go immediately to Mr. Trumbull, and
give him my royal assurance that in the worst possible event
of the law, his life will be safe.' The assurance of course
softened in a great degree the rigors of a winter's confinement,
and enabled him to proceed with his studies."

It was during this confinement that Mr. Trumbull, among
other pictures, copied that beautiful *copy* of the "St. Jerome,"
which is mentioned in the life of West as being executed by
him from the exquisite original of Correggio, at Parma. Mr.
Trumbull's is perhaps equal to his master's, and certainly one
of the gems of the art.

There is something, to me, inexpressibly beautiful in the
testimony borne to West's character, and to the force of truth
from the lips of one whose lips were unaccustomed to falsehood. This interview between George the Third and his historical painter, is highly honorable to both; and the account
of it from the lips or pen of West would have been a treasure.

"In June," proceeds the narrative, "at which time a turn
had taken place in the affairs of the two countries, and the
government began to relax their severity, Trumbull was admitted to bail by a special order of the king in council, on
condition of quitting the kingdom within thirty days, and not
to return during the war. His securities were West and Copley."
Did not Mr. West procure this order?

"Crossed," says the narrative, "over to Ostend, thence to
Amsterdam, and embarked. Temple accompanied him to
Ostend, and sailed for Boston, where he arrived in about thirty
days; and Trumbull in about fifty landed at Corunna in Spain.
Had sailed for Philadelphia, but fell short of water and provisions, and put back to Corunna. Finding an American ship
there bound to Bilboa, took passage in her, and arrived in the
beginning of December, and arrived at ———, in the middle
of January, whence he found his way home. Fatigue, vexation
and disappointment, brought on a fit of illness which confined
him to his father's the principal part of the ensuing summer.
At the close of the summer again visited the army then at
Verplanck's point, and entered into an arrangement with his

brother and others, who were contracting for supplying the army with provisions, and passed the winter at New Windsor as storekeeper.

"In the spring of 1783 the news arrived of the preliminaries of peace having been arranged. He was then at Lebanon. Conversation with his father, who was desirous to have him make choice of a profession, wished the law — leading profession in a republican government — gratify ambition, etc. — reply — 'So far as I understand the law, it is rendered necessary by the vices of mankind. A lawyer must be distinguished for his acuteness and skill in extricating rogues from the consequences of their villany, and as I view the life of a lawyer it must be passed in the midst of all the wretchedness and meanness of —' etc. — then went on to give an idea of an artist's life — enlarged on the honors and rewards bestowed by the ancients, particularly the Athenians, and in modern times referred to Copley and West. 'My son, you have made an excellent argument, but its operation is against yourself, and only serves to satisfy me that in the profession of the law you might take a respectable stand; and in your case you have omitted one point as the lawyers call it.' 'What is that, sir?' 'That Connecticut is not Athens.' He then bowed and left the room, and never afterwards interfered in the choice of life.

"In January, 1783, he (the painter) embarked from Portsmouth, New Hampshire, and in January, 1784, landed in Portsmouth, England, and immediately proceeded to London, where he was again kindly received by Mr. West, pursued his studies undefatigably, and in 1785 had made such progress as to copy for Mr. West his celebrated picture of the Battle of La Hogue. The first original composition of his own was painted immediately afterward, and he chose for his subject Priam bearing back to his palace the body of Hector — the figures about ten inches in height. The picture is now in the possession of the widow of Mr. Gore, to whom it was presented, at Waltham, near Boston, and is devised to Harvard College, where he (the painter) was educated."

In June, 1784, the writer found Mr. Trumbull the established successor of Gilbert Stuart in West's apartments. The picture of Priam with his son's corse was in miniature oil, a style in which Mr. Trumbull was afterwards unrivalled as an historical painter. The figures were of a size similar, or nearly so, to those in his "Bunker Hill" and "Death of Montgomery." Another original picture, painted by Mr. Trumbull, was a full-length figure of a soldier of the king's horse guards, for which one of Mr. West's hired models, who belonged to that corps, furnished person, costume, and horse. The figure was of a greater size than that in which Mr. Trumbull best succeeded.

In the year 1786, Mr. Trumbull finished his picture of the Battle of Bunker's Hill. I saw this beautiful picture in various stages of its progress, and when finished, in the painting rooms of Mr. West. The similarity of the subject leads to a comparison with two pictures previously painted by Mr. Trumbull's countrymen, and both familiar to him — the "Death of Wolfe," by West, and the "Death of Major Pierson," by Copley; and however masterly the picture of the younger painter, it fails in the comparison. Neither is it equal to his next picture, the "Death of Montgomery." "The Death of Wolfe" was produced by West at an early age, when thrown upon his own resources, in his own painting room, without an adviser or instructor, and adventuring upon what was then a new species of historical composition — an heroic action or subject in modern costume. West has therefore not only the merit of producing by far the best picture, but of originating a new style. Another great advantage possessed by the "Death of Wolfe," is that the painter has represented the triumph of his heroes. whereas Trumbull chooses for his picture the moment of the overthrow of his countrymen, and the triumph of their enemies. The death of Doctor Warren, however amiable, accomplished, and intelligent he may have been, is an incident of minor consequence compared with the repeated defeats of the veterans of Great Britain, by Prescott, Putnam, and the brave undisciplined Yankee yeomen their associates, before the hill was carried by reinforcements sent from Boston. Surely one of these moments of triumph might have been chosen by an American painter for his picture. *Then* Prescott, Warren, and Putnam would have been the heroes, instead of Small, Howe, and Clinton. Then, instead of Major Small (who is in fact the hero of the piece) arresting the bayonet of an English grenadier who is about to stab a dying man, we might have seen the gallant and chivalrous action of Putnam striking up the musket of his neighbor when levelled with deadly aim at this same Major Small (once his companion in arms), when retreating from the murderous fire which his soldiers would not face.

The imitative spirit is shown in the modern-dressed historical compositions which followed West's "Death of Wolfe"; he has a dying man in the center of his composition, and the dying Major Pierson, Doctor Warren, General Montgomery, etc. etc., follow in the train. But see the enormous difference in the interest and character of the dying men. Wolfe died triumphant, surrounded by his friends in the moment of victory, knowing that France had lost America by the successful efforts of his genius — that the chain which extended from the Gulf of St. Lawrence to that of Mexico, encircling the English colonies with links of French bayonets and Indian tomahawks, was broken and annihilated forever. But the dying men of the other pictures are nothing more than — dying men.

It is well known that the story of Bunker Hill, as told by Mr. Trumbull, was and is particularly objected to by many of the inhabitants of Boston and its neighborhood. It has been called "The triumph of British valor and humanity"; and the painter has been censured for taking Major Small's version of the affair, rather than that of the Americans concerned in it. We have before us several letters, written by a venerable gentleman, of high standing in our literary world, from which we extract a few passages on the subject. After censuring the costume of Prescott, and his situation in the picture (he is represented as a feeble old man, with a slouched hat and plain coat and underclothes, more like a Quaker than a soldier, and placed in a situation little corresponding with command), he says: "The whole picture is apocryphal from beginning to end, and unworthy of the gentleman I much esteem. Besides, General Dearborn, one of our delegation in Congress, has in manuscript the life of his father, Major-General Dearborn, who I have heard again and again contradict all the leading points of that picture." "Bunker Hill is two and a half miles from the table on which I am now writing, and I know the circumstances of that eventful battle better than the painter of it."

The composition, coloring, and touch of Mr. Trumbull's "Bunker Hill," are admirable. The drawing and attitudes of the figures, likewise admirable, are inferior to his next picture, of the same miniature size, the "Death of Montgomery, at Quebec." In this the grouping is better than that of the "Bunker Hill." The figures are accurately drawn, and the attitudes finely diversified. The *chiaroscuro* is perfect. But I cannot help feeling that it is the commemoration of another triumph of Britain over America. I must further remark that the truth of history is violated in misrepresenting the spot where Montgomery and his brave companions fell. When a man becomes a "graphic historiographer," he has a duty to fulfil that cannot be dispensed with. If the historian or the "graphic historiographer" cannot tell the whole truth, he must not at least violate the known truth.

These two beautiful little pictures were carried to the city of Washington in 1816-17 (as we shall hereafter notice), and shown to the members of Congress, as inducements to employ the painter in patriotic works for the capitol: but although their merits gained employment for the artist, the senators and representatives saw at once that such subjects were not fitted for the decoration of the rotunda. Had the "Battle of Bunker's Hill" represented the true point of time — the triumph of our militia and their gallant leaders over the disciplined veterans of Britain, there can be no doubt that the picture would have been copied for the nation.

The fourth and last historical composition which Mr. Trumbull finished while under the eye of West, was another triumph of the arms of Great Britain over her enemies. " The Sortie from Gibraltar " is perhaps the best of Mr. Trumbull's works.

Mr. Trumbull had proved that he could succeed in historical composition on the miniature scale, which was best suited for the purposes of the engraver. The American Revolution had terminated happily for the cause of justice and humanity. It was popular on the continent of Europe. The immense traffic in prints which had been established by England, presented a field for the accumulation of wealth. To paint a series of pictures on subjects connected with the American Revolution, was obviously a speculation worthy of attention. Pine, an English artist, had already gone to America for the purpose. It could not escape the attention of Mr. Trumbull's mind that he would have advantages over every rival. To paint the events of the struggle for freedom in America, and by a copartnership with European engravers spread prints of the size of the original pictures, was a feasible project, offering both fame and fortune. No man could better advise in the execution of such a plan than West, who had long circulated prints from his pictures wherever art or literature were known. Under such circumstances, and with such views, Mr. Trumbull made his arrangements for carrying into effect a project, of which every artist must lament the failure.

Let us now recur to the narrative. Mr. Trumbull says: "The success of this picture," the Priam and Hector, "induced him to commence a project which had long been floating in his mind, of painting a series of pictures of the principal scenes of the Revolution. He began with the 'Battle of Bunker Hill,' which was composed and finished in the early part of the year 1786. In the three subsequent months of the same year, the 'Death of Montgomery before Quebec,' was composed and painted. The pictures met with general approbation, not only in London, but in Paris, Berlin, Dresden, and other parts of the continent. They were as soon as possible placed in the hands of eminent engravers, for the purpose of being" published from the press. "Among others, they were seen by Mr. John Adams, then in London, and Mr. Jefferson in Paris, to whom the project was communicated of painting a series of national pictures, which was highly approved, and by their concurrence the subjects were chosen (several of which have been since executed), and he proceeded to arrange and adjust the composition of those subjects.

"Finding that the painting of Bunker Hill had given offence in London, and being desirous to conciliate, he determined to paint one subject from British history, and selected the 'Sortie of the Garrison of Gibraltar.' Of this the first study was made in oil, twelve by sixteen inches, and was presented to Mr. West (figures carefully finished), as an acknowledgment for his kindness. Then a second picture was painted, twenty by thirty, carefully and laboriously finished, with the intention of having it engraved. This picture was sold to Sir Francis Baring for five hundred guineas, who contracted for the purchase of a series of pictures of American subjects at the same price, subject to the contingency of the higher powers. He found that the possession of the pictures proposed would give offence in a very high quarter, and therefore retracted. Having engaged Mr. Sharpe, the first engraver of the age, to engrave the picture, he was tenacious of rendering the composition as perfect as in his power, he therefore rejected that picture, and began another six feet by nine. This picture occupied the principal part of the year 1788, and was finished in the spring of 1789, when it was exhibited by itself in Spring Garden, London, and received great applause. This picture was engraved by Sharpe, and has since been purchased by the Athenæum of Boston, where it now is."

The reason given by Mr. Trumbull for choosing this subject, "must give us pause." "The painting of Bunker Hill had given offence in London, and being very desirous to conciliate," he painted a third victory of the English over their enemies, to appease them for having painted the two which preceded it. *Who* had been offended by the triumphs of Howe and Carleton over Prescott and Montgomery, that were to be conciliated by the triumph of Elliot over the French and Spanish, allies of America? But so it is — and this conciliatory painting, after being offered for years to the conciliated people, is finally purchased by the citizens of Boston. That it *is so*, is matter of congratulation to Americans.

We see that Mr. Trumbull painted his subject three times — the first given to Mr. West, very small — the second sold to Baring, and the third and largest now in Boston. If, after painting these pictures, Mr. Trumbull had been lost to the world, there would have been just reason to exclaim, as it respects his reputation for painting, "Now to die, were now to be most happy"; for certainly the world would have said, "Had he lived, he would have been the greatest artist of his age." The world would have lost many beautifully painted miniature heads, and pictures of merit by this consummation — all we mean to say is, that Mr. Trumbull's reputation as a painter has not been enhanced by anything he has done since the "Sortie."

In 1787 Mr. Trumbull was in Paris; and in the house of Mr. Jefferson, our minister to France, he painted the portrait of that eminent statesman and patriot, and likewise the portraits of the French officers who assisted Washington in the capture of Cornwallis at Yorktown. We now return to the narrative:

"In the meantime the present constitution of the United States had been framed, and the first session of Congress was appointed to be held in New York in December, 1789; the time had therefore arrived for proceeding with the American pictures. (He had already obtained the portrait of Mr. Adams in London, and Mr. Jefferson sat to him for his in Paris.) Sailed for America, and arrived in New York, November, 1789, and proceeded to paint as many of the heads of the signers of 'The Declaration of Independence' as were present, and of General Washington at Trenton and Princeton."

These portraits, of such persons as had been in Congress at the signing of the Declaration of Independence, or had afterwards signed it,* and of Washington, for the pictures of the

---

* Mr. Trumbull, in a work published by him in 1832, says, that Adams and Jefferson, advised him to introduce the portraits of those who afterwards signed, *as if present* at the time of the important resolution; that is, to violate historical truth.

Battles of Trenton and Princeton, are among the most admirable miniatures in oil that ever were painted. The same may be said of the portraits in the small picture of the surrender of Cornwallis.

Mr. Trumbull at this period published a prospectus of his intended work, and solicited subscriptions for the prints of Bunker Hill and Quebec. He obtained nearly three hundred subscribers, at six guineas, for the two prints, and half the money paid at the time of subscription. In May, 1794, he returned to England, as secretary to Mr. Jay, and was announced by that gentleman to the English ministry as Colonel Trumbull. In 1796 he received the appointment of agent for impressed seamen; but Mr. Jay having concluded a treaty with Great Britain, by which commissioners were to be appointed to carry into effect an article respecting illegal captures, Mr. Trumbull was chosen as a fifth by the four commissioners who had been chosen by the two governments, and he accepted *that* as preferable to the first. Between 1794 and 1796, it will be seen that Mr. Trumbull was engaged in mercantile speculation. But I am anticipating his own narrative, to which I now return:

"In the summer of 1790 he painted the full-length portrait, in the council room, City Hall, New York, of General Washington, size of life; and in 1791, that of Governor George Clinton, in the same room."

These two large full lengths are in a style totally different from that Mr. Trumbull afterwards adopted; and the last-mentioned is, in my opinion, the best large-sized picture he ever painted. It represents the Revolutionary governor in his capacity of general, defending Fort Montgomery, on the Hudson: it is strikingly like, with an heroic and historical expression, and the distant figures are beautifully touched in.

"In 1792 he painted another full-length portrait of Washington for the city of Charleston, with a horse; and in the background a view of that city. At the same time he painted another, which is now at the college at New Haven, to which it was presented by the State Society of the Cincinnati. This

latter portrait is regarded, by the artist, as the finest portrait
of *General* Washington in existence. It represents him at the
most critical moment of his life, on the evening before the
battle of Princeton, meditating his retreat before a superior
enemy. At the time this picture was painting, Signor Ceracchi
executed a bust, of which there is a colossal cast in the collection of the American Academy of the Fine Arts. The best
evidence that can be given of the correctness of both these
productions of art is to be found in the close resemblance they
bear to each other, although executed by different hands and
in materials so dissimilar."

The reader will remark, that Mr. Trumbull emphasizes the
word "General." This refers to Stuart's portrait, which was
painted a short time after, and is presumed to represent President Washington. But Washington was president when
Trumbull painted his portrait, and when Ceracchi sculptured
his bust. Let it be further remarked, that the original bust of
Washington, by Ceracchi, is not colossal. It is the size of life,
is very unlike the colossal, and is in the collection of the late
Richard Meade, Esq. This last mentioned is very similar to
Stuart's original picture, and very like the heroic original,
but totally unlike the picture at Yale College; which, as a
picture, has much merit, and was painted in Mr. Trumbull's
best days.

The narrative proceeds: — "A few other portraits were
painted about this time; but the years '91, '92, and '93, were
principally spent in painting original portraits for the historical
pictures. In the accomplishment of his great design he travelled
from New Hampshire to Charleston, in South Carolina. The
head of General Lincoln, at the surrender of York Town, was
painted in Boston. Edward Rutledge, —— Hayward, and
William Washington, were painted in Charleston. The heads
painted at this period are in the small set of pictures now
at New Haven. They are the originals of the whole work, and
were all painted from the living men — persevering in the
object of obtaining authentic portraits."

CHAPTER IV.

TRUMBULL — *Continued.*

"DIFFICULTIES had existed between the late belligerents ever since the war, and they were of the most embarrassing character. Mr. Jay was appointed minister to Great Britain, for the purpose of bringing these subjects of mutual complaints and grievances to an end," negotiating a treaty of amity and commerce, etc. "and Mr. Jay appointed him his secretary. This afforded T. an opportunity of attending to the finishing of his three large copper plates, which were at that time engraving in London, Copenhagen (struck out), "and at Stutgard, in Germany, and at an expense of upwards of 3000 guineas." *

"The result of that negotiation is well known to have terminated in a treaty, signed on the 19th of November, 1794. The manner in which Mr. Jay conducted the negotiation rendered the duties of the secretary merely nominal. After the signing of the treaty Trumbull went to Paris; and he saw, from the condition of the continent, that all hope of profit from the sale of engravings was at an end. His calculation had been on a more extensive demand on the continent of Europe than elsewhere for American historical pictures. The war had overwhelmed all Europe, and painters and paintings were not in demand. In consequence of which he gave up his professional pursuits and embarked in commerce, until August, 1796, when he returned to England."

At this period, as Mr. Trumbull expressed it to Mr. Herring, "he made some lucky hits in the French funds." We have reason to believe, that at this time he purchased many valuable pictures by the old masters, some of which he afterwards brought to America.

---

* In 1833 these plates are said to be in the possession of Illman and Pilbro, engravers, at New York. Pilbro says, he bought them of some one in London, within a year and this person purchased them of another, who found them at a pawnbroker's.

The narrative proceeds to say, that "he was appointed one of the commissioners under the treaty; for the execution of the seventh article. This placed him in a new and difficult situation. The British commissioners, Sir John Nichol and John Anstey, Esq. were two of their most eminent civil lawyers, and the two Americans, Mr. Gore and Mr. Pinkney were likewise eminent lawyers: it was easy to foresee that these gentlemen would frequently differ with respect to the rights of the two countries, and it would remain with the fifth commissioner to decide." It might appear, from this statement of Mr. Trumbull, that he was appointed by the goverment of the United States, as well as Mr. Gore and Mr. Pinkney, but it was not so; the appointment was by some agreement between the British and American commissioners conferred upon him.

P

"An arduous duty for a man who had not been educated for the legal profession. It placed him under the necessity of going through a course of reading on the law of nations and maritime law.

"They were met at the threshold by a most important question. What cases were to come before them? and what their powers? On these points the commissioners of both nations were in direct opposition, when," says Mr. Trumbull, "I proposed to Sir John Nichol this question, 'Have you any objection to leave this to the decision of the lord chancellor?' To which he replied, 'None in the world,' I rejoined 'Neither have I, Sir John.' An audience of the lord chancellor was requested and the time appointed.

"When all the commissioners attended the question was proposed to him by Sir John Nichol — to which the chancellor immediately replied, 'Sir John, the American gentlemen are right. The parties who framed this treaty, in appointing this commission, intended to create a court with powers paramount to the courts of either nation, in order that the subjects of both might there find impartial decisions, conformable to justice, equity, and the law of nations. You, gentlemen, are vested with powers, such as have rarely been given to any court upon earth; I hope you will use them carefully and wisely.' Multitudes of complaints were made by the subjects of both nations, and were carefully examined and decrees made on each separate case on its own merits. The commission was not concluded until the beginning of the year 1804. The number of cases examined amounted to between three and four hundred, and the amount awarded to be paid by the British Government exceeded ten millions of dollars. The awards against the United States amounted to about half a million. In all cases of importance written opinions were recorded; one copy of which is in the hands of Colonel Trumbull. The principles laid down and acted upon in those opinions will hereafter form an important part of the maritime law of nations, and have already been of value to many individuals in the settlement of claims against Russia and other governments."

I have an interesting account of Mr. Trumbull's visit to the European continent during the period he was enjoying the honors and emoluments of a commissioner under the treaty negotiated by Mr. Jay; a part of the following was given to me in manuscript by Mr. Herring as written under Mr. Trumbull's dictation and part communicated from memory. The last being the first in order, I shall give it first.

"During the existence of the commission and previous to the year 1800, Mr. Trumbull took advantage of one of the adjournments with which the commissioners indulged themselves when wishing to recover from the fatigues of debates 'in which the parties differed continually,' to visit the continent: and as the adjournment was for some months, he resolved to travel to Stutgard, where his picture of 'Bunker Hill' was in the hands of the engraver. He first proceeded to Paris, desirous, among other things, to procure passports from the French Government. Upon applying he was put off from time to time, and at length upon receiving a hint that he was in danger in consequence of some suspicions entertained by the police, he decamped for Amsterdam, having the good fortune to find a vessel ready to sail and a captain willing to take him. At Amsterdam he applied to the French ambassador

for passports to Stutgard, and obtained them. This enabled
him to visit that and other places, and to take possession of his
painting and the engraved plate.

"Germany being at that time the seat of war, our artist met
with various adventures, one of which is particularly interesting. He arrived in his carriage at the only inn belonging to
a village on the Rhine, which was in the possession of a division of the French army. The inn was fully occupied by officers,
and there was no bed for the traveller. Boniface, however,
recollected that an aid of the general, who had his quarters
in the house had been recently sent off, and perhaps might
be absent for the night. He was willing to accommodate the
traveller, but must first have permission from the general.
Accordingly he was sent to inquire of, and receive commands
from his excellency. He returned with an orderly sergeant,
and a message from the general, who wished to see the applicant for his aid's bed. On being introduced, he was questioned
as to his country. 'America.' 'From what part?' 'Connecticut.' 'And the town?' 'Lebanon.' 'Ha! You must know
then my old friend Governor Trumbull?' 'I am his son.'

"The general was rejoiced to meet on the banks of the
Rhine, the son of one whose hospitality he had enjoyed in
another hemisphere, and the traveller found himself in excellent quarters, and among friends. The commander of this
division of the French army, was one of those officers who had
accompanied Rochambeau and learned his first lesson of
republicanism in the native country of the painter.

"The artist returned to France with his pictures, and as he
could not proceed to England without permission, and the time
of the adjourned meeting of the commissioners was fast approaching, he addressed a letter from Calais to Talleyrand,
requesting a passport. He received no answer, and proceeded
to Paris." His difficulties in that city I transcribe from the
manuscript, which begins abruptly:

"From a Frenchman whom he had known in Boston, who
expressed great pleasure at seeing him in Paris, and after some
conversation, asked, if he had seen the minister? 'What

minister?' 'Citizen Talleyrand, certainly.' 'I sent letters to him from Calais to which he made no reply and should have thought it impertinent to have called upon him under those circumstances.' 'O, you are very much mistaken — he will be very happy to see you — he wishes to see you very much — I have seen him this morning — he would be very happy to see you.'

"So, Colonel Trumbull called upon the minister, and was very politely received, and invited to dine; and he did dine that day with him. He sat next to Lucien Bonaparte, and near to Madame de Stael, who was very prompt to make inquiries, and launched at once into political subjects. Talleyrand, however, interrupted her by observing, 'This is no place madam, to talk politics.'

"The time was approaching when it was necessary for the commissioner to be in London, and he accordingly applied for a pass at the *bureau de police;* but he was put off. He called again but could not succeed. Being puzzled with this unexpected difficulty, he went to Mr. Pinkney and told him of it, but was assured that he could not help him, and that it was not unlikely that in twenty-four hours they would meet in the Temple.

"Trumbull at last made up his mind to call again on Talleyrand, to take leave, and, if he found a convenient opportunity, to obtain his aid in procuring a passport. Talleyrand at once took him into his private bureau, and began to talk on the subject of the difficulties between the nations, and particularly of the money demanded of the American deputies, and attributed the high tone of the American Government to British influence. Trumbull observed, 'Mr. Talleyrand, you have been in America, and know our constitution as well as I do, and you must know that these gentlemen can do no less than they have been instructed to do by their government.'

"Talleyrand fiercely thumped his fist upon the table, and exclaimed, 'But they must.' Whether in the ardor of his thoughts he had forgotten his diplomatic caution, or had acted a part for the purpose of having it communicated to the

American commissioners, can only be judged by those who know the character of the minister, and they will not hesitate to admit, as most probable, that he had made his calculations for effect. The strange turn which had been given to the conversation, and its rough termination, cut off all hope of Talleyrand's interference in the obtaining a passport; he accordingly applied again to the police office, and was told if he would ascend the grand staircase, and turn into a low door on the left, he would there find a person who would do his business.

"He went as directed, and entered a room in which was seated a little, thin, sharp old Frenchman, who was alone and writing. 'We shall meet in the Temple within twenty-four hours,' flashed on his mind. 'I shall be caught by this old spider.'

" 'What does the citizen want?' Trumbull informed him. 'What is your name?' 'John Trumbull.' 'Ah, you are very well known here.' He then went on with his writing, and paid no further attention to the application. And when Trumbull became satisfied with waiting, he retired — unmolested.

"The time appointed for the meeting of the commissioners in London was drawing nigh, and if he was detained, another would be selected *by lot* in his place. What could he do? Who did he know, of all in Paris, who would have an influence with the powers in the ascendant? 'David the painter — the very man!' He took a carriage and called on him, and was received with great cordiality, and asked about his great work — how the engravings progressed. He told him that 'Bunker Hill' was finished, and he had been to get the plate and picture, and had them in Paris, and that he was anxious to proceed to London, but did not appear to be as well known as he formerly was, concluding by asking David to assist him in procuring a passport.

"David requested him to take a carriage, and bring his picture immediately. He did so: and David accompanied him to the police office taking the picture along with them. On entering the office the same persons were there as before, and a whispering was observed among them, and looks of wonder that citizen David should lean on the arm of that man who could not get a passport. 'Which is the secretary's office?' demanded David, with authority. He was shown to it. He then introduced Colonel Trumbull, as a friend; vouched for him as a republican as good as himself; told his profession and his business in Paris; and requested that a passport might be furnished. The secretary promised to have it done immediately, and after a moment wished the minister to be informed, and his consent obtained. They were then ushered into the apartment of the minister (*of police*), and the picture produced. 'This gentleman,' said David, 'saw the battle of Bunker Hill and has painted it. I saw the picture ten years ago. He has been to have it engraved.'

"The minister was very polite; authorized the passport; but added, that 'he was almost tempted to use his power to prevent it, that he might detain so excellent an artist in the country.' Mixing up with his unwilling consent the smoothest flattery.

"No sooner was his passport ready than he took post horses and away with speed lest another change should detain him. On arriving at *St. Denis*, while changing horses, a motley crowd assembled around the carriage, and amongst them was a man distinguished by a military uniform and peculiar figure, being upwards of six feet one or two inches, in height, thin, and of a Don Quixote appearance, with a sword almost as long as himself dragging along the pavement in a brass scabbard. This figure approached the carriage and looking in, inquired, 'Is the citizen alone?' Trumbull's first thought was, 'I am entrapped!' "

After some inquiries and answers, which Mr. Herring repeated verbally, the narrative proceeds, " 'Is the citizen English?' 'No, I am an American.' 'The carriage is English?' 'Yes, I have been residing some time in England, and brought the carriage from that country.'

"These inquiries and answers at last led to the singular question by the stranger if he 'might be permitted to take the vacant seat as far as Chantilly?' The request, of course, was granted. When the horses were ready they proceeded, and the *militaire* asked a number of questions as — where his fellow-traveller had been, and of the persons he had seen in his route. On Trumbull mentioning a certain officer, the soldier exclaimed, 'Ah, he was a fool! I was a private in his regiment. I now command it.' It was Trumbull's intention to have proceeded beyond Chantilly; but his companion told him it would be unsafe. 'Wait until morning, and I will give you an escort through.'"

Here the manuscript fails me, but Mr. Herring terminated the adventure thus: "The painter concluding that he was a prisoner, complied with the suggestions of his companion as with commands, and awaited the result. The next morning at daybreak an escort of horse was ready and thus attended he proceeded. Having passed through the part which had been described as unsafe, to the traveller's surprise his guard left him to pursue his way at his pleasure. Still the fear of detention was not removed, and on his arrival at Calais, finding that the packet had just entered the harbor from Dover, so great was the fear of French republicanism which haunted the American commissioner, that he induced the captain, by an offer of one hundred guineas, immediately to return and land him on that shore where alone his safety could be assured."

If we look attentively at this narrative of difficulties, it will be seen that Trumbull did not ask Talleyrand for a passport — that he did not wait for an answer from the little old Frenchman at the police office — in short, that he had been imagining difficulties which had no existence. It appears further, that as soon as David applied for it, the permission was given. Notwithstanding which, the little old Frenchman and the French officer, six feet two in height, haunted his imagination as emissaries of tyranny, though both harmless — the first let him depart unmolested; the second gave him an escort to render his journey safe.

We have seen that the business which occupied the commissioners was concluded in the beginning of the year 1804. In the meantime an event had taken place which usually has the most important bearing on the life of man. During the existence of this commission Mr. Trumbull was married.

All I find in Mr. Herring's manuscript are these words, at the top of a page: "He was married in 1800-1." There is every reason to suppose that Mr. Trumbull meant to make England his home. His wife was an Englishwoman, and his only son an officer in the English army; but Mr. Trumbull returned to the United States, bringing Mrs. Trumbull with him, in June 1804.

In the month of June 1794, Mr. Trumbull had landed in England as secretary to Mr. Jay, and in a residence of ten years painted many portraits the size of life, assuming a style altogether different and much less happy than that he had formerly adopted.

Among the works of this period which have remained with the painter are portraits of Messrs. Gore and King; portrait of a lady; St. John and Lamb; the "Madonna *au Corset Rouge*," from Raphael; Infant Saviour and St. John; and a Holy Family.

On the occasion of this visit of 1804 to his native country, the painter brought a large collection of pictures, which had been, as is understood, thrown into the Parisian market as things of little or at least diminished value by the stormy waves of the French revolution; and were purchased by the artist in his visits to that capital. These pictures were placed on exhibition in the room afterwards occupied as a saloon in the Park Theatre, New York; but notwithstanding their great beauty and intrinsic merit, they did not attract sufficient attention to pay the charges of exhibiting, although the manager of the theatre gave the room rent free. This was the first public exhibition of original pictures by the old masters of Europe which had been made in America, and in many respects it has not been exceeded since. The artist at the same time exhibited as part of the collections his own fine picture of the "Sortie from Gibraltar," which is now in the Boston Athenæum.

After a trial of the want of taste in New York at that period, these pictures were repacked, and stored away until their owner returned again to London. They then followed him.

Mr. Trumbull, soon after his arrival in 1804, established himself in a large house, corner of Pine Street and Broadway, as portrait painter, in his second style. He stood alone in the northern and eastern division of the United States. Jarvis and Sully, though professing to paint, were tyros and unknown. Stuart was at the seat of government. Our wealthy citizens had their portraits painted, and the corporation of New York had their governors and mayors immortalized by Mr. Trumbull.

An auctioneer, once upon a time, had a variety of articles which he exposed for sale, perhaps in Wall Street, and among the rest some sheep. He dwelt at length, and with many flourishes, upon the invaluable bargains he offered, far below their value, and concluded his eloquent harangue with, "As to the sheep, gentlemen, they will speak for themselves."

So I would willingly say of the pictures painted during the painter's present visit to America, if my readers could all have the opportunity of appreciating their dumb eloquence. Some of these portraits of the head size are speaking likenesses; but of the generality, and of the whole lengths, they are wonderful proofs of the possibility of the same hand painting at one period beautiful faces and figures, worthy of the admiration of the amateur and artist, and while yet in the vigor of life, at the age of 48, producing pictures devoid of most things valuable in the art, and contrasts to his former work. Perhaps the worst of these pictures is the portrait of John Jay.

This could not last. Jarvis and Sully were rising. Stuart moved north. Applications for portraits became "few and far between," and in 1808, Mr. Trumbull again returned to England, loudly complaining of the taste, manners, and institutions of America. That he now intended to make England his permanent place of residence we presume.

In 1809, Mr. Trumbull was established in handsome style

in Argyle Street, London, and had some share of the portrait painting of the time, but not enough, and he again devoted himself to historical composition.

In respect to this portion of Mr. Trumbull's life, that is from 1804, all we find in the manuscript, dictated to Mr. Herring, is: "1808, the embarrassments of commerce affected the class of citizens by whom, in this country," (America) "the fine arts are chiefly supported, and he determined to seek abroad that employment which he could not obtain at home. Accordingly," (he returned to London and remained abroad until 1816), "during his residence in England he painted a number of pictures, with the hope of attracting some attention, but," says he, "everything American was unpopular. The War of 1812, was unpopular, and he failed completely. At the close of the war he returned to New York."

Now, during this same period, Washington Allston, and Charles R. Leslie, were likewise in London, and painting; and the reader has only to turn to the accounts these gentlemen give of the encouragement afforded to their efforts by Englishmen, and he will conclude that the true reason of failure is not given. Allston expressly says, "England has never made any distinction between our artists and her own."

When Mr. Trumbull returned to England in 1808, he carried with him several studies which he had made of the Falls of Niagara, with a view to have a panorama of that great scene painted by Barker, that species of exhibition being at the time fashionable and profitable in London.

I have heard Mr. Trumbull say, speaking of Mr. West, "For thirty years he was more than a father to me." Yet it is well known that after the failure of his prospects as an historic painter in London, and the rejection by Barker of his proposals for a joint concern in a panorama of Niagara, he spoke of Mr. West in a style of bitterness little according with the first-mentioned fact of paternal protection. That West secretly influenced public opinion against the efforts of the man he had made a painter, is so diametrically opposite to the uniform character and conduct of that benevolent and pure man, that the assertion, when I heard it made, astonished and disgusted me. He further charged his old master with influencing Barker to reject his views of Niagara. If the rival merits of the pupil could cause the master to fear his overshadowing popularity as an historical painter, still we are to look for a motive that might influence his conduct in thwarting the plans of a project as a designer of panoramas.

Mr. Trumbull's account of this transaction (as related by a highly respectable gentleman) is as follows: Mr. West, as was asserted, was overheard, at the theatre, in conversation with Barker, giving his opinion that the views painted by Trumbull were not fitted for a panorama, and discouraging the acceptance of his proposals. Barker, having rejected the plan, and this *overheard conversation* being reported to the disappointed painter, he repaired to Newman Street, and finding the old man, as usual, at his easel, opened his battery of reproaches, and told the story of the overheard dialogue.

The old gentleman continued his work until the complainant had finished — made a pause, and then mildly said, "All the difference from the truth in what you have stated, is, that I urged the plan, and the objections were made by Barker." But this did not satisfy — perhaps only irritated the disappointed man.* It is to be remarked that this is Mr. Trumbull's own version of the story. In connection with the anecdote, it may be well to quote the words of another pupil of West. Washington Allston says, "He was a man overflowing with the milk of human kindness. If he had enemies, I doubt if he owed them to any other cause than this rare virtue."

From this time until a subscription was filled for a picture of West by Lawrence, proposed by Mr. Waldo in New York, Mr. Trumbull spoke of West in terms of enmity. He was appointed to write the letter requesting the sittings, and he did it in the style of friendship.

It was not until after Mr. Trumbull's final return to the

---

* This passage has been submitted to the gentleman who originally related it, and he confirms the whole, adding, that by the pause before speaking, it was insinuated that West took time to fabricate an answer, and that the answer was a falsehood.

United States in 1816, that I had the most distant notion that he could feel enmity to his former teacher. Standing before a cast from Chantry's bust of West, I remarked, with a feeling of delight, "How like it is!" "Yes," was the reply; "it has precisely his Jesuitical expression." These few words let in a flood of light upon the hearer. They pierced like an arrow, and like a barbed arrow they remained fixed.

When afterwards I heard of the disappointed expectations of the artist, on presenting his master with the small study for his picture of the "Sortie," — that "it had not been exhibited and displayed as it might have been," and that the pupil expected the master to have relinquished his mantle, and covered him therewith; I had still more light shed upon me. Whether it was expected that West should ascend to heaven before his time to accommodate his grateful protégée, I know not; but I do know, that long after this period of disappointed expectation, the greatest and best works of the great painter were completed, and other pupils had arisen, much more able to sustain the "mantle," when he should be called from the cold world where his old age needed it.

But I must return to that portion of the artist's life, which passed between his return to England in 1808, and his last visit to America in 1816. During this eight years' residence in England, he made strenuous efforts to attract popular attention. But his style had changed since his happy state of pupilage under West. As we have seen in his own words, "he failed completely." Besides two elaborately finished pictures from Scripture subjects, which were exhibited at the British Institution, in the hope of prize or sale, the artist seized a moment of Russian popularity, and displayed "Peter the Great at Narva." When Scott's poems occupied public attention, he painted Ellen Douglass, her father, lover, and the old harper, which, although on the small scale, approached in nothing else to his first pictures. "The Knighting of De Wilton" was painted; and the picture of "Lamderg and Gelchossa."

But the two Scripture pictures above noticed seem to have engrossed a great portion of his time, study, and labor. The subjects are, "The Woman taken in Adultery," and "Suffer little children to come unto me," both now (1834) at New Haven. Both were painted on a small scale, and then enlarged to life size. These are the best pictures painted by the artist at this period, and far superior to his more recent works.

"The Woman taken in Adultery" is the best of the two. The figure of Christ is the best large historical figure by this painter, and is in many respects better than the Saviour in West's great painting of "The Healing in the Temple." For the distribution of the figures, the painter has judiciously followed the recommendation of old Richardson, where he points out the best mode of arranging the subject. The second picture, "Suffer little children," etc., is apparently more labored than the first; and is devoid of its aerial perspective. But the most striking defect is the palpable imitation of the Magdalen in Correggio's "St. Jerome," which the artist had copied (from West's copy) in the winter of 1800-1, and the utter failure in the attempt.

CHAPTER V.

Trumbull — *Concluded.*

In 1816 Mr. Trumbull returned to America, after having passed, for the second time in the enemy's country, a period of warfare successfully terminated by his fellow-citizens. The change which had taken place in the state of the arts during the last absence of the artist, rendered his prospects as a portrait painter sufficiently gloomy. In addition to Stuart, who had all the applications from the rich and the celebrated to the east, Sully was in high and deserved reputation, commanding the demand for portraits in Philadelphia and its neighborhood, and Jarvis was full of orders for private and public individuals in New York. Vanderlyn had likewise returned from the continent of Europe, and the admirers of the fine arts looked with mingled delight and admiration on his "Marius" and "Ariadne." And although Allston had not yet arrived, the fame of his success had preceded him, and he soon followed his great picture of the "Dead man revived by the bones of the prophet." Besides these prominent men, a number of younger artists were coming forward, many of whom soon displayed skill, which threw the waning talents of Mr. Trumbull in the shade.

The pictures brought home by Mr. Trumbull attracted attention to him as an historical painter, and he now judiciously determined, as the capitol at Washington was rebuilding, and the nation animated by recent triumphs, to make an effort for employment in commemorating the heroes of the Revolution, by exhibiting his early pictures at the seat of government.

A preparatory step was the revival of the American Academy of Fine Arts at New York, the consequence of which was his election as its president, and a nominal sale of several of his pictures to the institution over which he presided.

I was among the first and warmest in recommending the application to Congress. I looked with delight on the miniatures painted in 1786-7-8 and 9, and anticipated more delight from the same when enlarged and rendered more powerful by the charm of magnitude. Members of Congress seemed to calculate upon the same scale, and of the vast increase in difficulty between the small and the great, and the possibility of deterioration in an artist's abilities, while in possession of his physical powers, I was as ignorant as any member of Congress.

Mr. Trumbull proceeded to Washington during the session of 1816-17; and the fine compositions of "Bunker Hill," and "Montgomery," with the admirable miniature portraits of the signers of the Declaration of July 4th, and the heroes who terminated the Revolution at York Town, procured an order for four pictures, for the rotunda of the capitol, the architect of which made his design to accommodate eight, each 18 feet by 12. Appropriations were made for the payment of thirty-two thousand dollars, or eight thousand dollars for each, a part paid in advance, as I understand, and the remainder in due time. This magnificent national encouragement of the fine arts, and tribute of gratitude to the sages and warriors of the Revolution, met the full approbation of every portion of the republic.

But although the paintings of "Bunker Hill" and "Montgomery's Defeat," contributed by their excellence to facilitate the order for four pictures, Congress did not choose to ornament their halls with the triumphs of their enemies and rejected those subjects. They chose what is called the "Declaration of Independence," "The Surrender of Burgoyne," "The Surrender of Cornwallis," and "The Resignation of Washington," when his great work was accomplished.

As the "Declaration" and "The Surrender of Cornwallis," were composed, and the heads finished on the small scale, the painter began the series, by the large picture of the first subject, which, when finished, he exhibited in New York, and then in all the principal cities of the Union; this gave an opportunity to the citizens of seeing their picture without the expense of a journey to Washington.

Public expectation was perhaps never raised so high respecting a picture, as in this case: and although the painter had only to copy his own beautiful original of former days, a disappointment was felt and loudly expressed. Faults which escaped detection in the miniature, were glaring when magnified — the touch and the coloring were not there — attitudes which appeared constrained in the original, were awkward in the copy — many of the likenesses had vanished. The arrangement of the whole appeared tame and unskilful — and people asked, "What is the point of time?" — "It is not the Declaration," — "No, it is the bringing in of the Declaration by the committee." It was then found that men who were present at the scene were omitted; and men not present, or who had not even then taken a seat in Congress, were represented as actors in the great deliberative drama. Men said, "Is history thus to be falsified, and is this record to be placed in the capitol to contradict the minutes of Congress and the truth?"

However, these murmurs died away. The painter received several thousand dollars by exhibiting his picture before he delivered it at Washington, and it was received and paid for. It retains enough of the original to make it valuable for likenesses of some distinguished men, and proved by far the best of the series which had been ordered by the government.

In the second picture of this series, which had likewise been partly finished about 1790, in its original beautiful miniature form, the painter again violated truth, by introducing Lord Cornwallis in the scene of the surrender; and finding that so gross a violation of known fact was objected to, he gave the figure another name, and in his catalogue says, generally, "the principal officers of the British army."

On another occasion, when a person who had witnessed the inauguration of the first president described the scene to Mr. Trumbull, "Here stood Washington, in a suit of brown American broadcloth; there stood Chancellor Livingston, prepared to administer the oath prescribed by the constitution; and

here stood Mr. Otis, supporting the Bible," the painter remarked, "I would place a more important personage in that
situation." Thus the truth of history is to be sacrificed to effect
or flattery.

Horace Walpole has said, "I prefer portraits really interesting, not only to landscape painting, but to history. A
landscape is, we will say, an exquisite distribution of light and
shade, wood, water, and buildings. It is excellent — we pass
on, and it leaves not one trace in the memory. In historical
painting there may be *sublime deception*, but it not only always
falls short of the idea, but it is always *false*. Thus it has the
greatest blemish incidental to history. It is commonly false
in the costume, always in the grouping and attitudes, which
the painter, if not present, cannot possibly delineate as they
were. Call it fabulous painting, I have no objection. — But
a real portrait, we know, is truth itself; and it calls up so many
collateral ideas, as to fill an intelligent mind more than any
other species." Now, although Mr. Trumbull did not, and
could not, see any of the scenes represented by him, he had
the advantage of seeing the costumes of the persons, and of
painting the portraits of many of the men, although some years
after the transactions. He had an opportunity of knowing,
from Mr. Jefferson, Mr. Adams, and others, and from the
minutes of Congress, who were present when the committee
brought in the Declaration; and Count Rochambeau, or other
French officers in Paris, and Washington and his officers,
could have told him every minutiæ of the surrender at York
Town. The pictures should have been portraits of the *events*,
as faithful as of the *faces* of the men. That the painter should
fail in copying the features he had put on canvas in early life,
is only to be lamented; but just disappointment was excited
and expressed when men found that the walls of the rotunda
were to contradict the records of history.

The second picture of the series was finished and was carried
the same round for exhibition, but with somewhat diminished
profit. Still, I believe, thousands were added to the thousands
paid for it by the national government.

So far the artist had had his early painted models to guide him, but no farther. The "Surrender of Burgoyne" is altogether the work of his declining years, except as he had made beautiful miniature portraits of many of the officers present, when he had his original powers, and was fresh from his studies with West. It is a lamentable falling off, even from his two immediately preceding it. It was exhibited as the others, but with less profit.

The last was another fresh composition, still worse in the conception and execution. Several female figures are introduced, as witnesses of the resignation of that commission under which the hero had fought the battles of his country: but instead of adding grace and beauty to the scene, they are prominent in deformity.

Let not foreigners, or men of after days, take these pictures, because of their situation, as a standard by which to measure the arts of design in our country at the time they were painted. It was my duty to show the causes which led to the employment of their painter, and I have faithfully done so. The government judged of the painter's ability from what he had done in early life. They looked for improvement rather than deterioration. The progress of the arts had been great, and good painters existed; but the advantage of having the portraits of the men of other days in his possession, and the exhibition of compositions made near thirty years before, under the eye of West, very naturally induced the statesmen of 1817 to accept with joy the proposals of Mr. Trumbull. I have mentioned American artists existing at this time, whose works will give the true standard of the art of painting at the period of painting the four great pictures which are now (1834) in the capitol.

It is necessary to mention, that before the place designed for their reception was prepared, they were deposited in some lower apartments and occasionally seen; and that some ruffian, to express his disappointment or malice, cut through the canvas of one of them with a sharp instrument. The author of this atrocity was never discovered. When the rotunda was finished, the painter, with the concurrence of government, repaired to Washington, to see his pictures put up and retouch them. In this service he attended for a considerable portion of one session of Congress, urging his suit for the filling of the remaining panels, at the same time making a small picture of the Resignation of Washington; and unfortunately painting on other small pictures, particularly the original miniature "Battle of Princeton." When the sum to be appropriated to this service was in question, the painter was offered the wages of a member of Congress. He replied, "I am not a member of Congress, and never expect to be. I am a painter. — In New York my price for a portrait, of head size, is one hundred dollars; and one such picture occupies one week. I expect to be paid one hundred dollars a week for the time I have attended here."

I do not pretend to give the exact words, but such substantially is the fact, as related to me by a member of Congress then and there present, who gave the painter credit for the answer and his adroit management. It is unnecessary to add that the demand was paid.

That the painter demanded, in New York, one hundred dollars for a head or bust-size portrait is true; and true that he might paint one a week — but the deduction from the premises may be doubted.

When Mr. Trumbull first applied for the painting of the designs for the rotunda, his application was for eight pictures, the number which would fill it. It will be evident at once, from what I have said, that I consider it a most fortunate circumstance that this contract was made for four only. The artist has repeatedly made application for the honor of filling the remaining four panels; and on every renewed effort our journals have teemed with enumerations of his superior claims to all other artists in America for such patriotic employment. One publication intended for this purpose came avowedly from himself, and, in justice to his character, will be inserted. — (The letters to the President of the United States, as published with the resolution of the directors of the American Academy of the Fine Arts.)

In the year 1830 I attended a meeting called by the opposers of Mr. Jackson's administration, respecting the rights of the Indians. I was told that Colonel Willet was to preside. I found Mr. Trumbull in his place: the veteran, who had served with honor through the Revolutionary contest, could not be had. Shortly after this meeting Mr. Wilde, in Congress, said, "The painter had better keep to his palette," or words to that effect. And in the *American*, New York, 20th Jan. 1830, Mr. Trumbull indignantly spurns at the title. I publish the letter to Wilde, and the introductory letter to the editor.

"New York, 20th January, 1830.
" *To the Editor of the American,*

"May I beg the favor of you to publish in your paper the following copy of a letter which I have thought it my duty to address to the Hon. Mr. Wilde, in Congress, the original of which I sent to him by the mail two days ago, and which I now wish to make public in consequence of the publicity of his attack.

"After having devoted ten of the best years of my life, in very early youth and in middle age, to the active services of my country; and having employed the intervals of military and political occupations in acquiring an elegant art, for the very purpose of preserving through its means the memory of the great events and illustrious men of the Revolution; I did hope to enjoy some repose during the fragment of a life which can remain to a man who has passed its ordinary limits. It appears cruel as towards me, and disgraceful to themselves, that so many men in Congress should have continued to tease me with a repetition of paltry personal squibs. They may rest assured that, however painful the task may be, yet, so long as my intellect and my hands are spared to me, I shall never fail to return an answer.

"Yours truly, JOHN TRUMBULL."

"New York, January 16, 1830.
" *Hon. Mr. Wilde, in Congress,*

"Sir, — In the newspapers of this day, I observe a sketch of the debate which took place in the House of Representatives on the 11th instant, on the subject of the memorial from this city, relating to the Cherokee Indians, and which was signed by me as chairman of the meeting. I am very much obliged to you for the favorable terms in which you speak of me as an artist; but when you recommended to 'the painter to stick to his palette,' you perhaps were not aware that I had not been always, nor merely, *a painter*.

"You might not know, that in August, 1775, I was appointed an Aid-de-camp of General Washington; and that I am the eldest of the few survivors who ever had that honor.

"You might not know, that in July, 1776, I was appointed Adjutant-General of the Northern Department, with the rank of Colonel, under the command of General Gates; and that, of course, I am now one of the oldest surviving colonels of the Revolutionary army.*

"You might not know that, in 1794, I attended Mr. Jay, as his secretary, in his very important, though unpopular embassy to England.

"And probably you do not know the triumphant result of the 7th article of the treaty then negotiated by him, relating to the subject of ' irregular or illegal captures.'

"The papers relating to that subject were deposited, by the American commissioners, in the department of state, in 1804. It did not suit the policy of the government, at that time to give publicity to a result which was so favorable to the commercial part of the nation, and so honorable to Mr. Jay: and as those papers perished when Washington was burnt, it is probable that you are not accurately acquainted with the facts. I beg leave to state them to you.

"The commission to which was referred the subject of 'irregular or illegal captures,' was composed of five members: — Mr. Gore and Mr. Pinkney, on the part of the United States; Dr. Nichol and Dr. Swabey (two of her most eminent civilians), on the part of Great Britain; and I was the fifth commissioner, representing both nations. This commission was clothed with authority paramount to all courts of prize of both na-

* The preceding pages render any comment unnecessary upon these assertions.

tions. It was very natural for the two commissioners of each party to think their own government generally right; and such was the fact on all important questions — of course, all such questions remained to be decided, and were decided, by the fifth commissioner.

"In very many cases, the decisions of the courts of both nations were over-ruled by us and reversed; and the government of Great Britain actually and faithfully paid, under our awards, to citizens of the United States, *more than ten millions of dollars*.

"It is not to be supposed that I hazarded such a course in such society, during seven years, in the city of London, and supported my decisions by written opinions, without having devoted some time to the study of the law of nations.

"If you had known these facts, perhaps you would not have thought it so extraordinary that the painter should now risk an opinion on a question which he regards as one strictly of international law.

"I reason thus: — By the Constitution of the United States, treaties are the supreme law of the land, obligatory not merely on all the individuals, but on all the States which compose the nation.

"The power of making treaties is vested *exclusively* in the President and Senate.

"Many treaties have been made between the Presidents and Senates of the United States and the Cherokee nation.

"A treaty can be annulled only by the consent of both the contracting parties, or by the violent and lawless conduct of one.

"The Cherokee nation, one of the parties in this case, far from giving their consent to a dissolution of existing treaties, earnestly insist upon their fulfilment.

"Therefore, the present attempt to set aside these treaties, by any act of the government of the United States, or by their supineness or connivance, does appear to me to be a direct and most unfair appeal to the law of the strongest — a principle which I am very reluctant to see acted upon by the government of my country, in this or any case.

"Thus thinking, and presuming that I am a free citizen of a free country, I cannot be persuaded that I have acted improperly in expressing my opinion on this important subject to the representatives of the nation: and I presume that every gentleman who took part in the memorial in question will most cordially subscribe to these opinions.

"Permit me to add, for the information of Mr. Thompson, and whomsoever it may concern, that the meeting, of which I had the high honor to act as chairman, was not held in a grog-shop, but in the most spacious hall in this city, which was literally filled by the most respectable of its inhabitants.

"I am, etc., etc.

"John Trumbull."

After the completion of the large picture of the Declaration, the artist employed the first American engraver for talent, to give more extended circulation to that composition by his burin. He engaged A. B. Durand, Esq., after having failed in a negotiation with a celebrated Italian engraver, of the name of Gondolfi. Mr. Trumbull applied to Heath, of London also, who demanded a price equal to $6000. Mr. Durand agreed to engrave it for $3000. He was then a young man, and justly thought that the work gave him an opportunity of coming before the public, in connection with a popular subject, and that although it would exhaust at least three years of his time, he had better accept an inadequate compensation for the exertion of his talents, and gain, as he had reason to expect, an addition to his fame as an engraver. In 1829, Mr. Trumbull said, that in 1790 he got 270 subscribers for his two prints of "Bunker Hill" and "Montgomery," in the United States, at three guineas for each print, and in 1819, he could only obtain the same number for his print of the "Declaration of Independence." From this he inferred that as the population increases, the taste for the fine arts decreases. Fortunately for Americans the plate was engraved from the small original picture, and the engraver has preserved the real portraits of the eminent men introduced. We speak without hesitation on this point, having known most of the originals. Mr. Durand likewise corrected the drawing of several parts of the picture, by consent, and with the approbation of the painter.

The perseverance with which Mr. Trumbull pursued his plan of painting *more* great pictures for the government, not only to fill the four remaining panels of the rotunda, but to fill the president's house, and the engines he set at work with even more assiduity than when he made his successful application to Congress, are subjects of admiration. Presenting himself at the seat of government, he again, as at the former period, procured what is called his biography, to be circulated *there* and elsewhere in the newspapers. In December 1826, the *National Intelligencer* announces that the four great pictures are in their places in the capitol — that Col. Trumbull is at Washington — that his powers are undiminished, and promises his biography. On the 29th of December 1826, there appeared in the New York *Times*, "Biographical notices of Colonel Trumbull, author of those paintings of subjects from the History of the Revolution, which are now placed in the great hall of the capitol of Washington." The writer then praises the pictures, but acknowledges that "since they have been removed to the seat of government" they "have been bitterly criticised." After going through the military and civil services of *Colonel* Trumbull, the biographer eulogizes the *four pictures* in which "this nation," he says, "possesses a work which no other people have yet possessed." He then proceeds: "We are happy to hear, from the proceedings of the House of Representatives, that there is an intention to fill the remaining vacant spaces in the Grand Hall with other paintings of Revolutionary events, and hope sincerely that the importance will be felt, of employing the few remaining years of this *veteran soldier* and artist in this work. *No one else devoted his youth to the necessary studies. No one else has given years of thought and labor to the preservation of the memory of the great events of that distant day. He alone appears to have made it the study of a long life;* and strange will it appear to other nations, and to posterity, if under such circumstances, half of this magnificent room should be filled with *imaginary scenes delineated by men who have no personal knowledge of the events*, and who have hitherto scarcely given the dream of an idle hour to the subject." So are mankind deceived by bold assertions, without any foundation in truth.

Mr. Trumbull's best pictures are "imaginary scenes"; they could be no other. His only advantage over better painters, of 1826, was that he had collected portraits of many men (after he returned from England, and the Federal Government was established), who had served their country in the field and the council. He has great merit in so doing, and has reaped the advantage.

This biography of 1826, must be taken in connection with the following letters addressed by Mr. Trumbull to the president of the United States, on the 25th and 28th of December, 1826, four days before the "Biographical Notices" appeared in the *Times* at New York.

"Washington, 25th December, 1826.

" *To the President of the United States.*

"Sir, — I beg permission to submit to your consideration the following plan for the permanent encouragement of the fine arts in the United States: public protection has already been extended, in a very effectual manner, to various branches of the public industry employed in manufactures of different kinds; and I wish to call the attention of the government to the fine arts, which, although hitherto overlooked, may, I trust, be rendered a valuable, as well as an honorable branch of the national prosperity, by very simple and inexpensive means.

"I would propose that whenever an event, political, naval, or military, shall occur, which shall be regarded by the government as of sufficient importance to be recorded as matter of history, the most eminent painter of the time, be ordered to paint a picture of the same, to be placed in some of the national buildings — that an artist of secondary talent be employed to make a copy of the same, which shall be given to the minister, admiral, or general under whose direction or command the event shall have taken place, as a testimony of the approbation and gratitude of the nation.

"It appears to me that this would operate as a powerful stimulus to the ambition and exertions of the national servants in their various departments, as well as an effectual encouragement to artists, and an honorable mode of exciting their unremitting endeavors to attain to the highest possible degrees of eminence.

"I would next propose, that the most distinguished engraver of the day should be employed to engrave a copperplate from the painting so executed, and that one thousand impressions, first printed from this plate, be reserved by government for the purpose hereafter designated; the remaining impressions which may be printed, to be sold, and the proceeds applied to a fund destined to defray the expense of the plan.

"This part of the plan is founded on the experience of individuals who have pursued the business of publishing and selling engravings, many of whom, after paying the painter, the engraver, the paper maker, the printer, and all the various expenses of publication, have acquired considerable fortunes in reward of their enterprise and exertions.

"This was particularly instanced by the late Alderman Boydell, of London, who (himself an engraver), in the beginning of the reign of George III. found England paying annually to France and other nations, for this article of ornamental furniture, engravings, near $200,000, and lived to see (in consequence of a judicious encouragement of the fine arts by the sovereign and his own individual exertions), England receiving from France and other nations, a balance considerably exceeding that sum, making a difference in favor of England of more than $400,000 a year. Reasoning on this experience, it is manifest that this nation may be probably indemnified for the entire expense of the project, by the sale of those impressions which may be taken from the plates after the first thousand, which would remain to be disposed of as follows: —

"Every minister of the United States, going abroad on a

mission, should be furnished with one (or a set) of these reserved engravings, as an article of his outfit; they should be
handsomely framed and hung in the most public and elegant
apartments of his foreign residence — not so much for the
purpose of ornament, as of showing the people among whom
he resided, at once an historical record of important events
and an evidence of our advance, not only in political, naval,
and military greatness, but also in those arts of peace which
embellish and adorn even greatness itself.

"Every minister of a foreign nation returning home from a
residence among us, should also receive one (or a set) of
those prints, in a handsome portfolio; and the same compliment might occasionally be paid to foreigners of distinction
visiting the country from motives of curiosity or a desire of
improvement, in the discretion of government.

"An historical record of memorable events, and a monumental tribute of gratitude and respect to the distinguished servants of the nation, would thus be preserved in a series of paintings of unquestionable authenticity; the principal works
adorning the public edifices and placing before the eyes of
posterity the glorious examples of the past, and thus urging
them to that emulation which may render the future yet more
glorious; the smaller works in possession of the immediate
descendants of those who had thus received the thanks of the
country, decorating private houses with the proud evidence of
individual service and of national gratitude, and thus kindling
all the talent and energy of succeeding generations to elevate,
if possible, at least not to diminish the honor of the name and
nation; while the engravings in a more portable, more multiplied and less expensive form would disseminate through the
world evidence of the greatness and gratitude of the United
States.

"Talent for all the elegant arts abounds in this country, and
nothing is wanting to carry their votaries to the highest rank
of modern or even ancient attainment, but encouragement and
cultivation; and although all cannot hope to rise or be sustained in the most elevated rank, still the less successful com-

petitors would become eminently useful by turning their abilities to the aid of manufactures. It is the overflowing of the schools and the academies of France which has given to the manufacture of porcelain at Sevres, and of ormolu time-pieces and ornaments in Paris, that high pre-eminence over the rival attempts of other nations, which drives them almost entirely from the markets of elegance, and thus becomes the source of very considerable wealth to France.

"The history of the United States already abounds in admirable subjects for the pencil and the chisel, which should not be suffered to sink into oblivion: the last war especially, is full of them, and it seems to me that this is the proper field for the present and rising artists to cultivate; the field is not only fertile and extensive, but is hitherto untouched, and seems to solicit their patriotic labors and to chide their delay. They are cotemporaries and familiar with the actors and the scenes they are called to commemorate, and can therefore fulfil the duty with enthusiasm, a knowledge of facts, and a degree of absolute authenticity, which ensures success and would give real value to their works. Nor should it be forgotten, that the stream of time is continually, though silently, bearing away from our view, objects, circumstances and eminent forms, which memory can never recall.

"The public buildings offer fine situations for the display of works of this nature, not only in various apartments of the capitol, but in the house of the president, where the great room now furnishing, would with more propriety and economy be enriched by subjects of national history, executed by our own artists, than loaded with expensive mirrors and all the frivolous and perishable finery of fashionable upholstery.

"By giving, in such way as I have here taken the liberty to suggest, a right direction and suitable encouragement to the fine arts, they may be rendered essentially subservient to the highest moral purposes of human society, and be redeemed from the disgraceful and false imputation under which they have long been oppressed, of being only the base and flattering instruments of royal and aristocratic luxury and vice.

"I do not pretend to originality, sir, in submitting to you these ideas; Athens in ancient times, and Venice, in the best days of that republic, acted on these principles to a certain extent. All civilized nations have made the arts useful auxiliaries of history, by the means of medals; and it is even said, that this very system was proposed to Louis the XVI. of France and approved by him, but prevented from being carried into effect, by the long train of succeeding calamities. I have only attempted to adapt the general idea to the circumstances of our country and times, and I cannot but believe, that not only artists and manufacturers would derive great advantage from the adoption of some such plan, but that the honor and the essential interests of the nation would thereby be eminently advanced.

    "With very great respect,
      "I have the honor to be, sir,
        "Your most faithful servant,
          "JOHN TRUMBULL."

      "Washington, 28th December, 1826.

"*To the President of the United States.*

"Sir, — Permit me to place before you an estimate of the expense which would be incurred by the government of the United States, in carrying into effect the plan for the permanent encouragement of the fine arts, which I had the honor of submitting to you in a letter dated the 25th instant. Taking for the purpose a single event for commemoration, with which it would perhaps be proper to commence.

The United States Dr. for a painting to be placed in the large room of the president's house; the size not to exceed 6 by 9 feet, nor smaller than 4 by 6 feet, with figures half the size of life,	$2,500
For a copy of the same half the dimensions, to be given to whomsoever,	500
For an engraved copperplate from the same, in size 14 by 21 inches,	2,500
For paper and printing two thousand impressions at 50 cents, one thousand to be retained, and one thousand for sale,	1,000
	$6,500

The United States Cr. by proceeds of sale of one thousand impressions at 10 dollars,		$10,000
Deduct the usual commission on sales, 25 per cent.	$2,500	
For possible losses and damage,	1,000	
		$3,500
		$6,500

"The above statement is founded on my own personal knowledge and experience; and thence it is demonstrated, that if only one thousand impressions of the plate should be sold, the account would be balanced, with no other expense to the nation than the interest of 6,500 dollars, during the interval between paying the several articles of charge and the receipt of the proceeds of the sale of prints. And you will permit me to add, that one thousand impressions are a small number to sell of good works published by individuals; and that a greater number would probably be sold of a work published under the orders and authority of the nation, and thus bearing the stamp of perfect authenticity.

"I have stated the price of the principal picture at that sum, which I should have been delighted to receive for a similar work at the time when I painted the 'Battle of Bunker's Hill,' in 1786, and which I believe would be satisfactory at this time to distinguished artists, in Paris or London, and I have fixed the price of the copy by the same rule. I should have been happy to have received that sum in 1785, for a copy I then made for Mr. West, of his celebrated picture of the 'Battle of La Hogue.'

"The price at which I have estimated the engraving of a copperplate, 14 inches by 21 in size, is suggested by that which I paid to Mr. Durand for engraving the Declaration of Independence, 3000 dollars. The size of that plate is 20 by 30 inches, nearly one-third larger than that proposed in my estimate. I presume that 2,500 dollars for the smaller plate proposed would command the first abilities in the country.

"The price of printing, in like manner, is estimated by my own experience: each sheet of the Declaration, on grand eagle paper, cost me nearly 75 cents for paper and printing. That is much larger, and of course the labor and expense of printing is much greater, than is requisite for the contemplated purpose.

"I propose pictures of moderate dimensions, as being best suited to the apartments in the president's house, or the committee rooms of the capitol: and I propose copperplates smaller

than that of the Declaration; because the sale of that print
is impeded by the necessity of large and expensive frames and
glasses, or portfolios for their preservation. Should it be
thought more consistent with the dignity of a national work
to adopt a larger size for the copperplate, a corresponding
larger sum must be paid to the engraver: but, as in that case
it would be proper to increase the price of the impressions sold,
no difference unfavorable to the plan would arise, in respect
to my estimate.

"I have allowed one thousand dollars for *possible* loss or
damage on the sale of the prints; but loss to that extent is by
no means *probable*, and any saving on that article of the estimate would go in diminution of interest. So that it appears,
that with very little expense, beyond the mere *patronage of
government*, the fine arts may be stimulated and encouraged,
the national edifices decorated, authentic monuments of national history preserved, elegant and attractive rewards bestowed on the meritorious servants of the public, and the
national glory essentially advanced.

"With great respect I have the honor to be,
"Sir, your most faithful servant,

"JNO. TRUMBULL."

These letters, and the biographical notices pointing out
"the most eminent painter of the time," did not produce the
intended effect. Mr. Trumbull returned from attending Congress, and in April, 1827, as the minutes of the Academy over
which he presides inform us, "read copies of two letters pro-
posing a plan for the permanent encouragement of the fine
arts, by the national government," etc. etc., "*and requested* that
these copies" (in his own handwriting) "might be deposited
among the archives of the Academy." Whereupon, the board
of directors, consisting of fifteen persons, of whom three were
artists, including the president, resolved that five hundred
copies of these letters should be printed and distributed for the
benefit of the fine arts; which was accordingly done. In
these letters, the price which Mr. Trumbull fixed as a remunera-

tion to the first engraver in the United States, is founded on that which he gave Mr. A. B. Durand, that is, three thousand dollars. It is well known that Mr. Durand agreed to take that sum, merely as a young man's first step to celebrity, as the engraver of a popular subject, and that Heath demanded six thousand; so that the president, perhaps, notwithstanding the prospect of making cheap presents to distinguished individuals, might have been led into an unprofitable speculation. I will remark on the passage in these letters which asserts that works having been ordered by the nation, bear "the stamp of perfect authenticity," that it appears to be meant as an answer to those who have asserted from their own knowledge, that, although the author's pictures were ordered by Congress, they did not represent the truth of history.

About the time of completing the last of the series of pictures for the capitol, Mr. Trumbull became a widower, and soon after gave up the house in which he had painted those great works (the north corner of Park Place and Church Street), and failing in his efforts to procure an order for more pictures from government, he employed his pencil in painting portraits of many of his friends, gratuitously, and in making copies from the works of older artists, with, generally, variations to please his own taste.

On Monday, June 14, 1824, Mr. Trumbull opened for exhibition his last picture for the government, the "Resignation of Washington." It was exhibited six weeks; and the *Commercial Advertiser* told the world that "its exhibition had not paid room rent." Mr. Trumbull then went with his picture to Albany, intending, as I understood, to travel with it until he placed it in Washington. This is a sad contrast to the profit which his first picture for Congress gave from exhibition.

I have mentioned his admirable copies made in London, when under the roof of West. It is a curious and singular fact, that as the talent of this artist declined for original composition, so his powers for copying failed; and both appear to have decayed simultaneously. The number of Madonnas and holy families from his pencil is a proof of his praiseworthy perseverance, and of an utter blindness to the change which his judgment had undergone. I have seen exhibited, in the same place, the exquisite copies of the "St. Jerome" of Correggio and the Madonna of Raphael, with the holy family, painted as his academical gift to the institution over which he presides — and I defy the annals of painting to show a greater contrast.

A more unfortunate employment of the artist has been, after an interval of almost half a century, to complete, as he calls it, those pictures begun in 1787 or 8, or 1790, by painting in figures and heads which had been omitted. In every instance the recent touch is a blot, and the works injured by his misapplied industry.

Fortunately, the miniature original of the "Declaration" had very few heads to be finished. The Battles of Princeton and Trenton had more to fill up, and consequently have suffered more.

We now return to the manuscript dictated by Mr. Trumbull to Mr. Herring for publication, and partly published in Longacre and Herring's "National Portrait Gallery." "At the close of the war he returned to New York. In 1816 he was engaged by the government to paint the four large pictures now in the rotunda of the capitol at Washington, on which he was occupied seven years. Since which he has been principally employed in the ordinary pursuits of an artist's life; and though now at an advanced age, is still pursuing his design of completing his series of copies of his national pictures on a uniform scale of six feet by nine. Finding the government not likely to order the complete series, nor any individual desirous to possess them, he has, within the last year, given the entire set of the original paintings to Yale College; and a building has been erected by the president and fellows of that institution for their preservation."

I think it is due to the president and fellows, and the institution generally, to say that this gift was, and is a bargain, by which the artist receives fifteen hundred dollars annually during life, either from the receipts of the exhibition or otherwise.

The building cost $4000, and there are two galleries, one appropriated to Mr. Trumbull's paintings exclusively, the other containing Smibert's "Berkeley Family" (which I found far superior to my recollection of it; the dean, the amanuensis, and the artist, are finely painted), and a number of portraits, some good, and some good for nothing. The galleries are both well designed, and the pictures show to the best advantage.*

* I will here give the titles of the Trumbull pictures, from the catalogue drawn up by the artist, with such remarks as are suggested by a recent visit in August 1834: —

No. 1. "Preparation for the Entombment of the Saviour," painted 1827. This is a copy with intended amendments.

No. 2. "The Battle of Bunker's Hill," painted in Mr. West's house in 1786. A perfect contrast to No. 1, both in drawing and coloring, and full of excellence and beauty. It is much injured by the cracking of the paint, and has been repaired by the artist. This is a jewel.

No. 3. "The Death of Gen. Montgomery," painted immediately after No. 2, in the same place, and under the same eye, and even more perfect. A brighter jewel, but injured after the same manner.

No. 4. "Battle of Princeton." An instructive sketch.

No. 5. "The Declaration of Independence." The heads painted in 1787-9, and very beautiful, but the composition not so good as the two last, and much of the drawing very inferior. Still the greater number of the heads renders it very valuable.

No. 6. "Capture of the Hessians at Trenton." All that is good in this picture was painted in 1789 and shortly after. What is good is very good, but unfortunately the artist undertook, in after life, to finish it, and every touch is a blot. To look at the hands and compare them to the heads, excites astonishment. Washington's head and Smith's are jewels — the hands are very bad.

No. 7. "Copy of Correggio's St. Jerome." This is a jewel; but I think copied from West's copy. This was painted when the artist was a pupil of West's, in 1781.

No. 8. Copy of Raphael's "Madonna della Sedia," "painted," says Mr. Trumbull, "in London, in the house and under the eye of Mr. West."

No. 9. "Madonna au Corset Rouge," copied in 1801.

No. 10. "Death of General Mercer at the Battle of Princeton." I presume from the excellence of this composition, as I saw it in 1790, that it was designed under Mr. West's roof and eye — if not very shortly after. The artist has, as he calls it, "accomplished his original purpose"; but it is not so — he has accomplished the destruction of his sketch. The heads of Washington and some few near him, have all the merit of Mr. Trumbull's miniature heads of that time (1787-8-9, etc.), but the foreground figures are all comparatively bad.

No. 11. "Surrender of General Burgoyne." This is a copy in miniature from the large picture at Washington; and both being the work of late years, both are, compared with former work, very poor. Let any one of common sense, or sight, compare this with the artist's work done in West's house, London, or soon after, and the contrast will strike beyond previous conception.

No. 12. "The Death of Paulus Emilius," painted at Lebanon, 1774. Mere boy's work.

No. 13. "Surrender of Lord Cornwallis." Most of the heads painted in 1787-8-9. They are exquisitely beautiful miniatures. See the head of Rochambeau. The head of Washington has been finished lately.

No. 14. "Resignation of General Washington," copied from the large picture at Washington.

Mr. Herring's manuscript concludes thus, after mentioning the gift to Yale College, and the building erected to preserve the paintings — "in which they will be united by a number of pictures, by the most distinguished painters of various periods — Trumbull gallery."

No American painter has ever received from government such patronage as Mr. Trumbull; and in the decline of life he receives, as a reward for his military services, a pension, which, though not adequate to his merits, may, when added to the income from his pictures at Yale College, afford those comforts and enjoyments which old age so much requires to smooth the passage to the tomb.

No. 15. "Our Saviour Bearing the Cross," etc. This is a match for No. 1.

No. 16. "Our Saviour with Little Children," painted in London, 1812. I have spoken so fully of this picture and "The Woman taken in Adultery," that I pass them over here.

No. 17. "Peter the Great at Narva," painted 1811. A picture of no merit.

No. 19. "St. John and Lamb," has much beauty, and was painted in 1800.

No. 20. "Portrait of General Washington," painted in Philadelphia, 1793. Without merit of any kind.

No. 21. "Knighting of De Wilton," painted in London, 1810. A labored picture of little merit, except armor and drapery painting.

No. 22. "Portrait of Alexander Hamilton." Not like.

No. 23. "Holy Family," composed in London, 1802 — finished in America, 1806. Beautifully painted, but without originality of thought.

No. 24. "President Dwight." Not a good portrait or picture, compared to the artist's early works.

No. 25. "General Washington," a full length, painted in 1792. This is, in many respects, a fine picture, and painted in the artist's best days.

No. 26. "The Revolutionary Governor of Connecticut, Jonathan Trumbull," father of the artist. I presume a good portrait.

No. 27. "Infant Saviour and St. John," painted in London, 1801. Beautifully executed, but without originality.

No. 28. "Portrait of the Hon. Rufus King." A poor portrait, although painted in 1800.

No. 29. "Lamderg and Gelchossa," painted 1809. A labored picture without merit.

No. 30. "Portrait of Mr. Gore," painted 1800.

No. 31. "Maternal Tenderness," painted 1809.

No. 32 to No. 42. Miniatures in oil, painted in the artist's best days, from 1790 to 1792, and only rivaled by the exquisitely beautiful heads painted in the small historical pictures from 1786 to 1792. These are studies for the artist.

No. 43. Five heads. Oil miniatures, painted 1827, in imitation of the former happy style, but forming a perfect contrast.

Mr. Trumbull unfortunately believed, that in 1827 his sight and his judgment enabled him to paint as in 1786 or 1792, and in consequence has injured the small historical pictures of that period to a lamentable degree. Let the student admire and profit by the early works of this artist; but beware of the opinion that there is anything to imitate in the later efforts of his pencil: let him look at the hands in the "Death of Montgomery" and those of later date, and he must understand me.

CHAPTER VI.

WINSTANLEY—S. KING—ARCHIBALD ROBERTSON—CERACCHI
— TROTT — PAUL.

WILLIAM WINSTANLEY.[0]

THIS young man was understood to have come to New York on some business connected with the Episcopal Church.

He was of a good family in England, and had received a gentlemanly education. At his first arrival he was well received among our first and best citizens, and was intimate at the house of Bishop Benjamin Moore. He became well known to the public in 1795, by painting and exhibiting a panorama of London, as seen from the Albion Mills, Blackfriar's Bridge. This was the first picture of the kind ever seen in America, and was exhibited in Greenwich Street, New York.

In another part of this work it is stated that a friend of mine furnished the money either in part or the whole, to enable Barker to get up the first panorama ever executed, which was of Edinburgh. Barker afterward painted the panorama of London, and had it engraved and published in six prints of 24 inches each. These prints were brought to America by Mr. Laing, the brother-in-law of my friend, and were, through Mr. Alexander Robertson, lent to Winstanley. The reader may see in the biography of Stuart, how Mr. Laing was repaid. These panoramic prints brought him to the knowledge of Winstanley, as a painter, and having sold to General Henry Lee an original full length of Washington, by Stuart, he sent it to Winstanley as understanding the best mode of packing it, as it was purchased for the president's house at the seat of government. Winstanley immediately copied it, and sent the copy to General Lee, keeping the original; by and from which to manufacture more Stuarts, and finally Mr. Laing lost the amount of the original picture.

77

0   Winstanley was last heard of in London in 1806.

Winstanley painted portraits, landscapes — anything — and in 1801, this swindling genius, as appears by a puff direct in Denny's " Portfolio," announced the publication of eight prints by subscription, select views, to be engraved in London from oil paintings by Mr. Winstanley, "an artist of genius and reputation, whose landscapes in oil are greatly admired by the connoisseurs."

It was probably at this period that he borrowed the five hundred dollars from the Boston merchant, and gave him as security an original Stuart painted by himself. This is the last notice I have of William Winstanley.

S. KING.[01]

This gentleman, although he painted portraits for many years in Newport, Rhode Island, might perhaps have escaped my notice, if a great painter had not mentioned him as one who encouraged the efforts of design in his schooldays. He had not that skill which would entitle him to historical notice, but if he stimulated in any degree the genius of Allston, he deserves immortality. He was an able and ingenious man, and has contributed his mite to the progress of American art, by giving instruction to Washington Allston, and imparting some knowledge of the rudiments of the art to Miss Anne Hall, one of our most excellent miniature painters, and a National Academician.

Mr. King painted professionally in 1790, and when Allston returned, an accomplished artist in 1809, he had the pleasure of reminding the good old man of the kindness he had, as a child, received from him.

01 Samuel King was born in Newport, R.I., January 24, 1749. Married August 26, 1770, Amy, daughter of Samuel and Amy Vernon. Died December 30, 1819, at Newport, R.I. He made at least one miniature (that of Rev. Ezra Stiles, President of Yale College) in 1770 and finished a portrait in oil of Stiles the following year (1771). He passed the winter of 1771-72 in Salem, Mass. In 1780 King copied a portrait by Peale of Washington, belonging to John Hancock, which was sent to France. King had as pupils Gilbert Stuart, Washington Allston, Malbone and Charles B. King. Among the portraits by King are those of Rev. Gardiner Thurston, 1721-1802 of Newport, R.I.; Dr. David King, 1774-1836; Rev. Ezra Stiles of Yale College; Rev. Edward Taylor, 1708-1777 of Westfield, R.I., and Mrs. Richard Derby.

ARCHIBALD ROBERTSON.

Archibald Robertson arrived at New York on the 2d of October 1791. He was born in the village of Monymusk, eighteen miles from Aberdeen, Scotland, in 1765. His father was an architect and draftsman, and practised the art at that place.[1] Two brothers, Alexander and Andrew, are likewise artists, the latter has long been, if not the best, equal to the first miniature painter in the metropolis of Great Britain.

Archibald showed an early disposition for the fine arts. I have seen designs of Mr. Robertson's for historical compositions which evince good knowledge of drawing, *chiaroscuro*, and expression. One from Shakespeare, of Falstaff and his companions, has much of these qualities and pleased me most. Lord Archibald Grant encouraged his attempts at drawing, and after he had completed his education at Marshall College, Aberdeen, Grant invited him to Edinburgh to study the arts of design, and thither he went in 1782. At that time there was no academy of fine arts in that city, and Archibald associated himself with Weir and Raeburn, then like himself students of painting, to form a school for mutual improvement. Raeburn was about the same age with Robertson and afterwards attained that eminence as a portrait painter which gained him the appellation of the Reynolds of Scotland.

Robertson, Raeburn, Watson, and Weir had as associates some engravers of Edinburgh, and they obtained permission from the manager of the theatre to occupy the green room for their school on such evenings as it was not in use, which were three in the week. Runciman, who was the teacher of the drawing school of the college, lent them casts and directed their operations. He is well known among painters for his pictures from Ossian and other works, which place him almost on a level with Barry and Mortimer, at least in the minds of his countrymen, who speak of Barry, Mortimer and Runciman as the pride of Ireland, England and Scotland. The college drawing school was a free school. The associates studied from

[1] Archibald Robertson was the son of William Robertson. He died in New York City in 1835.

the life, and hired a porter as their model. It was a school of mutual instruction. Raeburn is well known to fame. George Watson is now his successor in Edinburgh. He was the youngest of the associates. Before going to Edinburgh the young painter had received instructions from Peacock in miniature, Nesbit in water color drawing, and Wales in oil.

Having passed two years in Edinburgh he returned to his own climate to restore his impaired health, which accomplished, after practising his art in Aberdeen and Edinburgh, he, in 1788, went to London. He carried among other letters one to Sir Robert Strange. The engraver was not home when he called, but his wife, a Scotchwoman, received her young countryman very cordially and went with him to Newman Street to introduce him to Benjamin West. The great historical painter was found at his *chevalet de peintre*, or easel, working upon one of the pictures commemorative of the Order of the Garter. West received the young man with that amenity which characterized him, and continued his occupation while conversing with his visitor, as was his wont. He asked Robertson what were his views in respect to the art. Whether he intended to pursue historical or portrait painting, and being informed that the latter was his object he recommended application to Reynolds, saying, "I seldom paint portraits, and when I do, I neither please myself nor my employers."

Robertson was delighted with the urbanity of the painter, astonished by the facility and rapidity with which he was executing the work on his easel, and determined to follow his advice by seeking an introduction to the great portrait painter.

To Sir Joshua he was introduced by Sir William Chambers the architect, and was received as he could wish. Reynolds was then the president of the Royal Academy and pointed out to him the steps necessary for his introduction to that school; the first of which is to make a drawing from the plaster figure for presentation to the counsel or keeper. We need not say that in Europe an academy is composed of those who can teach the arts or sciences it is instituted to promote. Robertson said he had no plaster figure to draw from, and the artist

directed him to choose one from those in his *studio* and make
use of it. The young Scot chose the crouching Venus and
triumphantly bore the goddess to his own chamber, eager to
devote himself to the study of beauty and the *antique*.

His drawing gained him admission to the schools of Somerset
House. He studied the portraits of Reynolds and copied several of them in miniature. Returning to Scotland he exercised
his profession at Aberdeen successfully, until he was solicited
by Dr. Kemp, of Columbia College, New York (through the
medium of the venerable Dr. Gordon of Kings College, Aberdeen), to come and settle in America. The advice of his friends
and his own inclinations determined him to visit the *terra
incognita*. Not until he had made up his mind for this voyage
of discovery did he make any inquiries respecting the country
or its inhabitants, or indeed think anything about it. It was
a land of savages where some Europeans had fled from oppression or poverty or debts, and others had transported
Africans, and convicted felons, in chains. The information
the young painter received was such as to induce him to believe that except in the seaports the country was a wilderness,
and the inhabitants wild beasts and Indians. He thought himself fortunate in meeting a lady whose husband had been
taken prisoner with Burgoyne, and had with the captured
army been marched from Saratoga to Virginia. She was at
New York, doubtless expecting to receive her husband in
that British garrison, after he should have marched in triumph
from Canada, and assisted in dividing the eastern States from
their brethren of the Union. She was disappointed; and now
solicited and obtained permission to pass through the tract
of country which separated her from the place of her husband's
captivity. She unwittingly confirmed Robertson in the opinion
that America was a country of savages, for she told him that
having been fortunate enough to carry from the city a large
stock of needles and pins, she found them of greater use to
her than money, they being so eagerly desired by the inhabitants she encountered in the course of her journey. This
would of course remind the young man of the avidity with

which the savages, discovered by Cook, sought for like articles, and even beads and nails, and confirmed him in the notion that all beyond the precincts of the cities was a land of wild beasts and wild men.

The reader will observe the manner in which this fact (the avidity with which pins and needles were sought for), told without explanation, might operate. The lady knew the cause doubtless of the high price set upon needles and pins, by the people among whom she journeyed from New York to Virginia. The people of America had, before the era of their emancipation from the bonds of a foreign parliament, been prohibited the exercise of ingenuity or skill in most articles of manufacture, or had, from the sparse nature of the population, been induced to depend upon Great Britain for the products of her manufactories; and being, at the time she spoke of, cut off from all foreign commerce by the armies and fleets of England, they were literally put to their shifts to make a shirt, and unable, in some instances, to pin a garment except with thorns, unless supplied by some visitor like herself, or by smugglers and illegal traffickers with New York or other garrisons of their enemy. She only reported the fact without comment or explanatory facts, and the young painter drew his own conclusions. When he arrived at New York in 1791, he expected to find some whites, but was utterly astonished on landing to see the same forms and complexions he had left behind on the other side the Atlantic, except here and there the face of an African. It is probable that he did not see an Indian for years after his arrival, and then as much of a raree show to his adopted countrymen as to himself.

In the month of December following his arrival in the United States, he went to Philadelphia, then the seat of government, to deliver to Washington the celebrated box made of the wood of the oak tree that sheltered Wallace after the battle of Falkirk. This token of regard for the character of the president, had been committed to the charge of Mr. Robertson by his friend the Earl of Buchan.

We extract the following from the "Atlantic Magazine":

"Philadelphia, January 4. On Friday morning was presented to the president of the United States, a box, elegantly mounted with silver, and made of the celebrated Oak Tree that sheltered the Washington of Scotland, the brave and patriotic Sir William Wallace, after his defeat at the battle of Falkirk, in the beginning of the fourteenth century, by Edward the First. This magnificent and truly characteristical present is from the Earl of Buchan, by the hand of Mr. Archibald Robertson, a Scots gentleman, and portrait painter, who arrived in America some months ago. The box was presented to Lord Buchan by the Goldsmiths' Company at Edinburgh, from whom his lordship requested, and obtained leave, to make it over to a man whom he deemed more deserving of it than himself, and the only man in the world to whom he thought it justly due. We hear further, that Lord Buchan has, by letter, requested of the president, that, on the event of his decease, he will consign the box to that man, in this country, who shall appear, in his judgment, to merit it best, upon the same considerations that induced him to send it to the present possessor.

"The inscription, upon a silver plate, on the inside of the lid, is as follows: — 'Presented by the goldsmiths of Edinburgh, to David Stuart Erskine, Earl of Buchan, with the freedom of their corporation, by their deacon — A.D. 1790.'

"The following is the letter which accompanied the box that was presented to General George Washington, by Mr. Robertson, from Lord Buchan.

"'Dryburgh Abbey, June 28th, 1791.

"'Sir — I had the honor to receive your excellency's letter relating to the advertisement of Doctor Anderson's periodical publication, in the *Gazette* of the United States: which attention to my recommendation I feel very sensibly, and return you my grateful acknowledgments.

"'In the 21st number of that 'Literary Miscellany,' I inserted a monitory paper respecting America, which, I flatter myself, may, if attended to on the other side of the Atlantic, be productive of good consequences.

"'To use your own emphatic words, "may that Almighty

Being who rules over the universe, who presides in the councils of nations, and whose providential aid can supply every human defect," consecrate to the liberties and happiness of the American people, a government instituted by themselves for public and private security, upon the basis of law and equal administration of justice, preserving to every individual as much civil and political freedom as is consistent with the safety of the nation: and may He be pleased to continue your life and strength as long as you can be in any way useful to your country!

"'I have entrusted this sheet inclosed in a box made of the oak tree that sheltered our great Sir William Wallace,* after the battle of Falkirk, to Mr. Robertson, of Aberdeen, a painter, with the hope of his having the honor of delivering it into your hands; recommending him as an able artist, seeking for fortune and fame in the New World. This box was presented to me by the goldsmith's company at Edinburgh, to whom, feeling my own unworthiness to receive this magnificently significant present, I requested and obtained leave to make it over to the man in the world to whom I thought it most justly due; into your hands I commit it, requesting of you to pass it, in the event of your decease, to the man† in your own country, who shall appear to your judgment to merit it best, upon the same considerations that have induced me to send it to your Excellency.

"'I am, with the highest esteem, sir,
"'Your Excellency's most obedient
"'And obliged humble servant,

"'General Washington,   "'BUCHAN.
    President of the United States of America.'

* Sir William Wallace, at first a private gentleman, unsuccessfully attempted a revolution in Scotland, nearly on the same grounds with that more recently accomplished in America, to expel the English and their adherents, who had usurped the government. Having gained a victory over the forces of Edward the First, at Stirling, he was soon after attacked by Edward at the head of 80,000 foot and 7000 horse; whereas the whole force of Sir William did not exceed 30,000 foot; and the main division of his army was tampered with by a traitor, and rendered of no use to the patriotic army. Not long after the battle of Falkirk, Sir William was made prisoner by some of Edward's partisans, carried to England and beheaded.

† The general, with great wisdom, has desired the box to be returned to his lordship with this answer, "That it is not for General Washington to point out the worthiest citizen of the United States."

" 'P. S. — I beg your Excellency will have the goodness to send me your portrait, that I may place it among those I most honor, and I would wish it from the pencil of Mr. Robertson. I beg leave to recommend him to your countenance, as he has been mentioned to me favorably by my worthy friend, Professor Ogilvie, of King's College, Aberdeen.' "

Mr. Robertson says that, although "accustomed to intimate intercourse with those of the highest rank and station in his native country," his embarrassment on being introduced "to the American hero," was so obvious, that Washington entered into familiar conversation, with a view to putting his guest at his ease, and introduced him to Mrs. Washington, whose urbanity and ceaseless cheerfulness fully accomplished the general's intention.

Previous to sitting for his portrait, in compliance with Lord Buchan's request,* the president invited the artist to a family dinner, which he thus describes in a memorandum before us: "The dinner at three o'clock was plain, but suitable for a family in genteel circumstances. There was nothing specially remarkable at the table, but that the General and Mrs. Washington sat side by side, he on the right of his lady; the gentlemen on his right hand and the ladies on his left. It being on Saturday the first course was mostly of eastern cod and fresh fish. A few glasses of wine were drank during dinner, with other beverage, the whole closed with a few glasses of sparkling champagne, in about three-quarters of an hour, when the general and Colonel Lear retired, leaving the ladies in high glee about Lord Buchan and the Wallace box."

The president sat to Mr. Robertson for a miniature, as did Mrs. Washington. From the miniature of Washington a larger picture was painted by the artist for Lord Buchan, "in oil, and of a size corresponding to those of the collection of portraits of the most celebrated worthies of liberal principles and in useful literature, in the possession of his lordship at Dryburgh Abbey, near Melrose, on the borders of Scotland."

To conclude the history of the Wallace box, we give Wash-

* See Cunningham's character of this *noble*-man, as quoted by me in this work.

ington's answer to Lord Buchan, and an extract from the hero's will.

"Philadelphia, May 1, 1792.

"My Lord — I should have had the honor of acknowledging sooner the receipt of your letter of the 28th of June last, had I not concluded to defer doing it till I could announce to you the transmission of my portrait, which has just been finished by Mr. Robertson (of New York), who has also undertaken to forward it. The manner of the execution of it does no discredit, I am told, to the artist; of whose skill favorable mention had been made to me. I was farther induced to entrust the execution to Mr. Robertson, from his having informed me that he had drawn others for your lordship, and knew the size which best suited your collection.

"I accept, with sensibility and with satisfaction, the significant present of the box which accompanied your lordship's letter.

"In yielding the tribute due from every lover of mankind to the patriotic and heroic virtues of which it is commemorative, I estimate as I ought the additional value which it derives from the hand that sent it, and my obligation for the sentiments that induced the transfer.

"I will, however, ask that you will exempt me from compliance with the request relating to its eventual destination.

"In an attempt to execute your wish in this particular, I should feel embarrassment from a just comparison of relative pretensions, and fear to risk injustice by so marked a preference. With sentiments of the truest esteem and consideration, I remain your lordship's most obedient servant,

" G. WASHINGTON.

"Earl of Buchan."

Extract from the will:

"To the Earl of Buchan I recommit 'The box made of the oak that sheltered the brave Sir William Wallace after the Battle of Falkirk,' presented to me by his lordship in terms too flattering for me to repeat, with a request 'to pass it, on the event of my decease, to the man in my country who should appear to merit it best, upon the same conditions that have induced him to send it to me.' Whether easy or not to select the man who might comport with his lordship's opinion in this respect, is not for me to say; but conceiving that no disposition of this valuable curiosity can be more eligible than the recommitment of it to his own cabinet, agreeably to the original design of the Goldsmith's Company of Edinburgh, who presented it to him, and, at his request, consented that it should be transferred to me, I do give and bequeath the same to his lordship; and in case of his decease, to his heir, with my grateful thanks for the distinguished honor of presenting it to me, and more especially for the favorable sentiments with which he accompanied it."

Mr. Robertson sent his picture to Europe by Col. Lear, and received the thanks of the Earl of Buchan. From 1792 to 1821, Mr. Robertson exercised his profession in New York, and likewise taught drawing and painting in water colors. He married Miss Abrams (an only child, and understood to be a fortune), and is surrounded by a numerous family. Good fortune and prudence going hand in hand, he retired from business at the last-mentioned period.

In 1802, he was one who assisted, with his advice, in the project of forming an academy of fine arts, and about the same time published an elementary book on drawing.

In 1816, when a second attempt was made to establish an academy of the fine arts, and an association was chartered under the title of the American Academy, Mr. Robertson was elected a director. The association consisted principally of lawyers, merchants, and physicians, with a few artists, and Mr. Trumbull was elected president. Mr. Robertson joined with another artist in recommending the establishment of schools, but the president overruled the measure, and defeated it by his influence with the board of directors, who being mostly not artists, were governed by his opinions, and the institution became merely a society for the exhibition of pictures, and so continues to this day.

Mr. Robertson found oil painting injurious to his health, and confined himself to water colors and crayons. Several portraits of this description, painted soon after his marriage, we have seen with pleasure; and he had great facility in the management of water colors on ivory. His exertions in his profession advanced the arts of design, and he is entitled to the gratitude of the country as one of those who forwarded the progress of the fine arts.

As an architect, though never professionally such, he has shown his skill on several occasions by plans for public buildings. He was among those who presented designs for the city hall of New York. Mr. Robertson enjoys health and affluence, the reward of prudence and temperance; and at an advanced age retains his love for science and the arts, united to an activity of body and mind, giving him power to advance their interests.

GIUSEPPE CERACCHI.

This great sculptor and enthusiastic republican was born at Rome about the year 1740. He was employed by the Pope, in conjunction with Canova, in designing and executing sculpture for the Pantheon. Louis Simond, in his travels in Italy, speaks of the monumental busts of the great artists of Italy, with which the Pantheon is decorated, as having been executed by "Canova and Ceracchi."

He left Italy on a visit to England, and arrived in London in the year 1772. He was well received by Sir Joshua Reynolds, then President of the Royal Academy, whose bust he executed in marble with great success and credit. He was the instructor, in modelling and sculpture, of the Hon. Anna Seymour Damer; who executed many works in marble, of sufficient merit to draw forth the praises of Horace Walpole, who compares her (and makes her equal) to the authors of the antique busts which have come down to us. Ceracchi executed a full-length figure of Mrs. Damer, "as the Muse of Sculpture"; in which, says Walpole, "he has happily preserved the graceful lightness of her form and her air."

The author of the " Life of Nollekins " says (vol. II. p. 19.
London edition, 1828) — "During the time I was under the
tuition of Mr. Nollekins, Signor Giuseppe Ceracchi, a Roman,
often visited the studio. He came to England in 1773, with
letters of recommendation from Nulty, a sculptor at Rome;
was employed by Carlini; and when he first exhibited at the
Royal Academy, his residence was stated to be at that artist's
house, in King Square Court, now Carlisle Street, Soho Square.

"Mr. R. Adam, the architect, employed Ceracchi to model
a *basso-relievo*, fourteen feet in length by six feet in height,
of the Sacrifice of Bacchus, consisting of twenty figures, in
Adams's composition, — a mixture of cement with oil, which
is now called mastic, and similar to that used on the columns
of the Theatre in the Hay Market, for the back front of the
house of Mr. Desenfans, in Portland Road; at whose decease
it was sold by auction to the proprietors of Coade's artificial
stone manufactory, in that part of the New Road called
Tottenham Court; and it is very tastefully modelled.

"The bust of Sir Joshua Reynolds, sold by the figure-casters,
Mr. Northcote informs me, was also modelled by Ceracchi.
Baretti, in his 'Guide through the Royal Academy,' when
describing the Strand front of Somerset House, thus speaks
of him: — 'The two figures nearest the centre were made by
Signor Carlini: the two at the extremities, by Signor Ceracchi,
an Italian sculptor, who resided some time in London, whose
abilities the architect (Sir William Chambers) wished to encourage and keep among us; but the little employment found
in England for sculptors, however excellent, frustrated his
intentions.' Ceracchi had, when I was taken to see him, very
extensive premises at No. 76, Margaret Street, Cavendish
Square. He was a short thin man, with a piercing black eye,
and a very blue beard. He was the Hon. Lady Damer's master
in sculpture, as that lady declared to me herself.*

"Ceracchi, highly gifted as he certainly was, met so little
encouragement in this country, that, after disposing of his

* He modelled a statue of his pupil, which, since the decease of Lord Fred. Campbell, has been carved in marble, and placed in the hall of the British Museum.

property in Margaret Street, he quitted England for Rome; where he continued to practise, as a sculptor, until the breaking out of the French Revolution,* when he became so violent a partisan, and so desperate, that he was condemned to death, as the leader of the conspirators connected with the infernal machine contrivance; and was guillotined at Paris in 1801. — Ceracchi continued so frantic to the last, that he actually built himself a car, in which he was drawn to the place of execution in the habit of a Roman Emperor. David, the French painter, with whom Ceracchi had lived in intimacy, was called to speak to his character; but he declared he knew nothing of him beyond his fame as a sculptor."

An ardent lover of the rights of man, Ceracchi conceived the design of erecting a monument to Liberty in the United States of America, and for this purpose crossed the Atlantic. In 1791 he arrived in Philadelphia, and prepared the model of a great work, designed to be one hundred feet in height, of statuary marble, and the cost was estimated at thirty thousand dollars.

The Congress, then sitting in Philadelphia, did not feel themselves authorized to expend the money of their constituents in erecting a monument of this description, and the sculptor was disappointed in respect to the government encouragement he had relied upon. He had, in the meantime, become acquainted with the first men of the United States, and had executed a bust, in marble, representing, with truth and characteristic dignity, the likeness of that great and good man, Washington. This beautiful piece of art and faithful portraiture, which is (with the exception of Gilbert Stuart's original painting, now in the Athenæum at Boston) the only true portrait of our hero, was purchased of Ceracchi by the Spanish ambassador for one thousand dollars, and sent to Spain, where it having been rejected by 'the Prince of the Peace,' for whom the ambassador intended it as a present (but who probably thought such a bust as little suited to his cabinet as that of Brutus or Socrates would be), this excellent

* This is erroneous, as will be seen.

piece of art remained with the ambassador, and after his death, with his widow; of whom Richard Meade, Esq. of Philadelphia, with true taste and patriotism, repurchased it, for the same sum received by Ceracchi, and sent it back to its native land.

General Washington not having the power, except in his private capacity, to forward Ceracchi's great plan of the monument, but admiring the model, and wishing to serve the man, advised him to try to obtain a subscription by private individuals, the amount of which should cover the expense. He accompanied this advice with a letter recommending the artist and the intended monument, and placed his name at the commencement of the subscription list.

The ardent sculptor was too impatient to await the success of this plan to raise the necessary fund, and returned poor and disappointed to Europe, in (I believe) 1795.

During the time Ceracchi remained in this country, he modelled and chiseled many busts of distinguished gentlemen connected with the Revolution, some of which I can particularize; and first the admirable marble bust of Hamilton, in the possession of that great man's family — the bust of Jefferson, deposited at Monticello — that of George Clinton, the Revolutionary governor of New York — another of Egbert Benson — one in terra cotta of Paul Jones, and another of John Jay. The artist took to Paris, with the model of the intended monument, many other models in clay — some of distinguished men — but in his wreck all have been lost, and no trace of them remains. This unfortunate, or imprudent and misled man of talents, when oppressed by poverty, and disappointed in his hopes of assistance from the government of the United States, or of adequate employment from our citizens, made several unjustifiable efforts to relieve himself from pecuniary embarrassment. He requested sittings from distinguished individuals, who, thinking to do him service, sacrificed their time to what they thought his wish to possess their portraits, and he, having finished their busts in marble, demanded large sums, as though he had been employed, or the work ordered. In this manner it is said that Alexander Hamilton's invaluable likeness was executed, and that eminent statesman and soldier yielded to the unexpected demand.

I find, in Dr. Hosack's "Medical Essays," an account of another attempt of this nature recorded. In vol. 1st, p. 202, the doctor, in a biographical memoir of Hugh Williamson, M.D., says: —

"Joseph Ceracchi, an Italian statuary of great celebrity in his profession, finding the turbulent state of Europe unfavorable to the exercise of his art, had come to this country. This gentleman exercised his talents in erecting honorary memorials of some of our most distinguished public men.

"He, at that time also, as appears by a correspondence in my possession, applied to Dr. Williamson, then a member of Congress, for permission to perpetuate in marble, the bust of the *American Cato*, as Mr. Ceracchi was pleased to denominate him. I beg leave to read the originals:

" 'Mr. Ceracchi requests the favor of Mr. Williamson to sit for his bust, not on account of getting Mr. Williamson's influence in favor of the National Monument; this is a subject too worthy to be recommended; but merely on account of his distinguished character — that will produce honor to the artist, and may give to posterity the expressive features of the American Cato.'

"To this note Dr. Williamson replied in his appropriate caustic style:

" ' Mr. Hugh Williamson is much obliged to Mr. Ceracchi for the polite offer of taking his bust. Mr. Williamson could not possibly suppose that Mr. Ceracchi had offered such a compliment by way of a bribe; for the man in his public station who could accept of a bribe, or betray his trust, ought never to have his likeness made, except from a block of *wood*.'

"Mr. Williamson, in the meantime, cannot avail himself of Mr. Ceracchi's services, as he believes that posterity will not be solicitous to know what were the features of his face. He hopes, nevertheless, for the sake of his children, that posterity will do him the justice to believe that his conduct was upright, and that he was uniformly influenced by a regard to the happiness of his fellow citizens, and those who shall come after them."

Ceracchi became a citizen of the French Republic, and not brooking Bonaparte's successful schemes for the overthrow of all liberty, and establishment of his despotism, the sculptor entered into a conspiracy for the destruction of the First Consul, before he should have riveted the chains already forged for the nation.

It has been repeatedly asserted that he was concerned in the infamous attempt to murder by the justly denominated *infernal* machine, but it was not so. He had entered into a conspiracy with Georges and others, and he was either to assassinate the tyrant when sitting to him for his bust, or to aid others in doing it. So far had he been deceived and blinded by his fierce passion for what he justly considered the prime blessing of man, political liberty, that he had persuaded himself that it was justifiable, or meritorious, to become a deceiver, a traitor, and a murderer, even in the sanctuary of his own apartment.

One account of this nefarious affair states, that Ceracchi had apartments in the opera house, where he received his sitters and executed his statuary, and that in this place the murder was to have been committed; but the plot being discovered, the artist was tried, convicted, avowed his intention, and justified it to the hearers as he had justified it to himself, and was sentenced to death, but was not guillotined or publicly executed, but removed to some bastile, where he ended life in oblivion — when or where it is not said.

Madame Junot gives another version of the conspiracy to assassinate Bonaparte; and I insert, from her memoirs, the passages relative to this extraordinary affair, and misled man. Junot, at that time commandant of Paris, had endeavored to persuade his wife and her mother not to go to the opera on the 11th of October, he knowing that the first consul was to be there, and that the conspirators intended *there* to murder him. The ladies, however, persisted in going, of course not knowing Junot's motives, which he would not divulge. Junot left them.

"When he returned to the box, his countenance, which all

day had been serious, and even melancholy, had resumed in a
moment its gaiety and openness, relieved of all the clouds
which had veiled it. He leaned towards my mother and said,
very low, not to be heard in the next box, 'Look at the first
consul, remark him well.'

" 'Why would you have me affect to fix my eyes on him?'
said my mother, 'it would be ridiculous.'

" 'No, no, it is quite natural. Look at him with your glass;
then I will ask the same favor from Mademoiselle Laurette.'
I took the opera glass from my brother, and looked at him in
my turn.

" 'Well,' said the general, 'what do you observe?'

" 'Truly,' I replied, 'I have seen an admirable countenance;
for I can conceive nothing superior to the strength in repose,
and greatness in quiescence, which it indicates.'

" 'You find its expression, then, calm and tranquil?'

" 'Perfectly. But why do you ask the question?' said I,
much astonished at the tone of emotion with which the general
had put the question.

"He had no time to answer: one of the aids-de-camp came
to the little window of the box to call him out. This time
he was absent longer; and on his return wore an air of joy:
his eyes were directed towards the box of the first consul, with
an expression which I could not understand. The first consul
was then buttoning on the gray coat which he wore over the
uniform of the guards, the dress which he then always wore,
and was preparing to leave the box. As soon as this was
perceived, the acclamations were renewed, as vehemently as
on his entrance. At this moment Junot, no longer able to
conquer his emotion, leaned upon the back of my chair, and
burst into tears. 'Calm yourself,' said I, leaning towards him
to conceal him from my mother, who would certainly have
exercised her wit upon the subject: 'calm yourself, I entreat
you. How can a sentiment altogether joyful produce such an
effect upon you?' 'Ah!' replied Junot, quite low, but with an
expression I shall never forget, 'he has narrowly escaped death!
the assassins are this moment arrested.' "

After their return home, Junot informs his wife's mother "that Ceracchi and Aréna, the one actuated by republican fanaticism, the other by vengeance, had taken measures to assassinate Bonaparte.

"We have yet only taken Ceracchi, Aréna, and I believe Demerville. They are just taken, but they were not the only conspirators."

Junot gives the following account of a scene between himself and Fouché on the subject: —

"And what do you think he said upon this resolution of the first consul to go to the opera? He blamed him as I did, but what was the motive? 'Because,' says he, 'it is an ambush!' You suppose, no doubt, that this deprecated ambush was for the first consul? No such thing; it was for those honest rascals, whose necks I would wring as willingly as a sparrow's, and with no more scruple, after what I have learned of them and the honorable functions which I find them exercising. He made an oration, which, I believe, was taken from his collection of homilies; by which he proposed to prove, that affair might be prevented going to this length. As I had already had a very warm discussion, upon the same subject, with a personage whom the First Consul will know, I hope, some day for what he is (and the time is happily not far distant), and as I know that this personage and Fouché had been emulating each other in their interference in this affair, I was desirous that my way of thinking should be equally known to both of them. I therefore constrained Fouché to explain himself clearly, and to tell me that it was wrong to lead on these men to the moment of executing their design, since it could be prevented. That was his opinion.

"'And thus,' said I, 'you would replace in society those who have evidently conspired against the chief of the state; and that not to force him to resign his authority, not to remove him from it, but to murder him — and to murder him for the satisfaction of their own passions. Do you believe that Ceracchi — content to die, if, in sacrificing himself, he can kill the First Consul — putting him to death to glut an inordinate passion, in obedience to a species of monomania — do you believe this madman will be cured by a simple admonition, or by an act of generosity? No: he must kill this man, whom he looks upon as a tyrant, and whom he will never be induced to see in any other light. Or do you believe that Aréna, during so many years the enemy of General Bonaparte, will abjure his hatred against the First Consul, because the latter has taken up the character of Augustus? No: It is his death they desire. Listen to the expression of Ceracchi, in buying a poniard: "I should like a knife better: the blade is solid and sure, and does not foul the hand." To leave a determined assassin like this to his blood-thirsty contrivances, what is it but to insure tomorrow the full execution of the project you have averted today?

"'This is not my first knowledge of the Arénas. The First Consul, who is thoroughly good hearted, is willing to forget the evil they have always been forward to do him; but I have not so forgiving a soul. I remember his arrest in the South: I have heard the particulars of the 18th Brumaire, and I am completely acquainted with the circumstances of the present affair. Certainly I tremble to see the First Consul go to face the death which, notwithstanding all our cares, he might encounter: but, on the other hand, I saw but this means of cutting through the net they had cast around him. His existence would be rendered miserable, supposing it was preserved.— There would be daily new conspiracies — a hydra, constantly reviving. When Fouché,' continued Junot, 'found that I saw through him, notwithstanding his cunning, he had recourse to the sentiments of humanity. He! Fouché! He harangued me in the style of a homily: and all this with that head that one would have supposed he had stolen from a skeleton. Oh! what a man! And the First Consul will place faith in his words! At length we shall see the conclusion of this affair, which he and another called child's play — reason in all things.'

"With respect to Ceracchi, nothing you could say of him would surprise me. Permon, who knew him in Italy, intro-

duced him to me at a ball at M. Delanoue's. Since then I
have sometimes seen him at Madame Magimelli's, at Auteuil.
I acknowledge his exaggerated notions have made me tremble;
while his distaste of life, and his profound melancholy, made
him interesting. Albert observed that his heart must have
been profoundly wounded by the injuries with which he
imagined Italy had to reproach Bonaparte: 'For I have
seen him,' said he, 'weep with enthusiasm in only speaking
of him.' And when he was required to model his bust, or
rather, when he himself requested permission to execute it, he
was so much affected in delineating the traits of him whom he
believed destined to regenerate the world, that I have heard
it asserted by persons who knew the fact, that he was compelled to abandon the task. This man had a soul of fire!"
Madame Junot says: —

"I had also seen this Ceracchi, and witnessed some of his
ebullitions of enthusiastic republicanism at Madame Magimelli's; and I confess he had not produced upon my mind the
same disagreeable impressions that he had upon my mother's.
I pitied him warmly, for it was impossible not to perceive that
his excessive sensibility must render him miserable."

Lucien Bonaparte is reported to have said, "How can
such strokes be averted? Jaques, Clement, Ravillac, Damien,
Jean Chatel — all these men executed their projects; because,
in forming them, they held their own lives for nothing. If
Ceracchi had been alone, as was his original intention, my
brother had been no more. But he thought, by taking associates, to make his success more certain. He deceived himself."
This is all I can find respecting Ceracchi.[0]

BENJAMIN TROTT.[00]

Mr. Trott is one of the few artists who have shrunk from
rendering me that assistance which even a few dates would
give in raising, what I hope and believe will be, a monument
to the arts of America. I give my own knowledge, and such
as flows incidentally from the communications of artists, who

0 Giuseppe Ceracchi was executed for his part in the attempt to assassinate Napoleon,
January 30, 1802.
00 Benjamin Trott died on November 27, 1843.

have not hesitated to furnish me with materials and help to put them together.

Trott commenced his career, as a portrait painter in miniature, about the year 1791; which will allow us to guess that he was born not far from 1770. In 1793 he painted a good miniature head, and practised successfully in New York when Gilbert Stuart arrived there from Dublin, in company with Walter Robertson. Walter Robertson was a native of Ireland; and I believe Trott first saw the light in or about Boston. Robertson's style was very singular and altogether artificial; all ages and complexions were of the same hue — and yet there was a charm in his coloring that pleased, in despite of taste. Trott's manner was more in the old way and more natural. Robertson was employed very much in copying Stuart's portraits; and with his coloring, and Stuart's characteristic likenesses, he was at the pinnacle of fame for a time. Stuart did not like that another, with another set of colors, should be mounted above him, on his own shoulders; and for that reason, and the more natural coloring of Trott, preferred the latter, assisted him by advice, and recommended him. — Trott's blunt and caustic manner was probably to Stuart's taste.

Notwithstanding Stuart's approbation, Trott longed to be able to imitate the coloring of Walter Robertson; and I remember to have seen in his possession one of the Irishman's miniatures, half obliterated by the Yankee's experiments, who, to dive into the secret, made his way beneath the surface like a mole, and in equal darkness.

He followed or accompanied Stuart when he removed from New York to Philadelphia; and that city was his headquarters for a great many years. His copies on ivory, with water colors, from Stuart's oil portraits, were good — one from the "Washington," extremely beautiful and true.

Who Trott's early instructors were, or whether he had any instructors, other than such as pictures and occasional contact with painters afforded, I know not. He certainly had attained a great portion of skill before he made his appearance in New

York. A well-painted miniature is to me a source of delight, and some of Mr. Trott's are of great beauty. I speak of the miniatures of the painter in his best days — for the days of decay generally attend the artist as well as his work.

In 1805 Mr. Trott visited the western world beyond the mountains, travelling generally on horseback, with the implements of his art in his saddle-bags. This was a lucrative journey. He returned to Philadelphia in 1806, at which time I was there with my friend Charles Brockden Brown; and I became somewhat intimate with Trott, and pleased with the pungency of his remarks and amused by the eccentricity of his manners. At this time his reputation was at its height, and he might have commanded more employment than he did, but he was visited by a most mischievous notion, a disease of the mind, which occasionally affects painters — this was a firm conviction, that some vehicle had been discovered for conveying colors to the ivory, which gave force, clearness, and every good quality; but that it was kept secret by those who used it, and gave great advantages to certain colorists. This megrim having taken possession of his brain, the consequence was that the time which if spent in drawing and practising with pure water, would have produced the effect he wished, was wasted in filterings and chemical experiments. He pursued a phantom, as alchemists of old sought the philosopher's stone — and with the success — to the same encouragement of irritability of temper, already too sensitive, and the waste of property and more precious time. I must however acknowledge, that by his distillations and filterings he produced some of the cleanest pigments that ever I used; and he bestowed upon me specimens of all the necessary colors for miniature.

In 1806 he justly considered that he had nothing to fear from my rivalry — he would not have been so liberal towards Malbone. The fame of this young painter annoyed Trott, for he had none of that feeling which rejoices at a rival's success, nor of that self-confidence which perhaps causes the generous sensation. Malbone proposed an exchange of specimens with him, probably to show the different manner by which two eminently successful artists arrived at their respective excellence. But Trott considered and denounced it, as an insidious mode of comparison with his own: forgetting, that if such an advantage could be taken by one, it was equally in the power of the other. Though not acknowledged, this jealousy shows a consciousness of inferiority, or at least a fear of the humiliating truth.

In 1808, Mr. Trott and Mr. Sully were joint tenants of a house in the metropolis of Pennsylvania, pursuing their respective branches of the art. Mr. Sully, who long knew Trott, says, that he was in all things extremely sensitive; and in many things generous and truly right minded.

When Sully returned from Europe, in 1810, he again took a house in conjunction with Trott. But during the violence of the opposition made by the associated artists to the Pennsylvania Academy of Fine Arts, Trott, led by Murray, spoke harshly of Sully, because, being a director of the academy, he did not join the association in their opposition.

In 1812 Mr. Trott exhibited, at the Academy, several miniatures of great merit. "The works of this excellent artist," says a writer in the " Portfolio," "are justly esteemed for truth and expression. In examining his miniatures, we perceive all the force and effect of the best oil pictures; and it is but fair to remark, that Mr. Trott is purely an American — he has never been either in London or Paris." The same writer compares Trott's miniatures to Stuart's oil paintings: without going so far, I can speak with approbation of two of his portraits, which had extraordinary merit, that of Benjamin Wilcox, Sully's friend, and a friend of the arts; and a lady in a black laced veil. Very dissimilar in manner, but both very fine.

In 1819, when passing through Philadelphia, I found Trott preparing to go south, Philadelphia had become too cold for him. He went to Charleston, South Carolina, and some one has remarked, that at the same time there were in that city three artists of the names of Trott, Rider and Canter. He returned to Philadelphia, and was generally to be found there until he made a mysterious marriage; and not having the effrontery to announce as "Mrs. Trott," a person whose origin he was ashamed of, he, after suffering for some time, took refuge in New Jersey, whose laws offered him a release in consequence of a limited term of residence, and he resided for some years in obscurity at Newark.

He did not return to Philadelphia, where his business and reputation had suffered, but removed to New York; and his miniatures having become poor, and appearing poorer in comparison with those of younger artists, he tried oil portraiture with no success. He painted a few oil portraits in New York; but although he had enjoyed intimately the opportunity of studying Stuart, and was an enthusiastic admirer of his manner, nothing could be more unlike Stuart's portraits than those painted by Trotter.

After remaining in New York some years, rather in obscurity, generally shunning his acquaintance, he went to Boston, probably his native place, in the year 1833, after an absence of perhaps more than forty years.

Trott was rather inclined to be caustic in his remarks upon others (especially artists), than charitable. He would introduce a bitter remark with a kind of chuckle, and "upon my soul I think," and conclude with a laugh, "I think so, upon my soul I do." If he saw any one in the street approaching, with whom he had a temporary *miff*, or feeling of offended pride, or who for any other cause, or no cause, he wished to avoid, he would turn the first corner or cross the street, and this was so frequent, that any one walking with him would be surprised or amused by the eccentricity of his proceeding: if he had time and opportunity he would say to his companion, "come this way," if not, he would leave him abruptly.

Of the full medium height, thin, with a prepossessing countenance, Mr. Trott had qualities which ought to have led to better results. An early marriage with one whom he could honor and present to his friends, without blushing and without effrontery as his wife, would probably have secured to him respectability and domestic happiness.

Jeremiah Paul.

This was one of the unfortunate individuals, who, showing what is called genius in early life, by scratching the lame figures of all God's creatures, or everything that will receive chalk or ink, are induced to devote themselves to the fine arts, without the means of improvement, or the education necessary to fit them for a liberal profession. They arrive at a certain point of mediocrity, are deserted, and desert themselves.[1]

About the year 1791, Paul commenced as portrait painter, after having copied prints, and even made some enlarged oil

[1]The following letter hitherto unpublished gives a different estimate of the merits of Paul as an artist. It also calls attention to the feelings of resentment which the publication of Dunlap's criticisms of Trumbull occasioned at the time. A reproduction is given of Paul's painting of the Washington family after a contemporary engraving published in London.

"Philadelphia, February 21st 1835.
"Colo. John Trumbull,
    "Sir,
    "May I be permitted the privilege of asking your assistance in some particulars, so far as you are informed, relating to a very unwarrantable attack upon the characters of numerous Artists, in a late publication by one Wm. Dunlap of New York, whose vehemence against you appears to be somewhat particularly directed to gratify his spleen.
    "His dastardly and unwarrantable calumny against my late estimable friend, Mr. Jeremiah Paul, and Mr. Jennings, known to you also, stating untruths in what he terms their biography, together with other artists, but more particularly those of Philadelphia, has determined me to answer his base falsehoods, and I am endeavoring to be strengthened upon the ground I have taken.
    "My wish is to call your recollection to the circumstance of your having shown me in early life, specimens by Mr. Paul (then unknown to me), and if you please the opinions you then and since have formed of that Gentleman's abilities.
    "Coming from such a source, Sir, it cannot fail to be received with the honorable credit it will deserve, by cultivated, informed and reflecting minds, and it will afford me much gratification to boast such auxiliary defence, in favor of my friend against the vilest slanders!
    "I have understood, also, that you have noticed in public print Mr. Dunlap's vituperations against yourself; be pleased Sir, to inform me when I may see them, and if you shall think proper to give me any knowledge of circumstances touching your own history opposed to Mr. Dunlap I shall feel proud to be considered worthy of the communication.
    "It will be impossible to disconnect your name in my observations, blended as it is, with acts of which I shall be obliged to speak; and as your talents have long since commanded the homage of my high respect, I hope to receive approbatory marks of your not being offended, if not being countenanced by you upon so righteous an occasion.
                "With very great respect,
                        "I have the honor to be,
                                "Sir,
                                "Your most Obt. Servt.
                                        "James Akin."

pictures from the engravings of West's pictures. I remember Cromwell dissolving the Long Parliament. "Take away that bauble."

John Wesley Jarvis mentions him thus, in a letter to me: "About 1800, there were four painters in partnership," this was in Philadelphia, "Jeremiah Paul was good," Jarvis must mean compared to the others, "Pratt was pretty good — he was generally useful," he was far superior to Paul. "Clark was a miniature painter — Retter was a sign painter — but they all would occasionally work at anything, for at that time there were many fire buckets and flags to be painted. When Stuart painted Washington for Bingham, Paul thought it no disgrace to letter the 'books.' "

When Wertmüller's "Danae" made a noise in our cities, Paul tried his hand at a naked exhibition figure, which I was induced to look at, in Philadelphia, but looked at not long. Neither did it answer Paul's purpose. Our ladies and gentlemen only flock *together* to see pictures of naked figures when the subject is Scriptural and called moral.[1]

In 1806, I found Paul in Baltimore, painting a few wretched portraits, and apparently prostrated by poverty and intemperance. This is the last I have known of him. He was a man of vulgar appearance and awkward manners.

J. R. Lambdin, Esq. a pupil of T. Sully's and native of Pittsburg, in a letter to me, says that Paul "Visited Pittsburg in 1814, painted many good portraits and better *signs*. From the sight of one of the latter I date my first passion for the profession I pursue: it was a full length copy of Stuart's 'Washington,' and was elevated over the door of a coffee house, in a diagonal corner opposite my mother's house." Again, "Paul introduced to the admiration of the citizens the exhibition of phantasmagorias, and, *I believe*, painted the first scenery, to the first theatre erected in the west. He died in Missouri about the year 1820."

[1] A "Venus and Cupid nine feet by seven feet," "taken from living models," was exhibited at the office of James Akin the engraver, No. 22 Mulberry Street, in 1811. This picture was painted by Paul.

CHAPTER VII.

THE SCHOOL FOR THE FINE ARTS — THE COLUMBIANUM —
THE NEW YORK ACADEMY OF THE FINE ARTS —
PENNSYLVANIA ACADEMY OF FINE ARTS —
SOCIETY OF ARTISTS OF THE UNITED STATES.

ACADEMIES (real and nominal) of the fine arts, form an important item in the progress of the arts of design. The first attempt at such an establishment was

THE SCHOOL FOR THE FINE ARTS.

Charles Willson Peale, in the year 1791, attempted to form an association under this title. Ceracchi, the great sculptor, joined in the scheme, but it proved abortive. Mr. Peale made a second attempt, and called the intended institution

THE COLUMBIANUM.

In this he was rather more successful. He collected a few plaster casts, and even opened a school for the study of the living figure, but could find no model for the students but himself. The first exhibition of paintings, in Philadelphia, was opened this year, in that celebrated hall where the Declaration of Independence was determined upon and proclaimed. The pictures were borrowed from the citizens. This association of artists, of whose names I find only Charles Willson Peale, Joseph Ceracchi, and William Rush, held their meetings at the house of Mr. Peale. Some other artists, principally foreigners, joined in this plan; but the foreign artists, and Ceracchi at their head, separated from the Columbianum, and after the first exhibition it died. Ten years after Mr. Peale's first attempt, some of the most enlightened citizens of New York, with a view to raising the character of their countrymen, by increasing their knowledge and taste, associated for the purpose of introducing casts from the antique into the country. These worthy citizens, though none of them artists, called themselves

The New York Academy of the Fine Arts.

At a meeting of these gentlemen, Dec. 3, 1802, Edward Livingston was requested to take the chair, and by ballot the following persons were elected: — Edward Livingston, *president*, Col. Wm. Smith, Dr. Jos. Brown, John B. Prevost, Wm. Cutting, Wm. M. Seton, and Stephen Van Rensselaer, *directors*, Robert L. Livingston, *treasurer*, Dr. Peter Irving, *secretary*. It was resolved to form laws, to apply for an act of incorporation under the title of "The New York Academy of the Fine Arts," and to extend the shares to five hundred, to be paid by instalments.

The charter was not obtained until 1808.* The words "New York" were exchanged for "American," and the word "Fine" was omitted. We had then these gentlemen of every profession, but that of an artist, constituted by law an academy of arts. By this charter, dated Feb. 12, 1808, to continue in force twenty-five years, Robert R. Livingston and others then being, and such as may become members, are constituted a body corporate, with the usual privileges, their income being limited to $5000 the year: the stock not to consist of more than one thousand shares at $25 the share: the management to be with a president, vice-president, and five directors. The first officers were Robert R. Livingston, *president*, John Trumbull, *vice-president*, Dewitt Clinton, David Hosack, John R.

---

* Robert R. Livingston, Esq., when residing in Paris as ambassador from this country, purchased by order of these gentlemen, and sent to New York, the following plaster casts: — The Apollo Belvidere — Venus of the Capitol — Laocoön — Gladiator — Silenus — Grecian cupid — Castor and Pollux — Germanicus — Hermaphrodite — Venus of the Bath and Torso of Venus — with the busts of Homer, Demosthenes, Niobe, Euripides, Hippocrates, Artemisia, Cleopatra, Alexander, Bacchus, Roma, Seneca, Augustus, Cicero, Brutus, and Xenophon.

I copy this from a list furnished by John G. Bogert,[1] Esq. When these casts arrived in New York, a building on the west side of Greenwich Street, which had been erected for a circus or riding school, was hired, and the statuary opened for public exhibition. This did not attract much attention; and the funds of the society suffering, the casts were packed up and stored. After the charter was granted, the use of the upper part of a building, once intended as a house for the president of the United States, but occupied as the custom house, was loaned to the *Academy*, and the casts removed thither. They were again removed, packed up, and stored, until 1816.

1 For Bogert read Bogart

Murray, William Cutting, and Charles Wilkes, *directors*. It will be observed that there was now *one* artist in the association, Mr. Trumbull. The casts and books were removed to the upper story of the custom house, which was granted rent free, and there exhibited for a time, then repacked and re-stored, sleeping quietly with the association.

In the meantime the importation of casts into New York, and the name of an academy of arts, produced important effects in the sister city of Philadelphia. We have seen above, that *the artists* of Philadelphia made the first move in the cause of the fine arts; but were too few, and too poor probably, to establish an academy. If they had succeeded, a *real academy* would have been opened, with schools for various branches, and teachers for the schools.

In 1805, Jos. Hopkinson, Esq., stimulated by a view of the casts executed in Paris after the antique, which were in the possession of the New York Academy, and, by his own taste and patriotism, proposed to several gentlemen of Philadelphia the establishment of a similar institution. They undertook it with zeal, and executed it with promptitude. Seeing that the nominal academy of arts was useless, and attributing it to the want of a building for the casts, they erected an elegant and appropriate building, while the necessary measures for procuring plaster casts from Europe were pursued, and in April, 1807, the Pennsylvania Academy of Fine Arts was opened, a charter having been obtained in 1806, and a president and directors elected, among the latter were two artists. On this occasion an address was delivered by Mr. Clymer, the president of the institution. At first, statues and busts alone were thougth of for exhibition; but Mr. Robert Fulton, of New York, having purchased a portion of Alderman Boydell's great Shakespeare Gallery, and other excellent European paintings, placed them with the Pennsylvania Academy, for their use and the public gratification. The great attention which these pictures excited, suggested the idea of establishing annual exhibitions for the advantage of the academy and the improvement of public taste.

In May, 1810, a number of artists and amateurs of Philadelphia formed an association, which they denominated "The Society of Artists of the United States." They drew up a constitution, which was signed by sixty persons. They were invited by the members of the Pennsylvania Academy, to hold their meetings in the building erected by those gentlemen, and they accepted the invitation. In six months the society increased to upwards of one hundred, and they proposed an union with the academy, so as to form but one institution; this, however, was found impracticable at the time, and shortly after an arrangement was made, and a written agreement entered into, and signed by five members of each institution, by which, for a consideration of two thousand dollars, proposed as the wish of the society, the members of the society became entitled to "free admission to the academy in like manner with the members thereof"; to the right of using the specimens of art; to "the right of making their annual exhibition in the rooms of the academy for six weeks; during which time the academy also to be open to the inspection of the visitors of the exhibition," and to the most commodious rooms and the use of the property generally for the schools of the society.

On the 6th of May, 1811, the first annual exhibition of the *Society of Artists of the United States*, in conjunction with the directors of the academy, was opened to the public; previously to which an oration was delivered by Jos. Hopkinson, Esq. The receipts of the exhibition, during the stated period of six weeks, amounted to eighteen hundred and sixty dollars. After which, by concurrence of the two associations, the exhibition was continued one week longer, for the benefit of the sufferers by fire in Newburyport, Massachusetts — four hundred and ten dollars was received, and appropriated to this purpose.

On the 8th of May, 1811, an oration was delivered *before the Society of Artists* and the public, by Benjamin H. Latrobe, Esq., and on the fifth of June following, a committee was appointed by the Society of Artists to confer with a committee

of the Pennsylvania Academy, on the subject of a more intimate union of the institutions; but a difference of opinion
produced a resolution of the society, that it was best to continue a "distinct and independent institution."

Thus it will be seen, that a real Academy for teaching the
fine arts, was formed, under the title of "Society of Artists,"
while the associated patrons of the arts were by law called the
Academy. The first exhibition of the "Associated Artists"
was made, by agreement, under the roof of the "Pennsylvania
Academy of the Fine Arts," in 1811. This exhibition I attended, but my notes on the subject are very meagre. A Ceres,
by Wertmüller, is mentioned with dissatisfaction — a street,
by Strickland, the architect — and "Views on the Schuylkill,"
by T. Birch.

The Society of Artists, and the Pennsylvania Academy,
both opened schools; and the consequence of a want of union,
between those who held the purse and those who possessed the
knowledge, was, that the schools languished and failed. The
Society of Artists, after a time, dissolved; and the Pennsylvania Academy of the Fine Arts became, and has continued,
merely an institution for collecting and exhibiting pictures and
statuary. As such it is valuable, and tends to the civilization,
refinement, and good taste of the public: but it is an academy
only in name.

In October, 1824, the artists presented some by-laws, which
they wished the Academy to adopt, they being willing to co-
operate with that institution; but the Directors insisted on
the privilege of rejecting academicians, though elected by that
body to fill vacancies; and that the President, an eminent
lawyer, shall judge of the qualifications of an applicant to become a student. This answer stopped all proceedings at that
time.

In 1828 the resident artists of Philadelphia appointed Messrs.
John Neagle and James B. Longacre to draw up a memorial,
which was signed by twenty-seven artists, and presented to
the Pennsylvania Academy of the Fine Arts, in which they
enumerated their grievances. They complain that they have

no voice in hanging their works for exhibition — that their works are mingled with those of old masters, and injured by the prejudices of society — that the annual exhibitions are not attended, because the Academy keeps an open exhibition all the year — that the casts intended for the student are made part of the exhibitions — that they have no voice in the appointment of the keeper — that the rooms granted to the use of artists were appropriated by the keeper to his private use — and generally, that although their works must eventually support the Academy, they are treated as ciphers. The Board of Directors appointed a committee to reply to this memorial, and the reply was signed by Jos. Hopkinson, president. The reply tells the artists how much the patrons have done for the arts; notwithstanding which, "a few artists, of a restless and ambitious temper, and impatient for personal authority and distinction, propagated opinions that artists only should have the government of an Academy of Arts." They say what is groundless, "that experience was opposed to this theory"; — they insinuate the danger of placing their property under the management of artists. They say that no artist, "in any country, ever received, or expected any other return for the exhibition of his pictures, than the introduction of them to the knowledge of the public, and the fame and emolument he would derive from that knowledge." All this is intended in good faith, but exposes the ignorance of these gentlemen in the history of the arts.

John Trumbull received in New York from the Academy $200 for the use of pictures for one exhibition. The artists of England have and do receive pecuniary emolument and relief from the funds accumulated by the exhibition of their works. But the artists of Philadelphia did not ask any remuneration for exhibiting their works, they asked just consideration, distinction, and honorable treatment. The directors tauntingly tell the artists that having been paid by their employers for their pictures, they are at the disposal of purchasers, and may be borrowed for exhibition without any debt due to the artist. The directors claim the right to elect the teachers, i.e. lawyers, physicians, and merchants elect the competent lecturers and masters in schools of art! The whole reply, though professing to wish to give satisfaction, is very little calculated to produce that effect, and consequently the rejoinder of the artists, signed by order of the resident artists, "John Neagle and James B. Longacre," expresses their diminished hopes in, and expectations from the directors, as their opinions relative to artists and their rights are so opposite to those entertained by the professional artists of Philadelphia. They touch on the subjects in controversy and conclude, "We are not prepared to accede to any terms whatever which will compromise the respect which we owe to ourselves or the obligations we feel to sustain to the utmost of our power the dignity of our profession."

It was the intention of the artists to have an exhibition of their works under their own direction, and they applied for Sully & Earl's gallery, which was offered for half the clear proceeds. This plan fell through, and I believe the affairs of the academy have declined, and artists coldly look on and occasionally exhibit their works in the apartments of the institution.*

By an Artist of Philadelphia.

"The Pennsylvania Academy of the Fine Arts" in Philadelphia, Chestnut Street, between Tenth and Eleventh Streets, north side. This institution owes its origin to a few gentlemen of Philadelphia — seven lawyers, one carver, two physicians, one auctioneer, one wine merchant, and one painter constituted the first board of officers. Incorporated 28th March, 1806. The property was divided into 300 shares, of 50 dollars each. A building was erected on a lot on ground rent. Within a few years an addition to the academy was erected on the east for the statues, now called the "Antique Gallery." In 1810, a society of arts was formed, called the "*Society of Arts of the United States.*" There was one also called the "*Columbian Society of Arts.*"

"The '*Academicians,*' a body of artists, were organized and were attached to the academy on the 13th March 1810. I do not know how long they acted in concert with the academy, but Mr. Edwin, who was one of the original academicians, told me that *diplomas* were promised to them by the board of directors, and that at some public meeting, where ladies were invited, each academician received, with great pomp and ceremony, a paper tied with a pink riband, which were thought to be the diplomas, until they reached home and went to exhibit the honors conferred upon them to their families and friends; when, lo! to their disappointment and chagrin, each had a piece of *blank paper!* I believe this was the death blow to all zeal on the part of the artists of that day. This fact I never knew until after I had become an academician.

"When the artists complained of the trick played off upon their credulity, they were promised soon '*righty dighty*' ones, but to this day no one has ever been thus honored by the board.

In another chapter I shall continue the subject of academies
as attempted in New York.

"The first exhibition held in the Pennsylvania Academy was in 1811, since which
an exhibition in the spring has been held annually, except 1833. This year no artist
was in the board after the death of Mr. Rush, the ship carver.

"By reference to the catalogue of the first exhibition in 1811, I do not find the title
P. A. or Pennsylvania Academy. The printed book, however, says they were organ-
ized in 1810. The catalogue of the third exhibition in 1813, is in the name of ' *Columbian
Society of Artists.* '

"I find the titles P. A. in the catalogue of the 2d exhibition in 1812. The duties
of the academicians were unattended to for years, and the titles ceased to be printed
with catalogues until the year 1824, when several artists were elected by the old academicians and most of these elections were confirmed by the directors. I called the
meeting which led to this step at my own house. Mr. Rembrandt Peale being one of
the party, and Sully another, it was suggested to reorganize the body of academicians
— we did so after our election by the academy, and our first meeting in the academy
(as academicians), was on the evening of October 18, 1824.

"The artists of Philadelphia themselves are much to blame. They want firmness
and consistency, and now they exercise no authority in the academy. Mr. Sully has
backed out from the Board of Directors, and so did I before him. I don't think he will
ever serve as an officer again. Mr. Inman was, the other day, elected a director, and
he is the only painter in the board, and whether he will truckle to these aristocratic
gentlemen, remains to be seen.

"I believe George Murray, the engraver, was the ring leader in mischief, in the
early history of our academy, but this was long before my time; he died before I had
entered as an artist. Mr. Sully can say much of the early history, and he will not say
a great deal, I think, in favor of Murray."

CHAPTER VIII.

ALEXANDER ROBERTSON — CANTIR — BELZONS — JAMES
EARL — ROBERTS — EDWARD TRENCHARD — WALTER
ROBERTSON — FIELD — WERTMÜLLER — WILLIAM
BIRCH — VALLANCE — THACKARA —
LAWSON — JENNINGS.

ALEXANDER ROBERTSON.[0]

THIS gentleman was born at Monymusk, near Aberdeen, in
North Britain, in the year 1768.[1] His father was an architect
and draftsman, and his elder and younger brothers, Archibald
and Andrew, are both artists. Andrew stands in the first
rank of miniature painters in London, and as far as my knowledge extends, is the first *in the rank*. Of Archibald I have
spoken above. He arrived in 1792, and finding that America
was a land of performance as well as promise, he wrote for
Alexander to join him in New York. Andrew was then a
child; previous to embarking for America, Alexander passed
five months in London in the summer of 1792, and took lessons
in miniature painting from Shelly. He embarked at Liverpool,
and in the autumn met his brother in New York, where he
had some practice as a miniature painter, and had established
a drawing school under the title of "The Columbian Academy
of Painting." Mr. Alexander Robertson associated with his
brother in this institution, and afterwards when conducting a
similar establishment of his own, has been the teacher of
many successive generations in the rudiments of the arts of

---

[1] Alexander Robertson, fourth son of William Robertson, was born May 13, 1772,
and came to New York in 1792 for the purpose of painting a portrait of Washington.
He died in New York in 1841. In the *American Minerva* New York, May 4, 1795, and
in the *Morning Chronicle* of October 1, 1802, appeared the following announcement:
"Archibald and Alexander Robertson, Columbian Academy of Painting Paints Portraits, Miniatures, instructs in Painting," etc.   [0] Alexander Robertson died in 1841.

112

design. Mr. John Vanderlyn received his early instructions
at the "Columbian Academy." In 1816 Mr. Robertson was
elected secretary to the American Academy of Fine Arts.

If Mr. Robertson had been no otherwise instrumental in
furthering the progress of the arts of design in this country, we
owe him much for freely communicating to us a very valuable
manuscript treatise on miniature painting, detailing every part
of the process, with instructions for each successive sitting.
This was written by his brother Andrew for Alexander's use,
but through his liberality, has assisted very many of our first
artists in that branch of the art.

Mr. Robertson sketches and paints landscape in water
colors with great facility. He has been the instructor of
many young ladies who are distinguished for talent and skill.
Miss Hall stands very prominent among our best painters of
miniatures, and was for a time his pupil. Several ladies under
the tuition of Mr. Alexander Robertson, have attained skill in
the painting of landscape in oil. A copy from Ruysdael by
Miss Storer, I remember as exciting my surprise and giving
me much pleasure.

Mr. Robertson married Miss Provoost, a niece of Bishop
Provoost, and is surrounded by a large and worthy family.
He is himself one of the most amiable men of my acquaintance.

Allan Cunningham in his "Lives of Painters," tells us that
Raeburn "was elected an honorary member of the Academy of
Fine Arts at New York," and goes on to say, "the secretary,
Robertson, says in his intimation to Raeburn of this transatlantic honor, that 'the institution is in a flourishing condition,
and the collection of paintings is rapidly increasing. In addition to such pictures as the funds of the society permit it to
purchase, the friendly donations of many of the honorary
members will enable it to boast of specimens of most of the
distinguished artists of the day.' In 1821 he was elected an
honorary member of the Academy of Arts of South Carolina.
The communication of Cogdel, the secretary, is in a strain
more to our liking than that of his brother secretary of New
York: no hint of the donations of works by new members."

Mr. Alexander Robertson is not to be charged with the eleemosynary spirit and hint of this letter. It was the common mode adopted by this nominal academy, to procure presents from persons of distinction, whether artists or not. I do not know that the pope was made a member of this society of physicians, lawyers, and merchants, but his friends Napoleon and Lucien Bonaparte were, and paid the admission fee duly and punctually. Raeburn, simple soul, thinking that he had to deal with a school of artists, took the hint, and sent to New York a very fine head, the portrait of an American gentleman, at that time in Edinburgh, which is a monument of his talents and liberality, and a model for every student of the art of portraiture.

Mr. Robertson still teaches drawing and painting; and another, and another generation, may profit by his instructions.

Joshua Cantir.[0]

This gentleman came to Charleston, South Carolina, in 1792 from Denmark, and became a resident. He had received his education as an artist, under a professor of the academy at Copenhagen. He painted and taught drawing for many years in Charleston. "He was," says my correspondent, "devotedly attached to the art, and possessed talents, which, under more favoring circumstances, and with that professional competition which he did not find at that time in South Carolina, might have raised him to a higher standing among artists than he actually enjoyed. He died in New York."

M. Belzons [00]

Was a native of France, and painted miniatures and other portraits in Charleston, South Carolina, in 1792. I should probably never have heard of him, if he had not been the first instructor, for a short time of Thomas Sully, whose sister he had married. M. Belzons had lost his fortune, and been driven to America by the French Revolution, the source of so much present misery and future good; and he employed that skill, which had been attained as a source of amusement, or an ele-

[0] Cantir (or Canter) died in New York City November 1, 1826.
[00] Jean Belzons was around about Charleston until 1812. After that there is no record of his location.

gant accomplishment in France, to the purposes of gaining a
reputable subsistence in a foreign country for himself and
family.

EARL.[1]

An English gentleman painted portraits in Charleston,
South Carolina, about the year 1792. Mr. Sully when a boy
saw him; and when he went to England, visited his widow and
gave her an account of him and his death by.yellow fever,
after he had embarked his property to return home.

JOHN ROBERTS

Was born in Scotland 1768, and came to America in 1793.
Possessed of remarkable talents, and receiving a good education, he turned every advantage to little account either for
others or himself by instability, and the want of that prudence
which is supposed to be one of the good gifts bestowed upon
his countrymen. He was truly eccentric, and probably prided
himself too much upon his eccentricity.

He was (says my informant) a good mathematician — passionately fond of music, and complete master of most instruments. — A musical club was formed in New York, where he
resided, of which my friend Charles Rhind, our first consul
to the Porte, and through whom our treaty of commerce with
that power was formed, Benjamin Trott, the distinguished
miniature painter and others of my acquaintance were members; they met in a room adjoining the Methodist meetinghouse; in John Street, and struggled with all the instruments
they could muster to overpower the discords of their neighbors
— but inflated minds acting upon inflated lungs, put down the
united efforts of fiddles, flutes, clarionets, and trumpets, and
they were obliged to give up the contest and remove to another
place of meeting.

[1] James Earl, brother of Ralph Earl, Sr., was born in that part of Leicester now
incorporated as Paxton, Mass., May 1, 1761. Like his brother he went to England
and there married, in 1789, the widow of Joseph B. Smythe of New Jersey, an American Tory. James Earl returned to America and shortly thereafter died suddenly of
yellow fever at Charleston, S. C., in August, 1796. His professional life as a portrait
painter was spent in England and South Carolina.

The ingenuity of Roberts in mechanics was as great as his taste for the fine arts. He made engraving tools, and even invented new to answer the exigencies of his work. His friend Trott had executed a beautiful miniature of Washington from Stuart's portrait of the hero, and Roberts engraved a plate from it, but after he had finished his work to the satisfaction of his friends, he was retouching it, when Trott came in, and some misunderstanding taking place between the engraver and the painter, Roberts deliberately took up a piece of pumice and applying it to the copper obliterated all trace of his work; then taking the miniature, he handed it to its owner, saying, "There, sir — take your picture — I have done with it — and with you." A few impressions, taken as proofs, only exist. He designed and engraved the frontispiece for David Longworth's edition of " Telemachus," published in 1797-8.

While he was engraving the "Washington" from Trott's miniature, he invented a new mode of stippling, produced by instruments devised and executed by himself, and which I have been assured, were "of such exquisite finish and workmanship, that a microscope was necessary to discover the teeth in some of the rollers." He made a printing press for proving his work. He painted in miniature and drew portraits in crayons; but being engaged in constructing an organ on *a new principle*, and in contriving improvements on the steam engine for propelling boats, he abandoned the fine arts, and would only paint or engrave to procure the very little money he wanted for living and making experiments.

A correspondent says, "In music he was a master on several instruments. He was the founder of the Euterpean Society (which still exists), and for several years led the orchestra thereof as first violin. Sometimes he took the clarionet, which he played with uncommon sweetness, at others he would take the flute, and he spent much of his time at the pianoforte and organ, both of which he touched like a master. He was much engaged in mechanics — he invented an economical stove, the patent of which he gave to an iron founder for a single casting, the moulds of which he made himself. He also invented a bellows of singular power, which he used in forging iron and steel. In his mathematical studies he devised a system of algebra, which he believed would render that science as simple as common arithmetic. He was an optician, and made improvements in preparing glasses or lenses to use in his new style of engraving. He was seized with apoplexy while descending the stairs of his dwelling, fell to the bottom, fractured his skull and died immediately, in the year 1803, at the age of thirty."

The reader may ask where are his works? Of what utility to science or art, his inventions? With all his extraordinary powers he brought nothing to perfection. Truth obliges me to say that with a mind so comprehensive, and body fitted to second its dictates, he seems to have forgotten the purposes for which such gifts are bestowed, and the source from whence they came — he abused them — he became intemperate, and it is most probable that the fall which ended his short life, was caused by alcohol rather than apoplexy. The low estimation in which artists were held at that period in our cities, where trade is the source of wealth, and wealth the fountain of honor, was both cause and effect in respect to that conduct I have been obliged to record: — that time is past. Artists know their stand in society, and are now in consequence of that conduct which flows from their knowledge of the dignity and importance of art, looked up to by the best in the land, instead of being looked down upon by those whose merits will only be recorded in their bank books.

EDWARD TRENCHARD.[1]

This gentleman was born in Philadelphia, and being the son of an engraver, received his first lessons in the art from his father. Not satisfied with the knowledge to be obtained at that period in America, he visited England, and brought out Gilbert Fox to practise with him, and teach him the art of

[1] A stippled engraved portrait of Count Rumford published in 1798 bears the signature of E. C. Trenchard as engraver, and Edward Trenchard's name appears among the signers to an agreement in Philadelphia for the establishment of a school or academy of architecture, sculpture, painting, etc., in 1794.

He died on November 3, 1824. He was the nephew, not the son of James.

etching. As I am informed, Mr. Trenchard was afterwards an officer in the navy of the United States.

WALTER ROBERTSON.

An Irish gentleman, who came to New York in the same ship with Gilbert Stuart.[1] The captain of the ship related that Stuart frequently quarrelled with Robertson when the decanter had circulated freely after dinner, and *in his cups* made use of abusive language. Robertson took the following method to keep the peace. He went to his berth, and returned to the cabin with a pair of pistols. "Mr. Stuart, we'll pass over what has gone by; but the first time you use ungentlemanly language to me, you will please to take one of these and I'll take the other, and we'll take a pop across the table." It is said the hint was taken, rather than the pop.

Robertson's style was unique; it was very clear and beautiful, but it was not natural. He went to Philadelphia before Stuart, and painted a portrait, in miniature, of Washington; which Field, another miniature painter and engraver, engraved and published, with decorations by Jno. Jas. Barralet. It was altogether a failure; and so little like the General, that one might doubt his sitting for it. His copies from Stuart's oil portraits pleased very much. After painting in New York and Philadelphia he went to the East Indies and there died. — His portrait of Mrs. Washington, engraved for the National Portrait Gallery, is like, and very creditable to him.

R. FIELD. [02]

An English gentleman, who engraved in the dotted style (or stippling), and painted very good miniatures. Field and

1 (From Dublin, Ireland, in 1793.) He painted a miniature of Washington and copied several portraits by Stuart. Robertson died in the East Indies in 1802.

02 Robert Field was born in Gloucester, England and emigrated to America in 1794. He painted miniatures in this country and made a number of stippled engravings, including a portrait for the first American edition of Shakespeare's works (Philadelphia, 1795). In 1808 he went to Halifax, Nova Scotia, where he painted large portraits. In 1816 he went to Jamaica and died there three years later.

Robertson both annoyed Trott. Of Robertson he said, his excellence depended upon the secret he possessed — the chemical
composition with which he mixed and used his colors; — of
Field, that his work was too much like engraving.

Mr. Field painted more in Boston, Philadelphia, and Baltimore, than in New York. He was a handsome, stout, gentlemanly man, and a favorite with gentlemen. He went from the
United States to Halifax, and I have not heard of him since.
I remember two very beautiful female heads by him; one of
Mrs. Allen, in Boston, and one of Mrs. Thornton, of Washington. In a preceding biography I have mentioned the head of
Washington, engraved by him. This picture has the merit of
not representing the General with a wig on, as Heath's engraving does; but the countenance is unlike Washington's.
And one remarkable deviation from the General's costume adds
to the belief that he did not sit for it — it is painted with a
black stock, an article of dress he never wore. I believe, when
president, Washington never wore his military dress; when he,
as General, wore it, he *always* wore it, but with a white cambrick
stock.

Adolph Ulric Wertmüller.

This artist was introduced to me by Mr. Gahn, the Swedish
consul, soon after his arrival in this country; and from Mr.
Gahn I have expected a promised notice of him, as he knew
him well and came to America with him. I have been disappointed, and take my information from the "Analectic Magazine" of 1815.

"Adolph Ulric Wertmüller was, by birth, a Swede, the son
of a respectable apothecary of the city of Stockholm. Having
acquired the rudiments of the art of painting at home, he removed to Paris for the purpose of further improvement, where
he studied and pursued his profession for several years. He
appears to have acquired considerable reputation on the continent of Europe. He was elected a member of the Royal
Academies of Sculpture and Painting, at Paris and Stockholm; and, in addition to these unsubstantial honors, he re-

ceived a more solid reward, in such a share of public patronage as enabled him to amass a considerable fortune. This he had placed in the French funds, and in the hands of a Paris banker; but, in that general convulsion of all financial and commercial concerns which took place in the early part of the Revolution, he lost the greater part of his fortune. He then determined to escape from the storm which threatened such general destruction, and try his fortunes in another hemisphere. In May, 1794, he landed at Philadelphia. In this country his paintings were admired, he received many attentions, and President Washington sat to him; but the arts were then strangers among us, and we were not yet rich enough for patronage. He remained here until the autumn of 1796, when he re-embarked for Europe, and returned to Stockholm, where he resided for several years. Misfortune still pursued him; he lost a large sum by the failure of a great house in Stockholm; and, in disgust, he again returned to America, and arrived at Philadelphia in 1800. Here he exhibited his large and beautiful picture of Danaë, from which he derived a handsome income. About a year after his arrival he married a lady of Swedish descent, who brought him a considerable property. After a few years' residence in the city of Philadelphia, he purchased a farm at Marcus Hook, on the Delaware, and removed thither, where he lived in ease and comfort until his death, in 1812.[1]

"Not long after his death, most of his pictures were sold at auction in Philadelphia. A small copy of his 'Danaë,' by his own hand, was sold for five hundred dollars; and some time after the original picture was sold, in New York, for fifteen hundred dollars.

"Wertmüller had studied his art with great assiduity and ardor: he copied with accuracy the models before him, and imitated with success the masters on whom he had formed his taste.

"His 'Danaë' is his greatest and most splendid production.

[1] Adolph Ulric Wertmüller was born in Stockholm, Sweden, February 18, 1751, and died at Claymont near Wilmington, Delaware, October 5, 1811. In August, 1794, Washington sat to Wertmüller for his portrait. In 1801 he married a granddaughter of Gustavus Hesselius the artist.

It is indeed his great work; and for that very reason it is, on every account, to be regretted, that both in the subject and the style of execution it offends alike against pure taste and the morality of the art.

"As in literature, so also in the other productions of cultivated genius, the connection between a corrupted moral taste and an unchaste, false style, is so strong, that, did not frequent experience teach otherwise, one would think it impossible that an artist, who feels the dignity, and aspires to the perfection of the noble art which he loves, could ever stoop to the pollution of that art, and the debasement of his own powers."

This artist painted in New York, and more in Philadelphia. It is said that William Hamilton, of the Woodlands, employed him to copy the old family pictures, and then destroyed the originals.

WILLIAM BIRCH

Came to America in 1794.[02] He was born in Warwick, England. He was an enamel painter, and settled in Philadelphia, where he died. I remember seeing a miniature of Washington, executed by him in enamel; which I thought very beautiful, and very like Trott's copy from Stuart's original picture. My impression is, that it was copied from Trott. Birch could design.

JOHN VALLANCE [03]

The name of Vallance is connected with that of Thackara, as they worked in partnership, as engravers, for many years. Dobson's Encyclopedia bears their marks on many a plate. Alexander Lawson says of him, "he had attempted to copy a head of Franklin, and also one of Howard, with some success.

02 William Russell Birch was born on April 9, 1775 and settled in Philadelphia in 1794 when he dropped his middle name. He made about sixty miniatures in enamel of the portrait of Washington by Benjamin Trott after Stuart. He was also an excellent engraver, having practised the art with success before coming to this country. He engraved a series of "Views of Philadelphia" in 1798-1800 and also a smaller series of plates illustrating seats in the United States. He died on August 7, 1834.

03 John Vallance was a native of Scotland, born 1770, died in Philadelphia June 14, 1823. He came to the United States about the year 1791, and was one of the organizers of the "Association of Artists in America," established in Philadelphia in 1794, and a member of the firm of Tanner, Vallance, Kearny & Co., engravers.

He was certainly the best engraver at this time (1794) in the United States; and had he been placed in a more favorable situation, he would have been a fine artist."

JAMES THACKARA.[1]

The partner of the above, but inferior to him as an engraver. He was a long time keeper of the Pennsylvania Academy of Fine Arts; not as the term keeper is used in England, but merely having charge of the property. Mr. Thackara is a respectable citizen.

ALEXANDER LAWSON.[2]

Of this gentleman, my valuable correspondent, Mr. John Neagle, says, he is "the best engraver of birds, in America. He engraved for Wilson's Ornithology."

In a letter to a friend who had requested Mr. Lawson to give him a memorandum respecting his first efforts, and the state of the art of engraving at the period of his arrival in America, he writes: —

"I was born near Lanark in Scotland, in the year 1773. Trifling circumstances gave me very early a love for prints, and my schoolmaster drawing a little (though he gave me no instruction in it), increased my fondness; so that my books had as many houses, trees and birds in them as sums. I went to Manchester, in England, when sixteen. A print store was near us, where some of the first prints were kept; — and my intimacy with a bookseller, who showed me all the best works with engravings, caused me to become enthusiastically attached to the art.

"I read all the books on art I could meet with; but they were of little use. My first efforts at engraving were made on smooth half-pennies with the point of my penknife; and at this I

[1] Thackara was born in Philadelphia, March 12, 1767, where he died August 15, 1848. He served apprenticeship to James Trenchard, whose daughter, Hannah, he married.

[2] Lawson was born in Ravenstruthers, Lanarkshire, Scotland, December 19, 1773, and died in Philadelphia, August 22, 1846. He married Elizabeth Scaife of Cumberland, England, June 6, 1805, and had two children, Oscar A. and Helen E. Lawson, both of whom became proficient in the art of engraving.

became pretty expert. I soon after obtained a graver, which
was made by a blacksmith from my description of the instrument, as I understood it to be from a figure I found in a book.
We made a clumsy affair of it, and it worked very stiffly; but
it was a step forward.

"When in the country, where I often was, I used to amuse
myself of an evening in ornamenting the pewter tankard, out of
which I drank my ale. A gentleman who called upon me
about three years ago (after I had been thirty-six years in
America), told me that when in the West Riding of Yorkshire,
while putting up at an inn, he happened to mention that he
was going to the United States, and the landlord immediately
brought forward a tankard of my ornamenting, which he said
he had preserved carefully ever since I was at his house, and
intended so to do as long as he lived."

This is one of the many little incidents which sweeten the
cup of life; and I doubt not but the knowledge of the value
set upon this early work of his art, gave more pleasure to the
artist at the age of threescore than the most flattering reception given to the most perfect production of his graver, when
he by dint of study and perseverance, in the land of his adoption, had placed himself at the head of one branch of his profession. It came from afar, associated with the recollections of
youth, bright hopes, and his former home. The artist thus
proceeds — "I bought a graver at last. I had *points* made for
etching, and tried that. I then got a mezzotinto tool, and tried
that mode of engraving — I tried everything, and did nothing
well, for want of a little instruction. I was then connected
in trade with my brother; but loving art better than trade, and
taking different views of political questions from those of my
brother, I gave up my share in the business, and in my twen-
tieth year, embarked· at Liverpool for Baltimore, where I
arrived on the 14th of July, 1794. I staid in that city one week,
and then came to Philadelphia, where I have remained ever
since. Thackara and Vallance were partners when I came to
Philadelphia. I engraved with them two years. They thought
themselves artists, and that they knew every part of the art;

and yet their art consisted in copying, in a dry, stiff manner with the graver, the plates for the Encyclopedia, all their attempts at etching having miscarried. The rest of their time, and that of all others at this period, was employed to engrave card plates, with a festoon of wretched flowers and bad writing — then there was engraving on type metal — silver plate — watches — door plates — dog collars and silver buttons, with an attempt at seal cutting. Such was the state of engraving in 1794."

In conversation Mr. Lawson said that while he worked with Thackara and Vallance he improved himself by studying drawing. He afterwards worked for Dobson, and engraved the plates for the supplement of the Encyclopedia.

He likewise worked for Barralet, the painter and designer, and afterwards formed a kind of co-partnership with him, but was obliged to quarrel with the eccentric Irishman before he could get any share of profits. Mr. Lawson is a tall, thin man, of large frame, and athletic; full of animation, and inclined to be satirical, but, as I judge, full of good feeling and the love of truth. Krimmell and Wilson he speaks of in rapturous terms of commendation, both as to talents and moral worth. Murray, on the contrary, with great asperity.

Mr. Lawson engraved the Rev. John Blair Linn's plates for his poems, the designs by Barralet. He likewise engraved the plates (and beautiful they are) for the nine volumes of Wilson's Ornithology, and Charles Lucien Bonaparte's four additional volumes. He is one of the many examples of a native of Britain coming to America and making himself an artist.

JENNINGS.

Of this painter all I know is, that he was in London practising *art* about this period. Colonel Sargent in a letter to me, says, "There was a Mr. Jennings, from Philadelphia, in London, to whom I had a letter from Colonel Trumbull. I know not what has become of him, though I had a letter from him some time ago informing me of his success in ' *manufacturing old pictures* for the *knowing ones*,' and that it was very curious to hear their observations upon the merits of these works of the old masters." Of course he was an impostor, leading a life of falsehood and deception; and probably ended it at Botany Bay, unless his meritorious knavery exalted him to a higher situation in the country of his adoption.[1]

[1] Samuel Jennings, a native of Philadelphia, painted a large and imposing allegorical picture in the year 1792, which he presented to the Philadelphia Library. It is called "The Genius of America Encouraging the Emancipation of the Blacks." It is not a work of great merit.

CHAPTER IX.

ANDERSON — HISTORY OF WOOD ENGRAVING.

A. ANDERSON.

THE first who attempted engraving or embossing on wood in America, was born in New York: but before I proceed to a notice of his life, I will give a memoir upon

ENGRAVING ON WOOD,

furnished me by Abraham John Mason, Esq., now one of our citizens, and practising the art in New York.

"As engraving and printing unquestionably had their origin in China, it will be proper first to give a sketch of the peculiar modes practised in that empire. The design is made on a thin, transparent paper, and pasted with the face downwards on the block; it is then engraved by cutting through the paper into the wood, leaving standing only those portions of the surface which appear black in the drawing. Their tools are similar in many respects to those of other block cutters, ancient and modern, consisting of a knife for outlining, with gouges, chisels, etc., of various shapes for clearing away the wood. They use them with much celerity, especially the knife, which they guide with both hands; their facility enables them to finish their blocks with great rapidity, and at an astonishingly cheap rate. The Chinese have never attempted the use of moveable types; all their books, illustrative or descriptive, being printed from wooden blocks, cut in the manner described, and this mode is to them far more economical, owing to the low price of workmanship of every kind.

"Their method of printing is simple, and peculiar to themselves. The block must be in a firm and level position, being first tightly fixed in a larger piece of wood to give it stability;

in front of this the paper is placed, cut to the proper size. The ink (which is merely a reduction without oil of that which is known as Indian ink) being distributed on a smooth piece of board, the workman takes a moderately stiff brush, which he dips into it, and rubs the block carefully therewith. The paper is next laid over, and rubbed with a second brush, which is soft, and shaped like an oblong cushion; the paper not being sized, a gentle pressure is generally sufficient, and which may be repeated, or regulated as occasion may offer. A third brush, very stiff, is used for cleaning the blocks. These brushes are curiously made of the fine fibres of the palm, or cocoanut trees. A set of these printing materials may be seen in the museum of the English East India Company, which are supposed to be the only specimens in Europe. In the manner described, without the aid of any press, have all impressions been taken in China, from the earliest periods to the present day. Their paper being so very thin, is printed on one side only, and each leaf in their books is folded in binding, and the edges turned inwards, and stitched with silk. There is much neat and curious execution about some of their cuts, but they seldom go beyond outlines, and are altogether deficient in the true principles of drawing.

"Much disputation has arisen as to the period when engraving was first practised in Europe. The earliest record rests on the authority of Papillon, the French writer, who gives a description of eight subjects, relating to Alexander the Great, having been cut on wood by twins of the name of Cunio, at Ravenna, as early as 1285.

"During the next, or 14th century, there is clear evidence of the practice, for printing playing cards, and figures of saints, etc. These were without doubt first executed in the Venetian states, and afterwards in Germany and the low countries to a great extent. The impressions appear to have been taken by means of a hand roller, the press not being known until the following century; in the early part of which the art was applied to engraving larger subjects of a devotional kind, with inscriptions. Several of these curious prints are still extant;

amongst them, in the possession of Earl Spencer, is the celebrated one of St. Christopher carrying the infant Jesus; this
is remarkable as being the earliest print bearing a certain
date, viz., 1423. The success of these gave rise to a more
extensive application of the art. Scriptural designs of many
figures were cut with descriptive texts on each block; they
were printed on one side only of the paper, and two of the
prints were frequently pasted together to form one leaf with a
picture on each side; entire sets were subsequently bound up,
and thus were formed into the block books so well known to
antiquaries. The Apocalypse of St. John, probably the first
of these works, appeared about 1420; one of the identical
blocks cut for it still exists in the library of Earl Spencer.
The latest and most noted of these books is the 'Speculum
Humanæ Salvationis,' produced about the year 1440, and being
partly printed from moveable wooden types, became the con-
necting medium that gradually introduced the invaluable art
of typography, which facilitating the production of books, was
the means of greatly increasing the demand for wood cuts for
primers, prayer books, etc. In 1457 Faust produced his
Psalter, printed with metal types, and initials in colors from
blocks. Of the principal letter, a highly ornamented B, an
accurate facsimile is given in Savage's 'Decorative Printing.'
Typography was introduced into England by Caxton in 1474,
who published his 'Game of Chesse,' Æsop, and other works
with wood cuts, the execution of which is quite barbarous,
when compared with continental engravings of the same period.
All cuts consisted of little more than outline until 1493, when
Michael Wolgemuth effected a great improvement in the art
by the cuts for his ' Nuremberg Chronicle,' in which he introduced a greater degree of shading, and the first attempts at
crosshatching. This was carried to much higher perfection by
his pupil Albert Dürer, who published in 1498 his Apocalypse in
sixteen folio cuts, and early in the 16th century, his 'Life and
Passion of Christ,' and other large works of high talent. In
1511, he produced the 'Fall of Man,' with thirty-seven small
cuts, and from that period until his death in 1528, he published a

variety of engravings on copper and wood, besides being an eminent painter. His pupil, Burgkmair, executed several rich works under the patronage of the Emperor Maximilian, many of the blocks of which still exist in Vienna, and form an ample refutation of the assertions of Mr. Landseer, and others, as to the practicability of effecting crosshatched work on wood. This 16th century was rich in able wood engravers in several parts of Continental Europe, amongst whom might be named Holbein, who published his celebrated 'Dance of Death,' 1538, Justus Amman of Zurich, Stimmer of Schaffhausen, Cesari Vecellio, a younger brother of Titian's; Porta, Salviati, and an innumerable host of others, whose skilful productions gave the art a high consideration with the best painters of the time. In England comparatively few works appeared, but amongst them should be noticed the first edition of the celebrated 'Martyrology,' published in 1563, the best cuts in which were probably done by foreigners, as we have record of only a solitary name or two of worth, until within the last sixty years. In the 17th century the art visibly declined, owing to the superior cultivation of copper engravings. Some few eminent artists, however, flourished, such as Van Sichem, Eckman, and Christopher Zegher, the latter of whom engraved many very masterly specimens from the designs, and under the direction of Rubens. By the year 1700, wood engravings sunk to a very depressed state; the French family of Papillon should, however, not be omitted, the elder of whom practised about the year 1670; his son John improved upon him, and was said to be the inventor of printing paper hangings, by blocks in 1688. He was the father of Jean Baptiste Papillon, who practised with much success as a wood engraver, but is more celebrated for his well-known work on the art in two volumes, published in 1766. With these and some few other exceptions, there is little worthy attention from 1650 until the era of the school of Bewick.

"Mr. Thomas Bewick began wood engraving in 1768; in 1775 he produced his cut of the Old Hound, for which the Society of Arts awarded him seven guineas, it being justly deemed so very superior to any specimens then executed. In 1785 he commenced his valuable Natural Histories, and published the 'Quadrupeds' in 1790, and the 'Birds' in 1797. These and his other works, all of which were richly embellished with cuts, effected by their great excellence the restoration of an almost lost art. Nearly contemporary with Bewick was Mr. Lee, of London, who produced many very neat specimens. Other artists soon arose, who effected still greater improvement in the art, by introducing a richer and more varied style of workmanship, which has led to the adoption of the art to so wide an extent as promises to be a sure prevention to its ever again sinking into neglect.

"Public lectures on this art were for the first time given in London, in 1829, by Mr. Mason, who subsequently delivered the same in the United States to the National Academy of Design.

"The theory and practice of this art, are in principle the reverse of engraving on copper; in the latter the lines to be printed, are sunk or cut in the plate; these being filled with ink, are by means of a rolling press, transferred in effect to the paper. In wood engraving, on the contrary, the parts that are to appear must be raised, or rather left untouched, and hence it is frequently termed relief engraving. In printing, the surface is only charged with ink, and the impression is taken as from types. The copper engraver rarely uses more than three tools of the kind which are termed burins or gravers. The artist on wood requires, according to circumstances, from ten to fifteen or eighteen, called gravers, tools for tinting and sculptures; the latter are used for cutting out the broader parts which are to be left white. The earlier artists cut on various kinds of wood, such as the apple, pear, etc; these being termed soft woods, are now only in request for calico printing and other manufacturing purposes, for as the style of work improved, these were abandoned, and box was tried on account of its superior texture and compactness, which have caused it to be the only kind used for every subject that can properly be termed a work of art. The surface of the wood to be engraved is carefully planed, scraped, etc., so as to render it as smooth as possible, in order to receive the drawing which must be put on the block itself, previously to commencing the engraving. The artist in its execution, has to arrange the strength and direction of the lines required for the various parts and distances, so that the printed impression, though composed of different series of interlineations, may present the same character in effect, as the original drawing.

"Much care is requisite, on the part of the engraver, to prevent a delicate design from being rubbed during the process of cutting; and it is usually covered with paper, which is removed by degrees as required. It will be apparent also how much depends upon the skill of the engraver, when it is considered, that, with every line cut by the tool, a portion of the effect of his original is removed, and his recollective powers and taste must be in constant exercise, to preserve the points of the design; and the block must be wholly engraved before any impression can be taken. The copper engraver, on the contrary, is enabled to take progressive proofs of his work, and has his original drawing, unimpaired, constantly before him. The latter has also another important advantage, in what is termed tinting; inasmuch as all his skies and flat backgrounds can be cut on the plate itself by mechanical means; and his various tints are thereby produced with every required delicacy. The wood engraver can have no such facility; all depends on the steadiness of the eye and hand, properly to effect the object, by cutting line after line individually, without any auxiliary assistance whatever.

"These brief explanations may serve to show the principles on which all engravings on wood are effected. Thus, whether the design relate to landscape, the human figure, or any other species of subject, it must be composed of an infinite number and variety of projecting portions of wood, produced by those delineations which, according to the judgment of the engraver, are best calculated to convey, when printed, the desired effect.

"The ancient mode of working was on the side of the grain, their wood being always cut the longitudinal way of the tree:

this method continued, for all wood cuts, till about the year 1725, when the present method was commenced in England, of cutting the tree transversely, or across. This plan presenting the end of the grain, admits, from its greater tenacity, of a finer kind of workmanship, and the application of the description of tools before named. The block cutters for paper hangings, etc. have their wood prepared in the same way as the old masters, and of course use similar tools; the chief of which is a knife, shaped somewhat like a lancet, with which the line has to be cut on both sides, and the superfluous wood has to be removed by gouges, chisels, etc. of various shapes, as derived originally from the Chinese.

"When we consider, that in this way all the finished works of the ancients were produced, it attaches a very great degree of merit to them; for the process seems evidently to have been a more tedious one than the modern: since, if a line be cut with the knife, it is necessary it should be met by another line before any wood can be taken out; whereas, in the present mode, the graver, as it cuts the incision removes the wood at the instant of operation.

"We have next to speak of the application of this branch of art to the imitation of colored drawings; or, as it has been sometimes termed, engraving in *chiaroscuro*. This is effected by cutting as many blocks as there are colors and tints in the original: and in executing subjects in this style, the first block engraved is that which embraces the outline, or most material parts of the subject, as a guide to the others; an impression being transferred to the requisite number of blocks, and the respective tints put in, so as to fit accurately when printed.

"One of the earliest known specimens of printing in colors is the letter B, in Faust's Psalter, produced in 1457. This was in two blocks, red and blue, which were very correctly adjusted. Towards the close of the 15th century the principle was adopted to a more finished extent, by the successful attempt at blending neutralized tints. Ugo da Carpi, of Rome, was amongst the first to effect this object; and the mode was so esteemed, that the greatest painters gave their attention to it, as a means of perpetuating their designs. Raphael, Parmegiano, Titian, Rubens, and others of note, in the 16th and 17th centuries, assisted by their designs, and in superintending their execution, in producing these works, and the many beautiful specimens extant exemplify the success of their efforts.

"From the middle of the 17th century, the art of wood engraving generally declined, and of course fewer subjects in *chiaroscuro* were effected. In 1688, this principle was applied, in France, to the production of paper hangings; which was introduced into Great Britain, by John B. Jackson, in 1750. This artist was the first Englishman who, with any success, practised engraving in this style. At first nothing was attempted that consisted of more than two blocks, but, before the close of the 18th century, the number was increased to five; which was never exceeded till the appearance of Mr. Savage's book on 'Decorative Printing,' in 1822. This work, which is throughout a fine specimen of art, has numerous examples in *chiaroscuro*, in 6, 7 and 8 blocks; and one in 14, copied from a design by John Varley. In all these, the artists' drawings are accurately represented, and the entire work is highly worthy a careful inspection.

"In this general sketch it has been quite impossible to notice the various points and capabilities of wood engraving, relative to its uses, application, and durability; or to name, with any justice, its many eminent professors, either ancient or modern. Its value is becoming daily more and more apparent in both hemispheres, by the demands on the talent of those who practise it. Its prominent points and beauties will hereby, by degrees, become more universally understood: this, however, can never be properly effected, till a thorough reformation shall take place in printing. Considering the innumerable works continually issued, illustrated with wood cuts, the public have, with very few exceptions, but little chance of duly estimating their merits; since, in the greater number of them, the engravings are printed in so heedless a manner as scarcely to deserve, by their appearance, the name of embellishments. There can be no doubt that publishers will, ere long, discover it to be their true interest to give more serious attention to this subject; which, as regards the reputation of the art, is of the most vital importance."

Having prepared the reader, by Mr. Mason's excellent memoir on the history, theory and practice of wood engraving, to appreciate the difficulties of the art, I proceed to the biography of A. Anderson, Esq., who introduced the art into our country and almost invented it. He was born in April, 1775, three days after the battle of Lexington, near Peck Slip in New York. After his school days were passed, his father placed him with Doctor Young to study the practice of physic; but he had from infancy devoted his play hours to drawing, and having attempted engraving, he was so fascinated by his success that he determined, as soon as he could, to "throw physic to the dogs," and become professionally an engraver. He did so.

John Roberts, the universal genius, a notice of whom I have given, at this time attracted attention. Doctor Anderson (for his medical title sticks to him to this hour), after trying various experiments, and making himself somewhat proficient in the art, gained an introduction to Roberts, and was received by him as a pupil. He worked as long as he could with Roberts, for the purpose of improving himself in drawing, and working with the graver, but the irregularity of the eccentric Scotchman, and his intemperance, forced him to give up the advantages he might have derived from his instruction.

Mr. Anderson confirms all that has been said of the surprising versatility and cleverness of Roberts — of his engraving — miniature painting — musical taste and skill — mathematical attainments — and dexterity in manufacturing tools, and musical instruments or mechanical machinery.

In the year 1794,[1] as a professed engraver, Mr. Anderson

[1] The earliest example of Anderson's engraving which we have seen is a very crudely engraved portrait of Thomas Dilworth, appearing as the frontispiece to Dilworth's "The Schoolmaster's Assistant," published by William Durell, New York, in 1792. In 1804 an edition of Bewick's "Quadrupeds," with cuts by Anderson, was brought

was engaged by William Durell, bookseller, and one of our early publishers, to engrave cuts for an edition of "The Looking Glass," the original engravings for which were cut by Bewick in wood. This led to the employment which distinguishes Anderson as our first engraver on that material. He worked through half the book on type metal and copper, and then commenced his essays on wood without other instruction than that derived from studying Bewick's cuts, which he was to copy. For this new art he had to invent and make tools. Perseverance, industry, and ingenuity overcame all difficulties, and he established himself as an engraver in wood. Soon after his first attempts, he cut a cameo for Sword's edition of Darwin. From that time Mr. Anderson has had constant employment, supported and educated a family, one of whom, a physician, takes the title of doctor partly from him — not entirely — for the inquirer after Doctor Anderson is sometimes asked, "Is it the engraver or the physician you would speak to?"

Mr. Mason thus speaks of him, "Of the leading artists here, the first notice is due to Doctor Anderson of New York, who may be termed the Bewick of America, and the father of his art in this country. This gentleman commenced in 1792 ('94) under every possible disadvantage: he at first cut on type metal, but hearing soon after that boxwood was used in England, he adopted it, and copied thereon some of Bewick's specimens. He persevered in the practice, and exhibited the highest ability, though for many years he received but little encouragement; but like his great English cotemporary, being an enthusiast in the art, he kept steadily and perseveringly on

out in New York. Of this production Thomas Hugo, in "The Bewick Collector" (London, 1866), writes:

"An edition in 8° was printed at New York in 1804, under the title of
  A General History of Quadrupeds. The figures engraved on wood, chiefly
  from the original of T. Bewick. By A. Anderson. First American Edition.
  With an Appendix, containing some American Animals not hitherto described.
  New York: Printed by G. & R. Waite, No. 64, Maiden Lane, 1804.
Some of the cuts in this volume are truly wonderful copies of the originals, and an inspection of them would stagger not a few who are accustomed to attribute to 'Bewick' every engraving of more than ordinary ability produced at the time when these were published."

Bayley & Goodspeed then comment, "Anderson's long and useful life was concluded by his death in Jersey City, N.J., January, 1870."

his course, and has the similar satisfaction of having witnessed
the progress of wood engraving to its present state of general
adoption. It is highly gratifying to know that this amiable
and talented veteran is still in full practice, and in the enjoyment of excellent health."*

Mr. Adams[1] of this city is also highly deserving of notice in
this place: he commenced the art regularly as a profession,
about eight years since; previous to which, he had merely
executed a few casual specimens. He has exhibited, in his late
productions especially, the most superior qualifications for
the art, displaying in his engravings a near approach to the
rich style of the modern English school. Although in New York,
xylography first arose in America, it has been greatly encouraged in other parts of the Union, especially Boston and Philadelphia, both of which cities have produced many able artists.
Of the introduction of wood engraving into Boston, the credit
is due to Mr. Abel Bowen, who began there in 1812, and has
continued the pursuit successfully; he has had several pupils
of ability (Mr. Hartwell and others), who now that the art is
becoming more generally understood, receive every encouragement in their professional practice. In Philadelphia wood
engraving owes its origin to Mr. William Mason.

---

* Mr. Anderson is fully entitled to be called "Doctor." He went through a regular
course of studies, and received the degree of Doctor of Medicine at Columbia College
in 1796: on which occasion he delivered an interesting inaugural dissertation on
"Chronic Mania." He then for a short time entered upon the duties of a profession of
which he promised to be a distinguished member. We have seen, however, that his
love of the arts of design, led him to relinquish the practice of a physician, and the honorable result of his labors as an engraver, leaves no reason to regret his change of profession.

[1] Joseph Alexander Adams, born in New Germantown, Hunterdon Co., N. J. Like
Anderson and Bowen, his predecessors and contemporaries in the art of wood engraving, he was self-taught. Linton commends his work for its "firm honest exactness
and clearness" and for "his graver drawing, mechanism of the art, disposition and
perfection of lines."

CHAPTER X.

MALBONE — TIEBOUT.

EDWARD G. MALBONE

BECAME by his own efforts a practitioner of portrait painting in miniature, in the year 1794. He was a native of the beautiful garden isle of Rhode Island, which had twenty years before given to the world Gilbert Stuart, and born at Newport in 1777. He discovered a propensity for painting at a very early period of life, as is not uncommon; but with him it grew with his growth, and strengthened with his strength, absorbing all other desires, and at length, becoming so predominant that he neglected every amusement, and almost every employment suited to his age, for the indulgence of his wishes to acquire knowledge in an art so genial to his taste.

In the "Analectic Magazine" for 1815, it is truly said, "whoever writes the history of American genius, or of American arts, will have failed to do justice to his subject, if he omit the name of Malbone." From Washington Allston, Charles Fraser, and Mrs. H. Whitehorne, Malbone's sister, I have received such information, as, combined with my own knowledge of the artist and his works, enables me to give his biography with more amplitude and accuracy than any that has heretofore appeared.

When a boy it was his delight to be wherever he could gain any knowledge of the object that his mind dwelt upon; and he appeared determined to pursue any light, that might guide him in his efforts to become a painter. He frequented the theatre, and having seen the effect of the scenery by lamplight, he anxiously sought to penetrate the mystery connected with these shifting pictures. He gained admittance behind the curtain by daylight, and the repetition of his visits, and

137

earnestness of his examination of everything belonging to the
scenery, attracted the attention of the artist who officiated in
that department, and he at length suffered the boy to assist
him with the chalk and the brush. After a time Malbone felt
bold enough to ask permission to paint a scene, and the request was granted. This was a great step on the ladder to
fame. An entire scene, probably a landscape, was produced
by the boy, and in due time and proper place exhibited.

This memorable event in the life of young Malbone, must
have occurred at the period of the history of American theatri-
cals, when the old American company was divided between
Hallam and Henry on the one part, and Wignell on the other;
leaving Harper to follow the suggestions of his great ambition,
which led him to seize upon this throne of Newport, and hold
his court in a palace, whose basement story furnished more
vulgar food to the citizens than that dealt out by the corps
above. The theatre and markethouse were the same; butchers
above and butchers below. But Harper was an intelligent
man, and likely to be pleased by the enthusiasm of young
Malbone.

The young painter thus made his *début* in a branch of art,
as dissimilar to that in which he was destined to become unrivalled, as can well be conceived; and the hand which in man-
hood guided the most delicate pencil, and touched with colors
of exquisite transparency, commenced by wielding the broad
brush of the scene painter, redolent from the tub where whiting, yellow ocher, Prussian blue, or rose pink, were mingled
with hot and half putrified glue.

Malbone triumphed; and it is probable that his scene was
the first thing approaching to nature, which the market for
butcher's meat and poetry had ever displayed, either from the
brush, the sock, or the buskin. The reward of the painter's
success was a general ticket of admission, which was the more
acceptable, as it gave him an opportunity of hearing in secret
the commendation of his own work — a reward most delicious
to authors and artists.

The young painter would doubtless visit the boxes, when-

ever his scene was to make its appearance; which probably
would be in tragedy, comedy, farce, and pantomime, or
wherever a landscape was wanted, whether for Bosworth Field,
or the island of Jamaica; he enjoyed the praises bestowed
on his work, on more occasions than he was entitled to. While
his companions in the theatre might suppose that he was
listening to the actors, he was listening to the compliments
bestowed upon the landscape, which by its contrast to the
other scenery, would long and often call the attention of the
spectators to its vivid coloring. This may remind some artists,
of the assiduous attention they have lavished upon the annual
exhibition at Somerset House, or Clinton Hall, if they had a
picture there exposed to the public; and of the eager watchful-
ness of eye and ear they have bestowed upon the visitors who
approached the place, where the painting on which their
hopes of fame depended, had been hung by the academic
hangmen — how eagerly sounds have been caught, and looks
watched — and if no signs of approbation could be gathered or
imagined, how the heart has sunk, and the injustice of those
secretly (or loudly) accused, who placed the picture in a bad
light, or too high, or too low — or destroyed its effect, by approximation to some overpowering rival production. But the
young scene painter had no rival to fear; and when his picture
received the full blaze of the row of footlamps, there was no
competitor to vie with it.

While the boy thus amused himself at the theatre, he filled
up his little intervals of leisure from school occupation, by
drawing heads at home, and at length, by attempting likenesses; and he soon devoted himself altogether to portraiture.

Allston, our great historical painter, younger than Malbone
by some years, had been sent from his native State of South
Carolina, for the improvement of his health, and was placed at
school in Newport; he did not, however, become acquainted
with Malbone until a short time before the young miniature
painter threw himself upon his own resources, at the age of
seventeen, and removed to Providence, then become the centre
of the wealth and commerce of Rhode Island. When Allston

was removed from school at Newport, to Cambridge College, he found Malbone in Boston, and renewed the acquaintance, which soon ripened into friendship. This was in 1796. Many years after, Mr. Allston, in a letter to a friend, speaks thus of the genius of Malbone. "He had the happy talent among his many excellencies, of elevating the character without impairing the likeness: this was remarkable in his male heads; and no woman ever lost any beauty from his hand; nay, the fair would often become still fairer, under his pencil. To this he added a grace of execution all his own." This just tribute to the memory of Malbone, will be found on another page of this volume, but I could not omit it in either place, without injuring both Allston and Malbone. In another letter Mr. Allston says of Malbone, "As a man his disposition was amiable and generous, and wholly free from any taint of professional jealousy."

"His rapid progress," says Mr. Fraser, speaking of Malbone's youth, "convinced him that he had talents, and gave alacrity to his endeavors. Prospects of fame began to open upon his mind, and that propensity which had hitherto been nourished by the mere force of nature, derived additional vigor from the hopes which increasing reputation and wealth inspired." He began now to be known and eagerly sought after as a miniature painter. Taste, feeling, and elegance marked every face and figure that came from his pencil; but more especially the forms of females. He visited the principal northern cities; the western had then no existence. New York, Philadelphia and Boston were in their turn favored by his residence. "In the winter of 1800, he came to Charleston, where his talents," I again quote from Mr. Fraser, who knew and appreciated him truly, "and the peculiar amenity of his manners enhanced the attentions which he received from the hospitality of its inhabitants."

Allston had returned to his native State that year, after finishing his education in the University of Cambridge, and adding stability to his constitution by passing the years of his nonage in the climate of the north. Mr. Charles Fraser, since an excellent miniature painter, was then a student at law, but his taste and inclinations were those of an artist. Allston, Malbone and Fraser, must have encouraged in each other the desire that led to their subsequent skill — Malbone, already a successful practitioner, was of course the leader.

Although Malbone delighted in conversation, and fully appreciated the frank manners and social habits of the South, the pleasures of the table never led him to neglect the more congenial occupation of his painting room. It was his regular habit to begin study before breakfast, and to occupy himself with the labor he delighted in for the greater portion of the day. Some years after he told the writer that eight hours were his average allowance in each day for his pencil. But in 1800 he painted many more hours in the day, never appearing to weary; and indeed so avaricious was he of time, that he contrived a method of painting by candlelight, making use of glasses, by the means of which he condensed the rays, and threw them upon the ivory. But this was merely an experiment, which did not answer as he wished. It serves, however, to show the ardor of his mind, and his perseverance in the pursuit of his favorite object. This ardent desire after excellence induced sedentary habits, which, although they sensibly affected his health, he could not, or would not discontinue; and the consequence was, that although his desires were pure, the inordinate gratification of them produced pain, disease and death.

In May, 1801, he sailed in company with his friend Allston for London, where he resided some months, absorbed in admiration of the paintings of celebrated masters. With a mind improved by study and observation, and animated by the enthusiasm of genius, he visited the different galleries of living painters, enlarging his ideas through the medium of their labors, and profiting by the study of those processes for the attainment of the wished-for effect, which were discoverable in their pictures.

In a letter to his friend, Charles Fraser, written at this time from London, he thus expresses his opinion of the artists whose works he saw there. "Mr. West is decidedly the greatest painter amongst them for history. Mr. Lawrence is the best portrait painter. Mr. Fuseli, from whom we expected so much, I was disappointed in." By *we*, he probably means Allston and himself. "After Lawrence, I think Sir William Beechey the next in portrait painting, and then Mr. Hopner.[1] Some of Mr. Copley's historical pieces I think very fine. So are Mr. Trumbull's, but I do not admire his portraits. Amongst miniature painters, I think Mr. Shelly,[2] and Mr. Cosway the best. Mr. West has complimented Mr. Allston and myself, and tells us we shall excel in the art. Yesterday was the first time he had seen a picture of my painting; to-day he conde-scended to walk a mile to pay me a visit, and told me that I must not look forward to anything short of the highest excel-lence. He was surprised to see how far I had advanced without instruction." He writes further: "I have not painted many pictures since I left Charleston; I am painting one now which I shall bring with me. It is 'The Hours; the past, present, and the coming.' "

This extremely beautiful picture is in the possession of Mrs. H. Whitehorne, of Newport, Rhode Island, the painter's sister, and although constantly hung up and exposed to the light, is as fresh and strong as when painted. I have seen it more than once, and never saw it without renewed admiration. Shelly, the miniature painter, mentioned above by Malbone as (with Cosway) the first of that day in England, painted a picture of "The Hours," from which a print has been pub-lished; and as Mr. Malbone saw Shelly's picture, the merit of entire originality in the composition of his "Hours" has been disputed. Mr. Fraser says on this subject, "He informed me that the idea was suggested to him by one of Shelly's that he had seen, although I always understood the composition to be Malbone's." Mrs. Whitehorne says, in her very interesting letter in answer to my inquiries respecting her brother, "I have heard him say that he selected two figures (and don't recollect from where they were taken), added a third, grouped them, and designed 'The Hours.'" Those who know the truth, taste, elegance, chaste drawing, and clear, strong color-ing of Mr. Malbone's pictures painted from nature, and espe-

1 For Hopner read Hoppner
2 For Shelley read Shelley

cially his female portraits, will not wish to rest his fame upon a composition even so fascinating as 'The Hours.'

"When in England," says Mr. Fraser, "he was introduced to the president of the Royal Academy, who, conceiving a high opinion of his talents, gave him free access to his study, and showed him those marked and friendly attentions which were more flattering than empty praises to the mind of his young countryman. He even encouraged him to remain in England, assuring him that he had nothing to fear from professional competition. But he preferred his own country, and returned to Charleston in the winter of 1801."

We have already seen how Malbone writes respecting the flattering and friendly attentions paid him by the amiable West. The American president of the English Royal Academy, some years after, when in conversation with Mr. Monroe, afterwards president of the United States, spoke thus of Mr. Malbone: "I have seen a picture painted by a young man of the name of Malbone, which no man in England could excel."

For a short time in the autumn of 1801, Malbone drew at the Royal Academy, Somerset House, and had as a fellow student a young Scotsman, who has since stood in the foremost rank of British miniature painters, Mr. Andrew Robertson, a younger brother of our fellow citizens, Archibald and Alexander Robertson. I have never seen anything of Robertson's that equals Malbone's pictures, unless it be the portrait of a young British officer, the son of Mr. John Trumbull, and in his possession. This I have always considered as a perfect specimen of portraiture in miniature.

On Malbone's return to America, the improvement he had made during this very short absence was manifest. After fulfilling his engagements in Charleston, he visited and painted in all our principal cities on the seaboard, and his company and his pictures were sought by all who could appreciate his conversation or his skill.

In the autumn of 1805, the writer, then endeavoring to recover the use of his pencil, after having laid it aside for near twenty years, by attempting to paint miniatures, found Mr.

Malbone successfully exercising his profession in Boston. His price for a head was fifty dollars. His health was then delicate. He suffered from a pulmonary complaint, but physical suffering did not change the mild and amiable temper of his mind, or impart any asperity to his manners. Eight hours of the four-and-twenty were devoted to the pencil, and those in which he mingled in society were not clouded by gloom or complaint.

The practice of the writer in his youth had been first in crayons, then in oil, and he was at the age of forty painting miniatures for subsistence without knowing the proper mode of preparing the ivory for the reception of colors. I met Malbone at the houses of Colonel David Humphreys, one of the aids of Washington, and long ambassador to Spain, and Andrew Allen, then British Consul, and I had exposed some of my work to the examination of the accomplished artist as to a master. He saw the difficulty and pointed it out. "You never can execute as you wish until your ivory is prepared to receive color." While at a dinner party at Allen's, he made an appointment for a meeting the next morning. "They persuaded me to drink some champagne," said he, when the meeting took place, "and my head is splitting." The champagne notwithstanding, he showed me the method of preparing the ivory, and furnished me with many valuable hints in addition.

By nature of a good constitution, although of a tall and slender form, his health declined so sensibly while he continued his confinement and application to his pencil, that he at length yielded to the solicitations of his friends, and broke from his studies to take *that* exercise in the open air, so necessary to the health, without which, man can neither enjoy nor communicate happiness. He repaired to the lovely island of his nativity; he endeavored to become an idler and a sportsman. It was too late. He had committed the fault, without intention and without guilt, which could be only atoned for by premature death. Nature has her rights, which, if violated by intemperate study, neglect of exercise, or seclusion from atmospheric air, the violation is punished as certainly as if what is usually called intemperance inflicted the injury. His frame had become too weak. The fiend that had fastened upon his lungs could not be shaken from his hold. His physicians recommended him to try a change of climate (a prescription which generally increases the sufferings of the patient, by removing him from the comforts of home and the care of friends), and in the winter of 1806, he took passage in a vessel for Jamaica and visited that island, but the change not producing the hoped-for benefit, he returned to the first port he could reach in the United States, which was Savannah, where he languished until the 7th of May 1807, when death relieved him from his sufferings, in the thirty-second year of his age.

The works of the miniature painter are, comparatively, little seen; they may be preserved for ages, but it must be as jewels of less real value are preserved, in caskets. Their possessors ofttimes do not know their worth, but show them as curiosities or likenesses of relatives, but on such occasions they may meet an eye that can estimate them as works of art. The works of Malbone are spread throughout our country — they are impressed with the seal of genius — the grace, purity, and delicacy of his character are stamped upon them.

The following letter from his sister, in answer to my inquiries, is too honorable to her and to her brother to be withheld from the reader of this work:

"Newport, March, 26, 1834.

"Sir, — Your letter of Jan. 9th, forwarded by Mr. Boggs, did not reach me until February 27th. It would be very gratifying to me to aid your wishes, in giving to the world an accurate biography of my lamented brother, Edward G. Malbone; but unfortunately I possess few sources of information, excepting the power of recollection. Although many years have rolled away, memory often prompts me to take a retrospective view of the interesting scenes of his early childhood. He could not have been more than six or seven years of age before any common observer must have noticed many peculiarities wherein

he differed from other children. Generally occupied in his own
pursuits, he could find but little leisure for play, the intervals
of his school hours being filled by indefatigable industry in
making experiments, and endeavoring to make discoveries.
He took great delight in blowing bubbles, for the exquisite
pleasure of admiring the fine colors they displayed; if he had a
curious toy he would invariably take it to pieces, and immediately imitate it so well that the difference was scarcely per-
ceptible; he actually created his own amusements, and not
only his, but those of his associates — being constantly engaged in various ways; sometimes cutting moulds and making
little toys of lead, then painting them, thereby greatly recommending himself to his young friends, among whom he distributed them. He would frequently raise his kites in the
evening with a long appendage of fireworks, of his own invention, attached to them, to explode for the pleasure of his
companions.

"He soon turned his attention to painting, copying any little
picture that pleased him; making his own brushes, and preparing his colors, even before he could discriminate between
the different shades, having never seen a paint box. He
would gather paint stones on the beach, and with the few
colors he could collect, labor till he could make them answer
his purpose. He was naturally very absent, appearing to be
wholly absorbed in his own reflections. I can never forget how
frequently we used to tease him to join in our plays, but he
would remain entirely inflexible to our entreaties, until we
were induced to ridicule his stupidity and laugh at his folly
in spending all his time in ruminating over all the old pictures
he could collect; he then would smile and reply, 'You may enjoy your mirth, but you shall one day see my head engraved';
always possessing such equanimity of mind that nothing
ruffled, or put him out of his course. About the age of eleven
or twelve, he commenced drawing figures of gods and goddesses,
with Indian ink, upon ivory or bone, purchasing common
handkerchief pins, and expunging the devices to replace them
with his own performances, but more frequently sawing out the

ivory or bone with his own hands, it being an article which
Newport, at that time, could not furnish. When the picture
answered his expectations he would take large brass wire, bend
it handsomely, and make the setting, which would somehow
find its way to the neck of the prettiest girl in the school, as
beauty was his particular admiration. This will give some idea
of his perseverance. His genius daily developing itself, he
labored under every disadvantage; his friends rather damping
his ardor, judging that it might interfere with his prospects
in future life, not anticipating in the remotest degree, that he
would arrive at that excellence which he afterwards attained.
But he himself was very sanguine, calculating to go to Europe
as soon as he was old enough. His acquaintance with Mr.
Allston commenced at an early period, growing into a friendship that terminated but with his life, opening also a new source
of happiness. He now became much interested in drawing
heads, applying himself closely, and visiting the theatre, by
way of relaxation, listening to the rehearsals, viewing and
making remarks upon the scenery, which, attracting the attention of the scene painter, he entered into conversation, and
showing a disposition to encourage him, he asked the liberty
of taking the brush, at which he discovered so much genius,
that, feeling gratified by the pleasure evinced by those present,
he voluntarily offered to paint a new scene. This was much
applauded, and it was so novel a thing for such a boy, that it
drew crowded houses. I never heard of any lessons in drawing, engagement as assistant, or any compensation (excepting
a general ticket of admission), until I met with it in the 'Analectic Magazine'; nor were his family circumstances so humble,
but that his father could at any time have placed him in a
different situation, had not the object been rather to discourage than promote his natural pursuits. It is true that
his family, from a combination of unhappy events, were living
in retirement, and suffering an accumulation of evils, not
however of a pecuniary nature, but from which resulted the
operating cause of the neglect of his early education; this was
the only misfortune, respecting himself, that I ever heard

him lament. He was now generally engaged in his own room, taking but little interest in what was passing around him, daily experience proving that his mind was wholly bent upon perfecting himself in the art of painting. About the age of sixteen he painted upon paper, Thomas Lawrence, which was so universally admired by every person of taste, who saw it, that his father could no longer shut his eyes to his decided talent, but having neither drawing nor painting masters in Newport, he sent the picture by a friend to Philadelphia, to a French artist (with a request to receive him as a pupil) who was so much struck with the performance that he immediately replied, 'De boy would take de bread out of my mouth,' requiring several years' services and so exorbitant a sum of money, that his father did not think proper to comply with his terms, flattering himself that some opportunity would present of placing him to more advantage. But this spirit of procrastination not being in accordance with the youth's feelings, at seventeen he determined to throw himself upon his own resources. Communicating his plans to no one but myself, he proposed a visit to Providence,[1] and immediately brought himself before the public as a miniature painter, and so warmly was he received, that several weeks passed away before he apprised his father of the step he had taken. He now wrote a letter to his father, and two to myself, which I regret its not being in my power to forward, having sought for them in vain; they were worth preserving, as they expressed his hopes and views for the future so powerfully, and at the same time so much filial obedience to his father's wishes. Continuing pleased with his flattering reception, daily improving, and successful in his likenesses, he remained in Providence thirteen months, until he was recalled by the sudden illness of his father, which terminated in death before he reached home. After the funeral, October 1795, he returned to Providence, continuing fully occupied until the following spring, when,

[1] Malbone went from Newport to Providence, R. I., in 1794 and established himself as a miniature painter and among his productions at this period was "The Birth of Shakespeare" after a painting by Angelica Kauffman engraved by Bartolozzi.

making us a visit, he received much flattering attention from the gentlemen of the town, particularly the British Consul, Mr. Moore, who exercised great hospitality towards him, losing no opportunity to introduce him to strangers of distinction, endeavoring to promote his interest, and being about returning to England with his family, kindly urged his joining the party, setting before him the advantages that must result from it — that it should cost him nothing, and when arrived in England he would make every exertion to forward his views among powerful friends. It was now that his affectionate heart shone forth in all its lustre; a youth of scarcely nineteen, to decline so favorable an opportunity, when all his hopes and wishes would have been so much gratified by the acceptation; but his three sisters were without a parent, young, and left in embarrassed circumstances, requiring a protection, and no earthly good could have tempted him to leave his country. A friend now advised his going to Boston in 1796, to which he acceded, and was immediately introduced to, and found friends in many of the most distinguished characters. His natural refinement and engaging manners being so prepossessing, that letters of recommendation seemed hardly necessary: his Boston friends appeared to vie with each other in the exercise of their hospitality. Had he availed himself of half their politeness, he must have had but little time to devote to his profession; it was, however, very gratifying to such a youth, and he ever cherished a lasting remembrance of their kind attention. This will show how highly he was estimated.

"His reputation now began to make some noise in the world, being constantly employed and always successful, merely allowing himself time to visit us once a year, and exerting all his powers to promote our happiness. In 1798 I was married. In the course of that year several of his friends were very urgent for him to go to Europe, offering to loan any sum of money he might require, without interest, which he declined, I believe, from an innate principle of self-dependence, shrinking from the bare idea of obligation, being predetermined to create his own fortune and rear his own fame. His younger sisters were now with me. The year previous, however, he visited New York (1797) for the first time — his good fortune still preceding him — making many friends and being liberally employed. But feeling an anxious desire to visit all our cities, the succeeding spring he went to Philadelphia, with equal success. In the summer the yellow fever becoming prevalent, obliged him to go into the country; even here he found full employment. After this he passed his time alternately in the different cities until 1800, the summer of which both Mr. Allston and himself passed in Newport, and perhaps it was the happiest of his life, being surrounded by the friends he loved best. In the autumn they both went to Charleston, S. C., his reception being as flattering as his most sanguine wishes could have anticipated, and enjoying the most delightful society; his acquaintance with Mr. Charles Fraser commencing here, he soon ranked among his warmest friends. His affairs being very prosperous he determined upon going abroad, and embarked about the middle of May 1801, for London, in company with Mr. Allston. His reception by the president of the Royal Academy was so flattering, that it could not fail to give him confidence in himself, holding out every inducement for him to remain in Europe; and having free access to the school of the arts his improvement was very rapid. He now painted the 'Hours' and several female heads, which were highly eulogized by the president, Mr. West, saying that no man in England could excel them, and that he had nothing to fear from professional competition; but his private affairs requiring his attention, he returned to Charleston in December of the same year.

"His reputation now standing very high, he was crowded with business. The summer of 1802 he returned to Newport. His sisters being all married, he occasionally visited the different cities, agreeably to the wishes of his numerous friends, yearly contemplating another visit to Europe; but being so fully employed, and devotedly attached to his own country, he found it difficult to put his wishes in execution until 1805, when he sailed for Charleston in December, with the intention

of going to London the following spring. But alas! in March
he took a violent cold, which settled upon his lungs; his sedentary mode of life contributing greatly to hasten on the disease,
which proved so fatal that medical aid was vain. He returned
to New York in June, very feeble and much emaciated, and
soon after to Newport, where he appeared to recruit a little;
laying aside his pencil, indulging in riding and exercise of
various kinds. Being very fond of field sports, in shooting, he
ran to pick up a bird; the act of stooping suddenly brought on
a hemorrhage, which confined him to his bed. His physicians,
anxious to save him, advised riding; and I travelled about the
country with him for some weeks; but not deriving any benefit,
the physicians recommended a warmer climate, which he very
reluctantly consented to try: considering it his duty, however,
while there remained a ray of hope to submit, although against
his own judgment, he accordingly sailed for Jamaica, December
1806. The voyage not proving of any advantage, and finding
himself rapidly declining, he was very anxious to return, and
took passage for Savannah, hoping to be able to reach Newport
as soon as the spring opened; but there he languished until the
7th of May, 1807, which closed his valuable life; his passage
being taken for Newport only two days previous, so anxious
was he to end his days among his dearest friends.

"His private character was truly unexceptionable: amiable
and excellent from the first dawn of reason; greatly beloved
by all his friends and acquaintance; the pride and delight of
his family — but he has passed away like a bright vision, leaving the sweet remembrance of his devoted affection and his
many virtues indelibly engraved upon the hearts of his few
surviving relations. He was born in August, 1777.[1]

"I have had several applications from gentlemen wishing
to collect particulars of his early life, two within a few months;
one from a gentleman in Albany, and one from an English
gentleman; but have furnished nothing excepting to Colonel
Knapp, I think in 1828 — sending him some newspaper biog-

[1]He was the son of John Malbone, grandson of Godfrey and Catherine Scott Malbone,
and great grandson of Peter Malbone, 1667-1738.

raphies, and at the same time mentioning some little incidents of his early childhood to the gentleman who forwarded the papers. You, sir, have probably seen his 'Lectures upon American Literature,' wherein he speaks very handsomely of my brother, not giving him credit for his manner of coloring however, which was in such high repute that it has been twice sent for from Europe since his death. Col. Knapp observes that his coloring fades like the hues of the rainbow; but at the same time says that he has only seen some of his early productions, which makes his apology. I wish he could see his 'Hours,' the tints being as vivid as when his hand gave the finishing touch, although it has hung up more than twenty years. His mode of coloring being peculiar to himself, and considered one of his greatest excellencies. Col. Knapp also observes that he shall reserve what information he has gained for a more ample page, when I trust that error will be corrected.

"A gentleman going to Europe the next year after his death, begged to be entrusted with several female heads of his; took them to the president, Mr. West, who asked the favor of retaining them awhile; — when the gentleman called for them, he said he could hardly bear to give them up, as he considered them invaluable. I hope, sir, if you ever come to Newport, you will call, that I may have the pleasure of showing you the 'Hours,' having no other productions of his in my possession, excepting a few unfinished heads. Mrs. Cosway's 'Hours' is quite new to me;* and being certain that my brother never arrogated anything to himself, do not understand it. I have heard him say that he selected two figures (and do not recollect from where they were taken), added a third, grouped them, and designed the 'Hours.'

"Trusting that this concise statement may be useful, I now refer you to the gentlemen named, Mr. Allston and Mr. Fraser, who can furnish much information, and am, sir,

"Respectfully yours,

"H. WHITEHORNE."

*I had mentioned Shelly's "Hours"; or perhaps by mistake, wrote "Cosway."

I continue my notice of this gentleman by a quotation from the author of his biography in the "Analectic Magazine":

"It too often happens that the biographer, after dilating with enthusiasm on the merits of the artist, is obliged with shame and mortification, to confess or to palliate the vices or grossness of the man. The biographer of Malbone is spared this painful task; all his habits of life were decorous and gentlemanly, and his morals without reproach. His temper was naturally equable and gentle; his affections were warm and generous.

"The profits of his profession, which, after his return from Europe, were considerable, were always shared with his mother and sisters, to whom he was strongly attached.

"In that branch of the art to which he had chiefly devoted himself, Malbone deserves to be ranked with the first painters of the present, or indeed of any age. The works of Isabey, the first living French artist in this way, are certainly not so good as his; nor is it believed that there are many English miniatures equal to them. This is not the empty praise of an unskilful panegyrist, but the sober opinion of practical artists.

"There is, in the European academies, a certain aristocracy of taste, which has somewhat unjustly degraded miniature painting to a low rank in the scale of the imitative arts; so that every underling designer of vignette title pages to pocket editions of the poets, has attempted to consider himself as belonging to a higher order of genius, than the painter who delineates 'the mind's expression speaking in the face.'

"Yet Reynolds entertained a very different opinion of portraiture as a field for the exertion of genius; and he pronounces the power of animating and dignifying the countenance, and impressing upon it the appearance of wisdom or virtue, to require a nobleness of conception, which, says he, 'goes beyond anything in the mere exhibition even of the most perfect forms.'

"This degradation of miniature painting is, however, in no small degree to be ascribed to the faults of its professors. They have generally limited their ambition to a minute and labored finishing, and a gay and vivid, but most unnatural brilliancy, of bright coloring. They content themselves with painting only to the eye, without addressing the mind, and their pictures are, therefore, portraits of Lilliputians, or, at best, of men and women, seen in a *camera obscura*, but never the 'pictures in little' of real and living persons. Now, Malbone had none of these faults, and almost every excellence which can be displayed in this kind of painting. He drew well, correctly, yet without tameness. He had acute discernment of character, and much power of expressing it. He had taste, fancy, and grace; and in the delineation of female beauty, or gay innocent childhood, these qualities were admirably conspicuous. His pre-eminent excellence was in coloring; such was its harmony, its delicacy, its truth. His miniatures have most of the beauties of a fine portrait, without losing any of their own peculiar character.

"In the arts, the miniature may be considered as holding the same relative rank that the sonnet does in poetry, and the peculiar merit of Malbone is precisely of the same kind with that of the poet, who, without violating the exact rules, or the polished elegance of the sonnet, is yet able to infuse into it the spirit, the freedom, and the dignity of the ode, or the epic.

"To all this he added the still rarer merit of originality; for he was almost a self-taught painter. Though, whilst he was in England, he doubtless improved himself very much by the study of fine pictures, and the observation of the practice of West, and other great painters of the day; yet it has been said by artists, that the style and manner of his earlier and later works are substantially the same, and those painted after his return from Europe are only to be distinguished by their superior delicacy of taste, and greater apparent facility of execution.

"The few pieces of larger composition, which his hurry of business left him time to complete, have the same character of grace and beauty.

"He occasionally amused himself with landscape. His sketches in this way were but slight, and are valuable only as they show the extent of his powers. There is one little piece of his which is said to be a mere sport of imagination: it possesses a singularly pleasing effect of pastoral sweetness.

"In the latter years of his life, he tried his hand in oil painting, in which he made a respectable proficiency. That he did not attain to great eminence in this branch, was owing, not to any want of talent, but to that of leisure and health; for so much of his excellence was intellectual, and so little of it purely mechanical, that with requisite application, he could not have failed to acquire distinction in any department of the art."

The biography of Malbone appears like a studied panegyric. I can sincerely avow that I never heard ill of him; nor do I know of an action in his short life that was not praiseworthy. If I had heard or known of his assuming a character that did not belong to him, or making any pretensions to *that*, which he was *not*, I would have exposed his turpitude unsparingly. If he had been addicted to vices, I would have recorded them. But truth and virtue were his guides; and all testimony agrees P that he was a good man, and a great artist.

Cornelius Tiebout.

Born in New York, probably about the year 1777,[01] began to show his propensities for drawing and scratching on copper at an early age, and made some progress in engraving on copper in 1790, while an apprentice with J. Burger a silversmith of New York. In the year 1794, he engraved several heads for my "German Theatre" then publishing; but it is believed that he received no regular instruction until he went to England about the year 1796. Mr. Rollinson, one of our oldest engravers at this time (1834), and still in the vigor of life, informs me that Mr. Tiebout was employed by Burger, during the latter part of his apprenticeship, in engraving, and on becoming free, immediately commenced as an engraver, and had as a pupil Benjamin Tanner, well known since. Mr. Tiebout en-

---

01 As plates engraved by Tiebout in 1789 exist this date may be regarded as doubtful. He was a prolific engraver and located in Philadelphia as late as 1824. He died in 1832.

graved for an edition of Maynard's Josephus published by Mr. Durell. In 1796 he went to London for instruction, and worked with Heath. He returned very much improved, for the old methods as described in the books, seem to have been previously his only guides. He engraved a head of John Jay, and the battle of Lexington, from a design by Tisdale. The latter has no claim to praise — it is feeble. Mr. Tiebout was the first American who went to London for instruction in engraving, and about the same time Alexander Lawson came to America and made himself an excellent engraver without instruction.

On his return from Europe, Mr. Tiebout chose Philadelphia as the place of his residence, and worked for Mathew Carey, and other publishers of books. After living prosperously and accumulating property, he engaged in a speculation for the manufactory of blacking, and was ruined. One among the many who leave the path they are accustomed to, and lose themselves. He exhibited in the Pennsylvania Academy in 1811-12 and 13. After his failure he removed to Kentucky only to die.

CHAPTER XI.

John Vanderlyn.

In my biographical sketch of Mr. Vanderlyn I shall make use of a memoir written by a friend of the artist, but as it is not the intention of my work merely to praise, I shall make use of my own knowledge, and give my own opinions both of the painter and his works. Mr. Vanderlyn's friend says:

"This distinguished artist was born in Kingston, Ulster County, in the State of New York, in October 1776. In the following year his native village was laid in ashes by the British troops, under the command of General Vaughan, and his family were among the principal sufferers; but however reduced in property, Mr. V.'s parents were still able to afford him, at the proper age, the benefits of a liberal education, at the Kingston Academy, then one of the most flourishing in the State, where he continued until the age of sixteen. His attainments at this period were such as to have qualified him for the pursuit of the liberal professions.* His eldest brother, Peter Vanderlyn was a physician of eminence in Kingston, and in the autumn of 1792, young V. accompanied him on a visit to the city of New York, and was introduced by him to the late Mr. Thomas Barrow, well known in this city at that time as a gentleman of cultivated taste in the arts."

Mr. Barrow was an Englishman, and originally a coach painter. He remained in New York during the Revolutionary War, and was the only dealer in good prints. His second wife was sister to Bishop B. Moore, and by this connection with the church he gained more than by his connection with the fine arts. He deserves a notice in this work as aiding their progress.

"Mr. B. was a large importer of engravings, and young V. from his early predilection for the art, was easily prevailed on to enter into the store and employ of Mr. B., and continued

* Does the writer mean that he did not pursue a liberal profession?

there for the period of about two years; it was here that his
taste for the art developed itself more fully; from his familiarity
and daily contemplation of the finest specimens of engravings
and inspired him with the hope of perhaps one day beholding,
and emulating at some future day their glorious originals. At
this period he occasionally attended, at leisure hours, the
drawing school of a Mr. Robertson, who had recently arrived
from England."

Mr. Archibald Robertson, here affectedly styled "a Mr.
Robertson," is mentioned in this work under date 1791, at
which time he arrived in the country. Vanderlyn received
three years' tuition at the school established by Mr. R. who
was well able to instruct him or any tyro in the art of drawing.

"It was also during his stay with Mr. Barrow that Stuart,
the celebrated portrait painter, arrived from England; and it
was then young V. became acquainted with him, and was permitted to copy some of his portraits, among which were those
of Colonel Burr and Judge Benson. In the autumn Mr. V.
returned to Kingston, carrying with him his two copies, and
disposed of that of Colonel B. to Major Van Gaasbeck, then
a member of Congress from Ulster County. After spending the
winter in Kingston, in the occupation of painting portraits,
he again, in the spring, returned to the city and engaged in
the business of portrait painting, and it was during the summer
here that he received an anonymous letter inviting him to call
at the corner of Church and Fulton, then Fair Street, which
proved to be the office of Colonel Burr; he was there directed
by the late Judge Prevost to Richmond Hill, then the residence
of Colonel Burr. He accordingly went thither without any
loss of time, and had his first interview with Colonel B. who,
after bestowing compliments upon his early skill and attainments in the arts, proffered him his aid to enable him to prosecute his studies at the first schools of Europe, after he had been
with Mr. Stuart for a short time. Mr. V. accordingly repaired
to Philadelphia, in which city Mr. S. then resided. After
spending eight or nine months with him, during which time
he copied a large picture by Van Ostade for his patron, Mr.

V. returned to New York, and executed a few portraits for Colonel Burr, among which were those of the French minister Adet, Albert Gallatin, and Miss Burr, Colonel B.'s daughter.

"In the same year, the fall of 1796, he embarked for France, arrived at Bordeaux, and without delay hastened to Paris, furnished with letters of introduction from the French minister to several men of distinction, and Mr. V. had also the pleasure to meet there Mr. Prevost, then secretary to Mr. Monroe, the American minister. Mr. V. was soon recommended to the school of Mr. Vincent, an eminent painter, and a cotemporary of David.

"In 1801 Mr. V. returned to his native country, bringing with him also a few copies from the first masters, and studies, which he had executed while in Paris. At this period, in 1802, he painted two views of the Falls of Niagara, which were afterwards engraved and published in London, in 1804. He also painted a portrait of Colonel Burr and another of his daughter, then the wife of Governor Allston of South Carolina.

"In the spring of 1803 he returned again to Europe, and was at this time commissioned by the American Academy to purchase a collection of casts from the antique, and such pictures as he might be able to procure from time to time. This institution had been then just established, and owed its origin to Chancellor Robert Livingston, then American minister to France; and the Hon. Edward Livingston, then mayor of our city was its president.*

"After remaining two months in France, he crossed over to England in company with Mr. Monroe, from whom he received the most friendly attentions and civility in London. In November of the same year he returned to Paris by the way of Holland and Belgium, in company with his countryman and brother artist, Washington Allston. He remained in Paris, on this occasion, two years. During this time he made portraits of Col. Mercer, of Virginia, and William McClure, Esq. of Philadelphia, whose life abounds with acts of the most disinterested liberality, the latter tendering him pecuniary aid

---

* See the article Academies in this work; where it will be seen that Dr. Joseph Brown, the brother-in-law of Colonel Burr, was one of the directors.

to enable him to visit Rome. He also painted for Joel Barlow, then residing in Paris, the death of Miss McCrea, which was his first essay at historical painting. About this time he met with Washington Irving, who was on his first visit to Europe. Mr. I. was travelling for his health, and came to France from Italy. He made a small sketch in chalk of this distinguished gentleman in the summer of 1805.

"Mr. V. left Paris in August of this year for Switzerland, where he tarried some weeks. He met his friend, Mr. McClure, at Geneva, and in company with him visited Ferney, Lausanne, Vevay and Clarens, classic ground, even before they were visited by the muse of Byron. He also visited the vale of Chamouny, at the foot of Mont Blanc, rambled amid the sublime scenes of Savoy, and extended his excursion into the cantons of Switzerland as far as Altorf on the road to Mont St. Gothard. In October of that year he crossed the Alps, by the pass of Mont Cenis, from whose summit he had the pleasure of his first view of the plains of Lombardy, and the beautiful sky of Italy. At Turin he stopped a few days, thence proceeded to Milan, where he visited the works of art of many of the Italian masters, and among others, the original 'Last Supper,' by Leonardo da Vinci, the wreck of a splendid painting, and one of the masterpieces of the art. From Milan he passed through Lodi, Placencia, Parma, where he tarried a short time, and was gratified with a sight, although too hurried fully to enjoy it, of some of the splendid frescos of Correggio in the churches. Passing through Modena and Bologna, he was gratified with some more works in painting, and then crossed the Apennines, the wild scenery of which reminded him of the style of Salvator Rosa, whose genius was nurtured by such scenes. He spent four or five days in Florence, a city rich in works of sculpture, architecture, and painting — noble and immortal monuments of her former wealth and greatness. The Florentine gallery is one of the most celebrated in Europe, and the churches are also adorned with splendid paintings by the early masters, all of which he now had an opportunity of beholding. He thence proceeded to Rome, by the way of

Sienna and the lake of Bolsena, and arrived there in the month of November.

"He was rejoiced to meet again with his friend Mr. Allston, who had preceded him by a twelvemonth to this seat of the arts, with views similar to his own, and they were the only American artists at that time in the city. He remained there upwards of two years, and occupied himself with zeal and enthusiasm in his favorite study, copying from the works in the Vatican, making sketches from nature, and visiting the numerous works of art which embellish that far-famed capital.

"During the second year of his residence at Rome, he painted his celebrated picture of 'Marius amid the ruins of Carthage,' which met the general approbation of the artists assembled there, and gave him reputation.

P

"In Rome it was customary for the foreign artists who resorted there for improvement in their profession, to meet together to draw from the living model, and Mr. V. with his friend Allston, attended an association, composed of young artists from different parts of Germany, Sweden, and Denmark. The French also had their own academy *de Rome*. While our young countrymen were studying their profession at Rome at their own expense,* and striving to obtain an art then but little cultivated at home, there were numbers of students from various parts of Europe, who had been sent there at the expense of their governments and their princes. Mr. V. was destitute of fortune, and could not have remained at Rome had it not been for the aid received from his friend Mr. McClure, already mentioned. Notwithstanding both he and Mr. Allston were without public patronage, and the éclat which always attends it, they were fully successful in contending for the honors of their art with the more favored protégées of the European monarchs. Mr. V.'s residence at Rome was, a part of the time, in a dwelling formerly occupied by Salvator Rosa, and he made a sketch of the garden, which is now in the possession of William Carter, Esq. of Virginia.

* I have omitted the words "and with no selfish views; but to add, if possible, to their country's renown," as savoring of something Mr. Allston would not join in.

"In 1808 he recrossed the Alps, and again returned to Paris. He exhibited his " Marius " in that capital, and received the Napoleon gold medal, which was awarded to him by the professors of the Academy of Artists, for having produced that painting, a work of the first merit. In the gallery of the Louvre, he made a copy of Correggio's admirable picture of Antiope, as large as life. This copy, placed alongside of the original, was greatly admired by the artists of the French metropolis."

I first saw this admirable copy at the house of John R. Murray, Esq. from whom, I then understood, Mr. Vanderlyn had received a commission to copy a picture for him. Murray admired it, but he said "What can I do with it? It is altogether indecent. I cannot hang it up in my house, and my family reprobate it." The artist had consulted his own taste, and the advantage of studying such a work, more than the habits of his country, or the taste of his countrymen.

"It has since been exhibited in the rotunda of our city. He also copied a head, with the hands and arms, after a female figure in the transfiguration of Raphael, now in the possession of Philip Hone, Esq.; also, two or three figures of reduced size from a picture representing Leda and the swan, by Correggio, which he sold in Paris to a gentleman of Salem, Mass.; also, he made a copy of 'Danaë,' of the size of life, after Titian, and which has likewise been seen and admired in the rotunda. In 1812, he painted 'Ariadne,' an original picture,* and also, from time to time, employed himself on portraits and minor works. At this period, when on a visit to Versailles, he formed the project of a panoramic view of its splendid palace and gardens, which was suggested by a visit which he made in 1814 to that celebrated residence of the monarchs of France. He was occupied in the sketches for some months, and these completed, he returned to the United States in 1815, having been detained for some time by the events of the war. He brought with him 'Danaë,' 'Ariadne,' and some smaller pictures,

* This picture has been purchased and engraved by A. B. Durand, Esq., himself an excellent painter, and our first engraver. This painting proved Mr. Vanderlyn's powers even more than the " Marius," and is in my estimation the finest figure of the kind I have ever seen. The engraving of Mr. Durand is worthy of it.

both originals and copies. 'Marius' and 'Antiope' were sent
home under the care of our Minister to France, General Arm-
strong, previous to the close of the war.

"Immediately on his return to his native country, he was employed in painting the portraits of some of our most distinguished fellow citizens, and among the rest, of Presidents
Madison and Monroe, Vice-President Calhoun, and of Governors Yates and Clinton. The portrait of Governor Clinton,
was painted for the Literary and Philosophical Society. He
has also painted two portraits of General Jackson, one for
Charleston, South Carolina, and the other for this city; also a
full-length portrait of President Monroe, for this city."

The word "immediately," in the preceding paragraph,
gives a false gloss to the whole, and prevents the reader from
forming a just estimate of Mr. Vanderlyn, and his condition as
an artist and a man for a long period. That he painted the
portraits mentioned, is true; but at times long distant from
each other; years intervening.

The pictures were of various degrees of merit, and generally
much inferior to what was expected from the author of the
"Marius," and the "Ariadne."

I have elsewhere described the manner in which John R.
Smith made his attack upon Mr. Vanderlyn, and his pictures,
before the directors of the incipient American Academy of Fine
Arts. He failed, but the instigator prevailed, and Mr. Vanderlyn's pictures were turned out. I am permitted to copy
from a letter of Mr. V's, some passages which ought to be
known. After noting some inferior symptoms of jealousy
he proceeds: "The instance which is more deserving of being
noticed and of which there can be no doubt, he (Trumbull)
was the prime mover, was, when I had my pictures in two
rooms of the old almshouse, forming a part of what was allotted to the Academy of Arts. I had obtained permission of
the president of the society, then De Witt Clinton, to have the
use of these rooms, and there was then no talk or appearance
that the Academy would soon be resuscitated, and my friends
Judge B. Provost and others, led me to believe that I should

not be disturbed in their possession, for at least six months.
I had these rooms fitted up as soon as they were vacated by
these former tenants, and spent fifty dollars in cleaning, painting, and coloring the walls. After my exhibition was open two
or three weeks, I went up the river, in July, leaving it in charge
of the keeper. During my stay in the country, I received a
letter from Mr. Murray, the vice-president, that they would
have need of the rooms, and requesting me to remove my
pictures. This appeared ungenerous, and was injurious to me.
I hastened to town and found one room already cleared. I
have sufficient reason for believing that it was through the
influence of Trumbull, with D. Hosack and Murray, that these
resolutions and measures were adopted. How far John R.
Smith was instigated by Trumbull, I do not now recollect. I
am not able to affirm that he was evidently encouraged to it
by Trumbull — I remember to have heard Smith say, that
he heard him use such language as 'damn the pictures, I wish
I had never seen them.'" In the same letter Mr. V. says,
"Trumbull made a proposition to two or three of my subscribers and trustees of the rotunda, during my absence at Washington, about two years after the existence of the rotunda,
when he had engaged in the government pictures; he understanding that the rotunda labored under a debt, still due to
the builder, made overtures to purchase the building without
consulting me; seemingly indifferent how far my interest was
affected. The trustees of course, could not listen to any such
proposition. Dr. Mott; Augustus Wynkoop; and C. D. Colden,
had all been spoken to for this purpose. When I mentioned
this affair to Mr. Allston, he could scarce believe it possible."

It was this gentleman's misfortune, that Mr. Trumbull returned to New York, after a residence of many years in England, in the year 1816; and *his* reputation did not rest alone
upon the pictures which he brought with him, but on those he
had painted in former days, and under the inspection of West;
(of which, very fine engravings were spread abroad), and on
the well-known unfinished, and nearly finished historical compositions which he had shown in 1790; besides the beautiful

miniature portraits of Revolutionary men, in former times, painted by him with great perseverance and activity. The association called the American Academy of Fine Arts, was revived, and Trumbull elected president. This was followed by his obtaining a commission for four pictures, at eight thousand dollars each, from Congress. Mr. Vanderlyn felt and knew that he was a better artist at this time than Trumbull; but *he* had the start of him; and the public knew nothing, and cared little about it. I remember well when Mr. Vanderlyn visited me at my house, and inveighed upon the injustice of giving all the government patronage to Trumbull, I answered, that he had a fair claim, as he had collected the portraits to be introduced, and no one else possessed them.

When the first exhibition was got up, Mr. Vanderlyn intended placing his noble "Marius" before the public, in the room fitted up in the old almshouse, but the place he wished was denied him by the president, and he exhibited nothing.

I now recur to the memoir again, and the first subject is that of panoramas. "While in Europe he had beheld panoramic exhibitions with admiration, and witnessed their success in Paris, as well as in London; and felt confident that if they were approved and popular in capitals, whose galleries abound in *chefs d'œuvre* of art, their success would be certain in our cities, where, comparatively, no such competition as yet existed. In fact panoramic exhibitions possess so much of the magic deceptions of the art, as irresistibly to captivate all classes of spectators, which gives them a decided advantage over every other description of pictures; for no study or cultivated taste is required fully to appreciate the merits of such representations. They have the further power of conveying much practical, and topographical information, such as can in no other way be supplied, except by actually visiting the scenes which they represent, and if instruction and mental gratification be the aim and object of painting, no class of pictures have a fairer claim to the public estimation than panoramas.

"It was under these circumstances that the corporation of

New York, in 1817, was induced to grant him the privilege of erecting a building for this object upon the public ground in the northeast corner of the park; and with a liberal and laudable motive of embellishing the spot, he proceeded to erect a building worthy of the merits of the institution and the character of our city; and to which he gave the name of the New York Rotunda. In the prosecution of his plan, he had the misfortune to involve himself in some pecuniary difficulties, arising from the excessive cost of the building. Eight thousand dollars was the estimated expense of the structure he had projected; and if ten thousand had sufficed, no difficulties would have ensued which could not easily have been surmounted. And those which did arise would probably have been surmounted, had he been present to superintend the progress of the work, which he was prevented from doing by other pressing and indispensable engagements, connected with the institution. The work, however, went on, and the building was erected at a cost of between thirteen and fourteen thousand dollars; all which was paid, with the exception of about three thousand five hundred dollars, which remained due to the builders and others who had furnished the materials; and it was this unliquidated balance which was finally the cause of his being deprived of the building, at a time when he had just begun to realize some of the hopes which he had formed at the commencement of the project.

"It was through the liberality of private individuals, some the personal friends of Mr. V., and all friends of the liberal arts, who were desirous of patronizing him, as well as of adding to the attraction and character of our city, that he was supplied with a principal part of the funds disbursed on the building, he himself furnishing about twelve hundred dollars out of his private resources. The lease of the ground granted to him by the corporation, was for nine years, with a nominal rent; and although there was no express clause of renewal, Mr. V. had received every assurance from the then mayor, the Hon. Jacob Radcliff, and several influential members of the board, that at the expiration of the first term, an extension would undoubtedly be granted, if he should desire it, and the institution answered public expectation. Thus was he induced to erect an ornamental structure, such as the rotunda in fact was, and as was admitted on all hands.

"He commenced his exhibitions, and there were presented, in succession, the panoramas of Paris, Athens, Mexico, Versailles (painted by himself), Geneva, and the three battle pieces of Lodi, Waterloo, and that at the gates of Paris. In addition to those panoramas, his own pictures of Marius, Ariadne, etc. etc. were also exhibited.

"The patronage which he received from the public was satisfactory, and he deemed that the institution would become a permanent one. In this, however, he was mistaken, for, after an ineffectual effort on the part of the Philharmonic Society, of the City Dispensary, and of the National Academy of Design, to get possession of the building, the Corporation of 1829, in despite of the petitions and remonstrances of Mr. V. and of his friends and patrons, finally resorted to summary measures to remove him from the rotunda, and which were adopted during his temporary absence from the city.

"This step having been taken, an effort was afterwards made to procure its recall; and in May, 1830, a petition, signed by Cadwallader D. Colden, Richard Varick, John Ferguson, and other gentlemen of the first respectability, who were among his patrons, was presented to the Corporation; praying that the building might again be appropriated to its original purpose, and that a new lease might be granted to trustees, to be chosen from among the petitioners, to see to the execution and fulfilment of such conditions as the board might prescribe; and also suggesting, that the creditors of the building should receive a portion of the receipts from the exhibitions, until their claims were liquidated; and that payment be guaranteed in such way as should be deemed equitable by the board.

"This petition, which protected the rights of the creditors, as well as those of Mr. V. was rejected; and the Corporation held the building, appropriating it, in the first place, to the use

of the Court of Sessions; and afterwards, it being found totally
unfit for that purpose, it was transferred to the Marine Court,
by which tribunal it continues to be occupied."

Of the merits of the case between Mr. Vanderlyn and the
Corporation, I am neither competent nor willing to constitute
myself a judge. Mr. Vanderlyn's recent employment by the
United States Government, and his triumphant success, gives
me sincere pleasure; and I hope that he may yet have the
honor of painting one of the pictures to fill the rotunda at
Washington, and show to posterity, that, in 1817, America had
a better painter than filled the first four compartments.

Mr. Vanderlyn made, I believe, several visits to the South,
and more than one to New Orleans. He put up a building
in that city, and had his panorama (perhaps more than one)
exhibited there. He likewise visited the Havana, and attempted an exhibition of his fine pictures of "Marius" and
"Ariadne," but without profit and without employment.

During these voyages and residences, the building Mr.
Vanderlyn had incurred a debt for the erection of, was generally
a useless and unprofitable thing.

After several pages respecting the rotunda and the corporation, the memoir of Mr. Vanderlyn's friend concludes thus:

* "Being deprived of the rotunda, and, in consequence,
involved in some pecuniary embarrassment, Mr. Vanderlyn
was obliged to recur to his only resource, that of portrait
painting, for his immediate subsistence."

That Mr. Vanderlyn has been "triumphantly successful,"
in his " Washington " for Congress, I sincerely rejoice; and *yet*
hope, that the corporation of the great city of New York will
remunerate the artist and others who may be losers by the

---

* It would appear from the wording of this memoir, that the rotunda was constantly used by Mr. Vanderlyn. On returning from a residence in Norfolk, in 1820, I
wanted a room in which to paint a large picture, and, on inquiry, was referred to the
rotunda. "But where is Mr. Vanderlyn?" I could obtain no knowledge on that
point. I understood the building to be abandoned to his creditors. "Who has the key?"
"Doctor Mott." I applied to him, and he put me in possession of the building for this
temporary purpose. Fortunately, before I put up my large cloth to paint on, some
friend of Mr. Vanderlyn let me know that he would return to New York, and I might
be considered an intruder, and I instantly abandoned the premises.

appropriation of the rotunda to the business of the city: for, whatever may be strict, legal right, there is a feeling of justice, which, though it may not touch the heart of a corporate body, will make itself familiar in the bosoms of the electors, who contemplate the actions of the common council.

Mr. Vanderlyn's friend proceeds thus: —

"He had the good fortune to be commissioned by Congress, in the spring of 1832, to paint a full-length portrait of Washington, to be placed in the Hall of Representatives, and an appropriation of $1000 was made for the purpose. That painting has now been completed, and has added to the fame of the artist, while it reflects credit upon the discrimination of those who selected him for the task. On its being exhibited in the capitol, the House of Representatives immediately and unanimously voted him an additional compensation of $1500.

"In 1833, Mr. V. presented a petition, for the second time, to the corporation of New York, soliciting the restoration of the rotunda, and a renewal of the lease, or such remuneration for his losses, as, under all the circumstances, that body might deem reasonable and just. This petition, after a delay of many months, has been finally acted upon, and its prayer denied."

Mr. Vanderlyn published an address to his subscribers in 1824, pamphlet form; and another pamphlet in 1829, after the loss of the building. These efforts remain without effect.[1]

[1] John Vanderlyn died at Kingston, N. Y., in the autumn of 1852.

CHAPTER XII.

BARRALET — TISDALE — CLARK — FOX — TANNER —
MARTIN — REED — MARTEN — GROOMRICH — FAIRMAN.

JOHN JAMES BARRALET

PROBABLY arrived from Dublin and took up his abode in
Philadelphia about this time.[1] He was certainly established
as a painter and designer before the year 1796. He was on
the wane, and appeared as an old man to Edwin when he first
knew him, which was in 1797. Mr. Barralet was by birth an
Irishman, but of French descent, and spoke the language of
his father's country fluently, having all the volatility of France
united with Hibernian prodigality and eccentricity. He was
a French Irishman. He was a man of talent without discretion
or anything like common prudence; prodigally generous, and
graspingly poor. As represented to me, he had the wildest
portions of the French and Irish characters whimsically
united in him. Mr. Barralet had been in good employ at
home in his native city of Dublin, and a teacher of drawing
in a public institution. In the earliest part of his American
career (although lame from some accident, probably in childhood), he was a beau of much pretensions, powdered to the
extent of the fashion of the day, and ruffled to the finger-
ends. In latter life he was a sloven to as great a degree.

His employment in Philadelphia was principally as a designer for publishers of books. Mr. Longacre (now one of our
most respectable artists) when a boy and a pupil of Murray's,
the engraver, was sent to assist Barralet in painting a trans-

[1] John James Barralet was born about 1747 and died in Philadelphia January 16,
1815. Barralet came to Philadelphia about 1796 (see Westcott, "History of Philadelphia") where he engraved a few plates and painted portraits and landscapes in water
colors. His name appears in the Philadelphia directories for 1797-1807 and 1813-14
inclusive, sometimes as "engraver," but more frequently as "artist."

parency which Murray was preparing to display in honor of
Perry's victory on Lake Erie. Young Longacre strove to
accomplish his master's views, but in vain; the work was
exhibited half unfinished, for Barralet amused himself by
taking snuff and telling stories while his young assistant did
all the labor.

Alexander Lawson engaged in a copartnership with Barralet; but the union of the Scotchman, a downright matter-of-
fact, industrious and warm-hearted man, with this flighty
genius, was that of oil and vinegar. Barralet designed pictures and Lawson engraved them. Barralet always poor,
contrived to receive payment for the work, and kept, or rather
spent it. Lawson prudently withdrew from the connection.
Another cause of disagreement between the parties was, that
Barralet would put a finishing touch to Lawson's work.
Between them they furnished the plates for Linn's poems, and
Lawson says his partner ruined several of them by retouching
them. On one occasion the poet was discontented with a
design presented by Barralet, but knowing his violent temper,
and the unsparing use he made of improper language, oaths,
and imprecations, the young clergyman was afraid to speak
to him on the subject, and persuaded Lawson to represent his
wish for some alteration in the design — he did so — and the
designer raved like a madman, at the indignity of being
criticized by a Yankee parson.

"On my arrival in the United States in 1797 (says Mr. D.
Edwin), Mr. Barralet was established in Philadelphia as a
designer of picturesque drawings, etc. etc. a man of abilities,
and, as I was informed, had been, at an early period of his
life of much more. He was the first in the United States who
invented a ruling machine for the use of engravers, he spent
much of his time also in making a better black for copperplate
printers' ink than that in general use — an article then much
wanted. He was the most eccentric man I ever knew — he
was lame — (a dislocation of the head of the thigh bone) when
he walked it was, to use the common saying, 'dot and go
one,' and the surtout coat he constantly wore in bad weather

was dipped in mud on the lame side at every step he took. He took large quantities of snuff — was extremely irritable and passionate, and very dirty in his general appearance, he was also very poor, but had too much pride to complain of a poverty he could ill conceal.

"A friend of his called on business at his house, he waited in a room without fire, though the weather was very cold, till his return; when B. came home, 'By George,' says he (his usual oath), 'we must have some fire, come with me in the cellar and I will split some wood.' Unfortunately there was but one stick, and that very knotty; the old man, who never lost his courage, made repeated strokes at the log, but in vain; grown desperate, he at last placed it on its end, stood at some distance from it, brandished his axe in a threatening posture, and to give more force to his desperate and final attempt, he ran or rather hopped (disregarding the assistance of his lame leg) at the devoted log, on which he inflicted a severe blow, but alas! still without effect; he then desisted, wiped the sweat from his face, and addressing his friend, 'By George, I believe the weather is warmer than it was, come up stairs, I think we have now no occasion for fire.'

"He once requested General Moreau, when in Philadelphia, to sit to him for his portrait; Barralet was then a widower, with two small children, living in part of a house, and having no housekeeper, things were in a very deranged and dirty state, but in expectation of the great general, everything was put in as much order as his reduced circumstances would admit of. The general came, but before the drawing was half done, he thought he heard some low sounds of sorrow in the room, but could see nobody; the crying and sobbing became at last so audible, that Barralet could not help taking notice of them. In a rage he limped or rather flew to the closet, which he unlocked, discovering his two children, whom he had confined, to keep them out of the way of his sitter. 'What do you want, you torments?' says the father; 'A piece of bread!' cried the children. 'Look there now, look there now,' said he to the general, 'what trouble I have with these brats.'

Then taking down, from an upper shelf in the same closet, a loaf of bread, he cut each a slice. They wished to make their escape, but he thrust them back, relocking the door, with threats, in case they were not quieter; and before the drawing was finished, the crying, a slice of bread, and the scolding were repeated, to the great amusement of the general, who told the story to his friends."

Mr. Barralet exhibited a drawing of the "First Landing of Columbus," which gained him applause and employment. He displayed many other original drawings in the exhibitions of the Pennsylvania Academy. I have no traces of him later than 1812.

E. TISDALE,

Designer, engraver, and miniature painter. He has declined, by letter, giving me any dates or facts relative to himself; if, therefore, I err, he must excuse me — the world will care nothing about it. He was born in New England about half a century ago.[1] His "Battle of Lexington" was engraved by Tiebout in 1797, and it is a feeble affair. He designed and perhaps engraved the plates for Richard Alsop and Theodore Dwight's "Echo," in 1807. He is said to be a man of wit. Among his early designs are some for Judge Trumbull's "McFingal." He was known to me in New York as a miniature painter in 1805. He removed to Hartford and became a partner in what was called "The Graphic Company." The business of this company was principally executing plates for the banks. — Tisdale designed the vignettes, Brewster was the dye sinker, N. Jocelyn, Willard, and Huntington the engravers.

Tisdale visited New York in 1820, and painted miniatures, but continued attached to the Hartford Graphic Company until 1825. He not only designed but engraved one or more of their plates. He is the author of a political satire called the "Gerrymander," and made designs for it. This publication was meant to lash Mr. Gerry, who, with the New England men in Congress, supported the imbecile Gates, in his opposition to

[1] Elkanah Tisdale was born in Lebanon, Conn., probably in 1771, and was last heard of in 1834.

Schuyler and Washington in 1778-9, but not for that is he made the butt for Tisdale's shafts; but for not going with the New England men in 1811-12 and 13, in their endeavors to obstruct the measures of government when it was found necessary to chastise the insolence of Great Britain by the War of 1812.

THOMAS CLARK. [1]

An English engraver, who exercised his art in New York about this time and worked in the dotted or stippling style, engraving several of the plates for David Longworth's edition of "Telemachus," and for the same liberal publisher a large plate of the resurrection of a pious family.

Clark went south — became deranged — imagined that he was constantly pursued by a negro without a head, and finally committed suicide by cutting his own throat to get rid of his tormentor. Mr. Longworth deserves to be recorded with praise for being the first to introduce engravings in *belles-lettres* literature into the country. He did much with limited means.

GILBERT FOX [0]

Was born in London about the year 1776. It so happened that an American, who practised engraving in Philadelphia without knowledge of the art, went on a voyage of discovery to London and finding young Fox, in the year 1793, bound by an apprentice's articles to Medland, a well-known engraver of that city, conceived the design of purchasing the youth's time if he could induce him to cross the seas to Philadelphia, the place of the adventurer's abode, and teach him what he had learned from Medland. Fox's reward was to be liberty and good wages.

Trenchard, such was the American's name, succeeded: the youth wished for change of place and to be master of his own actions, before he knew how to guide them; the master was tempted by the price offered; and Gilbert was shipped to Philadelphia in 1795 by Trenchard, as an assistant to himself, and teacher of the art of etching, which was imperfectly understood among us at that time.

---

1   For Clark read Clarke
0   Gilbert Fox later turned to acting. He died about 1806.

Mr. Alexander Lawson says, that among engravers the general impression was, "that Fox was only to impart his art to Edward Trenchard, who had bought and imported him, but it soon spread and every one became etchers." Gilbert did not like confinement and work, and being a draughtsman, when his contract with Mr. Trenchard was fulfilled, he engaged as a drawing master to teach the young ladies of a boarding school. He was a pretty young man, had a sweet voice, and an irresistible lisp, and taught "love's dream" to one of his pupils, who became Mrs. Fox.

Contrary to all rational calculation the boarding school proprietors would no longer trust the Fox among their flocks now that he was caught, and he had to seek some other mode of gaining a living for himself and family. The stage, the refuge of the idle, became his. He had some knowledge of music, a good voice, and, like Murphy's Dick, had visited the London theatres and been a member of a spouting club. This was capital enough to trade upon, and he was received with applause at the Chestnut Street Theatre, Philadelphia.

"Poor Fox," observes one of his cotemporary engravers, "he had some excellent qualities, but prudence was not one of them." He is to be considered as one who forwarded the progress of engraving in America.

It is said that his father bequeathed him one thousand pounds. If so, it soon vanished. He was engaged as first singer for the New York Theatre[1] — (there then was but one) — he played some young heroes in tragedy, and occasionally engraved. The head of Kotzebue for my German theatre is his work, and he was employed by David Longworth, our most enterprising publisher. He was always in trouble from certain symptoms of dissatisfaction among his creditors, who would not be put off with a song, or be content to wait for the yearly benefit, which experience had taught was of no benefit to them.

---

[1] "Hail, Columbia" was written by Joseph Hopkinson for Fox and was first sung at his benefit in 1798.

B. Tanner[1] — Martin.[2]

B. Tanner, born, as I believe, in New York, was a pupil of Cornelius Tiebout. He did much work for publishers, and published maps. Martin was a most wretched pretender to crayon painting. He was an Englishman; and such was the low state of taste among the people, that he had employers. His success encouraged Jarvis to try, and he thus assisted the arts.

Abner Reed[3] — Marten.

Reed, born in East Windsor, Connecticut; was the teacher in engraving of W. Mason, who commenced wood engraving in Philadelphia long after the year 1796. Marten came from Sheffield, England, about this time, and attempted wood engraving in New York in 1798, but soon after died of yellow fever.

W. Groomrich.[0]

An English landscape painter of some merit, painted in New York about this time. I knew him personally. There was a good deal of sprightliness and oddity about him. He attempted to paint some portraits, but they could not be recognized. Many of his landscapes were got off by raffling. I remember a landscape in which he endeavored, without success, to introduce the brilliant and gorgeous tints which nature displays in our autumnal scenery, but the blending of nature was not found in Groomrich's imitations, nor that harmony which she always throws over her most vivid coloring. Groomrich looked at his hard and discordant coloring, and cried,

[1] Benjamin Tanner, an excellent engraver, was born in New York City, March 27, 1775, and died in Baltimore, Md., November 14, 1848. He was working as an engraver in New York in 1792; afterwards in Philadelphia in partnership with his brother, Henry S. Tanner, and later of the engraving firm of Tanner, Vallance, Kearny & Co.

[2] The *Diary*, N. Y. May 11, 1797, and the *Mercantile Advertiser*, March 30, 1808, advertise "Likenesses in Crayons or pastels by Mr. Martin from London."

[3] He was born in 1771 and died in 1866; one of the earliest American engravers to engage in bank-note work as in 1792 he made plates for the Hartford (Conn.) Bank. He was at one time in partnership with John Scoles. In 1803-08 he was located at Hartford. Willard, Pelton, Daggett, Barber and John Cheney received instruction in engraving from him. His early work was produced in Lansingburg, N. Y., and New York City.

[0] William Groomrich died on May 24, 1811.

"*There* are tints! *there* is effect! *there* is distance! — they could not understand this coloring in England."

He painted a view from Harlem Heights, with really a good distance. "What shall I do for a foreground?" said he; "I will dash a watermelon to pieces, and make a foreground of it." No bad thought.

He removed to Baltimore from New York, and Mrs. Groomrich opened a boarding school for young ladies with some success. Robert Gilmor, Esq. of Baltimore, speaking of Groomrich, says, "He painted here several good landscapes. He was a pupil of Lambert's."

GIDEON FAIRMAN.

"Gideon Fairman, a native of Newtown, Fairfield County, Connecticut, was born on the 26th day of June, 1774. At an early age he exhibited an extraordinary mechanical ingenuity and taste for the fine arts. His father having been reduced in his circumstances by twice losing his property by fire, and burthened with a large family, his son Gideon placed himself as an apprentice to a man of the name of Isaac Crane, a blacksmith and mechanic in New Milford, a few miles distant from Newtown. Shortly after there came to the town an English engraver of no great merit, of the name of Brunton,[1] to whom some rude specimens of young Fairman's genius were shown in the way of engraving, which (considering that he had never witnessed the process, and worked with tools of his own construction) were surprising indications of talent. Brunton pronounced his performances astonishing, and advised his father to encourage him in a pursuit in which he bid so fair to distinguish himself.

"After residing a short time at New Milford with his family, he determined to leave a place where he could obtain no instruction in the art of engraving. He therefore started on foot with eighteen cents in his pocket, and walked to Hudson

[1] Richard Brunton, a die sinker and an engraver of book plates, etc., who in 1799 was sentenced to an imprisonment of two years for counterfeiting Connecticut silver coins.

on the North River, where a married sister resided. From
thence he found means to reach the city of Albany, where he
bound himself apprentice to Messrs. Isaac & George Hutton,
jewellers and engravers. He was now about eighteen years of
age, and served out his time with them, after far surpassing his
instructors in the beautiful art which was afterwards to gain
him so high a reputation. At the age of 21 (1796) he commenced business for himself, winning the good opinion of all
by a natural grace of manner, joined to great intelligence and
a fine person.

"He relied on his merit alone for advancement, nor did he
ever relax his efforts in a long career of usefulness, until, at
the close of life, a series of misfortunes broke down suddenly
the energies they could not bend.

"In 1798 he married, and in 1810 having lost his wife, he
proceeded to the city of Philadelphia, where a company of
bank-note engravers was formed under the firm of Murray,
Draper, Fairman & Co.

"In this city he continued; and in a few years, by his unremitting attention to business, he amassed considerable wealth.
In the year 1819, he was induced to enter into another partnership with Mr. Jacob Perkins, and accompanied him to England,
where he resided three years. Not long after commencing
business in London, they took into partnership the celebrated
engraver Charles Heath. This connection, however, proved a
disastrous experiment to Mr. Fairman, who was disappointed
in his anticipations by the extravagant expenditure of one of
the parties in pursuing a career which has since involved every
one connected with him. When at last Mr. Fairman felt the
necessity of returning to his own country, he left the shores
of England with a sad foreboding of impending calamity at
home; and so the event proved; for within a few days' journey
of the city in which he had gained so just a reputation, a friend
hastened to announce his utter ruin through a spirit of insane
speculation on the part of the senior partner of the concern.
He was, therefore, under the necessity of stealing covertly into
the city, and taking the benefit of the insolvent law to secure

his personal liberty. These accumulated misfortunes depressed him not, but an unconquerable desire to retrieve, in some measure, his great losses, pay his liabilities, and provide for the wants of his family, caused him to give himself so unsparingly to his business, of all perhaps the most sedentary, and being always remarkably robust, he was suddenly struck down by paralysis and fell a victim to his exertions, on the 18th day of April, 1827, at the age of 52 years." [0]

Such is the memoir with which I have been favored by a friend. I first saw Mr. Fairman in Albany, apparently full of employment as an engraver, in 1805. Many years after I found him living in prosperity and splendor in Philadelphia. His small figures for bank notes were designed and executed with much taste. After his return from England I saw him snugly situated in Philadelphia, with a second wife; but it appears that his affairs had been irretrievably ruined by the unhappy conduct of Murray. He was to the last a man of uncommon physical powers, beauty of person, and elegance of deportment.

0   Gideon Fairman died on March 18, 1827.

CHAPTER XIII.

REMBRANDT PEALE — SARGENT — WOOLLEY — WEAVER —
HOLLAND — PIGALLE — EDWIN — SHARPLES.

REMBRANDT PEALE.*

THIS worthy man and accomplished artist, the second son
and third child of Charles Willson Peale, inherited from his
ingenious father a love of the fine arts and of mechanics. He
was born on the 22d of February, 1778, at a farmhouse in
Bucks County, Pennsylvania, whither his mother had fled from
Philadelphia at the approach of the hostile British army, his
father being then with a volunteer company (raised by his exertions, and of which he was elected captain) with the army of
Washington.

We have seen that C. W. Peale had returned from his studies
with West in 1774, and although his mind was engaged by
the dangers then approaching, and soon after by his services
rendered to his country, he was so devoted to the art he loved
that he named his son born in 1774 Raphael,[1] his second child

* I take this opportunity to add, from recent communications, some further particulars respecting the extraordinary family of the Peales. On Charles W. Peale's return
from Europe, he promulgated a doctrine which is true to a certain extent, that "any
person may learn to paint" — I say true to a certain extent. Any person with good
eyes and common sense may be taught to draw and use colors, but they may fall
lamentably short of the end desired, and which is the only thing to be wished in an
artist. So any one may be taught to make verses; but it is only God who makes a poet.
Peale persuaded two brothers to become painters. James abandoned the trade of cabinet making, and became a miniature painter in full employ. He likewise painted in
oil, and even attempted historical composition. I am told of *one* on the death of Mercer
at Princeton. Two of his daughters and a granddaughter are now professional artists.
Anna Peale, now Mrs. Staughton, of Philadelphia, is well known as a miniature painter.
Her sister Sarah, residing in Baltimore (says my informant), "practises the boldest
branch of portrait painting in oil, and their niece, Mary Jane Simes, herself a living
miniature, rivals her aunt in the same style."

[1] Raphael Peale, the first-born son of Charles Willson Peale, appeared as a portrait
painter, in oil and miniature in 1800. He was not very successful in his profession being
obliged to work for very small sums. He died in Philadelphia March 4, 1825. His
advertisement, appearing August 3, 1801, reads: "DEATH *Deprives* us of our *Friends*,
And then we regret having neglected an opportunity of obtaining their LIKENESSES.

Angelica Kaufman, and his second son Rembrandt. These were followed by Vandyk, Titian, Rubens, Sophinisba, Linnæus, Franklin, Sybella, and Elizabeth. The last named after her mother, Mr. Peale's last wife. Mr. R. P. says, "all these children but two were named after painters, though only two of the number adopted the profession. Raphael was a painter of portraits in oil and miniature, but excelled more in compositions of still life. He may perhaps be considered the first in point of time who adopted this branch of painting in America, and many of his pictures are in the collections of men of taste and highly esteemed." He died early in life, perhaps at the age of forty, after severe affliction from gout.

Rembrandt commenced drawing at the age of eight, from the drawing book, between school hours; and I have heard him say that so great was his love of the occupation, that he injured his health by swallowing his food without chewing, and laid the foundation of illness in after life. At thirteen he left school, and devoted himself day and night to the pencil. At that age, he painted a portrait of himself, his second attempt from the life.

In the year 1796 his father relinquished portrait painting, and recommended his son to the public as his successor; but the recommendation was not successful, and Rembrandt determined to enter the world as a painter by a visit to Charleston, South Carolina. At this early period of his career as a painter, he fixes the time of Washington sitting to him for his portrait, and says, in a letter before me, that this, with the aid of one painted by his father, "gave rise to the portrait which is distinguished by its place in the Senate chamber at Washington."

At Charleston he was employed until 1801, when he went to England, accompanied by his wife and two children, to study under the direction of Mr. West. While Mr. Peale was in

"Raphaelle Peale, *Portrait Painter* (in Miniature and Large), will deliver LIKE-NESSES At No. 28, POWEL – STREET, Which is between Spruce and Pine and running from Fifth to Sixth street.

"*Those who prefer* R. PEALE'S *work, must apply within six weeks. His Price is* TEN DOLLARS. — NO LIKENESS NO PAY.

"*August* 3, 1801."

ₚ London he published a memoir on the mammoth, which is
honorably mentioned and quoted by Cuvier. In London he
painted a few portraits, and returned to America, thinking to
abandon painting for agricultural pursuits; but success after
his return to Philadelphia prevented his exchange of the pencil for the plough. In 1804 Mr. Peale issued the following
advertisement:

"REMBRANDT. The names being merely to distinguish
individuals — and whereas few persons discriminate between
the peculiar names of my father, uncle, brother, or myself,
which creates a confusion disadvantageous to the distinct merit
of each as an artist, I am induced to obviate this on my part,
in being known only by my first name, Rembrandt; the adjunct
Peale serving only to show of whom descended. Therefore,
ladies and gentlemen desirous of viewing a few specimens of
my style of painting, may find me by the following direction: —
REMBRANDT, PORTRAIT PAINTER IN LARGE AND SMALL, head of
Mulberry Court, leading from Sixth, three doors above Market
Street. Dec. 4."

How careful ought public men to be, not only of their actions,
but of their words, especially words given to the world through
the press! This advertisement could not be omitted in a biography of Mr. Peale without injustice to the subject, for it displays the character of the individual at the time, more than
pages written by the biographer for the purpose.

In 1807 Mr. Peale visited Paris for the express purpose of
painting the portraits of distinguished men of that nation, and
"to feast," as he has said, "on the treasures Napoleon had
assembled in the gallery of the Louvre." Mr. Peale painted a
great number of French savants and military men, many of
which on his return were placed in his father's museum. This
not only gave him an opportunity of improvement, but introduced him to eminent men from whom he derived important
information, tending to increase his store of scientific, literary,
and philosophical knowledge. His style had improved, but
his health had suffered, and he returned home once more determined to purchase that blessing by the abandonment of

palette and easel, for the cultivation of the earth. To this determination he could not hold; and after two years more spent in portrait painting, finding it impossible to relinquish the objects of his early love and his life's pursuit, he returned to Paris in 1809, with a resolution which may be estimated by the circumstance that he carried with him a wife and five children.

The gallery of the Louvre was now completed and in its full splendor. Mr. Peale took lodgings in the vicinity, and spent all the time he could spare from completing his collection of portraits of eminent men, in studying the masterpieces of eminent painters; but he could not be content from home, and "notwithstanding an offer from Denon to give him employment for the government, he returned to America after a residence of fifteen months." He again set up his easel in Philadelphia as a portrait painter, but found leisure to compose his picture of the "Roman Daughter," which possesses great merit.[1] — This was exhibited at the Pennsylvania Academy in 1812, and elicited just encomiums; but the painter experienced wounds from the shafts of detraction, aimed by ignorance, idleness, and vanity.

A man of the name of Svemin, Russian vice consul, asserted, that the picture was a copy, and that he had seen the original in the rooms of Gerard, at Paris. A man of his standing in society was believed, and Peale considered as an impostor. He found himself treated with disrespect, without knowing the cause, and only by accident learned the accusation against him, and who was its author. He took Sully with him and called on Svemin; who, after prevarication, was obliged to acknowledge that he thought he had seen a picture at Gerard's like Mr. Peale's, and the excellence of Mr. Peale's composition had made him conclude, it could be no other than a copy of that master's work. He avowed himself mistaken, and offered any reparation he could make. Thus is the reputation of a painter, both as artist and man, made the sport of vanity, and a sacrifice to travelled coxcombry.

[1] The "Roman Daughter" was at one time in the possession of the "Boston Museum" and is now owned privately in Boston.

The figures of this picture are the size of life, and painted carefully from nature. It is now in the possession of Mr. Savage, of Boston.

The establishment of a Museum, and Gallery of Paintings, in the city of Baltimore, was now a favorite object with Mr. Peale, and he accomplished it. He continued there nine years; and besides painting many portraits, composed and executed, in large, the "Ascent of Elijah," and other works of magnitude. Finally, he painted his "Court of Death"; which having been exhibited throughout the United States with success, has made his name, connected with it, familiar with the public.*

* When Mr. Peale brought this picture before the public, he published the following in the *American Daily Advertiser*, of Philadelphia:

"To THE PUBLIC. — After my return from France, in 1810, I designed and executed the equestrian portrait of Napoleon, my first experiment in large. The favorable reception of this, in public exhibition, induced me to venture on an historical subject — the story of the Roman Daughter, the last scene of which had often been painted, but not the first day's intercourse as I conceived it. Although my own gallery then stood in need of novelty and addition, I yielded to the request of some of the directors of the Pennsylvania Academy of Fine Arts, and sent this picture, wet from my easel, to their exhibition in 1811. Its reception by the public was flattering to my reputation; but, being my first attempt at original composition, faults were discovered, which I was impatient to correct as soon as the exhibition closed. My friends were invited to see the alterations. I showed them the changes made successively from my first ideas. Struck with this unsuspecting display of unassisted invention, Joseph Hopkinson, Esq., gave me the first intimation of a report being in circulation that I was not the author of this composition, but had copied it in France. Perhaps with too much of the pride of conscious integrity, I would not inquire who were the propagators of this misstatement; but accident having made me acquainted with Mr. Svemin as the author, my moral character, more than my reputation as an artist, required that I should receive an explanation. For this purpose, I waited on him, accompanied by Mr. Sully, in whose presence he assured me that it was the *excellence* of my picture made him *suppose* that I had copied it — that he *thought* he had seen such a picture in *Gerard's* painting room in Paris, but did not remember the *situation*, nor the *attitudes* of the figures, by which alone a picture can be remembered. Mr. Sully was satisfied of the incorrectness of his previous assertion, and was witness to the acknowledgment of his error. I then published a few paragraphs in the papers, in which I took occasion to speak of the encouragement of the arts in America; and, in order to bring it to the test, engaged myself to make a present of the picture of the Roman Daughter to the Pennsylvania Hospital, if any person could prove (by comparison) that I had copied it in whole, or in part, from any painting, print, or drawing whatsoever. This was done with full confidence, that in a composition which was strictly my own original, no part of it could, even by accident, be like anything else. For, although historical painters from Raphael to West, have always been permitted to borrow ideas, and even figures — no such advantage was taken.

"My motive at this time for reviving the recollection of these circumstances, is, that many persons, who never read the vindication, still continue under the erroneous impressions. Now, when I present myself again before the inhabitants of my native city,* with a more important original composition, I think it necessary, and the occa-

Of this picture Mr. Peale says, in a letter before me, it was painted "on a canvas 24 feet long and 13 feet high, containing 23 figures of the full size. The idea of this picture was taken from Bishop Porteus's poem on Death. But instead of following the bishop, in the employment of the usual allegorical person- ages, I imagined a more original, impressive style of personifica- tion, at once philosophical and popular, and had the satisfaction to find, that it was equally understood and appreciated by the ignorant and the learned. It was exhibited in the principal cities during little more than a year, and produced the sum of $8,886; thus proving it to be a successful experiment. In New York it was recommended from the pulpits, and by the Corporation of the city, who went in a body to visit it."

Thus far the author of the picture, who deserves praise for the experiment, and seems to be satisfied with the result. — He represents the causes and victims of Death, who is shrouded in mysterious obscurity. War and its effects are represented by the principal group. The figure of Pleasure is beautiful, and I recollect it as almost faultless. Intemperance was well conceived, if memory serves me; and many of the figures, in half-tint, well executed.

From 1822 to 1829, Mr. Peale painted portraits in New York, Boston, and Philadelphia, with checkered success, as to employment; and then, accompanied by his son, once more

sion is peculiarly proper, to enforce the correction of an error, not more injurious to me than to my fellow citizens who are disposed to encourage the efforts we are making to advance the arts in our country.

"Not only the picture of the Roman Daughter, but the picture of the Court of Death, shall be given up for the same charitable purpose, should any one, actuated by such excellent considerations, detect so dishonorable an imposition. If this cannot be done, then ought every lover of the arts, and every gentleman who knows the value of character, interest himself in discountenancing a groundless aspersion against an artist, who would value no acquirements nor fame that were purchased at the expense of his integrity.

"The noble arts require a more liberal encouragement in our country. They are capable of a direction the most honorable and useful. But the state of our finances, and the recent establishment of our public institutions, do not permit the purchase of expensive works, which can only be brought forth by popular encouragement, as was practised in ancient Greece; and if they are viewed with corresponding justice, zeal and patriotism, no greater reward need stimulate the exertions of the artist.

"Witness THOMAS SULLY. REMBRANDT PEALE."

* I have stated, *on the authority of Mr. Peale*, that he was born in Bucks County, and not in Philadelphia, as here asserted.

visited France, and had the satisfaction of spending sixteen months in Italy, copying some of the works of the most celebrated masters. Most of these copies were purchased by Mr. Bussey, of Boston.

Mr. Peale says, "I gratified my national and professional pride, by taking with me my portrait of Washington; which, in Rome, brought to my room some of the most distinguished artists, professors, and amateurs. At Florence it was exhibited, with distinction, in the Royal Academy. In London, it was visited by artists and other distinguished persons: and after my return to America, without my solicitation, it was bought by an unanimous vote of the Senate, and placed in their hall, as the picture which had united the suffrages of most of the intimate friends and relations of Washington."

Surely this distinction, these suffrages, and a good price received for this picture, may satisfy the author of it. But as I have mentioned it elsewhere, and given my opinion that it is not a likeness of Washington, and expressed my disapprobation of the manner in which I saw it exhibited in New York, with a poor copy from Stuart's head of Washington, without frame, placed on the floor, beneath the highly decorated picture by Mr. Peale — I must here repeat that opinion and that disapprobation.

At the time of finishing this picture, it was announced as forthcoming at Washington. It was published in one or more of the journals that Mr. Peale had been for some time painting "a portrait of Washington, which was said to be, in every particular, the most admirably correct representation of the *character* and *expression* of this illustrious man that has been offered to the world."

In due time the picture is thus advertised at Washington city. After repeating the eulogies on its character and expression, it proceeds: — "The painter had the rare advantage of having painted an original picture of the great patriot whilst living, which he has improved by subsequent study of his subject, with such aids as he could obtain from a reference to the works of contemporaneous artists. All the surviving worthies, who knew Washington intimately, speak with enthusiasm of this fine painting, as the only true likeness they have ever seen of him: and as a work of art merely, our letters from Philadelphia describe it as unsurpassed. This painting being finished, has been brought to this city by its author, with a view to submit it to the inspection of the national representatives and others, at the seat of government; and particularly with a view to obtain the opinions upon it of those who were compatriots and personal friends of Washington, of whom so many are at this season to be found at the seat of government."

Opinions were obtained upon the portrait by presenting a certificate to those who had known Washington, and gaining their signatures. This certificate asserted everything the painter wished.

A certificate is, in my eyes, a proof of something deficient or amiss. A certificate can be produced with signatures of many of the best men of any country to anything. Mr. Peale, in this certificate affair, shares equally, perhaps, with those who signed it; many of whom have since declared, that they did not think the portrait like the original.

Thus is the sacred cause of truth trifled with, and certificates obtained from "honorable men — all honorable men," to deceive mankind, mislead opinion, and oftentimes to destroy health and life. Why is truth so little respected, when it is the only foundation upon which human happiness rests? I blame Mr. Peale for degrading himself by submitting to the expedient of a certificate, but I blame the signers more.

None see the anomalies of character more than the biographer; and if he is a faithful historian of nature, he will represent them. Mr. Peale's conduct in the above-mentioned affair stands in contradiction to his general character as a man.

We have seen that it was in 1827 that Mr. Peale's father died, and I sincerely hope left property enough to place all his children in situations that, with the talent and industry of the family, has made them independent of circumstances. In 1829, the subject of this memoir visited France and Italy, as said above, and on his return published a volume on the latter country. In this publication he has shown himself an acute observer, and, in many instances, an excellent describer; but Italy and the eternal city are such an eternal theme, that the veteran reader feels as if he were going over pages familiar to him, although perfectly original. Mr. Peale's observations on works of art are very valuable to the artist. In the autumn of 1832, he says, "I made my last visit to England. From Liverpool proceeding to Sheffield, where I painted a number of portraits. In the spring " (of 1833), "I established myself in London, and divided my time between my painting room and the various galleries of pictures and the rooms of artists. Here I deliberately went over a review of the whole of my preceding studies — defined, compared, and digested their various merits and defects, which I collated with the living testimony around me, and brought my judgment to a mature conclusion as to the course I should pursue in my future practice; believing that I was demonstrating, in the work I was then executing, that I had made, as a student of nature and art, a manifest advance in the art which I had loved from my infancy, and to which I had devoted all my time and means." Long may Mr. Peale continue to advance in his art — an art in which he has held a distinguished place for many years.

Besides the usual occupations of a painter, Mr. Peale applied himself to lithographic drawing, and obtained the medal from the Franklin Institute of Boston.* I have freely expressed my opinion of what I consider errors in Mr. Peale's conduct and publications; not with a view to his injury, but to his

---

* Mr. Peale has furnished me the following note respecting his study of lithography: "I was among the first of the artists who employed this admirable method of multiplying original drawings. My first attempt in New York was a head of Lord Byron, and a female head from a work of Titian. In 1826 I went to Boston and devoted myself for some time to lithographic studies, and executed a number of portraits and other subjects, and finally a large drawing from my portrait of Washington, for which I obtained the silver medal from the Franklin Institute at Philadelphia in 1827. Unfortunately the workmen, by some neglect, destroyed this drawing on the stone when but a few impressions were taken.[01] I instructed one of my daughters and my son in the art, and they produced some very commendable specimens."

01 As Peale drew two large lithographic portraits of Washington there is some doubt as to which one he refers.

benefit and that of others. He has, in 1834, removed to New York, where I hope his portraits will be justly appreciated, and his success answer to his wishes.[1]

At an early age Mr. Peale was induced to make experiments on gas light, and when Doctor Kugler succeeded in purifying gas, he being then an inhabitant of Baltimore, formed a company for lighting the city with gas, which was done in 1817. Baltimore owes to him the honor of being the first of our cities that adopted this great improvement.

The ever active mind of this gentleman leads him to exertions honorable to himself, and beneficial to mankind. He is now about to publish in New York a book on the principles of drawing, with illustrations, and he shows the connection between drawing and writing, giving rules which I have seen. This work will entitle him to the gratitude of the public. The book is calculated to enable the student to instruct himself in writing by the same process and at the same time that he learns to draw. It will be eminently useful in schools of every description. The author has displayed great knowledge and much thought on the subject. The transition from drawing to writing is finely pointed out and illustrated, and the work must be extremely useful. I hope it may be adopted in our schools, and thus the ingenious author remunerated.

HENRY SARGENT

Was born in the town of Gloucester, State of Massachusetts, in the year 1770.[2] At an early age he was instructed in the

---

[1] Rembrandt Peale died in Philadelphia, October 3, 1860, having written, nine days before his death, a letter to Mr. Charles Henry Hart, giving the following important data:

"Philada., Sept. 24, '60.

Dear Sir:

In answer to yours of this morning, I will state that my Original Portrait of Washington was painted in the fall of 1795.

The first copy of it is in the possession of Joseph Harrison, of Rittenhouse Square.

Besides having painted 39 copies of my Father's 'Washington' I have made 79 copies of my own of which some remain in my possession.

Respectfully yours,
REMBRANDT PEALE."

[2] Henry Sargent was born November 25, 1770, and died in Boston, February 21, 1845.

rudiments of Latin and Greek, at the celebrated Dummer
Academy (so named after Governor Dummer, who made
large donations to it), near Newburyport, in which town the
father of Mr. Sargent, an eminent merchant, then lived,
during the War of the Revolution: and after Boston was freed
from the British troops, Henry was removed from Dummer,
in consequence of his father's taking up his residence in the
capital of Massachusetts, and received the remainder of his
education at such schools as that town then possessed. At the
usual age, he was admitted into the counting house of Thomas
Perkins; and that gentleman going abroad, Henry was received
into his father's mercantile establishment; here he remained
until the age of nineteen or twenty. Up to this period he had
evinced no partiality for the study of any of the fine arts.

This is a very remarkable circumstance in the life of Mr.
Sargent: in short it is unparalleled. In thus keeping his
hands from chalk or charcoal, and his school books uncon-
taminated by pen or pencil monsters, Mr. Sargent stands
alone in the history of art. The reader of this work will have
remarked, that from the time of West to the present day,
every painter or engraver began to scrawl, scratch, pencil, or
paint as soon as he could hold anything wherewith he could
make a mark. There is reason to believe that Mr. Sargent,
when a boy, evinced taste for poetry and music, notwithstanding which, the talent or faculty for imitating forms remained
dormant, and the craniological bump undeveloped, almost to
the age of maturity, although several fine portraits by Smibert, and finer by Copley, adorned the walls of his father's
house. They had been familiar objects from infancy, and
"familiarity," says the proverb, "breeds contempt." Certain
it is, that these familiar objects produced no effect upon the
boy. He was first incited to attempt drawing by some rude
sketches in common chalk, made by one of his brothers on
the walls of their sleeping apartment. Success made him
continue the practice. He found he could outdo his brother,
and the walls were soon covered with their rival productions.
Thus was the dormant desire to imitate forms aroused; but

the ambition to become a painter was awakened, never to sleep again, by the following circumstance:

A house and ship painter was employed to decorate one of the ships of Henry's father, which was preparing for sea. The incipient painter, having outstripped his brother in the arts of design, determined to encounter this more formidable rival. The desire was irresistible; and seizing the opportunity of the ship painter's absence from his brushes and colors, which he had abandoned that he might gratify a more common but equally irresistible desire for dinner, young Sargent seized his tools, and produced the head of a sea nymph, to the great astonishment of the gaping sailors. The master of the paint pots "knocked under," and this essay with colors was so often repeated, and with such success, that the duties of the desk and the counting house became uninteresting and repugnant to the student of the fine arts. Sketches of "men and things" deranged or interrupted the sober avocations of mercantile life, which it is possible the young painter's father thought were more important, and would produce more solid advantages; but after a time the old gentleman was induced to consent that Henry should try his skill with more refined and suitable materials than the paint pot and pound brush. Palette, pencil, colors, easel, and maul stick were procured, and a room was allotted him in his father's house as an atelier, where he soon painted several portraits, and made copies of several pictures, among others was one from a mezzotinto print published by Copley, from his painting of Brooke Watson, or the "Youth rescued from a Shark." [1]

Trumbull, in 1790, visiting Boston after his second sojourn in England, saw the young painter's work, and commended this copy so highly, that it was at once decided by his friends that he should be permitted to study the art for which he had not only shown a decided preference, but had given proof of being qualified to pursue with success.

This praise of the copy above mentioned decided the fate of Henry Sargent, and he embarked for London in 1793,

[1] This copy is now (1917) in the Boston Museum of Fine Arts.

carrying letters from Trumbull to West, who received him
with his usual urbanity; made him an offer of his services,
— and placed his rooms, his pictures, and his casts at his disposal. Apartments were taken by Mr. Sargent in the vicinity
of Mr. West; and during his whole residence in London, he
always had free access to the great painter's house, and the
benefit of his advice on all occasions relative to art. He likewise received the kindest and most courteous treatment from
Mr. Copley, to whom he carried letters.

In London Mr. Sargent remained four years, during which
he pursued such studies as are usually recommended by the
Royal Academy. He would then have passed over to the
continent, but the bloody contest, then in full violence, made
his friends anxious for his return home, which he accordingly
did in 1797. In Boston he remained for near two years, but
such was the apathy then existing towards the arts, that he
often was discouraged, and has said, that sometimes he regretted he had ever undertaken the profession. He, therefore,
in 1799, was induced to accept of a commission offered him in
the army then about to be raised, of which General Washington, who had retired from the presidency, accepted the command, but which, until called into actual service, was placed
under the immediate direction of Major-General Alexander
Hamilton. With this army Mr. Sargent remained until it
was disbanded. The taste for military life thus acquired, distracted and drew off his attention from the arts. He received
several commissions from successive governors of Massachusetts, which were particularly complimentary, as they were
unsolicited and unexpected.

I well remember the finest body of light infantry I ever saw
out of regular service, going through their evolutions in the
mall, and on the common -of Boston, under the command of
Captain Sargent.

During the last war with Great Britain, he received the
appointment of aid-de-camp to the governor, with the rank of
colonel, and was appointed assistant adjutant-general when
the invasion of that part of our country was expected in 1814.

After the glorious termination of this war, which a second time vindicated our rights, and chastised the usurpations of England — a second time triumphantly proved that the free citizen has only to determine to conquer, and he will conquer in despite of monarchies, aristocracies, and their hirelings — Colonel Sargent received several military and civil commissions, equally honorable and equally unsolicited. He was appointed, in behalf of Massachusetts, to attend to the surrender, under the treaty of Ghent, of certain islands in the Bay of Passamaquoddy, by his Britannic Majesty's government, to Brigadier-General Miller, and the authority of the United States. It was said, justly, in the papers of the day, that "the President could not have appointed a more proper person to have conducted this affair, than General Miller, or the Governor, on behalf of the commonwealth, one more suitable than Colonel Sargent."

At a later period Colonel Sargent was twice chosen to represent the town of Boston, in the General Court, or State Legislature, but at length he was induced to decline any re-election, by a deafness occasioned by too close proximity to a cannon which was suddenly discharged. His various public avocations having no charms for him, he again turned his attention to the arts, and set himself seriously to work upon his great picture of "The landing of the Pilgrims."

I never saw this picture, but I saw in the painter's room the small picture, the study for it, on one of my visits to Boston. This was about the year 1806, shortly after Mr. Gilbert Stuart's removal to Boston. Mr. Sargent says in a letter to me, "I became very intimate with him, and obtained much useful information from him. In our frequent walks together, the conversation of course often turned upon the subject of painting. It was his opinion (often expressed) that the art was on the decline. I never argued with him, for as he was a vain, proud man, and withal, quick tempered, I chose rather to preserve his friendship as an artist. He once had just painted a very fine portrait, and I ventured to ask him if it was not under-sized. He answered in a very peremptory manner, 'No, not in the least.' I was silent, but a few months after I saw him about to make a copy of the same picture, he held in his hand a small instrument, and I asked him what was the use of it. He said, 'to enlarge the copy, as he thought the original too small.' I imputed this acknowledgment to the lack of memory, and was again silent, not willing to interrupt the good feeling that existed between us."

The large picture, of the Landing, was finished after several years of severe application, and was destroyed in the following manner: After having been exhibited to the public, it was rolled upon a *fresh cut unseasoned* pole, around which, it continued for a number of months, during which time, the sap so completely rotted the picture, that it fell in pieces in unrolling. The part next the wood was like mud. The extreme interest the public took in this subject induced the painter to undertake the arduous task of painting another of the same size. This the painter possesses. Colonel Sargent painted for exhibition, a large picture of Christ entering Jerusalem. I give from "Sketches of Public Characters," the following:

"Sargent's picture of the Landing of the Pilgrims was (I speak in the past tense, for I understand that it was destroyed by some accident) much admired in its day by the descendants of the Pilgrims, and spoken well of by those who did not feel any extraordinary sympathy for that race of men. The event of the landing of those few wanderers had nothing in it of very great sublimity or interest when taken by itself, unconnected with the past or the future in relation to that period. A handful of adventurers setting foot on an inhospitable shore, in an inclement season is, no doubt, a subject of sympathy, but not of wonder. The appearance of a northern sky in such a season of the year, was a fine object for the painter, and Sargent availed himself of it. He was northern born, and had lived, for the usual months of the year, under such a sky as our forefathers first saw on their first landing, a freezing atmosphere, rocks, ground, all covered with a mantle of snow, while a low and sickly looking sun threw a few faint rays on the ironbound, frost-bound coast. The dignity of the group was conspicuous in the picture. All they had suffered, all they were prepared to suffer, and what they hoped to effect, were well conceived and defined in the painting. The pious, Providence-trusting, resigned look, was there also. A little of the soldier was still seen in Miles Standish — yea, more of it than of the saint. The females were well displayed; not with Amazonian hardihood and fearless look; but yet there was no timidity, no shrinking weakness, no dread of the savages, nor of a more appalling foe; a long and dreary winter, without house or home, or any shelter for themselves or their little ones. They stood, they looked, they went forward, as those who believe that they have a God for their protector. That painter is good for nothing who cannot impress us with the moral sublimity of virtue, and give us the majesty of religion with all her sweetness. There is a spirit of prophecy in the hearts of the good in every undertaking, which, if it has no defined views, no tongue, but only speaking looks, yet it lives and dwells in every vein, and kindles in every eye, and has full possession of the soul, as certain as the soul has an existence; and the painter of this picture had genius enough to seize the thought and make the best of it.

"The next picture, from the same artist, was 'Christ entering into Jerusalem.' This was also a popular picture. It was remarkable for variety in the expression of the countenance of the hosannah-crying multitude. The face of the Saviour is wonderfully fine. An Indian chief once viewing the picture in the presence of the author of these remarks, looking steadfastly in the face of our Saviour, said, emphatically, *that is a good man*. The last and only remaining picture I know from Sargent, is the 'Dinner Party'; a specimen of the extraordinary power of light and shade; to exhibit which seems the great object of the artist in this painting. Sargent formerly took several portraits which were praised for their spirit and exactness."

The "Jerusalem" was sold for $3000, and as much was received for the exhibition. It is probably ruined by travelling with its owner. Besides the pictures above mentioned, Colonel

Sargent has painted "The Christ Crucified," which is in the possession of the Roman Catholic Society of Boston. The Dinner and the Tea Party are beautiful and finished pictures, and are in the possession of Mr. D. L. Brown, of Boston.[1] A large full length of Mr. Faneuil, belongs to the city of Boston, and hangs in the far-famed Faneuil Hall.[2] " The Tailor's News" and "Starved Apothecary," are from the same pencil.

When the "Dinner Party" was exhibited in New York, the association of gentlemen, called "The American Academy of Fine Arts," elected the painter an honorary member, and about the same time he received the honorary degree of Master of Arts from Harvard University.

Attention to mechanical inventions and other causes connected with the study of mechanics, have, of late years, in a great degree, diverted Colonel Sargent from application to his favorite pursuit. It has always, and continues to be, the highest gratification to him to indulge in the practice of painting, but his health will not now allow of so sedentary an occupation, except at intervals.

WOOLLEY.

This was an English painter, who made New York and Philadelphia alternately his home. He painted small portraits in oil, the last of which I saw in Philadelphia. He was called the Woolley painter. His best picture was Archy Gifford's sign, at Newark, a fox hunt, doubtless copied from a print.

[1] "The Tea Party" and "The Dinner Party" now belong (1917) to the estate of Mr. Winthrop Sargent of Boston, Mass., and Fishkill, N. Y.

[2] Henry Sargent did not make the large full-length portrait of Peter Faneuil belonging to the city of Boston and hanging in Faneuil Hall. At ameeting of the selectmen of Boston, November 28, 1743, the following was adopted: "Whereas the Town at their Annual Meeting in September 1742 Voted that the Selectmen be desired to procure the Picture of Peter Faneuil Esq. to be put up in Fanwuil Hall at the expense of the Town and upon Enquiry finding it would be much Cheaper to send to London to procure a frome for the same Voted that Mr. Agent Kilby be wrote to for to procure and send a neat Gold carved frame of Eight feet long and five feet wide by the first Ship at the charge of the Town." As Henry Sargent was born in 1770 it will be noted at once that he could not have made this portrait of Peter Faneuil. As John Smibert was the foremost portrait painter in Boston in 1742 and as he made the portrait of Faneuil belonging to the Massachusetts Historical Society and drew the plans for the erection of Faneuil Hall, it seems probable that he made the portrait of Faneuil now hanging in the hall that bears his name.

WEAVER.

Probably an Englishman. He painted portraits in oil, small size. He generally painted on tin, "inveterate" likenesses, hard as the tin and as cutting in the outline. He was one of those, who, by intemperance, disgrace, as far as they can, a liberal and honorable profession. His portrait of Alexander Hamilton attracted attention from the strong likeness, and was the property of Dr. David Hosack, but he gave it in exchange to Mr. Trumbull, and, as I am informed, Mr. Trumbull destroyed it.

JOHN JOSEPH HOLLAND.[0]

This gentleman was born in London about the year 1776. At the early age of nine, he was apprenticed to Marinelli, the scene painter of the opera house; who, pleased with the boy, taught him both the theory and practice of scene painting, made him a good water-color draftsman, and architect. He married very young; and Mr. Wignell found him at the opera house as a scene painter, shortly after the termination of his apprenticeship, and engaged him for the Philadelphia Theatre.

I knew Mr. Holland for years, and ever found him a warm-hearted, generous, unsuspecting man. Of the world, at the time of his coming to America, he knew nothing, out of the sphere of his immediate existence in London. Holland has in after time, often laughed at his profound ignorance of the country to which he was emigrating. Not having an opportunity of consulting Wignell on the subject, he brought out his household and kitchen furniture with him, fully persuaded that such articles, except of inferior quality, and at enormous prices, could not be procured in the savage country he was going to. The ship arrived at New York, in the autumn of 1796, and was moored at a wharf in the East River, late in the evening. Holland went ashore to reconnoitre, and happened to see neither negroes nor Indians. The ship was at the foot of Wall Street; and the young cockney determining to keep on a line which he could retrace, proceeded up that avenue. All was matter of astonishment to him. He saw

0 Holland died on December 15, 1820.

men who looked like Englishmen. The street was well lighted
with lamps. He walked on good flagstone pavement. He
saw lofty edifices on each side of him; and finally found in
front of him a handsome Gothic or half-Gothic church. This
church being a landmark, he ventured to turn a corner and
walk up Broadway, where the shops still blazed, and the
broad pavements resounded with the feet of passengers; — he
arrived at another church, and saw, amazed, the lofty Roman
Ionic columns of St. Paul's. He could go no further. The
desire to communicate the results of this expedition into foreign
parts, to his equally interested partner on shipboard, caused
him rapidly to retrace his way with wondering and delight;
that he might congratulate his wife upon their arrival at a
land of civilization.

Mr. Holland after residing several years in Philadelphia,
was engaged by Mr. Thomas A. Cooper, who had leased the
New York Theatre, to rebuild that edifice internally; which
he did to the entire satisfaction of the proprietors. In New
York he lost his wife, and married a second time, to a woman
of superior talents; the daughter of Mr. Jackson, of Staten
Island. He died still a young man, and left no children. He
was a man of taste in the arts; and his landscapes in water
color had great truth and force. He never attempted oil.
Two of his pupils, Mr. Hugh Reinagle, and Mr. John Evers,
have been distinguished as scene painters, and have produced
many landscapes of merit both in water and oil.

Though short in stature, Mr. Holland was well formed,
active, and athletic. In his personal appearance, always extremely neat. When he entered the workshop, he uniformly
changed his dress; and both by precept and example, forwarded
the business of his employers with wonderful dispatch. Streets,
chambers, temples or forests, grew under his hand as by
magic.

During the last war with England Mr. Holland shouldered
his musket, and did duty as a soldier. He likewise at that
time made drawings of the fortifications which were thrown
up to defend the city, both on Manhattan and Long Islands.

His faults (for he had faults) were the result of accidental circumstances, his virtues were his own.

M. PIGALLE.

A French artist of this name, designed and etched some plates in New York, about this time, "particularly," says my correspondent, Alexander Anderson, Esq., the Bewick of America, "a fine emblematic eagle, for the title page of Tiebout's 'American Battles.'"

DAVID EDWIN.

This eminent artist was the first good engraver of the human countenance, that appeared in this country. His portraits from Stuart, in the stippling style, are unrivaled to this day.

He is an Englishman, and born at Bath, in the month of December 1776. His father, John Edwin, the celebrated comedian, was the delight of the citizens of London, in my young days; and the support of O'Keefe's comedies and farces, as Lewis was afterward of those of F. Reynolds. John Edwin was, however, I have reason to believe, a better actor than a father. David was articled to Jossi, a Dutch engraver, who went to England to study a particular branch of the art, not practised in Holland. He was a thoroughbred artist, and "the most correct draughtsman of the human form," says his pupil, "I ever saw."

When David Edwin was twenty years of age, in the year 1796, Mynheer Jossi returned to Holland, and took his apprentice with him. Their place of destination was Amsterdam; but as the republican French were in possession of the country, the travellers entered Holland by the way of Embden. The Hollanders were at that time enamored with the new system of French democracy; and John Bull was out of favor. Edwin found that his English face and English dress were insuperable obstacles to all familiarity or friendly intercourse with the Dutch. He observed that most of his fellow passengers in the boat, had taken off their hats and wigs; substituting in the place of both the Dutch striped cap; he therefore doffed his hat, and mounted in its place a red woolen cap, which he had purchased before leaving London, as a *companion de voyage*, and a warm friend for the night. Unexpectedly it proved a most useful friend by day; for no sooner had he appeared in his new costume, than he heard from different parts of the boat the exclamation of "Bonnet rouge! Bonnet rouge!" and he was hailed as a true *sans culotte*, with the utmost cordiality by those who had before assiduously shunned him.

The young Englishman did not agree as well with his instructor after arriving at Amsterdam, as he had done in his native land; and before the term of his apprenticeship had fully arrived, they separated. Edwin at one-and-twenty years of age, found himself in a foreign country without friends or money, and looked anxiously towards the land of his birth. There was, however, no direct communication with England, and he determined to make his way from Amsterdam, to some port from whence he might find a passage to any part of Great Britain; not despairing of finding some mode by which to reach London. But he was doomed never to see his native country again.

A ship bound to Philadelphia was in the harbor, and the young engraver entered himself under the American flag, to work his passage as a sailor before the mast, to the country which was destined to be his future home; a country where at that time, 1797, the art he was master of was in its infancy. He accordingly embarked from Amsterdam, and assisted, as well as hands used to *points* and *gravers* and not to ropes could do, in navigating the American to *Havre*, and finally across the Atlantic, and up the Delaware to the place of his destination. It was in the month of December 1797, that David Edwin landed in Philadelphia, after being near five months on board ship as a fore mast-man, and he made his *entrée* upon this new scene in a new world, in his tarry round-about, and equally tarry trowsers; trudging after the captain through the streets of Penn's city, with the ship's letter bag on his shoulder, on the way to the post office.

The duties appertaining to the voyage having been discharged, the engraver prepared to cast his sea skin, and appear in his proper character. His sailor's dress he sold to one of his messmates, and with the aid of Delaware River water and Philadelphia soap, with a decent suit of London landsmen's clothes from his trunk or chest, he bade adieu to the ship, to seek his fortune on the shores of a new world. He had heard that his countryman, Mr. T. B. Freeman, resided in Philadelphia, and carried on his business as a publisher; and he waited upon him — stated his circumstances — his profession — his well-known name (well known to Englishmen from his father's celebrity), — and solicited employment. He was well received; in fact he was such a person as was wanted in America, especially in Philadelphia where the book-publishing business was in greater forwardness than in the more commercial metropolis of New York.

Mr. Benjamin Carr, mentioned by me in the "History of the American Theatre," was a friend of Mr. Freeman's, who was then about publishing a collection of Scotch airs selected by Carr; and Edwin was employed to engrave a title page. This was his first work in America; and at the time of commencing it he was destitute of the necessary tools, and could procure none in Philadelphia; the cause is not stated by my informant, certainly there were at that time several engravers in the city, and it would appear that some of them might have helped a brother in this state of destitution, as it regards tools. The engraver accidentally found in his seaman's chest, a graver which had been thrown into it at Amsterdam and forgotten. The shank of this tool, or that part which is inserted into the handle, he shaped as well as he could to his purpose, and commenced etching his plate therewith. As he proceeded with his work, he reversed the tool, tied a rag as a substitute for the handle, round the end he used as an etching point, and with this second contrivance finished the plate.

An engraver, at the time of Mr. Edwin's arrival in Philadelphia, had much to struggle with. He says in a letter before me, "copperplates were finished rough from the hammer;

no tools to be purchased, he (the engraver) had to depend upon his own ingenuity to fabricate them for himself, or in directing others qualified for the work; but worse than all was the slovenly style in which printing was executed. Often have I in extreme cold weather, waited hours for a proof, till the paper, oil, and even the roller could be thawed. The workshop of the principal printer in Philadelphia, was little better than a shell, and open to the winds. I once insisted that the printer should have the plank of his press planed and leveled, as it was impossible in the state it was now in to take off a tolerable impression; and the plate I wished printed had cost me much trouble in the execution; the printer resisted all my arguments for a long time, being himself perfectly satisfied with the state of his press: at length, and only in consideration of my paying the expense, it was that he gave his consent."

I have transcribed Mr. Edwin's statement of the rude imperfections attendant upon engraving and copperplate printing in Philadelphia in 1797. In New York, before that period, there were difficulties similar, no doubt; but as early as 1790, the writer, under the direction of Mr. Peter R. Maverick, found no difficulty in procuring tools for etching and engraving, and some prepared plates; and etched and scratched until he was satisfied that engraving required more skill, time, and patience, than he had to bestow upon it. Mr. Maverick was the best engraver then in New York; his competitors were indeed few and feeble. He was his own printer, and worked off his own proofs very comfortably, at his own press, in a comfortable workshop. In his printing he had an assistant. Mr. Edwin goes on to say, "Mr. Edward Savage, a portrait painter, was the only publisher of prints at that time. He published prints from pictures of his own painting, being sometimes painter, engraver, and printer."

Edwin engaged at one time with Savage,[1] and came on to New York, but how long he worked for him, or when he returned to Philadelphia, I do not know; probably he was in New York a very short time.

[1] See note, Vol. I, p. 381.

Mr. Edwin says, "At the time of my arrival in Philadelphia Dobson was publishing an edition of the Encyclopedia. It was thought a rash undertaking; and General Washington, on being asked to subscribe to the work, declared, that 'he thought Mr. Dobson a bold man.'" Now, as I was a subscriber to Dobson's work, I doubt not that Washington gave it every encouragement, being so much more able. The plates, at the time Edwin speaks of, were done by Thackara and Vallance, assisted by Lawson. Edwin, for many years, had all the portrait engraving in the United States.

"About the year 1801," he says, "I had the happiness of forming an acquaintance with Mr. Gilbert Stuart." I think he might have dated his happiness some years earlier, and been within the bounds of truth. "It took place on my undertaking to engrave a portrait of Dr. Smith (of the Pennsylvanian University), from Mr. Stuart's painting. The first meeting I had with the Doctor on the subject of the plate that was to be engraved, I shall not readily forget. The Doctor had been a schoolmaster; and although ignorant of the art of engraving, undertook to examine me on my capabilities. — He was old, hasty, and very irritable. He began in a broad Scotch dialect, by asking me if I could draw. But when we came to the price of the plate, I thought the poor Doctor would have gone distracted. He ran out and in the room, throwing at me angry and reproachful glances; and ended with the determination of paying me only half of my demand, which I accepted, considering the connection I should form with Mr. Stuart by undertaking the work of more value to me than any sum the Doctor could pay me for the plate."

At the commencement of the last war between America and Great Britain, Mr. Edwin informs me that there was no town of any consequence, from Maine to Louisiana, both inclusive, whose citizens were not in his debt for work done. He says, "I lost it nearly all; which, with a sickness, occasioned by an over-application to my business, caused in me a temporary disgust to my profession. I applied to Mr. T. B. Freeman, who, with his usual humanity, employed me as a clerk in his auction store. But, as they say, an old coachman loves the smack of the whip, so I, at most of my leisure hours, undertook small jobs in the engraving way: that of most consequence was my last — the last I ever shall engrave — the head of, I am proud to say, my friend and patron, G. Stuart, painted by Mr. John Neagle.

"Mr. T. B. Freeman meeting with difficulties in his business, I found myself, in the spring of 1831, of no further use to him, and quitted my station in his counting house. I then made some efforts to recommence engraving, but could get no publisher to trust me with a plate. In the winter of that same year I was seized with influenza (at that time a general complaint), which affected my head severely, and took from me the sight of one of my eyes, leaving me a prey to melancholy and distress."

Such is the account I received from this once excellent engraver; written in the month of April, 1833, at the age of 57. — A poor, broken-down, and prematurely old artist. In the month of June I visited Mr. Edwin, in company with my friend, Mr. Neagle; at which time he appeared in general good health and cheerful. An attempt was made to provide for his age, by procuring for him the situation of keeper of the Pennsylvania Academy of Fine Arts, when Mr. Thackara retired from the situation, but his friends did not succeed.

Since writing the above it has given me much pleasure to learn, that by a gift from Mrs. Francis (once of the profession of which Mr. Edwin's father was an ornament, and an old acquaintance of both Mr. and Mrs. Edwin), the old age of the engraver is amply provided for.[1]

JAMES SHARPLES.

This gentleman was an Englishman; and being of a Roman Catholic family, was educated in France, and intended, like John Kemble, for the priesthood; but, like John, he preferred

[1] Edwin died in Philadelphia February 22, 1841. His mother was Mrs. Walmsley, a milliner of Bath, England. A catalogue of his engraved work compiled by Mantle Fielding was issued (privately printed) in 1905.

the fine arts. He married before coming to this country; and on the first attempted passage was taken by the French, and, with his wife and three children, carried to France, and there kept as prisoners for some months. When liberated he made a more successful effort, and landed in New York about 1798.

He painted in oil; and I have seen a composition of his, wherein several of Doctor Darwin's family were portrayed: but his successful practice in this country was in crayons, or pastels, which he manufactured for himself; and suited, in size, to the diminutive dimensions of his portraits, which were generally *en profile*, and, when so, strikingly like.

He visited all the cities and towns of the United States, carrying letters to persons distinguished, either military, civil, or literary, with a request to paint their portraits for his collection. This being granted, and the portrait finished in about two hours, the likeness generally induced an order for a copy, and brought as sitters all who saw it. His price for the profile was $15; and for the full face (never so good) $20.

He painted immense numbers, and most of them very valuable, for characteristic portraiture. His headquarters was New York; and he generally travelled in a four-wheeled carriage of his own contrivance, which carried the whole family and all his implements, and was drawn by one large horse. — He was a plain, well-disposed man, and accumulated property by honest industry, and uncommon facility with his materials.

Previous to the establishment of his safe and methodical way of travelling, I witnessed a scene connected with this gentleman's itinerary movements which made a deep impression on me. I had joined the stage wagon, the usual travelling machine of those days, and with Mr. and Mrs. Sharples, with their three children (two boys and a girl), rode to Middletown, Connecticut, enjoying the picturesque beauties of the route with more zest, as my adult companions were capable of appreciating them. We stopped at the inn door, in the flourishing village of Middletown, about midday and in summer. I jumped out of the vehicle, to inquire for my friends of the Alsop family; and I soon saw the stage, with the horses at full run and no driver, pass me with the rapidity of lightning, the little girl alone in the carriage, and the distracted parents following, with outstretched arms and unavailing screams. On dashed the frightened horses with their light load, she perhaps unconscious of her danger; and soon deviating from the road, they struck the carriage against a post, overturned it with an awful crash, and, leaving it, pursued their race. All within sight of the accident ran to the spot with the distracted father and mother, looking to draw from the ruin the lacerated corpse of the child: when, on taking out the little creature, she was found perfectly unhurt, and restored to her parents as she had been left by them and the driver of the team to the mercy of four horses without guide or governor. I have travelled a great deal since then, but never saw a driver leave his horses without due security, but I thought of Middletown and the Sharpleses.

Mr. Sharples was a man of science and a mechanician, as well as a painter. In the first volume of the Hosack and Francis' " Medical and Philosophical Register " will be found a paper on steam carriages, confirming this character.

Mr. Sharples had acquired property without meanness, and looked to the enjoyment of easy circumstances in old age, when he died suddenly, at the age of 60, in New York, of an ossification of the heart, and was buried in the cemetery of the Roman Catholic chapel in Barclay Street. His widow, her daughter, and youngest son, returned to England, and long resided near Bath, after selling the *distinguished heads* (among which I had the honor to be numbered) at public auction.

The two sons both practised their father's art in America: James, the younger, presented me with a copy of my friend Elihu E. Smith's portrait before leaving the country. Felix resided and died in North Carolina.[01]

01 James Sharples was born in England in 1751. He had been educated in France for the Roman Catholic priesthood but forsook the church for the fine arts, returning to his native country where he married. In 1793 he came to this country and in 1796 his portrait in pastel of Washington was made in Philadelphia. This was the last sitting Washington gave to a painter. Sharples visited many parts of the country sometimes

painting in oil, but generally in pastel, and making his own crayons. He died in New York February 26, 1811.

George W. P. Custis says in a letter, written four months before his death, to Thomas William Channing Moors, of New York: "The finest and purest likeness of the chief is the original picture in crayon by Sharpless, done in 1796, and with the original by Peale in 1772, of the Provincial Colonel, forms the first and last of the originals of Washington most to be relied upon in the world. Stuart's is the great original of the first president of the U. S.; Peale's, of the colonial officer; Sharpless', of the man." In another letter to the same a month later, he says: "I assured Lord Napier, who made me an especial visit to inspect the treasures, that the Sharpless (original from life) was the best likeness of the man extant. Trumbull for the figure, Stuart for the head, and Sharpless for the expression, and you have all you can have of the portraiture of Washington." (The name is commonly spelled incorrectly Sharpless, as above.)

CHAPTER XIV.

John Wesley Jarvis

Was the best portrait painter in the city of New York for many years. He was, like many of our artists who are strictly American, born in England. The nephew of the great law-giver of Methodism, the place of his birth was South Shields, on the Tyne, and the time, the year 1780. His father emigrating to America, left him with his uncle until he was five years of age. Had he remained longer under the roof of that extraordinary man, even a few years, when the first, best impressions are made, it might have been well for the embryo painter. He might have been a preacher, and if so, one of the most popular in America. Or he might have been introduced to a guide, who would have made his talents a blessing to himself and the world. Even at the early age of five some impression must have been made upon the boy by the orderly mode of life he saw practised among those around him; an order and regularity which he in after life seemed to mock by the arrangements or disarrangements of his own ever shifting places of abode.

Jarvis's father having taken up his residence in Philadelphia,[1] the child was conveyed to that city, and there received his second education; for even at five years of age, the first must have been impressed upon the tender mind of his infancy. Was not the boy's conduct in the following transaction guided as his mind had been moulded in early childhood? Or was it the unsophisticated workings of that inclination to good which we receive from the Creator, that prompted his tongue and his action?

While John was yet an urchin, "with shining morning face,

---

[1] John Wesley Jarvis came to America with his parents to Philadelphia in 1785. He died January 12, 1840.

creeping like snail unwillingly to school," and munching a
huge piece of bread and butter, which he had demanded after
breakfast, more to prolong the time before he must resign his
liberty to the schoolmaster's despotism, than because he
wanted food — on his way to the dreaded mansion, he passed
an unoccupied building in Water Street, and his attention was
arrested by sobs coming from the house to which he was opposite, and which had been partly torn down, and so left for the
accommodation of the proprietor (until he saw the best time
for rebuilding) and of any vagrant who wanted shelter. Having ascertained the quarter from whence the signs of distress
came, John Wesley, still munching his luncheon, unconsciously
overloading his stomach (if a child's stomach can be over-
loaded), entered the deserted place with feelings of curiosity,
if not humanity (perhaps mixed, as most of our motives are),
but the latter soon prevailed, when he saw a little fellow,
younger than himself, seated on the broken floor and crying
bitterly. "What's the matter, little boy?" said the young
Englishman, suspending the operation of his masticators. The
tone of sympathy increased the sobs of the forlorn child.
"Don't cry! tell me what's the matter?" "I've lost my father,
and I'm hungry." The idea of being hungry, especially as
that was the last word, had more powerful influence on the
feelings of the commiserating boy than the loss of a father.
"Hungry," he cried, "why have you had no breakfast?" "I
have not had anything to eat since I lost my father," sobbed
the little sufferer. "When was that?" "Yesterday morning.
He went to sea in the "Sally" while I was playing up at the head
of the wharf." "Where's your mother?" "Mother's dead. I
slept here last night. I'm very hungry." "Here, take this, and
I'll get you more."

The little urchin fell to work upon the remains of the bread
and butter, and his friend sat down by his side comforting him,
and now and then asking him a question. Jarvis saw the bread
and butter, seasoned with tears, demolished, and then said,
"Come, I've got a father — he'll take care of you — come with
me." And willingly forgetting school, he took the little fel-

low's hand and trudged back to his home, to place him under the protection of one he knew from experience could give him bread and butter. The father of John soon found out the owners of the ship "Sally," and they received and took care of the little orphan until the return of his father.

It appeared that the father of the boy was mate of a ship bound to Europe, and intended taking this motherless child with him. He had made every arrangement, and, that the boy might be out of "*harm's way*," had ordered him to keep in his stateroom, where he thought him safe stowed away at the time the ship sailed; meanwhile the boy had slyly stolen on shore and joined in play, just without sight of the vessel, and when he looked to get back again, lo! she was gone.

With the father hours had passed in attending to his arduous duties before he thought of liberating his little prisoner; and we must imagine his feelings when the child was not to be found. The boy had been seen to go on shore. That quieted one of the mate's fears. The captain, a brutal man, would not put back — said the owners would take care of the boy — he would lose wind and tide — and the mate submitted. But when the ship had cleared the river and the capes of Delaware, and the pilot was about returning, the father of the lost boy threw his sea-chest and himself into the pilot boat and returned in search of his child. The owners commended his desertion, and found him another berth for himself and the little runaway.

We may imagine the feelings of the mate on his return, when he found his boy safe — and his gratitude to little John Wesley.

Such were the feelings — such the actions prompted by nature, before the world, or the miscalled pleasures of the world, perverted the heart or the instinct. Before I proceed regularly with the biography of John Wesley Jarvis, I will as a contrast to the above, repeat a story which Jarvis, when a man, often told of himself, as I am informed. Being on a party of pleasure in the neighborhood of New York, his attention was attracted to a sturdy boy who was playing near him, perfectly unmindful and independent of Jarvis and his companions, their wine, their cigars, or their bursts of merriment. The painter admired the boy, and with his usual playful manner and laughing eyes, addressed the child, and at the same time called the notice of the company to him. "What's your name, my man?" "My name's John, and I'm not your man." "That's a fine fellow — John? a very good name. It's my name too. Have you any other name?" "Yes, I have." "That's right! what is it?" "Wesley." "Wesley! John Wesley! that's my name too. Have you any more names?" "Yes, I have." "So much the better — the more the merrier. What's your other name?" "Jarvis." "That's odd enough — that's my name too. Who's your father?" "Jarvis, the painter — and mother says he is a very bad man."

I must go back to Philadelphia and the days of the painter's childhood. Jarvis has said, "In my schoolboy days the painters in Philadelphia were Clark, a miniature painter —Gallagher, a painter of portraits and signs, he was a German who, with his hat over one eye, was more *au fait* at walking Chestnut Street, than at either face or sign painting — then there was Jeremiah Paul, who painted better and would hop farther than any of them — another, who painted red lions and black bears, as well as beaux or belles, was old Mr. Pratt, and the last that I remember of that day was Rutter, an honest sign painter, who never pretended or aspired to paint the human face divine, except to hang on the outside of a house: these worthies, when work was plenty — flags and fire-buckets, engines and eagles in demand — used to work in partnership, and I, between school hours, worked for them all, delighted to have the command of a brush and a paint pot. Such was my introduction to the 'fine arts' and their professors.

"About this time I first saw Stuart, who occasionally employed Paul to letter a book — for example, the books in the portrait of Washington, which Jerry thought it no dishonor to execute: the two great men, however, quarrelled, and Paul threatened to slap Stuart's face — trusting. I presume, to being able to hop out of the way of his arm. Mr. Pratt was at this time, say 1790, an old man, and as he encouraged my visits,

I frequently passed my out-of-school hours at his shop, making figures of what passed for men and things by dint of daubing on my part, and imagination on the part of the beholder.

"Dr. Rush, seeing my propensity to have a hand in the manufactory of monsters, the many-colored offspring of this combination of genius, persuaded my father, as the time had arrived when I must learn something besides *learning*, or expect to starve with the Philadelphia market at my elbow, to make a painter of me. But I did not like the prospect of making one in a partnership of Paul, Pratt, Rutter, and Gallagher; and as I saw in the prints displayed at the shop windows, something much more perfect, and more to my taste, I preferred being an engraver. To this my father assented, and Savage being at that time the publisher of prints, some of which with his name to them I then admired, I was bound apprentice to the most ignorant beast that ever imposed upon the public. He painted what he called fancy pieces and historical subjects, and they were published as being designed and engraved by him, though his painting was execrable, and he knew nothing of engraving. He was not qualified to teach me any art but that of deception. There he was a master — at drawing or painting I was *his* master. Fortunately, as he could neither draw nor engrave, it was necessary for him to employ one who could, and who did not wish the honor of having his name affixed to the fancies of the Savage.

"Mr. David Edwin had arrived in America with more skill than money, and Savage engaged him to engrave for him. Not long after this my master removed to New York, and took Edwin with him. I followed of course. From Mr. Edwin I learned to draw and to engrave, and we worked for the fame and profit of the *great Savage*.[1] Yet I had no intention of becoming a portrait painter. Edwin returned to Philadelphia, and soon, by engraving some of Stuart's portraits, became known and extensively employed. I made all my master's pictures, engraved them, printed them, and delivered them to customers. I remained with him until my time of service ex-

[1] See note, Vol. I, p. 381.

pired, and, 'bating some pranks and unlucky tricks, I served him faithfully.

"I began to engrave on my own account; but Edwin visiting New York, asked me to go and see a great portrait painter, not long since arrived, and full of employment — with of course his pockets full of money. I went to the painting room of Mr. Martin, and found him overwhelmed with business. 'This,' said Edwin, 'is the best portrait painter in New York.' 'If that is the case,' said I, 'I will be the best portrait painter in New York tomorrow, for I can paint better than Mr. Martin.' And I have been at it ever since."

I reminded Jarvis of a portrait of Hogg, the comedian, very like, but flat and dingy, which I had seen when honest John Hogg kept a porter house in Nassau Street. "That was one of my first," said Jarvis, "and my old friend Gallagher, being then in New York, helped me. I was the best painter, because others were worse than bad — so *bad* was the best. There was a man of the name of Buddington, who shared in face making; but I beat him at it."

My first recollections of Mr. Jarvis, go no further back than about 1805-6. He had in conjunction with Mr. Joseph Wood for some time occupied rooms in Park Row, between the theatre and Beekman Street; here, he says, he taught Wood to draw "from the round," and as Wood applied himself particularly to miniature painting, he seized an accidental opportunity of introducing him to Malbone; and *his* instruction made Wood an artist. Malbone came into the painting room of Jarvis with some ladies, to see the pictures, and Jarvis having before seen him, entered into conversation, and took an opportunity to call in Wood, and introduce him as one wishing instruction in miniature painting. This led to the offer on Malbone's part to impart any knowledge he possessed; and to his instructing both Jarvis and Wood, in his mode of proceeding, from the preparation of ivory to the finishing the picture, and they both became painters of miniature.

Mr. Jarvis tells me that about this time he invented a machine for drawing profiles on glass. The outline being rapidly drawn on one side the glass, was blacked as rapidly on the other; and for each of these, he and Wood (both worked at it, and occasionally an assistant, hired by the day) had a dollar — they likewise made the profiles on gold leaf, shadowing a little by hatching — for each of these they had five dollars, and frequently shared between them a hundred dollars a day. This was of course while the thing was a novelty. These were piping times — and what with Jarvis's humor, Wood's fiddling and fluting — and the painting executed by each, they had a busy and merry time of it. But I fear *"merry and wise,"* was never the maxim which guided either.

The artists indulged in the excitements, and experienced the perplexities of *mysterious marriages;* and it is probable that these perplexities kept both poor, and confined them to the society of young men, instead of that respectable communion with ladies, and the refined circles of the city, which Malbone enjoyed: and I have reason to think, that these mysteries and perplexities caused the dissolution of the partnership of Jarvis and Wood on no friendly terms.

I remember Mr. Jarvis in a painting room in Broadway, nearly opposite the City Hotel, fully occupied in painting profile portraits on Bristol board at five dollars each; very like and very pretty. Portraits in oil, or miniatures on ivory, were done if required.

Those studies which are necessary to the formation of a good painter, were not neglected by Jarvis. He studied anatomy with Dr. John Augustine Smith; and when my friend Dr. John W. Francis returned from Europe, in the year 1816, bringing with him the splendid edition of Gall and Spurzheim, whose work my friend was warmly interested in, he showed it to Jarvis — Jarvis asked the favor of studying the book. He kept the volume many months. "When I afterwards saw him," says Dr. Francis, "he remarked, 'this book of Spurzheim's elevates our art to a science: it has principles of value to the artist. If I have any merit as a portrait painter, so be it; I may have depicted Lavater: but Spurzheim renders the artist the phrenological delineator. Look at even Houbraken's

heads; see the portraits in the " Spectator ": every forehead is
of the same height — every pericranium of the same rotundity
— every wig of the same form and dimensions.' " Jarvis may
probably be considered the first painter in this country who
applied phrenological science to the principles of the art of
portrait painting.

Jarvis studied Gall and Spurzheim assiduously. He thought
he saw in the science great advantage to the painter, and
entered into the views of the phrenologists most enthusiastically. He likewise studied modelling in clay, and a head of
Thomas Paine, who wrote "Common Sense," and played the
fool, is now in the library of the Historical Society, modelled
by Jarvis. These men were at one time intimates and house-
mates, — how much the painter profited by the precepts
and example of Tom Paine, in the latter stage of his existence,
the reader may judge. He could not but admire his genius;
and few things are more dangerous than admiration of a misled
man of uncommon talents.

Baltimore was the field in which our painter reaped a rich
harvest for more than one year. He left his family in New
York. I remember that in returning from Philadelphia, I
joined Jarvis in the Raritan steamboat, and he told me he
came from Baltimore, and should return again; but it being
late in April, he came on to New York to see to the moving of
his family on the first of May, according to the custom of
the place.

Jarvis could not, or would not see the merit of Stuart. He
occasionally had commissions to copy portraits by Stuart, and
it appeared to me, that with all his cleverness, he could not
imitate Stuart's coloring. I saw him at work upon a copy of
Judge Benson, and remarked the difference of tone. "I will
give the color of nature," said Jarvis, "that's not nature,"
pointing to the original. I have seen a letter of his, in which,
speaking of Stuart's pictures, he says, "I should like to set
my name down amongst those who do not think him so great,
as some say he is."

In the autumn of 1807, Mr. Sully's business in New York

had so slackened, that he offered himself to Jarvis as an assistant, — the latter having then the run. Jarvis said it was a great shame, that such a man should want to work as his assistant; but he gave Sully employment, and paid him liberally.

Mr. Sully once told me, that calling on Jarvis, he was shown into his room, and left to wait some minutes before he entered. He saw a book on the table amidst palettes, brushes, tumblers, candlesticks and other heterogeneous affairs, and on opening it, he found a life of Morland. When Jarvis came into the room, Sully sat with his hand on the book, which lay open on the table. "Do you know why I like that book?" said Jarvis. "I suppose because it is the life of a painter," was the reply. "Not merely that," rejoined the other, "it is because I think he was like myself."

What reflections do such a remark suggest! That a man could possibly derive pleasure from contemplating such an image as the life and character of Morland presents, and at the same time consider it as a likeness of himself, is incomprehensible. My readers probably know that Morland was a greater brute than the pigs he delighted to portray: but Jarvis was a man of far superior character, both for intellect and feeling, than Morland.

The last anecdote reminds me of the usual appearance of this eccentric man's painting room. Easels, palettes, some fresh set and others with dry paint on them, brushes, clean or otherwise, pictures finished, or half finished, or just begun, a table in the centre of the room with glasses, bottles, decanters, empty or half full, chalk, and scraps of paper, with or without sketches, and in the midst, perhaps, a lady's hat and shawl. Once, in addition to all this, when I entered his room at his request, I found his wife with her infant and a cradle, with all the etceteras of a nursery. This was not a *mysterious wife*, but a delicate and ladylike woman, before marriage Miss ——, and used to those comforts which result from order, and may be obtained at much less expense both of money and of time, than the *discomforts* arising from con-

fusion, carelessness, waste, and extravagance. Besides the
above-mentioned mass of heterogeneous materials, I saw a
side table with a set of musical glasses, on which he gave me
a tune with great adroitness. With the utmost profusion in
lavishing money, there appeared to be in Jarvis no notion of
order or comfort, and much less of elegance; on the contrary,
all around him evinced, if not a studied, at least an over-
whelming confusion — a chaos *hastening to destruction*.

Mr. Jarvis was fond of notoriety from almost any source,
and probably thought it aided him in his profession. His
dress was generally unique. His long coat, trimmed with
furs like a Russian prince or potentate from the north pole,
must be remembered by many; and his two enormous dogs,
which accompanied him through the streets, and often carried
home his market basket, will be remembered by all who were
children in New York at the time.

We shall see that later in life the painter visited the cities
further south than Baltimore; and by his humor, his convivial talents, his story telling, and his untiring capability of
remaining at the table, as well as by his talents as an artist
became the favored guest of the proverbially hospitable
South. Generally in New York in the summer, he received
his Southern friends in their annual passage to and from the
springs and the Canadas, and was happy to return, in his way,
their dinners and suppers. This was done with the same profusion and confusion as he ordered other affairs. One of these
dinners, as described to me by one of the guests, will serve to
elucidate his character, and I will attempt to repeat the
description.

Some Southerners having arrived, to whom he wished to
return civilities and do honor, the painter invited several
gentlemen of note to meet them. This was before his marriage
with the lady above named. He then had his rooms in Wall
Street, and Pierre Van Wyke, the recorder of the city, had
his office below, in the same house. With Van Wyke, as with
most of the gentlemen of the city at that time, he was intimate; and among others Van Wyke and G. C. Verplanck were

invited to meet the strangers. They sat down to a table pro-
fusely covered with every good and costly viand the market
could afford; venison, pheasants, and canvas-back ducks
tempted the appetite, although knives with broken handles,
and forks with one prong made the operations of carving and
eating somewhat awkward and difficult, and excited no little
surprise among the guests who were not aware of the painter's
habits. Wine was as plenty and of as great variety as the
meats, and the wine glasses of various sizes, but principally
of the largest calibre and most profound depth, such as would
not allow of the repetition of Sam Foote's pun — however old
the liquor — "Your glass of wine is very little of its age," —
it would not apply here. The mode of opening a bottle (decanters there were none) was by breaking off the top of the
cork and thrusting the remainder down the neck with a greasy
fork — a corkscrew would have smacked too much of order.

"Jarvis," said the recorder, "I want some small drink —
here's nothing but wine." "Give the recorder the brandy
bottle!" "No, no, give me some small beer, or some water."
"We don't know such things — there is porter and ale."
"Some ale, then." "Tom! give the recorder some ale." After
a pause, Van Wyke says, "Jarvis, where is this ale of yours?"
"Tom! why don't you give the recorder some ale?" "There's
no tumbler, sir." "No tumbler!" "No, sir." "Well, throw
the soap out of my shaving cup."

In the course of Mr. Jarvis's very extensive practice, he
painted the portrait of Bishop Benjamin Moore, of New
York; and that eminently worthy gentleman used to tell of
one of Jarvis's quick and humorous thoughts with great glee.
During one of the sittings, religion became the subject of conversation, and the bishop asked Jarvis some questions relative
to his belief or his practice. The painter, with an arch look,
but as if intent upon catching the likeness of the sitter, waved
his hand and said, "Turn your face more that way, and *shut
your mouth.*"

In the year 1808 (or 9), Mr. Jarvis married the lady mentioned in a preceding page, and I believe about the same time

raised his prices to $100 for a head, and $150 for head and hands. Some time before, I find by a letter of John Randolph, of Roanoke, that he paid Jarvis for his portrait $80. The size is not mentioned. It may be presumed that raising the price diminished the number of sitters in New York; be that as it may, the painter, in the autumn of 1810, visited Charleston, South Carolina, where he found no objection to his prices, and a welcome reception given to his inexhaustible fund of table entertainment.

In or about the year 1814, Mr. Jarvis had possession, I presume by purchase, of Wertmüller's " Danaë "; and exhibited it in the same house in which he painted, in Murray Street, near Broadway. Here Henry Inman became his pupil, or apprentice: but Jarvis had, soon after, better accommodations at the old Bowling Green house, built for the president of the United States at the adoption of the federal constitution — afterward assigned to the governor of the State, and for a time occupied by Governor George Clinton; but at the time of which we speak, divided between the collector of the customs, Jarvis, and the gods. The lower part of the building was the custom house, and in the upper the casts sent from Paris by Chancellor Livingston were deposited, and there Jarvis had his painting room. This was a good opportunity for the study of the antique, and no doubt was useful to the painter and his pupils. In the summer of 1813, Mr. Jarvis painted in Baltimore, and his pictures exhibited in Philadelphia are catalogued as of Jarvis of Baltimore.

When he went, for the first time, to New Orleans, he took Henry Inman with him. To use his own words — "My purse and pockets were empty. I spent 3000 dollars in six months, and brought 3000 to New York. The next winter I did the same."

He used to receive six sitters a day. A sitting occupied an hour. The picture was then handed to Henry Inman, who painted upon the background and drapery under the master's directions. Thus six portraits were finished each week.

This was said in the summer of 1834, after having passed

the previous winter at the same place, and returned a paralytic. The organs of speech which once kept the table in a roar, were no longer at the command of the enfeebled mind and imperfect memory, and could only by painful effort be brought to give sluggish utterance to disjointed language. He said he had not painted while at New Orleans last winter; he could not get a room to suit him; there were none but three-story rooms to be had, and ladies would not go up in the garret. "I roomed with Hill, who plays the Yankee characters; I used to go to the theatre every night through the mud. One night I fell down in the mud, and I lamed my arm; I could not get up again; and there I lay till three watchmen picked me up; one of them gave me my knife and I walked off. 'Why he is not drunk,' says one to t'other." Mr. Jarvis has often and habitually shown his care for, and love of his fellow creatures; he now knows that it is man's duty to care for his own prosperity — to love himself, that the love to his neighbor may be efficient. To preserve the gifts bestowed upon us is a duty, which if not performed, brings repentance. In a letter before me he thus speaks of the place where a few years ago every house was open to him, and he spent his thousands in a few months, and brought away thousands in his pocket. "New Orleans is more disagreeable than ever; I say nothing about the mud; but a lodging was not to be had. I did not know what to do. I thought I would have to cut my throat, get drunk, or sleep with a negro. But now I have a room to sleep in — they call it boarding — the weather has been decent these few days, so I went to market to see if there was anything in it. I saw some beef, alias carrion, a few pokes, *an owl*, some crows, a few toadstools, and a smoked dog." But with a constitution of uncommon strength, and uninterrupted health, it took years to produce this wreck — years, passed, as it would appear to some, in pleasure — to others in a mad pursuit of misery.

But it was immediately after Jarvis's two *first* visits to New Orleans that he painted those full-length portraits of military and naval heroes which will keep him in public remembrance for a short-lived immortality, by their situation in the City

Hall of New York, and their great merit. These pictures, by being the most difficult works he ever executed, tested the knowledge he had obtained by his exertions amidst apparent inattention to study and real waste of nature's gifts in dissipation. They are historical portraits, painted with skill and force — real representations of men and character; throwing most of the pictures painted for the city of New York previously, far in the background. In the year 1812 I remember meeting Jarvis in that room, afterward enriched by his pencil, and *even then* he anticipated painting full-lengths for the corporation of the city. The pictures then in the room were the governors of the State painted by Trumbull. "One of these days," said Jarvis, "you and I will be employed in painting for this room." "You may," I replied, "but there are no miniatures wanted." This was some time before I attempted to recover my oil brush. "We shall see," was Jarvis's rejoinder. He did see; and performed the task he was called to very much to his credit; although it is little to the credit of the *then* rulers of the city, that no specimen of Stuart's unrivaled pencil is to be found on the walls of its public hall.

After the war was over, and no more heroes were to be made by the cannon's mouth or the pencil's point, Jarvis continued to visit the South in the winter and return North in the summer, like the Carolinians and the snipe and woodcock. Having returned to New York from Charleston or New Orleans, he met an old acquaintance in the street and saluted him with the usual "How d'ye do?" The reply was, "Very well, I'm always well; and how are you?" "*Well?*" cried Jarvis; "*Well!* I have not heard such an answer to that question for many a month. We don't talk so in the South." "Why, what do they say there to a 'how are you?'" "Rather better today than I was yesterday; but not so well as I was last Wednesday."

To sing a good song is the bane of many a good fellow, and the merry story teller frequently makes his home a house of mourning, while he sinks an object of pity to a premature grave. It is an old Joe Miller joke that the fiddle of the company is hung behind the street door when the master visits his family; but I am afraid it is too true to be considered a joke.

I will endeavor to give the reader a faint idea of some of the stories which made the highly gifted man we are considering a Yorick at the convivial board. Not that I can give his words or convey any notion of his peculiar manner — a manner which gave point to a remark which, from another, might pass unnoticed.

In the year 1826 I met him in the Park on a rejoicing day. "When I see *our folks* at such times as this," said he, "it puts me in mind of the story of the young man from the interior, who, coming to New York, went on board one of our frigates, and it happened while he was there a salute was fired by the ship. 'By God!' he exclaimed, 'we are a great people!' "

An artist, now of high standing, told me that some years ago, as he was travelling in the stage to the seat of government, his attention was attracted to a fellow passenger by the utter want of decency in his appearance and conduct. His mouth was in a disgustingly filthy condition from his chewing a piece of a cigar, while streams of yellow saliva issued from the corners, descending upon and staining his shirt. During the ride this filthy figure took a miniature from his pocket and showed it to the young artist, asking his opinion. He praised it, but remarked something he thought wrong. "Aha! you are an artist." The young man felt that he ought not to accept the title and evaded giving an answer, but asked who painted the picture. "I did," and after a time his dirty companion announced himself as Jarvis. After arriving at Washington he met him at a ball, and was introduced to him. He was now dressed in black, and appeared like a gentleman. — "I observed," said the young man, "that he was well known to many, but always addressed with a familiarity little allied to respect."

Some of his humor was what is called manual; not precisely that refined wit which removes the chair from the expectant sitter and displays him prostrate for the delight of an enlightened company; but preserving so much of the character that one friend is exposed in his peculiarities or weaknesses for the amusement of other friends.

It will appear strange to many, and I confess that it appears strange to me, although the fact has been long known, that men of the first standing in our society, rich men, elderly men, with families at home, should habitually meet at a porter-house to drink beer or brandy, and seek amusement in the babble that beer and brandy generate. At a certain porter-house in New York Jarvis frequently appeared, and met several men much older than himself, with others, and amused one part of the company by *playing off* another. Three or four of these worthies had hobbies which they delighted to ride. A cashier of a bank made astronomy his study — a rich merchant directed the movements of the European armies — an old ship captain quoted poetry by the yard, and other prosers had nags equally unsuited for their bestriding. Jarvis's joke was to sit by the astronomer and drink and smoke until he had got him among the stars; then steal off unperceived, and set the merchant to moving armies, and the captain to moving heaven and earth with divine poesy, and thus, having got all the talkers involved in words and smoke, he would move to a convenient distance, and with those who were in the secret, enjoy the confusion of tongues and subjects, each smoking his cigar very seriously, and occasionally putting in a question to keep up the motion of the hobby riders.

It is said, that on seeing a tall, melancholy looking French-man walking very solemnly down Broadway, with a very large cigar box under his arm, Jarvis placed himself immediately behind, imitated his funereal step; and as he saw an acquaint-ance likely to join in the fun, he would by signs bring him to follow in the train; until he got up a string of some length, walking in solemn procession. The bearer of the box, on turning a corner, looked round and saw that he had a suite of attendants, of whose motives he could form no notion. He stopped — the procession stopped. "Gentlemens, vat you mean? Vat you mean, gentlemens?" Jarvis answered, "See-ing that you were a foreigner, sir, and no friends to assist you at the burial of your child, we thought to show our respect by attending the funeral."

While residing at the hospitable mansion of a southern planter, the owner being for some days absent, the painter played the following freak. The house stood a little way from the road; a gate being in front, and near it a large dog kennel, which had not for years had an inhabitant. Jarvis took paints and brush, and wrote on this doghouse, in front and on the sides, "Take care of the dog." It was then his amusement to see the passing neighbors or travellers approach, and suddenly stop — read the inscription, and cautiously cross to the other side of the road. If a horseman came cantering up, the speed was checked and the road crossed, or a spur given to the steed, and a quickened pace insured. — Those who wished to come to the house avoided the gate, and took a back way — "Take care of the dog," changed the course of the whole county. At length the owner of the plantation returned; and, startled as the rest had been, avoided the gate. "Why, Jarvis, what have you got in the dog kennel?" "A dog, to be sure! come and see." They went — and the painter took out of the dog house a puppy which had not yet seen the light. "Poor little fellow!" said Jarvis, "don't you think it is necessary to *take care* of him?"

At Charleston, South Carolina, where he long continued a great favorite, on one occasion, at a large dinner party, after the wine had circulated freely, and had banished form; and from some of the convivialists, not only form but discretion; it was proposed that the company should club, and make up a sum, which should be the prize to the man who told the greatest and most palpable *lie*. This was readily agreed to, and the prize sum deposited. The president began — and the monkey's tail, of a mile in length, was nothing to what he had seen in his travels. Lie followed lie; and as it is easy to heap absurdity upon absurdity, and extravagance on enormous exaggeration; and as easy to excite laughter and command applause, where champagne has been enthroned in the seat of judgment — each lie was hailed with shouts of approbation and bursts of merriment. One of the company, who sat next to Jarvis, had exceeded all the competitors, and unanimous admiration seemed to insure to him the prize. The *lie* was so monstrous and so palpable, that it was thought wit or ingenuity could not equal it. Still something was expected from the famous story teller, and every eye was turned on the painter. He appeared to be very serious; and placing his hand on his breast and bowing his head, he gravely said, "Gentlemen, I assure you that I fully and unequivocally believe every word the last gentleman has uttered." A burst of applause followed, and the prize was adjudged to Jarvis.

The habit of entertaining boon companions, and "setting the table in a roar," unfits a man for domestic comfort. Mr. Jarvis's marriage was not a happy one. A separation took place, and the mother withheld her children from their father. Legal interference made this unhappy state of things public and made the painter more and more reckless of the world's opinion, and apparently regardless of his own welfare.

It was about four years ago, *i.e.* 1830, that I met Mr. Jarvis in Broadway. I had not seen him for many months. He reproached me for not having called upon him. I told him I did not know where he lived. "Come with me and I will show you." Although it was not yet noon, I perceived that it was late in the day with Jarvis.

We turned down Vesey Street, and walked towards his quarters; and by the way he expatiated largely upon a plan he had for painting two large pictures for exhibition. "In one," said he, "I show the effects of bad habits, and strong liquor. I will paint a farmhouse with everything around it going or gone to ruin: fences down — gates broken or unhinged — windows shattered, and old hats and petticoats for panes of glass — the man of the house in rags and bloated, reeling home from a tavern — his wife sallow, dispirited and sick — the children neglected, filthy, and crying for bread. In the other picture I will exhibit the effects of industry and temperance, on another farmhouse and its inmates. The house and fences neat and painted white; — all serene around, and in the distance a golden harvest. The white house, shaded by luxuriant fruit trees, the man full of health and vigor, having returned from the field, has his blooming children around him, and is plucking cherries for them, while his wife, full of health and smiling with content, looks at him she loves, and invites him in to his meal. In short, such a place as the abode of temperance must be."

By this time we had arrived at the abode of the artist, who could conceive and describe these scenes, and a commentary on the text was given. In the front room was an easel, a palette and brushes, with the paint dried upon them. Two or three bad unfinished portraits on the floor, confused furniture in scant quantity, and a little dirty boy. The painter threw open a door, and invited me into a back apartment. It was small, and on one side was a bed, and on the other a pile of wood. Opposite to the door was a kind of cupboard. The centre of the room was occupied by a table with bottles and glasses. He opened the cupboard, and took out a decanter of brandy, a pitcher of water, and two tumblers, for which he found room on the table. "Come," said he, "drink?" "No," I replied, "I belong to the white house." "Well, well," said he, filling a tumbler more than half full of brandy, "if you will not drink, you shall see me drink," and adding some water, swallowed the whole. The result of such conduct has been seen. At the age of fifty-four, an age at which men, with half the vigor that he had been blessed with by nature, are strong in body, and more strong in mind than at earlier periods, his mind and body are destroyed. The excellent artist cannot paint — the tongue which delighted the hearer is paralyzed — the memory which furnished ideas for a rich imagination to combine, is no more. With a frame of iron, and constitution of steel — with a mind to contrive, and hand to execute — nature had endowed this extraordinary man; but the good gifts were misused, the blessing of health and strength counteracted by poisons, and the name of John Wesley Jarvis, a man of great talents and kind disposition, can only be used "to point a moral or adorn a tale."

Mr. Jarvis was never a hypocrite nor a sycophant. His manners were not what are styled courteous, but they were always frank. In prosperity and adversity he met the first and best of the land as an equal. He did not disparage the works of other artists, either by words or by smiles which conveyed a sneer of contempt. Stuart alone he made war on — but it was open war on one who could defend himself. I never knew him to refuse his advice or assistance to an artist. To me he was always friendly, as an artist and a man. The depreciation of his powers has been long gradually more and more apparent, and it is due to truth that the cause should be pointed out, and particularly due to every professor of the fine arts.

I shall conclude my account of Jarvis with an extract from a communication concerning him from Dr. Francis:

"Dr. Syntax never with more avidity sought after the sublime and picturesque, than did Jarvis after the scenes of many-colored life; whether his subject was the author of ' Common Sense' or the notorious Baron Von Hoffman. His stories, particularly those connected with his southern tours, abounded in motley scenes and ludicrous occurrences; there was no lacking of hair-breadth escapes, whether the incidents involved the collisions of intellect, or sprung from alligators and rattle-snakes. His humor won the admiration of every hearer, and he is recognized as the master of anecdote. But he deserves to be remembered on other accounts," continues Dr. F., "his corporeal intrepidity and reckless indifference of consequences. I believe there have been not a few of the faculty who have exercised, with public advantage, their professional duties among us for a series of years, who never became as familiar with the terrific scenes of yellow fever and of malignant cholera as Jarvis did. He seemed to have a singular desire to become personally acquainted with the details connected with such occurrences; and a death-bed scene, with all its appalling circumstances, in a disorder of a formidable character, was sought after by him with the solicitude of the inquirer after fresh news. Nor was this wholly an idle curiosity. Jarvis often freely gave of his limited stores to the indigent, and he listened with a fellow feeling to the recitals of the profuse liberality with which that opulent merchant of our city, the late Thomas H. Smith,* supplied daily the wants of the afflicted and necessitous sufferer during the pestilence of 1822.

"We are indebted to Jarvis for probably the best, if not the only good drawing of the morbid effects of cholera on the human body while it existed here in 1832. During that season of dismay and danger our professional artists declined visiting the cholera hospitals, and were reluctant to delineate when the subject was brought to them. But it afforded a new topic for the consideration of Jarvis, and perhaps also for the better display of his anatomical attainments, he with promptitude discharged the task. When making a drawing from the lifeless and morbid organs of digestion, to one who inquired if he were not apprehensive of danger while thus employed, he put the interrogatory, 'Pray what part of the system is affected by the cholera?' 'The digestive organs,' was the reply. 'Oh no, then,' said Jarvis, 'for now you see I am doubly armed — I am furnished with two sets.' " [1]

[1] In the original edition several pages were devoted to dinner-table stories related by Jarvis on various occasions. These are here omitted as having no relation to art, to Jarvis, or to any persons connected with the subject of the book and as unnecessary to a further knowledge of Jarvis' peculiarities.

* This distinguished merchant was proverbially known as a man of unbounded liberality in the days of his adversity as well as of prosperity. During the prevalence of the yellow fever in 1822, he almost daily visited the abodes of sickness in different parts of New-York, and he often appropriated, of his own private funds, some fifty, one hundred, or more dollars in the course of the day, to the relief of the afflicted sufferers.

CHAPTER XV.

Wood — B. H. Latrobe — Sully.

Joseph Wood.

Mr. Wood was born at Clarkstown, Orange County, State of New York. His father was a respectable farmer, and wished his son to follow in his steps.

When Joseph was fifteen years of age he had gleaned some tidings of painters and their high estate, and feeling confident in his powers with the pencil, he determined to seek his fortune in New York.

He was attracted by some miniature pictures in the window of a silversmith's shop. He offered himself to this silversmith as an apprentice, and was received. These miniatures seem to have decided his future employment; for being permitted to attempt to make a copy of one, he so far succeeded as to encourage him in the hope of becoming a miniature painter. Working as a silversmith and attempting to paint, occupied the youth for some years, at the end of which, Wood had become acquainted with the eccentric John Wesley Jarvis.

Jarvis and Wood for a time carried on business together, having rooms near the Park Theatre. Their principal occupation was in profile likenesses, but by degrees Jarvis had employment in oil portraits, and Wood having improved, got work in miniature.

Wood's biographer says, in the "Portfolio," Malbone gave him instruction, and "While he (Malbone) lived, was Wood's best friend, and when he died, he left him an example in his life, and a pattern in his works."

The friends, Jarvis and Wood, separated. Wood had for a long time his painting rooms in Broadway, and executed work enough to have secured a fortune. Such was his rapidity, that he has often finished a portrait in one day.

Mr. Wood, about the year 1806-7, removed to Philadelphia, and from thence to Washington, the seat of government, where he died at the age of fifty-four.

BENJAMIN HENRY LATROBE[0]

Was a native of England, the youngest son of the Reverend Benjamin Latrobe, an English Moravian clergyman, and Anna Margaret Antes, the daughter of a gentleman of Pennsylvania. The childhood of Benjamin Henry, which was passed under the age of eleven, at school in Yorkshire, gave indications of his future eminence as a draughtsman and architect, for even then he made drawings, generally original, from buildings which attracted his attention. From Yorkshire, he was sent to a Moravian seminary in Saxony, and thence to the University at Leipsic. In 1785, after three years of intense study, Mr. Latrobe left Leipsic, for the purpose of travelling, but was tempted to enter the army of the King of Prussia, and served as an officer for one campaign. He then made the tour of Europe, and studied the works of the masters in the art which he loved. On his return to England, he studied architecture and civil engineering, and immediately distinguished himself.

In 1790 he married Miss Lydia Sellen, and was appointed surveyor of the public offices in the City of London. He lost his wife in 1793, and that event, and the part he took in the great political divisions of the day, induced him to think of the United States as the future field for the exertion of his abilities, and as the country of his choice. In November 1795 he embarked, and after a passage of nearly four months, arrived at Norfolk in March 1796. Delighted with Virginia he remained in Norfolk and Richmond, until November 1798. In this interval among other professional exercises, he planned and built the penitentiary at Richmond, and examined and reported on the Dismal Swamp Canal.

In 1798, on a visit to Philadelphia, when in company with the President of the bank of Pennsylvania, the conversation turned upon the banking house then proposed to be built.

0   Latrobe died on September 3, 1820.

Mr. Latrobe made a sketch of a design, while the conversation was going on, and left it with the president, without thought of the future.

In July 1798, he received a notice that his plan for the Bank of Pennsylvania was adopted, and a request to furnish instructions for the workmen. It is needless to speak of the universal approbation which this beautiful edifice has received. To superintend its erection, Mr. Latrobe removed to Philadelphia, and soon after undertook the water works which he triumphantly executed. At this period he married Miss Mary Hazlehurst. He was, in 1799, engaged in making surveys relative to a canal for uniting the waters of the Chesapeake and Delaware Bays: his report was adopted, and the work begun, but was not finished, as the subscribers did not pay up their shares. These waters have been united by a more expensive route. In 1803, Mr. Latrobe was called to Washington by Mr. Jefferson, to complete the works begun under former administrations, and was appointed surveyor of the public buildings. Little had been done for the buildings, until Mr. Jefferson in 1803 by his influence, caused the determination in Congress to proceed to their completion, and by him Mr. Latrobe was selected to carry the resolution into effect. To finish upon another's plan, and in conflict with the interests of all who had preceded him, raised difficulties in the way of Latrobe, and he was met by opposition at every step, and assailed by misrepresentation from every quarter. But the president duly appreciated his merit, and gave him his undeviating support.

In 1808, Mr. Latrobe commenced the south wing of the Capitol, the exterior of which, of course, had to conform to the north wing, as designed by Dr. Thornton, but the interior was finished on Latrobe's plan. The navy yard being also under Mr. Latrobe's direction, he planned and erected the buildings and machinery connected therewith. In 1809, he surveyed and superintended a canal which passes through the city, uniting the main stream of the Potomac with the eastern branch. This construction reflects honor on Mr. Latrobe's skill and ingenuity.

In 1811, the south wing of the Capitol was finished; but

the approaching war caused the suspension of the public work. Mr. Latrobe has been praised for what has been termed, a new order of architecture. In the small vestibule of the east entrance of the north wing of the Capitol, the vaulted roof is supported by columns representing the stalk of the Indian corn with its fruit. The column being the stalks bound together, and the capital, the ears of corn with the husk open. In 1813 Mr. Latrobe resigned his situation at Washington; his reasons will appear in note A, appendix. Freed from the service of the United States, Mr. Latrobe devoted his attention to the great object of supplying the city of New Orleans with water on a plan similar to that which had been so successful at Philadelphia. This work had been proposed to Latrobe in 1809 by Mr. Jefferson, and the plan matured by consultation with Governor Claiborne. The engines were to be made at Washington, and sent by sea to New Orleans, where Mr. Latrobe sent his eldest son and pupil to receive them and construct the work; the War of 1812 rendered this dangerous, and the architect removed to Pittsburg, to carry on the work, and transport the materials by river communication. With this project was combined another in conjunction with Robert Fulton; and Latrobe became agent of the Ohio Steamboat Company. In this undertaking he was unfortunate; misunderstandings arose between him and Fulton, afterwards amicably explained, but in the meantime Latrobe was ruined; his spirits sunk, for the first time in his life, and he abandoned himself to a state of profound despondency. Not only was he disappointed by the failure of efforts for steam navigation, but in the great project respecting New Orleans.

In this state the peace of 1814 found Mr. Latrobe, but to his mind it brought no consolation. Mrs. Latrobe, however, had seen by the papers that a law had passed for rebuilding those edifices, which a barbaric enemy, in an irruption for the purposes of destruction, had laid in ruins. Unknown to her husband she wrote to his former friends, stating his situation, and asking their influence for his reappointment to his former office. She had the gratification of carrying to her husband the answer, that the subject had been already under consideration, and there never had been a moment's hesitation as to his being appointed to rebuild the Capitol. A letter from Mr. Latrobe in answer to one from Mr. Jefferson, will be found in the appendix (Note B), and is one of the most impressive documents relative to the destruction of Washington city, that has yet met the public eye.

In 1817, Mr. Latrobe received the intelligence of the death of his eldest son, Henry S. B. Latrobe, whose life was sacrificed to the New Orleans Water Works, as was ultimately that of his father. In 1818, Mr. Latrobe finding himself uncomfortably situated under the direction of a commissioner appointed by Congress, who was ignorant of science or art, and could not appreciate an artist, resigned and removed to Baltimore. He had, however, left specimens of his taste and skill by the erection of St. John's church, and Christ's church at Alexandria, as well as many private dwellings. In Baltimore he was employed to plan and erect the Roman Catholic cathedral, the greatest monument to his architectural fame, though not, perhaps, so perfect as the bank of Pennsylvania above mentioned. The exterior of the cathedral still wants one of its towers to lighten the dome by contrast. He likewise designed the Baltimore Exchange. Mr. Latrobe after quitting the public employ again, turned his attention to the New Orleans Water Works, and to complete them, removed to that city. He had the prospect of completing this great undertaking and making a fortune for his family, when the same cruel disease of the climate, which had deprived him of his son, robbed the world of his valuable life.

The character of Mr. Latrobe's architecture is simplicity and perfect proportion. The Grecian model had his preference, and the book he most frequently consulted was Stuart's "Athens." The uncommon facility with which he used the pen and pencil gave him great advantages, and his profound knowledge, rendered his sketches perfect models for the workmen.

Mr. Latrobe was above the middle height, and his early

military campaign had impressed itself upon his manner and
carriage. He was a profound mathematician, and a skilful
linguist, ancient and modern. He was a scientific musician,
and well versed in the natural sciences of geology, etymology
and botany. He never left home without his sketch book,
and his family possess drawings of scenery accumulated in his
journeys. His career in the United States, though a proud
one for his children, was rendered painful to himself, and was
finally cut short when it would have resulted in fortune for
them, as well as fame to him, which was already secured.
This country has felt, and must continue to feel the benefit of
his exertions, not only personal, but through his pupils, Mills,
Strickland and Small, and those to whom his example and
instructions must *descend*.

THOMAS SULLY.

This gentleman, who has long stood at the head of his profession as a portrait painter, and whose designs, in fancy subjects, all partake of the elegant correctness of his character,
and the rich store of knowledge he has accumulated, was not
born in America; but is one of the many artists who have been
brought in childhood to a country whose institutions or manners do not place the painter in the rank of the mechanic, and
among whose inhabitants is not found a class or *caste* who look
down with contempt upon the man of science and taste,
because he receives money for the product of his talents;
a caste who call the giving of employment to such men (their
superiors in knowledge) *patronage*. But he was born in a
country rich in science, art, and literature, where such a
caste does exist. In a late British Review of the first character
it is said, "If the tenth son of the lowest baron were to follow
painting as a profession, there would be many well-meaning
persons who would hold up their hands in surprise and horror
at the degradation of such a step. They could scarcely be
more shocked at his keeping a shop, than at the idea of his
painting for money. Painting is considered as a mechanical
art, and the man of rank would be considered to lose caste by

following it." We all have to thank our fathers who have
rescued us from such a state; for if we had not been made
independent of England, the same absurd and arrogant
aristocratical caste would have been established in America.

The evil spirit exists here as elsewhere; but is kept down
by our democratic institutions; and when the aspirants assume
the airs of superiority, they are *put down* by the spirit of
common sense.

Thomas Sully was born in Horncastle, Lincolnshire, in the
month of June 1783. He has told the writer that his earliest
recollections were connected with his maternal grandmother,
with whom he was placed in charge at Birmingham by his
parents, they being comedians, and attached to some of the
provincial theatres at the time, and of course unsettled wanderers. But their merit gaining for them a permanent establishment, by an engagement at Edinburgh in Jones and Parker's
Theatre, little Tom was removed to the capital of Scotland;
but, as he has said, never lost his attachment to the good old
lady who had taken charge of his early infancy. When he
revisited England, after many years' absence, a man, a husband, and father, his first care was to see the guardian of his
helpless years, to recall to memory the incidents of his childhood, and to employ his pencil in sketching. the antique
building, whose every door and window, every nook and corner,
recalled some scene of that period, that link in the chain of
existence when all was novelty — when every object presented
to the senses a subject for inquiry, and a lesson in the most
important part of man's education. "At this window," said
Sully, pointing to the sketch, "I was hired to remain stationary
one rainy day, for a given time, and my reward was to be
sixpence. I stood, like a hero, looking straight forward at an
old brewhouse, when the rain having undermined its founda-
tions, it fell with a crash — to my great delight; for in addition
to the novelty of the scene presented, the accident gave me my
liberty."

In the year 1792, the painter's father was induced, by the
liberal offers of Mr. West, then, and for years afterwards,

manager of the Virginia and Charleston, South Carolina, Theatres, to remove with his family to the United States. Mr. West was the brother-in-law of the elder Sully, who brought with him four sons, of whom Thomas was the youngest, and several daughters. The oldest son, Lawrence, was a miniature and device painter for many years in Virginia, and will be hereafter mentioned in connection with Thomas. The second, Matthew, although an excellent draughtsman, preferred the stage and followed his father's profession, and was long the favorite comedian of the Southern States. The third son, Chester, tried the stage in very early life; but not liking it, or not succeeding to his wishes, abandoned the profession, and devoted himself for a time to a less dangerous one, as practised among Americans, the sea. He went several voyages before the mast; but his companions of the forecastle did not suit him, and at the age of nineteen (his parents had been some time dead) he bound himself apprentice to a cabinet maker in Portsmouth, near Norfolk, Virginia, and obtained the power, by industry, to support himself, and become the respectable father of a well-educated family. One of the daughters of the elder Sully married Monsieur Belzons, a French miniature painter settled in Charleston, who, although a very poor artist, was the first instructor of the subject of the present memoir.

From the above dates it will be seen that Thomas Sully was brought to this country a child of nine years of age. The profession of Lawrence Sully, that of miniature and device painter, created and fostered in the breasts of several of his brothers and sisters the desire to become painters. Lawrence's ability in his art was but moderate, but it appeared otherwise to the younger branches of the family. Thomas was especially desirous of becoming an artist, and has said that for years he looked up to the productions of Lawrence as the summit of perfection.

Thus it is with us all, at all times. Man, individually or in society, considers *that* as true and beautiful at one period which he sees and knows to be false and deformed at another. The childhood of an individual and the childhood of a people are in most things similar. Each commences its career in ignorance, gropes in darkness and uncertainty with tottering steps, is guided or misled by the crafty who assume the office of teachers, and can only get a glimpse of the true and the beautiful at distant intervals, when, as he gathers strength, if not perverted from that desire for truth which the Author of all good has implanted in his heart, he will eventually see the loveliness which resides in perfection, and will aim unceasingly to attain it.

The individual whose name and life has suggested these reflections, is an instance of the power of that desire, and the effect of virtuous perseverance through uncommon difficulties, to the attainment (if not to the full accomplishment of his wishes) at least to the high and commanding eminence which may encourage thousands to follow and emulate him, not only in his works of art, but in the suavity of his manners, the blameless tenor of his life, and his benevolent exertions to forward the views of all who apply to him for instruction.

In 1783 Thomas was sent to the same school with Charles Fraser, in Charleston, and the similar propensities of these boys caused intimacy. Fraser, though like himself, a beginner in the art of face-making and spoiling copy books, became Sully's leader and teacher. Mr. Sully has said of Mr. Fraser, "he was the first person that ever took the pains to instruct me in the rudiments of the art, and although himself a mere tyro, his kindness, and the progress made in consequence of it, determined the course of my future life."

The desire which Thomas felt to imitate his brother Lawrence's productions, was not immediately indulged. He was placed by his father, in 1795, in the insurance broker's office of a Mr. Mayer; but the broker complained to his father that although he was very industrious in multiplying figures, they were figures of men and women, and that if he took up a piece of paper in the office, he was sure to see a face staring at him; in short, that Tom spoiled all the paper that fell in his way, or that he could lay his hands on; and concluded by advising, that instead of a merchant or broker, he should be made a

painter. Accordingly, the youth was placed for instruction
with Mr. Belzons, a French gentleman, who had recently
married into Mr. Sully's family. Mr. Belzons had emigrated
from France in consequence of the revolution, and having lost
his property, had made a profession of the art which had been
studied as an accomplishment. Although he was enabled to
support his family in Charleston very respectably by the pencil,
he was neither in skill nor temper the best qualified person to
teach the young painter. In fact, he was a very poor artist,
and like many of his lively countrymen, had not learned to
control his passions.

Tom had been directed to superintend the cleaning of Belzons' gallery, and accordingly took his seat with a box of water
colors (a present from his sister), and all the requisites for the
work he was engaged upon, nothing doubting that by sitting
at his table and prosecuting his studies at one end of the gallery, while the servant was scrubbing the other, that he was
doing his duty and obeying his teacher. While thus innocently
and properly employed Belzons entered, and either mis-
taking Sully's employment for neglect of his orders, or put out
of humor by some previous occurrence, he in a violent rage
assailed the young painter with opprobrious language, at the
same time dashing the precious box of colors to pieces, and
strewing the floor with pencils, drawings, and fragments of
what the youth deemed his dearest treasure. Tom looked in
despair upon the wreck, and might have submitted to what
appeared utter ruin; but when Belzons, his passion increased
to frenzy by indulgence, roused the youth's indignation by ac-
cusations which he knew to be unjust, and finally attempted to
strike him, the spirit of the land of his fathers and the land of
his adoption blazed forth, and with an agility and power of
muscle the assailant was not prepared for, Tom with one blow
floored his master; and when in the blindness of fury he repeated his assault, again prostrated him, doubtless to the great
delight, if not edification, of the black who was plying the
scrubbing brush. The French combatant seemed to gain
strength, like the antagonist of Hercules, from his repeated

falls, and his rage being in no wise abated, the man would probably have overpowered the boy by superior weight and power; but at this crisis Mrs. Belzons, a beautiful woman, attracted by the noise, entered and rushed between her husband and brother. Tom left the gallery — found his hat — and without further accommodation, departed with a determination never to put himself again in the power of his brother-in-law.

This event took place early in 1799, when Sully was sixteen years of age. His parents were dead. His brother Lawrence settled at Richmond. The youth was thrown upon the world, and all his previous plans dissipated. He had left Belzons' house without money, or anything else except the clothes he had on. It was not likely that he would slacken the cords of resentment against oppression and insult, or that Belzons, while he felt Tom's blows, would seek to lure back so pugnacious a pupil. We may imagine the feelings that made him avoid all his acquaintance that day; and, for lack of other shelter, he slept the night following in the Exchange, a public building, the upper part of which was enclosed and locked against, and the lower left open to, the destitute of every description. The next day something must be done. Tom found that to be tolerably comfortable, he must eat as well as sleep; and though stomach-full when he thought of his wrongs, there was nothing in that turbulent feeling which supplied the want of food, or created sensations of pleasure.

He sallied forth from his wretched lodging and met a friend, who could enter into his feelings; to him he related his story, and asserted his determination not to return to Belzons. His conduct and resolutions were approved, and present protection afforded him.

The "John Adams," United States ship, was at this time fitting for sea. Mr. Read, the navy agent, became interested for the youth, and offered his interest to procure a midshipman's berth for him. The offer was accepted: our painter was within an ace of becoming a sailor, but his brother Lawrence inviting him to come to Richmond and become his pupil, the love of art prevailed over the love of variety and wandering; and after submitting the question to the benevolent Mr. Read, it was resolved that he should go to Virginia, and pursue his studies as an artist. But Lawrence had not remitted money to transport him from Charleston to Richmond. Tom was without a cent, and was too delicate to mention the circumstance to his Charleston friends; but he had a person and address which, together with unblemished character, recommended him to strangers as well as acquaintance, and gained him friends throughout life.

He found in the harbor of Charleston a vessel belonging to Norfolk, commanded by her owner, Captain Leffingwell. Sully applied to him for a passage, promising to pay at Norfolk. Leffingwell received him willingly, took him not only into his vessel, but on their arrival at Norfolk into his house; until his brother should remit money to pay the debt, and wherewithal to pass up James River, this was in due time done, and Tom was at home again.

Mr. Lawrence Sully appears to have been a man struggling with poverty, and not possessing that skill as an artist, or that energy and felicity in resources which would have enabled him to place an amiable wife, and numerous family of children, in such eligible circumstances, as a man of ordinary ambition must aspire to. The talents of his young brother were of more importance to him, than his instructions could be to the ingenious youth who now commenced as miniature and device painter.

In the year 1801, Mr. Lawrence Sully removed his family to Norfolk, and of course Thomas went with him. At this time the younger brother was the better artist, and the main support of the household. But not content with ivory and water colors, and stimulated by the sight of some portraits and other pictures by Mr. Henry Benbridge, who was then exercising his pencil in the Borough, Tom determined to try oil, and made his preparations accordingly. An original picture by Angelica Kaufman, still in the possession of Mr. Sully, strengthened this determination, as in it he had a subject to copy. He resolved as soon as possible to abandon miniature painting in water

colors, and to become a painter in oil; and the first effort was
to make a copy from Angelica; but so ignorant was he of the
materials he was about to use, that he ground his pigments
in olive oil, and to his great surprise found that they would not
dry. Fortunately there was a sign painter in Norfolk who explained the mystery, taught him that vulgar flaxseed oil
would do him better service, and put him in the way of renew-
ing his labors with better success. The praise lavished on this
effort encouraged Tom to try portraits from life, of a small
size, in imitation of Mr. Benbridge. His first sitter for an oil
portrait was Mr. William Ormsted.

The young painter who looked up to an artist who had been
educated at Rome, with an awe approaching to idolatry, found
means to gain access to that mysterious temple, a painter's
atelier; and was received with a benignity more corresponding
to the gentlemanly education and attainments of the being
he approached, than to his own hopes. Benbridge, for it was
his sanctum sanctorum he had entered, encouraged his efforts,
instructed him by painting his portrait, and explaining his
palette, its arrangement, and the application of the tints
while the work was going on; and behaved as a genuine artist,
if a gentleman (as the term implies), will always behave to
those who love the art, and appear worthy of it.

In 1803 the business of Lawrence Sully, and his credit,
failed in Norfolk. Richmond, the seat of the State legislature,
presented hope of resource, and thither he repaired, leaving
his family to the care of Thomas. This was in December, and
Christmas was at hand, a festival more observed in Norfolk,
than in any other portion of the United States. Originally
peopled by Englishmen and Episcopalians, the custom of the
parent country in celebrating this holiday was combined with
the hospitable profusion of the South; and with a custom long
prevalent in the borough of providing abundant stores on
Christmas eve, or the twenty-fourth of December, for the
approaching short winter which is there known only in its
milder form, never begins but with January. Christmas eve is
in Norfolk a fair; the main street as well as the market, is one

continuous exhibition of poultry, of which turkeys are the preponderating article; wild fowl, butchers' meats, Carolina hams, venison, and more eggs than are to be seen in New York at *poss* or Easter. Through the day and evening this portion of the ancient borough is one thronged mart for the sale of articles of food, and the produce of all the surrounding region seems crowded into the hospitable town to promote the festivities of "Merry Christmas," and provide for the few days of cold weather, expected with the new year. There are few in the United States who have not a turkey for Christmas dinner; but to judge by the Norfolk market at this time of preparation, one would suppose that every table would show two; and the provision of eggs for puddings and nogg, in the morning is always in equal proportion and profusion. But what was all this to poor Tom Sully? He could only look on, and while others anticipated the joys of the morrow, think, that in the house he had charge of there would be none of these good things to rejoice over. He had to furnish food for his brother's wife, and four infant girls, and no means to provide for the feast of the morrow, or the wants which winter brings in its train.

"Sally, what have we got in the house?" "There is some Indian meal, and some sweetmeats." "Capital!" said Tom, "we will have Indian cakes, and the children shall have the sweatmeats in the bargain." Youth, hope, and purity, were the Christmas guests, and Tom, after a dinner which neither dulled his intellect nor clogged his limbs, went to see his brother Chester, who was at this time serving his late-in-life apprenticeship, with honorable perseverance at Portsmouth. Tom told Chester of the state of his family — laughed at the Christmas dinner — and pointed joyously to the pictures engaged, but yet unpainted, which were to improve his skill and supply all deficiencies in the household establishment, which he felt determined to support and improve.

The brothers were taking their afternoon's walk, when suddenly stopping at a corner, Chester said, "Tom, go you on ahead to the market place, and wait for me — I'll soon join

you," and darting off, round the corner of a street that led to
the harbor of Portsmouth, left him. As directed, the young
painter, no way suspecting anything extraordinary, walked to
the market house, and there waited until his brother, heated
and flushed by some unusual exertion, joined him. Tom had
observed two sailors at some distance down the street Chester
had turned into; but had no notion that they were connected
with his brother's motives for leaving him; and his elder brother
had sent him forward out of the way, that he might not be
involved in the adventure which he now recounted. We have
seen that the young painter had pugnacious propensities,
which might be aroused to action, and the means to gratify
them. Chester, stouter and inured to the gymnastic exercises
of a seaman and an artisan, older, but equally active, was more
qualified for combat and more than equally ready.

"When I left you," said he, "I gave chase to two fellows
who had been my messmates, and to whom I had pledged my
word, that if ever I met them on shore, I would pay them in
full for the scurvy services they rendered the boy, over whom
they had a little brief authority."

"But there were two — why did you not take me with
you?"

"No, no — it was my own business, and I knew I could
manage it alone. I hailed them. 'Hallo my lads, bring to. I
will now quit scores with you both, and perform my promise.'
We had a crowd about us immediately. I chose the biggest
bully to begin with, and I said to the spectators, 'Gentlemen,
if you will take care of that chap, while I thrash this, I will
then thrash him for your amusement.' 'Hurrah!' they cried,
'we'll see fair play.' So, we set to. He could not hit me a
blow, and I soon found him ready to give me a receipt in
full. — 'Now for t'other lubber.' But he seeing that I paid in
hard coin, sneaked from the crowd who were too eager spectators, to be good watchmen, and had taken to his heels. So,
now let's cross over to Norfolk, and see Sally and the children."

The talents, industry, and amiable manners of Thomas enabled him to support Lawrence's family, and pay his debts; but

the accumulated house rent he could not discharge, and the furniture being sold by the landlord, Mrs. Sully and children followed her husband to Richmond.

Tom now began the world for himself, remaining in Norfolk; and with two persons of the names of Brown and Taylor, he took a house in company, and kept bachelor's hall. His year's receipt from his labors, was one hundred and twenty dollars; but with this he lived contentedly, and relieved the necessities of others. The house he lived in was in Church Street. One of the joint partners in housekeeping, before the end of the year falling in debt, was removed by his creditors to prison. Sully attended upon him, and by his exertions procured his release. In after times when the fame of the painter was bruited abroad, Taylor used to boast that "in early life he was among the first *patrons* of young Sully, in the Borough of Norfolk." The man who is blessed with taste and benevolence, and with riches to gratify both, cheerfully assists struggling genius through the impediments poverty throws in his way, and enjoys in conscious rectitude the reward which the good deed assuredly brings, but he never boasts or assumes the title of patron.

In August, 1804, Sully removed to Richmond, and joined his brother Lawrence again as a partner. The one pursued his miniature and device painting, the other painted portraits in oil. But Thomas soon felt the cravings after further knowledge, and the desire for that improvement from instruction which was not to be found in Richmond. He determined to visit the land of his fathers, and formed a rigid plan of economy, by which to accumulate sufficient to carry him to London; youthful confidence assuring him, that, once there, he could make his way, and see painters and pictures.

He began his approach to London by removing to Petersburgh; a very short step on the way, but a new field for his pencil. But while successfully painting, and acquiring property and friends, his brother Lawrence died, leaving his wife and infant children unprovided and unprotected. Inclination was sacrificed to duty; the young painter gave up all his hopes of improvement and dreams of pleasure, from travel and the treasures of art, and returned to Richmond, to become the protector of the widow and the orphan.

After faithfully acting as the brother and the uncle for more than a year after Lawrence's decease, he became the husband of his brother's widow and the legal father of his children. — This step was approved by all who knew him and his circumstances, and never repented by himself.

It happened that Mr. Thomas A. Cooper, in one of his professional visits to Richmond, sat to Sully for his portrait. — This led to a friendship for the painter, and an invitation, when Mr. Cooper became lessee and manager of the New York Theatre, so friendly and liberal, that it induced the young painter to remove with his family to that city, and gave the impulse which has ultimately carried merit to its deserved goal — fame and fortune.

In a letter from Sully to a friend, after mentioning his first acquaintance with the tragedian, he proceeds thus: — "I should be very ungrateful not to acknowledge Cooper to have been one of my greatest benefactors. His friendship encouraged me to remove to New York, where he thought I might learn more of the art, from the example and pictures of more experienced artists; and that I might feel a confidence in taking, for me, so adventurous a step, he pledged himself to secure me business to the amount of one thousand dollars; and, on my removing to New York, gave me authority to draw upon the treasurer of his theatre for money, as I might require it, to that amount."

"So shines a good deed in a naughty world."

Our great poet has said, that the evil deeds of men are written in brass — the good they do, in sand. May this *good* deed be written in brass!

When Sully presented himself to the manager in New York, his first words were, "Well, Mr. Cooper, here I am!" — "That's right!" said Cooper, "I am ready for you — work engaged — sitters waiting — you shall have a painting room in the front of the theatre, that will cost you nothing — and call

on the treasurer for money as you want; you have a credit
with him for a thousand dollars."

Mr. Sully remembers and feels this as he ought. The friends
of genius, the admirers of art, ought to remember and feel it.
To encourage and foster talent is conferring a benefit on mankind, and the world is indebted to the benefactor.

Thus, in 1806, Mr. Sully commenced his career anew, in a
metropolitan city, aided by the friendship of the most brilliant
histrionic artist the western world had seen. The writer of
these memorials of the fine arts of his country was then engaged as assistant manager in the New York Theatre, and that
situation brought him in immediate contact with Mr. Sully;
the acquaintance ripened into friendship, and has existed
undiminished to the present day.

Mr. Sully was yet a young man and a young painter. —
He had much to learn, and no one knew his deficiencies better
or felt them so strongly as himself; therefore, having energy
of character, he of course improved daily. Trumbull and
Jarvis were both painting in New York; and at that time the
first was the best portrait painter, though he did not continue
long so; his art was without feeling or nature — and Jarvis's
nature was soon supported by art. What Jarvis knew was
freely communicated: to derive advantage from the older
artist was not so easy of attainment. Sully sacrificed one
hundred dollars (that is, one-tenth of his borrowed capital),
for the purpose, and carried his wife to Trumbull's rooms, as
a sitter, that he might see his mode of painting, and have a
specimen from his pencil. He gained some knowledge for his
money, and probably learned to imitate the neatness with
which palette and pencils and oils and varnishes were used
and preserved; an art Jarvis never knew or thought of: and
he gained a model, which served him as a beacon, warning
him of that which it was necessary to avoid.

Of many anecdotes connected with Mr. Sully's portrait
painting, of this time, a few may amuse the reader. He was
surrounded by men whose profession is laborious, but who
in the moments of leisure indulge in the sportiveness of boys.

The painter had, as one of his sitters, Mr. Jas. Hamilton, of Philadelphia, a friend of his friend the manager; who, as actor and manager, was then in the enjoyment of the flood tide of success and unbounded animal spirits. Hamilton's portrait was nearly finished when Cooper entered the painter's room: and after looking over the artist's shoulder for some time, he said, "Sully, it is very like James, but" — and he paused.— Now, thought the poor portrait painter, here comes the usual *but*. He worked on, only saying, "Yes, I think it is like." "It has a very strange color," said the other. "How so?" "Don't you think it looks very green?" said the manager.

This is one of the ways in which artists are civilly told that they do not know what they are about. "No," said Sully. "Green! No — rather warm, perhaps, but certainly not green." "It has a strange appearance to me," said Cooper. "I have colored as usual — I have tried to give his complexion," said the painter. "It is very like, but there is a greenish tint — it's very like." And after some minutes' chat on other subjects the critic departed, leaving the painter to rub his eyes and look in vain for green in the flesh of his picture.

By and by Harwood called on him; and, after admiring the likeness, said, in his good-natured way, "But, Sully, don't you think all your half-tints are too green?" "Green! I see no green, except a little here; as we find it in all flesh, where the yellow mingles with the blue." "But all over — somehow — I suppose I am wrong; but the whole has a greenish hue, as if I saw James through a pair of green spectacles." "Perhaps I look green too." "No, not at all — it is very like — I dare say I am wrong." The subject was changed; but the "green-eyed monster" had got possession of the poor painter; and when Harwood was gone, the picture was turned upside down, and viewed at various distances, in search of green.

A well-calculated interval was suffered to elapse before Twaits made his appearance. "Good morning, Sully. — Bless me, how like James! — but he looks as if he had been at an alderman's feast, and the green fat of the turtle had tinged his skin."

It happened that one of the servants of the theatre was employed in the room putting up a stove; and hearing all this green criticism, he approached and gazed with lack-lustre eye. "Yes," said he, "it is green, sure enough."

Sully was by this time convinced that he could not see. He put down his palette — turned the face of the green picture to the wall, and with Twaits walked to the *green* room of the theatre: where the tragedian and two comedians reiterated their compliments on the successful likeness he had made of James Hamilton; but it was a pity there should be such a *green* tint about it. "I dare say it will not look so green when he gets it to the woodlands, and it is surrounded by trees and green fields," said Harwood. Sully declared his determination to remedy the color — he would repaint it. — "I have been at work so long, that I suppose I can't see. I work no more today. Tomorrow I will go over it again."

"Why, you pump!" said Cooper, "to let us three buckram men persuade you out of your senses. It is all a trick. The picture is better colored than any you have done. Go and finish it without changing a tint; and, Tom — hereafter believe your own eyes, in preference to any other pair, let them belong to whom they will."

About this same period, Mrs. Warren, late Mrs. Merry, had come on from Philadelphia, to delight the public of New York, as she had often done before, by the finished pictures she exhibited on the stage: she at the same time assisted Sully, by sitting for that likeness which was afterwards engraved by Edwin for the " Mirror of Taste."

She had had but one sitting, and had appointed four o'clock for the second, on a certain day, when she was to visit the theatre for her professional exertions. The painter had placed the newly begun portrait on his easel, at one o'clock, to prepare it for the sitting before he went to dinner; and becoming dissatisfied with his work, determined to rub it out, and commence anew with another sketch, to be ready for the lady's visit. The door was carefully locked, but the key most unwisely left in the lock — no lounger was to be admitted. But scarcely had he defaced the product of the first sitting, ere he heard the feet and voices of females on the stairs, and then a tap at his door. No answer. "Mr. Sully!" And he knew the "silver-sweet" tones of Mrs. Warren's voice. "It will never do to answer" — so communed the painter with himself. "I must work two hours before it is ready for the sitting." "Mr. Sully," was repeated in the same melodious accents. — Another was heard to say, "He is not here." "Yes, he is," said the first, "for I see the key inside of the keyhole. Mr. Sully! Why, he certainly has locked himself in and gone to sleep." "A capital hint *that* — I'll take it. I'll be asleep" — and he leaned back in his chair and was asleep instantly. "Try if you can see him through the keyhole." "I will. Sure enough, there he sits, fast asleep before his easel. Well, we will not disturb him." The ladies laughed at the drowsy artist and went off. The ever-industrious painter relinquished dinner to accomplish his purpose, and at four o'clock was ready for his sitter, who punctually came. Women are in *this*, as in most things, more true than men.

"Why, Mr. Sully, what a sound sleeper you are." "Oh no! not very." "Yes you are, and sitting before your easel too." "I never slept before my easel in my life." "But I saw you, so sound too, for I knocked and called upon your name, and made noise enough to raise any but the dead." "None so deaf as those who won't hear," said the painter, and then told the truth and his reason for not admitting her. "Well," said the lady, laughing, "that is too bad, Sully; but I suppose I must let your candor cancel the memory of your rudeness, in refusing to let me in — there is no apology like plain truth, so here's my hand — you are pardoned."

Anxious for improvement, Mr. Sully resolved to visit Boston, and see the great portrait painter as soon as circumstances would permit. In the year 1807, removing his family as far on the way as Hartford, he proceeded to the capital of Massachusetts. He took letters to Andrew Allen, Esq., British Consul; to Mr. Perkins, and several others. Mr. Allen was the friend of Thomas A. Cooper, whose letter of introduction

Sully carried. He was of the family of that Allen who was the friend of West in the days of his youth. Andrew Allen was a friend of the arts, and a frank noble-spirited gentleman. By such a man the young painter could be no otherwise than cordially received. He inquired into his wishes and his views, and thought how he best could gratify the one and forward the other. He had an appointment with Stuart for a sitting the next day, and it was arranged that Sully should accompany him and then return with him to dinner.

The next person to whom Sully delivered a letter was a rich merchant. He was in his counting house. He read the letter. "Mr. Sully, from New York — extremely happy to be of any service. Where do you put up? How long do you remain in Boston? John, take this letter to the post office. — You paint portraits — dull times in Boston just now."

As soon as the artist left the presence of the commercial magnate, he deliberately took all his remaining letters of introduction from his pocket, and as he walked to his hotel, tore them one by one, and strewed the fragments on the cold pavement, where they were received without one expression of desire to serve him, or any token of extreme happiness in consequence of his presence.

The next day Allen introduced him to Stuart, who received him with the utmost urbanity, and ever after treated him with liberality and kindness, imparting instruction as freely as he had received it from his own great master. Allen was placed in the sitter's chair, an awfully wearisome throne when the occupant is under the hands of many operators on the human face, but not so in the *atelier* of Gilbert Stuart. One of his patients being asked, after a sitting, if he was not tired, answered, "Yes, with laughing."

Sully, in after times, when describing his first interview with Stuart, has said, "I had the privilege of standing by the artist's chair during the sitting, a situation I valued more, at that moment, than I shall ever again appreciate any station on earth."

Before he left the painting room, Isaac P. Davis, Esq. came

in, a truly liberal, friendly and excellent gentleman, to whom
Sully had, by the omission of his friends in New York, brought
no letters (which, if he had, would have been preserved from
the pavement by the well-known character of Mr. Davis).
He was intimate with Stuart and with Sully's friends in New
York, and on being introduced, reproached him with not
bringing letters to him. Before the sitting of Allen was over,
an arrangement was made that Mr. Davis should sit to Sully,
and by the result Stuart was to judge of the nature of the
instruction most needed by the young artist.

Acordingly Davis sat, and the picture was carried to Stuart,
"He looked at it for a long time," said Sully, "and every
moment of procrastination added to my torment. He delib-
erated, and I trembled. At length he said, 'Keep what you
have got, and get as much as you can.'"

There is more encouragement in this oracular sentence than
at first view meets the eye. Most young artists have to get
rid of "what they have got," or the greater part of it, as well
as to "get as much as they can." For further encouragement,
Stuart showed him his palette, his arrangement of colors, and
his mode of using them. He advised him in respect to his
future proceedings, and recounted his own experience. There
was here no necessity for purchasing a picture by way of getting
a lesson; all was as it should be, and as it is with every liberal
artist — gratuitous.

CHAPTER XVI.

SULLY. — *Continued.*

IN the autumn of 1808 Mr. Sully returned with his family to
New York, and again set up his easel. He was improved in
theory and practice, but the tide had turned, or the stream had
taken another course. Jarvis had improved likewise, and
painted most decided likenesses. Trumbull who, as has been
said of Reynolds, "gave good dinners" while in New York,
had painted up his guests and returned to England, as the
discontents between us and that country multiplied, and as the
merchants slackened both in dinners and portraits. New
York being essentially commercial, the embarrassments in
trade no doubt affected Sully, while Jarvis, at that time the
better painter and better known, had full employment. Sully
was obliged to offer himself as his assistant in copying, preparing, filling up backgrounds, or laying in draperies. "It is
a great shame that it should be so," said Jarvis; but he frankly
accepted the offer, paid him liberally, and rendered him every
assistance in his power.

At this time of ebb tide (or rather low water) at New York,
Benjamin Wilcox, of Philadelphia, invited Sully to that
metropolis, and thither he removed with his large and increasing family. Mr. Trott, the miniature painter was then in full
practice in Philadelphia, and conjointly with him, Sully took
a house in the month of February 1809, in which they
both successfully pursued their respective branches of art in
harmony.

The interruption to commerce was felt by Sully after a
time in Philadelphia. His business nearly ceased. He had been
employed at $50 a head, and was full of work. He proposed,
by advice of his friends, to paint thirty portraits at $30 each,
and a list for that number was filled. Again he was in a kind

of eddy of prosperity, but he felt that he had arrived at that point beyond which he could not make his way unassisted towards the perfection he aimed at, and had determined to attain. This aid he thought could only be obtained in London.

The Pennsylvania Academy of Fine Arts was then in embryo. Gentlemen, many of whom were personal friends of Mr. Sully, had associated for the purpose of erecting a building, procuring casts from the antique, and good pictures, and thus becoming the benefactors of their country by encouraging the advancement of the arts. It was proposed to these gentlemen to employ Mr. Sully in the prosecution of this design; and he agreed, for the sum of $3000, to proceed to London and employ himself in making copies from paintings of the best masters accessible there, for the academy. He announced his intention of departing for Europe, and declined receiving sitters. Happily, the scheme proved abortive, for it is evident that the sum was not adequate to the purpose intended. Sully was blinded by his desire for improvement; but small as the amount was, the directors declined the project for want of funds to make the necessary advances.

Thus disappointed and thrown out of business, the painter's good friend Wilcox opened a subscription at $200 each signer, to be paid to Sully, and repaid by copies of pictures to be painted by him in London, and sent from thence to Philadelphia at the painter's expense, each subscriber being entitled to one picture from a master. Sully's inexperience, or thirst for the opportunity of studying the works of art, made him insensible of the inadequacy of the price he was thus setting upon his labors; he only saw the prospect of improvement.

Seven subscribers were obtained. Thus for $1400 a good painter undertook to support a large family in America, while he incurred the expense of going to England and remaining there during the time necessary to the painting seven pictures from the works of masters, and then transporting them with himself back to Philadelphia.

Mr. Sully, when mentioning this period of his life in a letter to a friend, says, "I will not dwell upon the slavery I went

through, nor the close economy used to enable me to fulfill
my engagement; but although habitually industrious, I never
passed nine months of such incessant application. Let me
never forget the disinterested kindness of Benjamin Wilcox on
this occasion. His generous offer of the use of his purse, gave
me a courage and a confidence that enabled me to complete
my engagement cheerfully."

It will be seen that the painter only called upon his liberal
friend for $500 during this experiment; two hundred, after
the nine months' residence in London, for the purpose of paying his passage back; and three hundred advanced to his
family during his absence. Although Mr. Sully himself would
not dwell upon the particulars of this arduous struggle, it is
doing a duty to the world to present them to the student as
the honorable and interesting characteristics of a true disciple
of the fine arts.

Mr. Sully having left $1000 with his wife, embarked on the
"Delaware" the 18th of June 1809, and arrived at Liverpool
the 13th of July following. Although his parents had long been
dead, his aged grandmother — then ninety years old — the
nurse and guardian of his infancy, still lived in Birmingham,
and still in the same house in which he passed his early proba-
tionary hours, the novitiate to life's motley mysteries. Sully
was not a man to forget his first duty, and he immediately
repaired to Birmingham.

While on this visit, recalling the events of childhood, and
wondering at the pigmy dimensions of every place around;
which, being traced upon his mind's tablet when that was of
its smallest size, had expanded with the growth of the material
to a greatness very much beyond the reality; he made inquiry
after the old lady who had petted and cherished him in days
of yore. "Here she comes," was the answer. He had difficulty
in making himself known; for although she remembered the
child, her mind could not unite that cherished image with the
appearance of the gentleman before her. Truly there was no
similitude. And that this gentleman had come from America
— a far-off country, of which she had no distinct notion —

and that this gentleman was the identical Tom Sully she used to carry in her arms, puzzled the old lady overmuch. In fact, this same business of identity has puzzled others as well as old women.

Mr. Sully carried a letter directed to Mr. West from William Rawle, Esq., of Philadelphia; but the first letter he delivered in London was to his friend and subsequently fellow student, Charles B. King. Long after Mr. Sully has been heard to say, "I resided under the same roof with him, and our painting room was in common during my stay in London: an intimacy of twenty years enables me to testify to qualities of heart and correctness of conduct rarely equalled for purity or usefulness."

When Sully first saw King in England, there was an immediate reciprocity of feeling, that produced a frank interchange of thought without hesitation or disguise. King had been some years studying in London, and could appreciate Sully's inexperience. "How long do you intend staying in England?" "Three years, if I can." "And how much money have you brought with you?" "Four hundred dollars." "Why, my good sir, that is not enough for three months — I'll tell you what — I am not ready to go home — my funds are almost expended, and before I saw you I had been contriving a plan to spin them out, and give me more time. Can you live low?" "All I want is bread and water." "Oh, then you may live luxuriously, for we will add potatoes and milk to it. It will do! we will hire these rooms, they will serve us both — we will buy a stock of potatoes — take in bread and milk daily — keep our landlady in good humor, and (by the bye) conceal from her the motive for our mode of life by a little present now and then, and — work away like merry fellows." And so they did. Thus making themselves excellent artists by a system of labor, economy, and independence as honorable as it was efficacious.

His friend King introduced Sully to the council chamber of the Royal Academy, and he has thus recorded the first impression made upon him in a note book, from which, by permission, this extract is made. He thus remarks upon the

pictures deposited by the academicians on their election: —
"The room is well stocked with works by Reynolds, Gainsborough, Fuseli, Stubbs, West, Lawrence, Owen, and many
others. Owen's manner pleases me much. It is cool, broad,
and firm, in some respects like Reynolds'. The color is laid
on in great body and with large brushes, so that no markings
or hatchings are visible. His coloring is cool in the lights
and warm in the shadows, beginning from almost pure white
to vermilion tints — to the cool half-tint from that graduated
to a greenish half-tint, which looks like ochre-black and vermilion, and which perhaps is rendered more green when
finished by glazing with asphaltum — the main shade of black
and vermilion broken with the green tint. In some places
Indian red is used instead of vermilion.

"Gainsborough's manner struck me as being exactly as Reynolds describes it. There is some resemblance to it in Stuart's
manner, only that Stuart is firmer in the handling. His dead
colorings seem cool and afterwards retouched with warm
colors, used then so as to resemble the freedom of water-
color painting. Many light touches of greenish and yellow
tints are freely used, and although on inspection the work
looks rugged and smeared, and scratched, yet, at a distance,
it appeared to me the most natural flesh in the room. The
specimens of Reynolds' pencil disappointed, and Opie's seemed
raw, crude and dirty. Copley more hard and dark than usual.
Lawrence's too much loaded with paint, and the red and
yellow overpowering. The ceiling of this room is painted by
West and Angelica Kaufman, by far the most delicate coloring
I have yet seen of the president's, and Angelica has closely
imitated it."

Such were the feelings of the young American painter in
1809, upon first seeing the works of the London academicians,
and such was his keen mode of observing and retaining the
result of his observations for comparison with subsequent
attainments.

The next thing was to deliver letters of introduction to
artists, and first to Benjamin West. His friend, King, went

with him, and the first introduction he had to this great painter
and benevolent man was in the gallery which leads from
his dwelling house in Newman Street, to the suite of rooms
beyond it, for painting. The two young men were standing
at the commencement of the gallery, which used to be hung
with the sketches of the master's great works. Sully heard
the steps of the great painter, but an angle of the gallery hid
him from sight. He fitted his eyes to the height of six feet to
catch the eye of the great man, but felt a momentary disappointment in having to sink them to the attitude of a little old
man, by no means answering to the picture his fancy had
drawn. But all sensations, except those of pleasure, were put
to flight by the reception he met. He was conducted to the
painting rooms, and saw in its incipient state, the great picture
of "Healing in the Temple," at which West (then approaching
his seventieth year) was at work with all the mental power of
youth.

From that time West was, to use Mr. Sully's expression
when in conversation on the subject, "like a father" to him,
and he had "the advantage of his instruction and the free use
of his pictures."

The letters Sully bore to Lawrence, Sir William Beechey,
and Hopner,[1] procured him a reception from those eminent
painters as courteous as could be wished. Beechey's advice
was always freely given, but in a blunt and sometimes almost
harsh manner. The young painter only saw Hopner once.
He was afflicted with the gout. Examining a picture in the
room, Sully, who had been encouraged by him to ask any
questions relative to his art, inquired *what yellow he used in
flesh?* "Yellow? None," was the laconic reply. "Indeed!
I thought yellow was necessary to balance the blues and
reds." "There is no yellow in flesh, sir." The lesson and the
manner taken together not only prevented further questions,
but forced the inquirer to conclude that there was no further
information for him in that quarter.

To Sir Martin Archer Shee he had brought no letters, but
was introduced to him by Mr. Marshall, who had been one of

1 For Hopner read Hoppner

Wignel and Reinagle's company in Philadelphia, and was now attached to the Haymarket Theatre. Shee was at this period an experimenter in macgylps, but of too liberal a nature to keep his discoveries to himself. He gave his composition of the article as the result of his labors and experience. "Macgylp, made of mastic dissolved in spirits of turpentine, and drying oil prepared by letting good linseed oil stand in a bottle over litharge, may be used safely if used sparingly." "Mastic," said he, "will not crack if used over colors *thoroughly dry*. The litharge used in making drying oil should be granulated. Drying oil which has stood a long time should be shook before using it. 'When taken, to be shaken.'"

The painting room of Sully and King was a good one, and as above mentioned, used in common. It is in Buckingham Place, Fitzroy Square, and has not only to boast of King and Sully, as occupants, but of Leslie and Allston.

As Sully had painted a head of his friend Davis, to show Stuart the point he had arrived at, so he carried to West a head of his friend King. The frank and friendly criticism showed that there was an indecision in expressing the anatomy of the head, which indicated a want of confidence in the painter of his knowledge of the internal structure, and the advice was to study osteology assiduously. This was precious advice, and was gratefully received and followed.

Having seen the lions of London, it was necessary to find the means of fulfilling his engagement by copying seven good pictures, and to do this, pictures must be found and procured. It is well known, that in England nothing of art is to be had or even seen without paying for it, and our student was to make $400 support him for as long a time as possible, and certainly until he had gained possession of seven paintings by a master or masters, and copied them. He had found in London an American, a liberal American, who was moving among the great and the rich, and of course possessed the passports to their locked-up treasures. This was John Hare Powell, Esquire, of Philadelphia. Powell offered him any assistance he might want, and obtained for him access to the collections of Angerstein and others of the aristocracy with whom he was on intimate terms. But he could not fulfill his contract by merely seeing pictures. He was told that if he went to France the best pictures would not only be open to his view and examination, freely and gratuitously, but that he would have the privilege of copying them at will. "I must go to France," said the young painter. But on consulting Mr. West, he said, "I understand that your object on your return is portrait painting." "Yes, sir." "Then stay in England. You wish to fulfill an engagement and improve yourself by copying some pictures. My collection, old and new, is at your service. There are specimens of the ancient masters and of the moderns. Take them as you want them, and come to me for my advice when you want it."

But for this offer, the young painter must have gone to France. English collections were out of his reach: he might look, by special favor and introduction, but he might not even take out a pencil and make a memorandum. He must have been thrown upon a foreign country with his scanty resources; and have lost the instruction of the best teacher living, but for the advice and generous offer of the American patriarch of painting. "Study portraiture in England above all schools." This wise counsel determined Sully; and the liberal permission to use his choice collection of old masters, as well as his own works, with the privilege of removing them to his own *atelier*, made everything easy to the ardent and industrious student. Nine months he labored, painting through the day, and drawing at the academy in the evening; husbanding his scanty resources, which even by the limitation of his sustenance to bread, milk and potatoes, would not have lasted so long, had not John Coates of Philadelphia employed him to copy some landscapes, which were in the possession of Wm. Penn.

The money arising from this additional copying, gave him power to prolong the time to the accomplishment of the contract; but notwithstanding this salutary aid, at the end of nine months his funds were exhausted; and for his expenses in returning home, he drew upon his good friend Wilcox for two hundred dollars.

The following letter from Mr. West shows his anxiety that Sully should have a longer time given him, to improve himself, and the high opinion he entertained of the young artist. It is from the "Portfolio."

"Newman Street, Nov. 3, 1809.

"Philadelphia I cannot name without being interested in all that has a connection with that city: this, my good sir, alludes to a young gentleman now studying painting under my direction as a professor of that art, whose talents only want time to mature them to excellence; and I am apprehensive, that his means of support are too slender to admit his stay at this seat of arts that length of time to effect what I could wish, as I understand it cannot be longer than the beginning of next summer. Could his friends unite in a way that would afford him the means of studying here another season, he would then secure the knowledge of his profession on that permanent basis, on which he would be able to build his future greatness in America — to his honor and the honor of the country.

"The young gentleman I allude to is Mr. Sully. I find him every way worthy and promising. I could not refrain from thus giving you my sentiments, when the success of Mr. Sully in his profession as a painter, is so much to be desired.

"I have the honor to be, my dear sir,
"Your much obliged,
"Benjamin West."

The friends of Sully, and he, like West in his early days, found or made friends everywhere; such is the force of talent joined to good conduct and conciliating manners. His friends Wilcox and Powell and others would have willingly advanced funds to prolong his stay in Europe: they knew nothing of his penurious mode of subsistence, and would cheerfully have placed him at his ease in his studies; but the just dread of debt and love of independence, made him prefer the shorter period for improvement, and the lenten fare of penury to the more liberal allowance of time and rich diet. Though fond of the theatre, he never indulged himself in seeing a play. Passionately devoted to music, and himself a skilful performer, he would never have heard a concert during this time, but that he met in London a friend who had a similar taste, and private concerts at his house.

The number of Americans who had attended the Royal Academy, attracted the attention and became a theme for conversation among the native students. When Sully had entered his name in the book as usual, several of the young men satisfied their curiosity by examining the entry, and when they read the words "from Philadelphia," the exclamation from each was heard, "another American."

Beside the labor of painting, and drawing at the academy, the friends Sully and King studied from a model hired to stand in their painting room; and the lesson Mr. West had given the young painter, when he carried his head of King to him, caused the additional labor of studying osteology by copying anatomical engravings at night, and of course by candlelight, to the lasting injury of his eyes. Such is the enthusiasm of genius directed to the object it loves.

The friendship of Hare Powell having opened some of the galleries of the rich to Sully, he made the best use his time would allow, for profiting by this privilege. He has said that notwithstanding the works of great masters which met his eyes at Angerstein's, his attention was arrested by the " Marriage a la mode," of Hogarth, and he could with difficulty tear himself away from them.* The pictures of Titian did not

---

* See Leslie's opinion on this subject in his biography. These pictures are two feet three inches high, and two feet eleven wide. Hogarth's portrait of himself, is two feet eleven by twenty-three inches. Rembrandt's "Woman taken in Adultery," is two feet nine, by two feet three, and cost Angerstein six thousand guineas. Mr. Sully preferred the "Adoration of the Magi," in this collection, to the "Woman taken in Adultery"; it was painted with the greatest facility. Rembrandt's ground of preparation was like the Venetians in general, white, over which he scumbled lightly a clear transparent warm color, over that he passed olive glazings, which became the principal ground color of his pictures; and like Adrian Ostade, he glazed the same olive color upon itself, so as to bring it to any depth or richness, and often produced his lights and shades by the means of one color only — his mode of producing his lights was always by masses of different colors, having affinity to each other, laid on pure; and which when examined seemed to be laid on by chance; but which all harmonized at a short distance. Those pictures which have been painted with most facility, have been most

afford him great pleasure until Sir Wm. Beechey directed his attention to the " Ariadne."

It may be supposed that he did not neglect the pleasure and profit which visits to West always afforded; who had at that time two works on hand, very dissimilar, his "Amor vincit omnia," † in the small room at the commencement of the sketch gallery; and the "Healing in the Temple," in one of the spacious apartments to which the gallery led. On one occasion when Sully was with him in the small room, the young man took up from a sofa the wing of a mackaw, and was examining it. "That," said West, "is the wing of one of my genii. I never paint without having the object before me, if it is to be had." An important lesson to all painters.

Sully having finished a copy from a Correggio, which had been entrusted to him by his kind benefactor, carried it to Newman Street, for his inspection. "It is very correct," said the master, "but what ground did you paint it on?" "A tan color." "That accounts for the only difference. The original is painted on a lilac." Sully begged to have the original again— took it home — and made a second copy on a lilac ground.

Thomas Sully had now been nine months in England; he had completed all the copies contracted for, and some more; he had painted four landscapes for Mr. John Coates; studied diligently at home and at the academy; and in March 1810, he embarked for New York on his way to his family. When he took leave of the good West, he requested him to visit, on his return to Pennsylvania, his dear native place, Springfield. "Inquire for Springfield meetinghouse," said the old man, "two miles from where the road crosses you, you will find the house." It was on this road that he had refused to ride on the

admired. Sully saw at Angerstein's a very good portrait by Van Dyck, of which he says, "It would seem that he used Naples yellow and white for the highest light — next, Venetian red and white; the gray tints are broken into every part of the flesh, and are apparently of blue black and white. Titian's practice of coloring is supposed by Ramsay Reinagle, to be as follows for making out the effect of his pictures. Raw umber, burnt umber, Venetian red, Indian red, and black: glazing the draperies, etc., and then heightening the scale of colors as the work progresses."

† A copy of this picture by Leslie was brought to this country by one of our travelling connoisseurs.

same horse with the boy who was content to become a tailor. Mr. Sully found the house, but not by the old gentleman's direction, for roads, as well as everything else, had changed their course in the lapse of sixty years. The house to which West bore such filial affection was at the time of Sully's visit owned by a superannuated man of the name of Crazier, who considered the queries of his visitors so intrusive and inexplicable, that he ordered them peremptorily to leave the place. Fortunately his son came in from his agricultural labors, and comprehended the desire of Sully and his companions to make inquiries respecting the great painter, who had made the township an object of note, and understood the meaning and the motive for making a sketch of the house. Two sketches of the building which would excite so many recollections, recall so many scenes — scenes so very opposite to those in which he had been an actor through a long life — were faithfully made by his grateful pupil, and sent duly and safely to his master and friend.*

* Having brought the biography of Sully to the time of leaving England, a few of the notes made by him on painters and paintings, their manners and materials, may be of use to such of our readers, as study the art.

"The best picture of Reynolds that I could see in London, was in Guildhall. The Governor of Gibraltar — Elliot. A portrait by Opie, on the same wall, pleased me exceedingly.

"Sir William Beechey uses a mixture of nut-oil, mastic varnish, and sugar of lead, well shaken and suffered to settle. This he uses in his light colors to make them dry.

"Ramsay Reinagle paints on paper which is pasted on linen; a narrow strip is left of the linen all round to allow for the changes produced by the weather.

"I find wax is sometimes used by the English painters, which is prepared by boiling the honeycomb, and extracting the wax with care, and then it is bleached in the sun. In order to mix it with the mastic varnish it is melted alone, and then the mastic poured to it. If a small lump is put with the white, all the other colors on the palette will partake of it — but no other liquid must be used while painting with this. Beechey has the custom of tempering his colors with a mixture of japanner's gold-size and turpentine. He invariably declines the use of any liquid to dip his pencil into, preferring to temper the color with the knife — should he require the color to be more liquid, he adds turpentine. When finishing the picture, no matter how large it may be, he brushes it over with a mixture of drying oil and spirits of turpentine, and then adds upon it a mixture of turpentine and gold-size; upon this mixture he retouches the work, and it serves as a varnish. I am persuaded this practice would hasten the destruction of the picture, and at all events change the tone." Mr. Sully has said that Mr. West followed the process last mentioned in his "Healing the Sick," and the defect of it was visible in 1822.

"Mr. West sketches on paper with umber and a reed pen; the effect is also put in with umber — next it is brushed over with size, and then retouched in oil colors.

"Mr. Shee condemns the use of yellow ocher in the flesh; thinks burnt terra de sienna

During the passage to New York, and in the month of April the ship was surrounded, and more than once in danger from ice islands. They were once saved by the prompt exertions of a passenger (a sea captain), who in the night happened to be on deck, and saw that the ship was running on an ice mountain, when the sleepy watch and helmsman were unconscious of the danger. He gave the alarm — took the command of the vessel — altered her course by force and authority — and received the captain's thanks when he had rushed on deck and seen the perilous situation he had been rescued from. Another sea captain was likewise a passenger, a rough and boisterous son of the storm, who had conceived an affection for the painter — that is, "taken a strong liking to him." The alarm of ice islands bieng given one night, and the well-known sound of confusion on the deck reaching him, he snatched Sully from his berth, and bearing him aloft in his

quite yellow enough, and for a very swarthy complexion glazing over the flesh with asphaltum is sufficient, and while the glazing is wet he touches upon it with a palette set for the purpose, which drying with the glazing, mixes and partakes of its hue. Umber he discards. Venetian red is a favorite color in the flesh. Blue black, Indian red, burnt terra de sienna, blue, vandyke brown, asphaltum, vermilion and lake. He observes that as colors are liable to change from yellow to brown, some allowance should be made in the first instance.

"Mr. West observed that Correggio generally painted on a ground of a pearly tint, composed of Indian red, black and white. In copying, it was essential to paint on a ground of the same tint with the original. Correggio as an ideal colorist was excellent, his pearly tone suited the chastity of his subjects.

"Titian's grounds were mostly of burnt umber and white, which is the nearest approach to the half tint of nature. Rubens used a white ground, and his coloring, which is uncommonly rich, is like metal, compared with the purity and truth of Titian.

"The English painters generally use absorbent grounds. Lawrence paints his common sized portraits in a broad flat frame painted yellow. This preserves the edges of the canvas from injury, and helps to determine what will be the effect of the picture when framed. Lawrence oils out the ground after making the outline, which he is more exact and particular with, than any portrait painter I know of. His room is lined with dark red — so were Owen's exhibition and painting rooms.

"A macgylp is made with water saturated with sugar of lead, an equal portion of mastic varnish, and three-fourths of linseed oil. It dries well. Ramsay Reinagle approves of oiling out a picture — in painting a dark complexion, uses white lowered with asphaltum. Brown ocher and Naples yellow are better for flesh than yellow ocher. Drying oil is not fit for macgylp after it has stood a month, without shaking the bottle well. An absorbent ground may be prepared with weak size, whiting, and a small portion of treacle."

So far Mr. Sully's notes. It may be added that oiling out a picture is a bad practice, and that burnt terra de sienna is yellow enough for nearly all complexions; perhaps this is what Hopner meant when he said, "There is no yellow in flesh."

Herculean arm, rushed upon deck, where the first thing he did
after placing him on his feet was to fasten down the hatches.
The alarm being over, Sully asked him the meaning of the last
act. "There were more than enough," said the sailor, "already
on deck to fill the boat, and I meant that all under the hatches
should stay there."

Returned to Philadelphia and to his family, the painter
occupied again the same house, jointly with Mr. Trott. Sully
felt that in portrait painting he had made little progress, except
that he had more of the theory, and that his general knowledge of his art was much greater. The public however saw
great improvement in his portraits, and he had the world of
fashion at his beck. That knowledge he had obtained was soon,
and ever after, apparent in all the productions of his pencil.

He was enabled to offer to his friend Wilcox the $500 he
had borrowed of him. "Why what have I done," said he,
"that you will not paint for me, as well as others? I don't
want the money — I must have pictures." The painter sent
him pictures nominally to the amount of the debt, but on any
estimate except that made to induce his friend to accept them,
to the value of half as much more. The copies for masters
made for, and sent at his expense to the subscribers, are now
the ornaments of their houses, and of ten times the value of that
very moderate sum the young painter received for them: but
that well-timed aid enabled him to gain the prize he aimed at.

In 1811, Charles R. Leslie's talent, since so fully developed,
manifested itself. Sully, ever ready to communicate to others
the knowledge bestowed upon him, either by the instrumen-
tality of men like himself, or by his own indefatigable exertions, encouraged the efforts of Leslie in every way. He
painted a head in the manner of Rembrandt expressly for his
instruction. He thus taught the boy the use of the material,
which he has employed so conspicuously to his own honor
and the delight of the world. For this service rendered, we
have heard Sully say that Leslie has never ceased repaying him
by presents of prints, drawings and other friendly tokens of
remembrance and good will.

But the effect of too close application to study began to show itself before the end of 1811, and rendered it necessary for Mr. Sully to make a journey to Richmond for the recovery of his health. This leads to a notice of an arrangement made by the painter to secure the services of an eminent physician for his family after he returned from this journey to Virginia. Dr. Dorsey very willingly agreed to attend as family physician, for the sum of $100 the year, to be paid in pictures. After a time the doctor protested against the bargain, and said "I must break off, Sully, this will not do." "How so?" "Because none of you will be sick." "Only let us remain well, doctor," said the painter, "and I am willing to paint to three times the amount for you."

A pleasant acquaintance of mine had the habit of introducing any subject whatever, by "speaking of a gun," a phrase similar to the French *apropos des bottes*. We shall come nearer the mark we aim at, by saying, "speaking of a doctor," and having related one painter's anecdote of a doctor, let it introduce another. Doctor Lewis, a very old gentleman was sitting to Sully for his portrait when Dr. Abercrombie came in. "So," said the latter, "sitting for your picture, Dr. Lewis, that's right!" "Yes," said the old gentleman, "I have settled all my affairs, and have nothing to do but have my likeness taken and die." In two months from the time he was a corpse.

This did not prove a sufficient warning to Dr. Abercrombie, who perhaps had not yet settled his affairs, for he soon after sat for his portrait. When he was adjusting himself to the fatal chair, the painter inquired, "How much time can you give me, doctor?" "I'll sit as long as you please," was the reply. "I can paint all day." "And I can sit all day." By and by, Trott came in, but finding a sitter, retired. After the longest time he had ever known or heard of for the operation, he returned, — found the doctor on the same spot, and withdrew. He came a third time, after a still longer interval, and there still sat the doctor, who saluted him with, "Well, Mr. Trott, don't you think I'm a good sitter?" "Good," said Trott; "yes indeed. You set like an old hen." This joke, may pass in common parlance because, in common parlance *sit* and *set* are frequently very improperly confounded.

Another easel anecdote, *apropos des bottes*. Monsieur Brugere, a French gentleman, who had lived in double blessedness, until his consort and himself were of a certain age, or a little beyond, called on the painter and engaged his portrait. The transaction, by agreement, was to be a profound secret, as he meant to surprise Madame Brugere, by presenting her with a duplicate of his beloved visage, as a New Year's gift. While this affair was going on the painter received a visit from Madame Brugere. Sully, on seeing her enter, thought the secret had fared the fate of most secrets, and was preparing to bring Monsieur's physiognomy from its hiding place; but the lady did not give him time to be a marplot. "Mr. Sully," said she, "you must paint my picture very quick; for I am determined to surprise Mr. Brugere very much by presenting to him my likeness on New Year's day, the first thing he shall see. Monsieur Brugere has long desired to possess my portrait — I have long time refused — but now I would surprise him, when he shall find it hung up before his face on New Year's morning. So you will paint my portrait, and we shall keep it very, *very* secret, from Monsieur Brugere and all the world." Thus this happy couple had hit on the same plan to increase each other's pleasure at the commencement of the year. Accordingly both portraits were painted, and both secrets remained inviolate and unsuspected. The painter contrived that the pictures should be carried to the house and placed in the parlor on New Year's eve, after the family had retired to rest — the same pretence for the secrecy of the proceeding, and the lateness of the hour, answering for each, and each plotting with the painter to deceive and surprise the other. A visit was soon received from the husband. "Aha! Monsieur Sully! *Mon Dieu,* how we have all played trick! I trick my wife — my wife trick me — you trick both. Very early on New Year morning Madame Brugere get up and go into the parlor. I listen, and I hear her exclaim very loud and laugh immoderately. So I go to her to enjoy the joke.

'Aha! my dear!' I say, 'is it like?' —'You shall look if it is like:' and there I found her picture by the side of mine. 'Aha!' said I, 'Sully has told you my plot, and you counterplot me!' but I found it was the same thought in two heads." "And the mutual desire to produce an agreeable surprise," said the painter.

Mr. Sully painted several full lengths about this time. One of the celebrated George Frederick Cooke, in the character of Richard the Third, he presented to the Pennsylvania Academy of Fine Arts. A full-length portrait of Samuel Coates, an active governor of the Pennsylvania Hospital, is placed opposite to one of Doctor Rush, in the building erected for West's picture of "Healing in the Temple," but in an antechamber. Coates's portrait he presented to the Pennsylvania Hospital; that of Dr. Rush he was employed to paint by the directors and paid for. This was in the year 1813.*

* "To THOMAS SULLY, Portrait Painter, Philadelphia.
"New York, April 16th, 1812.

"Dear Sir — I am desirous of obtaining a portrait of my friend Dr. Rush. I have an imperfect likeness of him in crayons, by Sharpless; but it contains nothing of the character of Dr. Rush, which it should be the object of the painter to delineate: in that respect yours is a *science*, not an *art*, as it is generally denominated. Believing that you duly appreciate the mind which animates the face of my friend, and that you have become familiarly conversant with his features, I have no doubt you will be enabled to furnish me with a portrait which will be gratifying to me, at the same time that it will afford me and your other friends an opportunity of seeing a specimen of the present highly improved productions of your pencil. I hope your engagements will permit you to confer upon me the favor I ask, in the course of the present season.

"I wish it to be a half length, to correspond with that of Dr. Bard, by Vanderlyn, which you have seen in my room. Your order for the same will be honored whenever you think proper to inform me of the amount, and to whom it shall be paid.

"Would it improve the picture by throwing into the background a distant view of your City Hospital or University, to which Dr. Rush's labors have been so much and so long devoted?

"I am, Sir, with regard and respect,
"Yours,
"D. HOSACK."

"To DR. BENJAMIN RUSH.
"New York, April 23d, 1812.

"My dear Sir — I have written to Mr. Sully, the portrait painter, of your city, requesting to know if his engagements will permit him, at this time, to execute for me a portrait of a much esteemed and respected friend. Finding that he is both ready to comply with my wish, and pleased with the subject upon which I have requested his pencil to be employed, it remains for me to ask the favor of you to oblige me by sitting to him for this purpose, whenever you may find it convenient. I am very sensible of the tax I lay upon your friendship, in asking from you this favor, incessantly occupied as you are by business. I already possess an imperfect sketch, by Sharpless, but it consists of mere features, exhibiting little or nothing of the character which I consider everything in a portrait.

"I have applied to Mr. Sully, believing that he duly appreciates his art in this respect, and that he, at the same time, is sufficiently acquainted with your *mind* as well as your *face*, to blend them on the canvas. You see I am fully apprised of the correctness of the observation by Sir Joshua Reynolds, that 'it is not the eye, it is the mind, which the painter of genius desires to address, that it is this *intellectual* dignity that ennobles the painter's art, that lays the line between him and the mere mechanic.'

"But I hope I am not imposing upon you the task of a *five* hours' sitting, the time occupied by Sir Joshua when he painted his celebrated portrait of your friend Dr. Beattie.

"Present me affectionately to Mrs. Rush and Miss Julia; I hope we shall be favored with a visit from them in the course of the summer. I am happy to tell you, that after the embarrassments which the delay of payment for the garden had temporarily created, my mind is once more at ease, and that my undivided attention is now given to my profession. My promised letter is only *delayed*, not forgotten.

"With great respect and esteem,
"I am yours,
"DAVID HOSACK."

CHAPTER XVII.

Sully — *Concluded.* House.

The yearly receipts of the painter has been stated, at the time he commenced oil painter in Norfolk: it was $120. His yearly earnings now, for some years, including the first after his return from England, were, from $4,500 to $4,120. This did not last; and before the year 1818 his business had most sensibly decreased. He lost much time by undertaking to make a large drawing of West's picture of "Healing in the Temple," for the directors of the Pennsylvania Hospital. — From this an engraving was to have been made: he was to receive $500 for the finished drawing. But after proceeding in the work for several weeks, he found that he should lose by the bargain, and begged to be released from it, unless an additional $200 could be added for his remuneration. The directors chose to annul the agreement, and the time employed upon the drawing was lost.

By invitation from the city of New York, Mr. Sully repaired to that city, and painted Commodore Decatur's full-length portrait, for which he received $500. This was the first painted of that series of full lengths which the common council of New York ordered, to commemorate the men who distinguished themselves during the short War of 1812: a war which, in its causes, characterized the insolence of Great Britain, and, by its events, proved that she was not the mistress of every sea, or conqueror on every shore — the latter had been before shown triumphantly on the same soil. Mr. Sully's "Decatur" is not the happiest effort of his genius or pencil.

The voices of all in America who understood or loved the fine arts, would have called upon Gilbert Stuart to have fulfilled the views of the city of New York, by perpetuating the resemblances, in form and character, of the defenders of the

country; and he had already commenced the full length of
the first who began the career of victory, the conqueror of the
" Guerriere "; but, from some misunderstanding with the officer,
or with the corporation of New York, or from some caprice
of the eccentric painter, the work was discontinued, and the
collection in the city hall of New York cannot boast a picture
from the hand of Stuart.

Mr. Sully was applied to by the common council of New
York to go on to Boston and paint the portrait of the officer
whose likeness Stuart had begun and left unfinished; and the
assurance was given, that the portraits of the other victorious
commanders, naval and military, would be ordered in succession. This was a glorious and golden opportunity for the
painter. But to go to the place where Stuart resided, — his
friend and early instructor — his elder, and undoubtedly, at
that time, his better as an artist, and paint a subject which he
had commenced — "Oh no!" said Sully, " it cannot be!"
However, as the journey was pressed upon him, and thinking
that he might find some means of serving Stuart, connected
with this project, he asked a little time before giving his final
answer. He therefore wrote to Mr. Stuart, reminding him
"that he had heard him often express his aversion to painting
backgrounds in their details, the draperies of portraits, and
the subordinate accessories of pictures; telling him that the
corporation of New York were determined to have a gallery
of portraits of distinguished men, for which he might be employed if he chose, and offering to be his assistant in the subordinate parts of the plan, and the whole should be under his
direction." Stuart never answered the letter. Sully declined
going to Boston, as required, and another was employed to
paint the pictures. Mr. Jarvis, who had not the same scruples
in respect to Stuart, went on to Boston, and achieved the work
which Stuart had neglected or refused: and in consequence of
the satisfactory likeness produced, was employed for a long
time in decorating the city hall of New York with full lengths
of successful commanders.

Some years after, Mr. Sully being in company with Mr.

Stuart at Boston, the latter proposed painting in conjunction, and almost in the words of Sully's former proposition, concluding with, "We can carry all the continent." Mr. Sully replied that he should be delighted with such a company scheme, and then asked him if he remembered his letter to him in 1814. He denied all knowledge of it. Upon which Sully remarked, "If we had undertaken that business at that time, sir, we should have painted" — Stuart interrupted him by exclaiming, "All those full lengths which that blackguard painted!"

The affair of the drawing commenced for the Pennsylvania Hospital mentioned above, took place in July 1818, and in October of that year he had another order, which produced still more unfortunate results. He was applied to by the legislature of North Carolina for two full-length portraits of Washington. In reply, he proposed the painting of one historical picture, in which some prominent action of the hero should be represented, and mentioned the crossing of the Delaware at Trenton. This was agreed upon. He wrote for the dimensions of the place the picture was destined to occupy; and not receiving an answer, proceeded with the work on a canvas of great dimensions: years were expended in the completion; applications for portraits almost ceased; money was borrowed to carry on the work, and when it was finished he was informed that there was no place fitted to receive it, and the picture was thrown upon his hands.

To paint a great picture, and this was such both in size and subject, the artist requires a lofty apartment, and many expensive adjuncts which may be dispensed with in the composition of smaller works. The time exhausted in studies and labor, especially where all is done by one person, as has heretofore frequently been the case in our country, probably amounts to years; and the expenses of the artist and his family, if he lives in that becoming style which his professional standing in society entitles him to, and even his interest may require, must be serious in the amount. Thus his picture costs him (without charging it with any of the capital expended on his education as an artist) some thousands of dollars, which, if paid by a purchaser, is thought a great price, although it merely suffices to repay the painter for the expense incurred while painting the work — and his talents and labor go for nothing.

Stuart used to say no man would paint history if he could find full employment in portrait. If mere gain is to be considered, he was right. Sully had committed two errors in this business: first, his ambition prompted him to put aside the painting of two full lengths which were offered to his pencil, for the sake of painting history. Here "vaulting ambition did o'erleap itself"; and secondly, prudence should have dictated to wait until he received an official answer respecting the size of the historical picture.

Mr. Sully had produced a fine historical picture, representing perhaps the most brilliant achievement of Washington, and in many respects in the most perfect style of art; but he found no purchaser for it, nor any profit from its exhibition. Unfortunately, Washington's portrait was not acknowledged as a likeness. The generation, who were its judges, generally formed their opinion of his countenance from the vile print published by Heath of London, and called Gabriel Stuart's "Washington" (certainly it was not Gilbert Stuart's), and from Trumbull's pictures of the general. This unfortunate picture was at length sold to Mr. John Doggett, a wealthy and worthy frame maker of Boston, for $500, and he sold it to Mr. Greenwood, the keeper of the Boston Museum; and it there remains rolled up, awaiting the time when it shall be justly appreciated. If it was an old instead of a modern picture, the winter landscape would alone stamp it as a jewel; but in the old pictures one good part redeems — in the modern, one part faulty condemns. When the painter hears this picture mentioned, he sometimes says, "I wish it was burnt." A small finished study, four feet by three, painted previous to the large picture, was purchased by Sir James Wright, and is now in Edinburgh, and another of the same size was purchased by Col. I. Ash, of Georgetown, South Carolina.

In July 1821, Mr. Sully first became personally acquainted with Washington Allston. Among the many projects suggested by the lack of regular professional business as a portrait painter, the noise which Granet's picture of the "Capuchin Chapel" made at this time, was the cause of one which Sully carried into execution with success. It was justly thought that a good copy would be a profitable exhibition picture, especially as the original was the property of a man of fortune, and not visited with the same freedom as one feels when paying twenty-five cents for admission — a kind of ease similar to one's enjoyment "in mine own inn." Thus thinking, Sully, having obtained permission of Mr. Wiggins of Boston to make the copy (a permission for which he was in part indebted to the suggestion of Mrs. Wiggins, that it would diminish the number of visitors who came to see the original painting — ladies do not like to have their carpets trodden by unhallowed feet), the painter repaired to the famous tri-mount town, and prepared for the task. When Sully spoke of the time necessary to make a copy of this very highly finished picture among his brother artists, Sargent gave him four months, Allston said five, Stuart six, but the indefatigable painter finished it in less than three. When he told Allston it was finished, he said, "You have made a sketch." "No; a carefully finished copy — come and see." It was acknowledged to be such. But the artist had worked ten hours every day; and such was his absorption in the labor he had undertaken, that, neglecting his premonitory feelings, he one day on leaving off, after having extended the time of labor, while preparing to clean his palette, fainted away from exhaustion.

M. Granet, the painter of the original which Sully copied as above, had been commissioned from Naples to paint a picture while he was in Rome, and took for his subject the choir of the Capuchin Church in the Piazzi Barberini, during divine worship. He was admirably successful. He had orders for, and executed ten copies of his picture. One of these was made for Mr. Wiggins, who brought it to the United States. The other copies by Granet are distributed all over Europe.

In this same year, 1821, Mr. Sully painted his fine full-length portrait of Mr. Jefferson for the Military Academy at West Point. For this purpose he visited the sage at Monticello, and in his house made a painting, head size, of the venerable ex-president. The painter was an inmate of Monticello twelve days, and left the place with the greatest reluctance.

Many are the vicissitudes which a portrait painter has to undergo even after he has attained eminence. How necessary is it for him to catch and hold fast a portion of the product of the flood tide, that when the ebb comes he may not be left stranded and destitute like a shipwrecked mariner. Perhaps no painter of Mr. Sully's acknowledged merit has experienced the fluctuations of fashion, or the caprices of the public, in so great a degree. At one time overwhelmed with applications for portraits, at another literally deserted, not because he deteriorated, as some have done, for all acknowledge progressive improvement to the present hour. In 1824 Mr. Sully's business had decreased fearfully, and his embarrassments increasing in proportion, had become so onerous that he had determined to leave America. He had pressing invitations to come to Edinburgh, and there take up his permanent residence. While he hesitated, a plan was proposed by some of his friends for a second visit to England, instead of a removal of his family. It was thought he might leave his family at home while he went to London and painted the portraits of eminent men, originals, and copies from good pictures by artists of known talents, of deceased worthies, the Lockes, the Newtons, the Miltons, the Cromwells, the Hampdens, and others that we claim as our countrymen, and revere as our benefactors. He was to be supported by sums subscribed for the purpose by those who wished such pictures, and who wished to encourage the art and the artist.

This plan was so far matured that the painter carried it in the form of a subscription paper to a wealthy, and professing friend for his signature. He was coldly received, and time asked for deliberation. Sully took his leave with his subscription paper in his hand; and if the patron looked from his window upon the man whose expectations he had raised but to disappoint, whose manly spirit rose as his hopes were crushed, he might have seen the heart-stricken husband and father tear the paper to pieces, and dash it in the kennel before his door.

He now thought of accepting invitations from Boston promising him employment, and having made known his intentions, packed up and made all ready for the journey, he was waited upon by Messrs. Fairman, Fox, and Childs, engravers, who were determined to prevent what they justly considered a loss to the city. "You must not leave us," they said. "I have no employment here." "If you had gone to England, you would have returned. If you go to Boston, and take your family, you will stay there. Will you paint our portraits?" "Certainly." It was agreed upon. The painter unpacked his materials, and from that time to this he has had uninterrupted success — full employment, increased prices, increased reputation, and increasing skill.

Mr. Sully is, as we believe and sincerely hope, anchored safely in port for life. He has portraits engaged in succession for years to come at liberal prices. His fellow citizens of Philadelphia justly appreciate him as an artist and a man. The late wealthy, eccentric, benevolent, and munificent Stephen Girard caused to be built in addition to one of his houses, purposely for the artist, an exhibition and painting room, and in that house he resides surrounded by his numerous family, and by all those conveniences which are so dear and necessary to a painter.

With a frame apparently slight, but in reality strong, muscular, athletic, and uncommonly active, Mr. Sully does not stand over five feet eight inches in height, but he walks with the stride of a man of six feet. His complexion is pale, hair brown, eyes grey, approaching to blue, and ornamented with uncommonly long eyelashes, and his whole physiognomy marked with the wish to make others happy. At the age of fifty-one, he enjoys the cheerfulness and activity of youth. Two of his daughters are married, one to Mr. John Neagle, a first-rate portrait painter, another, herself a painter, to Mr. Darley.

The oldest son of the artist has followed the example of his father in rejecting the counting house for the painter's *atelier*, and we doubt not will follow his example in industry and virtue.

Notes on Pictures and Painting,

By Thomas Sully, Esq.[0]

Charles R. Leslie, Esq., soon after he went to London, copied Hogarth's "Gate of Calais," and sent it to this country. Sully copied it, and says in one of his notes, that he "painted the figures in front at each side with color tempered with wax; especially the figure of the Scotchman, which, except a slight effect of burnt umber in the commencement, was wholly painted with wax colors, which is prepared as follows: to a dessertspoonful of mastic (varnish) add a piece of bleached wax, melted by fire; when this mixture is cold it will form a thin jelly, which may be either used as a magylp by tempering it with oil, or by adding it to the colors when ground in oil." Sully's copy from Leslie is in Sully and Earl's gallery, Philadelphia. The fate of Leslie's copy from Hogarth is singular. It was purchased at auction by a boy for two dollars, who did not know its worth, and willingly sold it to his master for a trifling advance. It is now in New York.

In April, 1826, Mr. Sully visited the collection of Joseph Bonaparte, at Bordentown, New Jersey. The remarks of the painter at this period of matured knowledge and judgment, are worthy the attention of the student. "Titian's plan does not appear to me to produce splendor of coloring by employing the brightest colors, but by the judicious and artful use of sober tints, and the practice of toning and glazing them. I am now speaking of the impression made upon me by an inspection of those examined on this occasion. Indian red appears to have been the principal red used in the flesh — in the fairest flesh a little improved with vermilion. I have little doubt that the dead coloring made with Indian red, or even colcothar in the flesh, then toned with raw umber and white in

0   Thomas Sully died in his ninetieth year, the 5th of November, 1872.

the lights, and glazed with asphaltum or mummy in the shadows, would be near the general preparation. But if in the dead color black were used in the gradations, perhaps toning with brown ochre and Indian red might be better. It is remarkable how much glazing has been used in the 'Lucretia,' which I examined closely. Even the whole drapery has been glazed or toned down. The effect is a subdued splendor, far preferable to the oily smoothness of the opposite system. Absorbent canvas seems to have been used; the colors much loaded. I again had occasion to remark that in large pictures very sober colors may be employed to produce richness of effect. A picture by Velasquez (a deer chase) has very much the aspect of a Titian, but there is not so much display of glazing and process; the unity of the tone seemed effected by beginning the whole picture with one color for the shade, and one for the light, which are afterwards finished upon. Murillo looks dirty and clouded in the tone and in the flesh; except in small pictures of a portrait size, *there* the flesh was rich and natural. Guido looked hard and liny near Titian, and very cold and weak. The large pictures of Rubens have much of Titian's good color in them, although generally of a higher scale."

In 1828, Mr. Sully, though standing so high in his profession, copied a head painted by Raeburn, for study. He says of it, "I found much use made of glazing colors of green, purple, asphaltum, and lake. The green made of Prussian blue and asphaltum; the purple, of Prussian blue and lake. After dead coloring near life, I tinted the flesh, white drapery, and background with yellow, red and blue tints: when dry, glazed and improved the shadows, and scumbled the lights, on which I improved the tinting and finished the picture."

In 1827, Mr. Sully says, "I have resorted to my first method in laying in the flesh, by dead coloring with Indian red and black — two tints with white and light red, and two tints of white, making out a broad effect of the head — including hair — a portion of the drapery and a portion of the background. I follow upon that with the following tints, in the order they are set down, beginning with the madder lake and so on; — using a light touch with a long-haired pencil.

Madder lake	Brown ocher	Cobalt and white
Vermilion	Brown and white	More white
Vermilion and white	More white	Black and brown ocher
More white	More white	Black and brown and white
More white	Cobalt	Asphaltum or Vandyke for the hair

"Yellow ocher, or Naples yellow, may be substituted for the brown ocher, or blue-black for the cobalt, or raw umber for the black and brown ocher tint. The background and drapery tinted in the same way; that is, with the Indian red, black and white; and, while wet, the colors broken in — except in masses of colored or dark drapery; these may be put in of the tone or depth of color, and glazed and retouched afterwards. The subsequent sittings are to glaze the shadows of the flesh, scumble the lights with light red and white, or any other fit tone, and retouch the complexion. I have painted, in this way, Dr. Abercrombie, and two copies of Guy Bryan, Esq."

Mr. Sully was incessantly making experiments, but not losing his time in search of nostrums and secrets. He made notes of the palettes of eminent men — he tried their practice, and finally came back to the above. He thus gives Raeburn's palette. After ivory black and white lead, follow the tints.—

1. Indian red	6. No. 5 and white	12. Black and Indian red
2. Add white	7. More white	13. Add white
3. More white	8. Raw umber	14. More white
4. More white	9. Add white	15. More white
5. Brown ocher and Indian red	10. More white	16. More white
	11. More white	

Finishing palette: —

1. Indian red and vermilion	7. No. 6 and more white	13. No. 12 and white
2. No. 1 and white	8. No. 7 and white	14. More white
3. More white	9. Raw umber	15. Ivory black and white
4. More white	10. Raw umber and white	16. More white
5. No. 1 and brown ocher	11. More white	17. Madder lake
6. No. 5 and white	12. Indian red and black	18. Asphaltum

"The foregoing memorandum, from Sir Henry Raeburn's portrait of Dugald Stewart, presented by Dr. P. Tilghman to our Academy, has induced me to remark, that it is a list of colors applicable to most complexions, varying, as occasion demands the tints Nos. 5, 6, and 7. In very florid complexions, as those of red-haired persons, or of very fair, a different scale is requisite; for such, perhaps, burnt terra de sienna and vermilion. Light red and Naples yellow, with vermilion and white tints would be better. In glazing, I found he had incidentally employed cobalt with the tint No. 12 (Indian red and black); cobalt with asphaltum; also asphaltum with No. 12. It is well to paint with daring boldness and strength in determining the head. In finishing with the different tints, more circumspection must be used."

In another note he gives the proportion of light and shade for large pictures. "The half, demi-tint; one-fourth, dark shade; and one-fourth, light. For small pictures, more dark shade, and less bright light."

Speaking of one of his pictures, he says, "By taking too much pains with the detail, I have lost breadth — by muddling the colors, I have lost clearness. I must give more local tint to the flesh; the cold tints bordering the shadows trench too much on the light — the face looks muddy."

In May, 1830, Mr. Sully writes thus: — "On careful inspection of several good pictures of the old masters in Abraham's collection, at New York, I find that the practice of touching the whole picture with a warm color, like terra de sienna, and, in some instances, with a dark color like asphaltum, was common to their practice. A fine copy of Correggio's 'Magdalene,' and a portrait by Velasquez (rather doubtful), were much toned. In the landscape by Hobbima, asphaltum has been used over all the surface, sky and all. In a landscape, said to be by Claude, I found much scumbling, of a lilac neutral tint, over the distance and middle ground — perhaps also the sky; and finally, the whole picture, sky also, was toned with raw sienna, or a color like it. The best picture in this collection is a Murillo: the colors are subdued, simple, little discrimination of tint: brown ocher, Indian red, and raw umber chiefly: the whole much toned: a very full pencil has been used: the colors, at least in the beginning, were stiff, the marks of the brush left — no softening tool employed."

In June, 1831, Sully visited Boston. Ever in search of improvement, not only by industrious application, but by the examination of the works of others, and the lessons received in conversation with the masters of the art, he has made a note of the remarks of Allston, whom he always designates as "number one." "Allston says that Stuart condemned vermilion, but could not relieve himself by a substitute. (He) was of the same opinion, and had used Venetian red; which, if of good quality and well washed, will answer every purpose if a glazing of madder lake be resorted to. In Italy they have a superior kind of madder lake, called *terra rosa*. The walls of Allston's painting room are colored with Spanish brown. Allston recommends emphatically, solid tinting in painting flesh, especially for large pictures that are to be seen at a distance. 'Paint pure, decided tints: if too raw, you may correct them by scumbling — glaze at pleasure.' Again, 'never use brown drapery to a dark or yellow complexion; it will look like a snuff bag.' He recommends the use of a very slight glazing of asphaltum to a portrait, face and all."

In 1832, he has this note. "Inman observes that his practice is to measure the face from the eyebrow to the chin. That as a general rule, to the end of the nose is one-half of the face from the brow to the chin. He observes carefully the distance of the eye from the brow and from the nose, as on these points much of the identity of the face depends. Stuart Newton in conversation told me 'he thought Lawrence's portraits over embellished — too theatrical — so that locality was sacrificed. (He) would prefer to see the individual with his exact and leading characteristic expression, but treated with an improved view. Reynolds, far the best portrait painter — he too had to contend with the complaint of want of likeness — Lawrence's portraits of females rather loose. (He) would like to see all portraits of women made beautiful, and *like* if possible. On account of their costume, etc., they are the best subjects for a painter of portraits.' "

It may be seen by these notes how attentive Mr. Sully always was to every opinion that might improve him; and it is hoped that by publishing these memoranda, made only for private use (but given by permission), many students may find hints for their coloring and for their conduct. I think them invaluable.

JAMES HOUSE.

This gentleman had in early life chosen painting for his profession, and practised taking likenesses in Philadelphia about this time. What changed his views I know not, but he entered the army of the United States, and I remember him long as Colonel House, and in 1814 commanding as fine a regiment as I ever beheld.[0]

0 House was a Brevet Brigadier General at the time of his death, November 17, 1834.

CHAPTER XVIII.

SIMOND — MARAS — GALLAGHER — MILES — MURRAY —
RAPHAEL WEST — ECKSTEIN — GUY — TUTHILL —
FRASER — STEWART — HUTCHINS.

LOUIS SIMOND. [0]

THIS gentleman, although not professionally an artist, had been so well taught in the course of a liberal education, and practised in this country for his amusement with so much skill, that he must be considered as one who contributed to the progress of the arts of design.

L. Simond was a native of Switzerland, who visited this country as a merchant; married in New York, and resided with us many years. On his return to Europe, he passed some time in England, and published a work on that country, particularly noticing artists and arts. Unfortunately for his reputation as a critic of painting, he had become intimate in New York with John Trumbull, who was, at the time of his visit to London, painting his unsuccessful historical large pictures in that city, and *then* the enemy of B. West. Simond uniformly condemns the works of West, except the "Death of Wolfe," and that, he hints, was stolen from a previous picture. Trumbull's pictures, then painting, are praised in the comparison. Without this clue, Mr. Simond's strictures on West would be unintelligible to those who know his taste.

His description of a night and early morning in London is very fine. He afterwards published travels in Switzerland and Italy.

M. MARAS. [00]

A Frenchman by birth, M. Maras visited America about the year 1800. In 1801-2 he painted poor miniatures in New York. A poor or bad artist flourishes best where the people

---

0 Louis Simond, who was born in France in 1767, died in Switzerland in 1831.
00 We know no more about M. Maras than the fascinating history given by Dunlap. There was a John Maras in New York in 1808. A Maras exhibited in Philadelphia in 1820.

are most ignorant; and M. Maras, with great judgment, transferred himself from New York to Constantinople, where he is
at the head of affairs in the department of the fine arts, and
painter to the sublime sultan. Charles Rhind, Esq., who
negotiated our commercial treaty with the porte, recognized in
the sultan's portrait painter, M. Maras from New York. The
present sultan, among his many reforms, patronizes the fine
arts (at least so far as to despise what the Mahometans consider a religious prohibition), and, in imitation of more civilized
monarchs, makes presents of his portrait in miniature to the
ambassadors of other courts. This gives Maras full employment. The sultan puzzled the painter by requiring him to
paint his sublimity on horseback, and the Frenchman was
mounting him on a creature more like an ass than a horse,
when my friend Rhind visited his rooms. He had possession
of the grand signor's magnificent sword and jewels, enough to
make him a nabob — if he could keep them.

GALLAGHER.[0]

A foreign artist, who painted portraits in Philadelphia at
this time, and perhaps earlier. When there was a lack of portraits to do, he painted signs. He had a dashy, sketchy manner,
and had been well instructed in the rudiments of drawing.
In 1807, Thomas A. Cooper employed him in New York as
scene painter; but however great Gallagher's taste for the arts
might be, his taste for lounging was greater, and, unfortunately
for him, Cooper had been used to the rapid and effective
manner of John J. Holland. He began a kitchen scene very
beautifully, and might have made it rival a Dutch picture, but
week after week passed, and the scene was not ready for the
stage. "Some time next year," said the manager, "I may
have *one* scene from Mr. Gallagher, and it will cost more than
a Van Dyck or a Titian."

Gallagher used to come every Saturday with the accounts of
the scene department in his hand, and walk the stage during
rehearsal to Cooper's great annoyance. "What does that
man do *here?* I will not pay him $30 a week to walk with his

0 Christian Gullager was born in Copenhagen, the 1st of March, 1759. The name was
then Guldager. After the 1807 episode he disappeared, only to reappear in Philadelphia,
dying there on November 12, 1826.

hat on one side, and his hands in his pockets!" Gallagher was dismissed, and I lost sight of him.

E. MILES.[01]

All I know of this gentleman is, that he painted miniatures in Philadelphia for many years, and (as I am informed by J. R. Lambdin, Esq., who was his pupil in 1823), was once miniature painter to the Emperor Paul of Russia, the mad autocrat.

GEORGE MURRAY

Was a native of Scotland and went up to London (certainly no rare case) a destitute lad. How he *got on* there my informant saith not, but he was taught engraving by Anker Smith. Entangled with the Liberty Boys, he found it prudent to leave England, and took refuge in our Southern States, where he commenced trader and married. He failed in his mercantile business and removed with his family to Philadelphia, where he resumed his professional employment, probably in 1800. His talents and knowledge as an engraver soon brought him into notice, and his necessities were relieved by employment for the plates of the Encyclopedia. He was particularly skilful in engraving animals, and the lions of the Encyclopedia are a fair specimen and a proof of his talents.

When bank notes became the currency of the country, Murray engaged in that branch of engraving and associated with Fairman, Draper and others, they formed the well-known company of Murray, Draper, Fairman and Co. in 1811. The company was prosperous, became rich, and Murray was the financier and apparent leader of the business. He at this time is said to have kept his carriage, and wore a breast-pin of the cost of $700. Not content with thriving in business, he engaged in purchasing houses and lots — their value fell, and he was ruined by the fall and his own prodigality.

He was a great agitator in the controversies between the

01 Edward Miles, who was court painter in England in 1794, was born at Yarmouth, England, October 14, 1752, and after painting in London from 1786 to 1794 went to St. Petersburg in 1797. He painted miniatures in Philadelphia from 1807 to 1828, the year of his death.

artists of Philadelphia and the proprietors of the building and statuary called the Pennsylvania Academy of Fine Arts. Mr. Sully, who had been elected a director of the Academy, and endeavored by every means in his power to make it useful, was a particular object for Murray's enmity, and he was finally obliged to call upon him and charge him with asserting false-hoods in respect to him. It is said to be painful even now to Mr. Sully to hear the name of Murray.

This reckless and improvident man died poor, about the year 1824.[1] "I have seen," says a correspondent, "his widow keeping a small huckster's shop where gingerbread and apples were sold." He is one of the men of genius who set themselves up as beacons to warn others from the rocks of folly.

RAPHAEL WEST.

In the year 1800 this gentleman, my old and intimate com-panion in London, most unexpectedly appeared in New York with his wife. Benjamin West and John Trumbull had made purchases from Mr. Wadsworth, of Genesee, of tracts of land on that paradise, the Genesee flats, near the bend which the Genesee River makes after coming from the higher lands to the west (and turning north flows through luxuriant meadows, which always reminded me of the poetical Elysium), and finally falls into Lake Ontario, near Rochester. The elder West wished his son to visit his purchase, and as we Yankees say, improve it. But of all creatures my friend Raphael was the least fitted for the task of a pioneer in America. Born and educated in London, he had never been out of its neighbor-hood; and though he had studied the noble oaks of Windsor forest, which he used to draw with anatomical precision united to all the beauties of the picturesque, he was a stranger to the appearance of the untamed forest, where only the Indian footpath gave token of the presence of man, and where instead of the deer, who in conscious safety approached and gazed at his drawings, he found the bear, the wolf and all those free

[1] A notice in *Poulson's Advertiser* of November 9, 1822, would seem to indicate the latter as the year of Murray's death.

rovers of the woods who at that time were the prey of the
Iroquois, or preyed upon the flocks and herds of the settler —
for then not only the spot to which the London painter was
destined but all that country of the west, now thronging with
human life and replete with human happiness, was a wilderness, uncultivated except where the Onondaga, the Oneida, the
Seneca, or some other individual of the Six Nations had
pitched a wigwam by the side of a stream; where the fertile
and inexhaustible soil gave maize without labor as a coarse
condiment to his venison. I do not mean that in 1800 there
were literally no settlements commenced in this great country,
but they were principally the squatters and pioneers of Yankee
population, and Raphael had the house of Wadsworth, at
Big Tree, to receive him, although the owner was still in
Europe. This place is now a paradise.

Raphael West was born in the year 1769, the oldest son of
the great historical painter. His portrait as a boy is introduced
by his father in the beautiful small picture of the family,
leaning on the arm of his mother's chair, who is looking at the
second son, Benjamin, an infant on her lap. His school education was entrusted to one of the numerous academies that surrounded London, and it seems to have been a favorite with the
Americans of that day, as Mather Brown, John Singleton
Copley (the son of the painter, and now Lord Lyndhurst),
and Raphael West, were schoolmates and playmates, when, as
Mather Brown told Leslie, "he and Raefe had often, while
bathing, given the chancellor in embryo a ducking in the
Serpentine River.*

Having mentioned the West family picture, I will repeat
what Mr. Charles R. Leslie has said respecting it, as connected
with my friend Raphael. "Of all Mr. West's pictures, *great* or
small, I prefer (perhaps you will laugh at me) the little one

* Let it be remembered to the credit of Lord Lyndhurst, that he did not forget his
early friend Raphael West, while chancellor, and when Raphael, after the death of his
father, was rather in straitened circumstances, Lyndhurst exerted himself with the
government, but in vain, to induce them to purchase some of the large pictures left by
Benjamin West. Lyndhurst offered Raphael a place, but it was not a sufficiently eligible
one, and was declined; and unluckily, for the places he could have given him, of more
consequence, Raphael was not qualified.

representing his own family. Sir Joshua Reynolds used to say, 'no man ever painted more than half a dozen perfectly original pictures in his life.' Certainly this one stands pre-eminent among Mr. West's half dozen. It is well known by an indifferent engraving, as large, I believe, as the picture, and represents a young mother (Mrs. West) soon after the birth of her second child. I know of nothing in the art more lovely than the mother and the sleeping babe. Near her stands, half reclining, a boy of nine or ten years of age (your old friend Raphael West) and on the other side sit two Quakers with their hats on, the father and brother of the artist, who leans on the back of one of their chairs." Does he not lean on his wife's chair? By the bye, had Allan Cunningham ever seen this picture, or even seen Mr. West, he could not, one would suppose, constantly speak of him as a Quaker. To return to Leslie. "I believe the picture represents the first visit paid by the father and brother-in-law to the lady, after the birth of the second son, and the silence which reigns over the whole is that of religious meditation. When Mr. West's pictures were sold, Mr. Newton and I agreed, if it should come at all within our means, to buy this one between us. But Raphael West, to whom it belongs, would not part with it. It was therefore not included in the sale. I did not know the reason at the time; but Raphael since told me, and added, with a feeling which does him honor, that as long as he could keep anything, he would not part with that picture. It is well known that when Benjamin West, a young man, left home for Italy, he had formed an attachment to a young lady of Philadelphia, of the name of Shewell. On his arrival in England from Italy, his prospects as an artist soon assumed so promising an aspect, that he determined to remain there, and wrote to his affianced bride, asking her to undertake the voyage to England, under the care of his venerable father. The lady and her intended father-in-law complied with the request, and in London, for the first time, the old gentleman met his eldest son, who was a watchmaker, settled in Reading, and at that time forty years of age. This son was born after old Mr. West went to

America, and the mother dying, the child was retained by her relatives. West married and remained in America until he came to bring a bride to his son Benjamin, one of the many children given him by his American wife."

Both the parents of Raphael West were Americans. Educated in the midst of artists and pictures, he was, when I became acquainted with him in 1784, one of the best designers, of the Academy figure from life, that England possessed. He did not apply himself with the necessary industry to painting which ensures success, but seems to have been discouraged by the overshadowing merit and fame of his father. "If I should attain the skill and excellence of my father," thought (perhaps said) the youth, "I shall not find another George the Third to be my employer and friend." Raefe helped me to do nothing; and I very frequently was a hindrance to his little application, by visiting the little room, in Newman Street, at the head of the gallery. After I left England he painted one of the pictures for Alderman Boydell's Shakespeare Gallery. This picture, "Orlando and Oliver," from "As you like it," was purchased and brought to this country by Robert Fulton, and is now in the possession of James Roosevelt, counsellor at law of New York.

In 1800 Raphael, as has been said, visited America, to improve wild lands, and although he did not exert his talents as a painter for the public, or exhibit any pictures during his stay, his taste had influence on the arts of the country (for the leaven cannot be mingled with the lump and produce no effect), and the drawings he brought with him, and those executed during his residence at Big Tree, and communicated or presented to his friends, must be considered as swelling the tide of western art by a copious though transient shower.

Disappointed, discouraged, and homesick, Raphael gladly broke from the Big Tree prison, to return to the paternal home in Newman Street. On his way he visited me in New York. His anger was kindled against Wadsworth, who, like a true American, saw in the wilderness the paradise which was to grow up and bloom there, but which was invisible to the London painter, and if possible, still more so to his London wife.

"Would you believe it, Dunlap, as I sat drawing by a lower window, up marched a bear, as if to take a lesson!"

The last time I saw my friend Raphael, was in the winter of 1802. His wife and himself were on a cold day surrounded by snow in a sleigh, and going to embark when I bade them adieu. Even the prospect of England in the distance, could not cheer his English wife; and I felt at the moment that for a husband to bring a wife from London to America, a lady used to London life, was as certain a source of misery to both husband and wife as ingenuity could contrive.

Thirty-two years have passed since my friends departed from these shores; and I am certain from what I know of Raphael West, that whether fortune has smiled or frowned, his good principles and excellent temper have insured him many a day of happiness.

I will here quote a passage from a letter of Mr. Leslie's in answer to my inquiries. "You know our friend Raphael possessed more talent than industry. His best picture, 'Orlando rescuing his brother from the lioness,' is, or was, in America. There is an old tree in it, drawn in a very masterly style. I have seen other drawings and etchings by him of some of the old oaks in Windsor Park, in a very grand manner. He also drew the human figure with a masterly and anatomical precision equal to his father, and I believe he often assisted him in his large works. He drew the whole of the outline of the 'Death on the Pale Horse,' upon the large canvas, having no other guide than a small sketch by his father, and he executed this in a style that left the old gentleman nothing to correct. I have seen a *Satan* painted by him. Bold and picturesque, but more grotesque than grand. It was like everything else he did, too much in the taste of Salvator Rosa. Peter Pindar, I am told, said of it, that 'It was a *damned thing*, but not the devil.'" Doctor Wolcott[1] was not content with endeavoring in vain to decry the father, but visited the son with his malice in hopes of better success. Leslie continues, "I do not remember the line among Peter's works, but it reminds me of a criticism of Fuseli on the picture of the 'Resurrection,' by

Mr. West. The Saviour (rather a heavy figure) was issuing from the tomb. There were angels above, one of them in an attitude of surprise. — In the exhibition, Sir William Beechey (who told me the story), asked Fuseli if he thought such an expression was proper to an angel on such an occasion. — 'Yes,' said Fuseli, 'the angel is very much in the right — he has expected to see the Messiah come forth, instead of whom he sees that great lubberly fellow, and is very much surprised.'" Thus painters talk of each other — *some painters.* I have had occasion to show Fuseli's bitter envy towards West. Leslie proceeds:

"Allston will remember that he and I were one day waiting in Mr. West's large painting room to see him, when the door opened, and a young girl of about fifteen came bounding in, but stopped suddenly on seeing strangers, blushed and ran out. We both thought we had never beheld anything so lovely. Mr. West entered soon after, and we asked him who the beautiful creature we had just seen was. He told us, she was his granddaughter, and added, '*She is a little Psyche.*' She is the only child of Raphael West. With features of Grecian regularity, blue eyes and light brown hair, her complexion 'Nature's pure red and white,' and a form perfect as her face, that first glimpse I had of her almost seemed like the momentary visit of an angel to the earth. This lady is now a wife and mother. She sat to me, since her marriage, for Anne Page, in a picture I painted of Falstaff and others at dinner, at Mr. Page's house. Her grandfather often painted her."

On the death of Benjamin West, his property was divided between his two sons — his only children, and the great picture of "Death on the Pale Horse,"[0] is the property of Raphael. The younger brother has the "Christ Rejected," and by coming with it to America realized a large sum of money from its exhibition. I believe a larger might be accumulated by the exhibition of the "Death on the Pale Horse" in this country. As it is, this property lies useless to its owner, whose principal revenue is derived, as I am informed, from his portion of the rent of the buildings in Newman Street.

0   Raphael Lamarr West died in England May 22, 1850. "Death on the Pale Horse," the great picture, is presently in the Pennsylvania Academy of Fine Arts. The original, small version is in the Philadelphia Museum of Art.

John Eckstein.[01]

"Eckstein," says my friend Sully, "was a thorough-going drudge in the arts. He could do you a picture in still life — history — landscape — portrait — he could model — cut a head in marble — or anything you please.

"I once visited his *atelier* with Washington Irving — it was lucky that I cautioned him not to express any emotion at the odd things we might encounter, or he would perhaps have been taken by surprise. Amongst the many strange versions of classic history was one, 'The Roman and Sabine combatants separated by the Sabine women.' One of the females had her infant clinging to her shoulder — the terrified brat was represented screaming with affright, and the artist had anxiously added a very usual circumstance with children when they cry, and no handkerchief convenient — a large bubble was appended to its nose — a most graphic symptom of grief.

"I know nothing of his dates. I found him when I removed to Philadelphia," (1800) "an old man, and he has been dead many years."

In 1812, he exhibited a model of an equestrian statue of Washington in Roman costume, and many drawings on historical subjects.

Francis Guy

Was originally a tailor of Baltimore. He attracted some attention by his attempts at landscape painting, and finally made it his profession and found employers.

Robert Gilmor, Esq., of Baltimore in a letter to me, says, "He began by copying my pictures and drawings, which are his best works. I have several of them. His blue he made of common coal-cinder."

Coal-cinder makes a blue-black, but is not sufficient for the blue of the painter. His style was crude and harsh, with little to recommend his efforts, which now would not be tolerated.

---

01 John Eckstein, "portrait painter, modeller in clay," appears in Philadelphia Directories of 1796 and 1797, and again in 1805 and 1806 and from 1811 to 1816. He was listed in Philadelphia as late as 1822, probably erroneously.

He exhibited several landscapes in the gallery of the Pennsylvania Academy as late as 1811.

TUTHILL.[1]

In the year 1812, as far as memory serves me, I saw for the first time this artist. He was then painting in Chatham Street, New York, was a married man, and had several portraits in his room. He told me that he had been to London to study the art; but his works bore little indication of that school. He likewise claimed to be a pupil of Mr. West's. I lost sight of him for many years, but met him again in Utica, much improved in manner, appearance and painting. He had been successful as an itinerant; and by presenting smooth and well-varnished pictures, with some resemblance to his sitters, he was accumulating property.

CHARLES FRASER.[2]

The love which this gentleman felt for the art, which he eventually pursues as a profession, was in early life controlled by those who had charge of his education and patrimony; for he had the misfortune to lose his father before he was nine years of age.

He is a native of Charleston, South Carolina; and from his earliest days, like most who have devoted themselves to painting, or any of the arts of design, was observed to use every substance which came in his way to make a mark, in endeavoring to imitate some of the forms presented to his sight. His wish was to become a painter, but those on whom the care of his education devolved, did not yield to his desire for instruction in that art. They perhaps did not feel authorized to sacrifice any portion of his patrimony, to qualify him for a pursuit whose results they might deem less certain, than those of (one of what are called the learned professions) the law; and had him educated accordingly.

[1] A. G. D. Tuthill was born in 1776 and died at Montpelier, Vt., June 12, 1843.

[2] Charles Fraser, son of Alexander and Mary Grimke Fraser, was born August 20, 1782, and died at Charleston, S. C., October 5, 1860. He painted a whole-length portrait of Lafayette for the city of Charleston in 1825. In the winter of 1857 an important collection of 313 miniatures by Fraser was exhibited at Charleston, S. C.

Mr. Fraser has expressed his regret at their choice. In a letter to a friend, he says, "It was to this timid and homebred feeling (if so I may call it), that I owe the circumstance of not having been educated as an artist. This unfortunate error by which the destiny of my life was directed, or rather *misdirected* will ever be, as it has always been, a source of regret to me."

In 1793 he met, in a schoolmate, a congenial mind, and having more skill than his companion, a boy recently from England, he became his instructor, and encouraged him in that, which, undoubtedly their schoolmaster considered a career of idleness. This English boy was Thomas Sully, who says, in a letter to me, Mr. Fraser was "the first person who took the pains to instruct me in the rudiments of the art." Mr. Fraser has done much for the progress of the arts of design, by his own pencil, and by his conduct as a man, and a gentleman; but if he had only been an agent in the good work of instructing and encouraging Thomas Sully, the world of art would have been incalculably indebted to him.

In the year 1798, Mr. Fraser, in accordance with the wishes of his guardians, entered a lawyer's office, but left it again in 1801, for the much more attractive study of his favorite art; but after three years he became discouraged, and resumed his legal studies in 1804. In 1807 he was admitted to the practice of the bar, and continued therein until 1818; doubtless during that time stealing an hour from the court of contention, to devote to the court of the muses.

Having by eleven years' practice as a lawyer, by diligence, punctuality, and the most conciliating manners, joined to probity above all suspicion, made himself in a great measure independent of the contingencies attending any failure or disappointment, in the pursuit he most loved; he commenced painting professionally in miniature, and has from that time found that his pencil has been in request so fully and constantly, in his native city of Charleston, that with the exception of two months passed in the exercise of his profession at Hartford, Connecticut, in the summer of 1831, his fellow citizens of South Carolina, and their visitors, have amply occupied his time. Those who have seen Mr. Fraser's miniature portraits will not be surprised that they have been in constant demand in one city.

Mr. Fraser is a gentleman of polished manners and fine feelings; with a person to attract attention and command respect. The friend and associate of Sully, Malbone, and Allston, he is of that class of artists, happily become common in this country, who receive and confer honor on the arts of design.

STEWART.[1]

Mr. Stewart painted wretched portraits about and before this time in Hartford, Connecticut. This gentleman had been (as I was informed at the time I saw him and his pictures), a clergyman. What turned him from the cure of men's souls, to the caricaturing of their bodies, I never learned. He was the first instructor in painting of S. L. Waldo, Esq.

HUTCHINS.

Mr. Hutchins has occasionally painted portraits in New York, but has attended to other pursuits which, perhaps, have prevented that progress he might otherwise have made. He has had a friendly instructor of late, in one of our first artists, A. B. Durand, Esq.

---

1 Rev. Joseph Stewart, a Congregationalist minister, who was born in 1750, painted portraits for a short time in New Haven, Conn., while studying for the ministry. In 1800 he established a museum in New Haven.[0]

0 Joseph Stewart should be Joseph Steward. Bayley and Goodspeed are misinformed about Mr. Steward; he was born in Upton, Mass., in 1753 and studied for the ministry after graduating from Dartmouth (1780). A serious illness led to his opening a museum in the State House, Hartford, in 1797. He had been painting as early as 1793.

Steward died on April 22, 1822.

CHAPTER XIX.

WASHINGTON ALLSTON.

THIS name stands, to use Sully's expression, "number one" in the catalogue of American painters, or at least can only be placed second to that of his great master West, to whom, if inferior in facility of composition, he is superior in color, and equal in drawing. Not only does Washington Allston stand proudly pre-eminent in the eyes of his country-men as an artist, but they see in him the virtues of the man, and the accomplishments of the scholar and the gentleman. If he surpasses, in any of the attributes of a painter, the great man with whom we have associated his name, and compared his attainments, none more readily than himself will allow that the glorious distinction was achieved by help of circumstances even happier than those which attended upon the ambition of West; and that the aid of his precursor was not among the least. The mantle of Elijah has fallen upon the shoulders of Elisha.

Washington Allston was born in the year 1779,[1] in the State of South Carolina. The climate not agreeing with his con-stitution, he was sent, by the advice of physicians, at a very early age (between six and seven), to Newport, Rhode Island, and was there continued at school until 1796, when he was transferred to Harvard College, Cambridge, Massachusetts.

Mr. Allston, on being questioned respecting his early efforts at designing, answered his correspondent thus: "To go back as far as I can — I remember that I used to draw before I left Carolina, at six years of age (by the way no *uncommon* thing), and still earlier, that my favorite amusement, much akin to it, was making little landscapes about the roots of an old tree in

---

[1] Washington Allston was born November 5, 1779, the son of William and Rachel Moore Allston, and died at Cambridge, Mass., July 9, 1843.

the country — meagre enough, no doubt; the only particulars of which I can call to mind, were a cottage built of sticks, shaded by little trees, which were composed of the small suckers (I think so called), resembling miniature trees, which I gathered in the woods. Another employment was the converting the forked stalks of the wild ferns into little men and women, by winding about them different colored yarn. These were sometimes presented with pitchers made of the pomegranate flower. These childish fancies were the straws by which, perhaps, an observer might then have guessed which way the current was setting for after life. And yet, after all, this love of imitation may be common to childhood. General imitation certainly is: but whether adherence to particular kinds may not indicate a permanent propensity, I leave to those who have studied the subject more than I have, to decide."

Without assuming to be deeper studied in the subject, the reader will remark, that in these delights of Allston's childhood appear the germs of landscape gardening, landscape painting, sculpture, and scenic composition. Less intellectual children are content to make mud pies, and form ovens with clay and clam shells as if to bake them in. Even when at play they are haunted by the ghosts of cakes, pies, and puddings.

Allston continued: "But even these delights would sometimes give way to a stronger love for the wild and the marvellous. I delighted in being terrified by the tales of witches and hags, which the negroes used to tell me; and I well remember with how much pleasure I recalled these feelings on my return to Carolina; especially on revisiting a gigantic wild grapevine in the woods, which had been the favorite swing for one of these witches." Here may be perceived the germ of that poetic talent which afterward opened and was displayed both by the pen and the pencil of Mr. Allston.

The European — or even the inhabitant of the Eastern or Middle States who has been born since the effects of our Revolution banished slavery from those portions of our country — cannot conceive of that species of education which is the lot of those who are surrounded in their childhood by swarms of

slaves of all ages; some born in the country, some recently
brought from Africa, scored with the marks perhaps of their
high barbaric origin, but all ignorant of the duties, or even
the decencies of life. All who have been born where negro
slavery existed, can realize the picture drawn by Allston of
his childhood, of the tales of terror instilled into his eager ear
by those who wished to please the young lord of the land, and
whose servility would make a deep impression upon young
master; cherishing self-love and self-importance if continued
beyond a very early age. Mr. Allston was peculiarly happy in
being removed from the place of his birth, before lessons more
pernicious than could flow from witch stories were taught by the
negroes of the household or the plantation. The writer can
vividly recall the words and actions of his father's negroes,
whose companion he was doomed to be until their words and
actions made impressions never to be erased.

Allston, in another letter to the same correspondent says,
"I concluded my last with the amusement of my childhood:
my next step will be to my boyhood. My chief pleasure now
was in drawing from prints — of all kinds of figures, landscape
and animals. But I soon began to make pictures of my own;
at what age, however, I cannot say. The earliest compositions
that I remember were the storming of Count Roderick's
castle, from a poor (though to me delightful) romance of that
day, and the siege of Toulon; the first in Indian ink, the
other in water colors. I cannot recall the year in which they
were done. To these succeeded many others, which have
likewise passed into oblivion. Though I never had any regular
instructor in the art (a circumstance I would here observe
both idle and absurd to boast of), I had much incidental instruction; which I have always through life been glad to
receive from every one in advance of myself. And, I may add,
there is no such thing as a self-taught artist in the ignorant
acceptation of the word; for the greatest genius that ever
lived must be indebted to others, if not by direct teaching, yet
indirectly through their works. I had, in my schooldays, some
of this latter kind of instruction from a very worthy and

amiable man, a Mr. King of Newport, who made quadrants
and compasses, and occasionally painted portraits. I believe
he was originally bred a painter, but obliged, from the rare
calls upon his pencil, to call in the aid of another craft. I
used at first to make frequent excuses for visiting his shop to
look at his pictures, but finding that he always received me
kindly, I went at last without any, or rather with the avowed
purpose of making him a visit. Sometimes I would take with
me a drawing, and was sure to get a kind word of encouragement. It was a pleasant thing to me, some twenty years after
this to remind the old man of these little kindnesses."

We may imagine that two such youths as Allston and Malbone — one a native of the beautiful island which gives name
to a State, the other preserved from disease by its salubrious
atmosphere, both full of love for the beauties of nature and art,
would, while thus thrown together, have an interchange of
thoughts on themes so dear to both; but these beings, so
similar in their taste, did not become intimate at this time.
On this subject Mr. Allston, in a letter to a friend, has said,
"I became acquainted with Malbone but a short time before
he quitted Newport, a circumstance which I remember then
regretting exceedingly, for I looked up to him with great admiration. Our not meeting earlier was owing, I suppose, to
his going to another school, and being some years older than
myself. I recollect borrowing some of his pictures on oiled
paper to copy. Our intimacy, however, did not begin till I
entered college, when I found him established at Boston. He
had then (for the interval was of several years) reached the
maturity of his powers, and was deservedly ranked the first
miniature painter in the country. Malbone's merits as an
artist are too well known to need setting forth by me: I shall
therefore say but a few words on that head. He had the
happy talent, among his many excellencies, of elevating the
character without impairing the likeness: this was remarkable
in his male heads; and no woman ever lost any beauty from
his hand; nay, the fair would often become still fairer under
his pencil. To this he added a grace of execution all his own.

My admiration of Malbone induced me at this time (in my freshman year at college) to try my hand at miniature, but it was without success. I could *make no hand of it;* all my attempts in that line being so far inferior to what I could *then* do in oil, that I became disgusted with my abortive efforts, and gave it up. One of these miniatures, or rather attempts at miniature, was shown me several years after, and I pronounced it '*without promise*' (this anecdote has found its way into 'Blackwood's Magazine'), not knowing it to be my work. I may add, I would have said the same had I known it. I may observe, however (for I know not why I should not be as just to myself as to another person), that I should not have expressed a similar opinion respecting its contemporaries in oil; for a landscape with figures on horseback, painted about this time, was afterwards exhibited at Somerset House.*

"My leisure hours at college were chiefly devoted to the pencil, to the composition equally of figures and landscapes; I do not remember that I preferred one to the other; my only guide in the choice was the inclination of the moment. There was an old landscape at the house of a friend in Cambridge (whether Italian or Spanish I know not) that gave me my first hints in color in that branch; it was of a rich and deep tone, though not by the hands of a master; the work, perhaps, of a moderate artist, but of one who lived in a *good age*, when he could not help catching something of the good that was abroad. In the coloring of figures, the pictures of Pine in the Columbian Museum, in Boston, were my first masters. Pine had certainly, as far as I can recollect, considerable merit in color. But I had a higher master in the head of Cardinal Bentivoglio, from Van Dyck, in the college library, which I obtained permission to copy one winter vacation. This copy from Van Dyck, was by Smibert, an English painter, who came to this country with Dean, afterwards Bishop, Berkeley. At that time it

* Doctor Waterhouse claims to have the first oil picture painted by Mr. Allston. In a letter dated November 16, 1833, the doctor says of Allston, "for whom I have always had the strong partiality of a friendship partaking of paternal; for he was under my special care during his college life, and I have in my possession his first essay in oil, being the portrait of my eldest son when a child."

seemed to me perfection; but when I saw the original some
years afterwards, I found I had to alter my notions of perfection. However, I am grateful to Smibert for the instruction
he gave me — his work rather. Deliver me from kicking down
even the weakest step of an early ladder."

Having gone through the four years' course of collegiate
studies, Allston was graduated A.B. in 1800, and returned
to his native State, South Carolina. In a letter to a friend he
says, "On quitting college I returned to Charleston, where I
had the pleasure to meet Malbone, and another friend and
artist, Charles Fraser, who, by the bye, now paints an admirable miniature. My picture manufactory still went on in
Charleston until I embarked for London. Up to this time my
favorite subjects, with an occasional comic intermission, were
banditti. — I well remember one of these, where I thought I
had happily succeeded in cutting a throat! The subject of this
precious performance was, robbers fighting with each other for
the spoils, over the body of a murdered traveller. And clever
ruffians I thought them. I did not get rid of this banditti
mania until I had been over a year in England. It seems that
a fondness for subjects of violence is common with young
artists. One might suppose that the youthful mind would delight in scenes of an opposite character. Perhaps the reason
of the contrary may be found in this: that the natural condition of youth being one incessant excitement, from the continuous influx of novelty — for all about us must *at one time be
new* — it must needs have something fierce, terrible, or unusual
to force it above its wonted tone. But the time must come to
every man who lives beyond the middle age, when 'there is
nothing new under the sun.' His novelties then are the *rifa-
cimenti* of his former life. The gentler emotions are then as
early friends who revisit him in dreams, and who, recalling
the past, give a grace and beauty, nay, a rapture even, to
what in the heyday of youth had seemed to him spiritless and
flat. And how beautiful is this law of nature — perfuming, as
it were, our very graves with the unheeded flowers of childhood.

"One of my favorite haunts when a child in Carolina, was

a forest spring where I used to catch minnows, and I dare say, with all the callousness of a fisherman; at this moment I can see that spring, and the pleasant conjuror Memory has brought again those little creatures before me; but how unlike to what they were! They seem to me like the spirits of the woods, which a flash from their little diamond eyes lights up afresh in all their gorgeous garniture of leaves and flowers. But where am I going?"

The answer will be "Not out of your path. The painter and the poet are alike, 'of imagination all compact!' You are both."

At the period of his return to South Carolina from college in 1800, Mr. Allston painted a head of St. Peter when he hears the cock crow, and one of Judas Iscariot. In May, 1801, at the age of twenty-two, he embarked with his friend Malbone for England. Malbone had passed the previous winter at Charleston; and whatever intimacy subsisted between these young painters at Newport and at Boston, a congeniality of taste must have increased when Allston met his matured friend in the place of his nativity. We have heard that Allston sacrificed his paternal inheritance to his love of the arts to which he had devoted *himself*. The product of the sale of his hereditary property was appropriated to the support of the student in Europe, and the furtherance of his enlightened ambition. He had generous offers from friends in Charleston, who, it would appear, wished to prevent any sacrifice of this kind, but the painter preferred independence and a reliance on his own resources.

In one of his letters to his friend, on the subject of his early life and prospects, he says, "There was an early friend, long since dead, whom I have omitted to mention, and I cannot but wonder at the omission, since he is one whose memory is still most dear to me. The name of this gentleman was Bowman; he was a native of Scotland, but had been long settled in Carolina. I believe I was indebted for the uncommon interest he was pleased to take in me to some of my college verses, and to a head of St. Peter (when he hears the cock crow) which

I had painted about that time. Be this as it may, his partiality
was not of an everyday kind; for when I was about to embark
for Europe, he proposed to allow me — nay, almost insisted
on my accepting — a hundred pounds a year during my stay
abroad. This generous offer, however, I declined, for having
at that time a small income sufficient for my immediate wants,
it would have been sordid to have accepted it. He then proposed to ship for me a few tierces of rice! That too I declined.
Yet he would not let me go without a present; so I was obliged
to limit it to Hume's 'History of England,' and a novel by
Dr. Moore, whom he personally knew, and to whom he gave
me a letter of introduction; the letter however was never
delivered, as the Doctor died within a few days of my arrival in
London. Such an instance of generosity speaks for itself. But
the kindness of manner that accompanied it can only be known
to me who saw it. I can see the very expression now. Mr.
Bowman was an excellent scholar, and one of the most agreeable
talkers I have known. Malbone, Fraser, and myself were
frequent guests at his table, and delightful parties we always
found there. With youth, health, the kindest friends, and
ever before me buoyant hope, what a time to look back on!
I cannot but think that the life of an artist, whether painter
or poet, depends much on a happy youth; I do not mean as to
outward circumstances, but as to his inward being: in my
own case, at least, I feel the dependence; for I seldom step
into the ideal world but I find myself going back to the age of
first impressions. The germs of our best thoughts are certainly
often to be found there; sometimes, indeed (though rarely), we
find them in full flower; and when so, how beautiful seem to us
these flowers through an atmosphere of thirty years! 'Tis in
this way that poets and painters keep their minds young. How
else could an old man make the page or the canvas palpitate
with the hopes, and fears, and joys, the impetuous, impassioned,
emotions of youthful lovers, or reckless heroes? There is a
period of life when the ocean of time seems to force upon the
mind a barrier against itself, forming, as it were, a permanent
beach, on which the advancing years successively break, only

to be carried back by a returning current to that furthest deep whence they first flowed. Upon this beach the *poetry of life* may be said to have its birth; where the *real* ends and the *ideal* begins."

Within a few weeks after Allston's arrival in London, he became a student of the Royal Academy. The first drawing he made from plaster, the "Gladiator," obtained him permission to draw at Somerset House; the third procured him the ticket of an entered student. He was immediately introduced to Mr. West; and in one of the valuable letters from which extracts have been made, he thus speaks of him: — "Mr. West, to whom I was soon introduced, received me with the greatest kindness. I shall never forget his benevolent smile when he took me by the hand: it is still fresh in my memory, linked with the last of like kind which accompanied the last shake of his hand, when I took a final leave of him in 1818. His gallery was open to me at all times, and his advice always ready and kindly given. He was a man overflowing with the milk of human kindness. If he had enemies, I doubt if he owed them to any other cause than his rare virtue; which, alas for human nature! is too often deemed cause sufficient."

Those feelings, which induced Mr. Allston to exclaim, "Alas for human nature!" are feelings similar to West's, and the *true* feelings of *nature;* that enmity which is generated by the contemplation of virtue, is foreign to man's nature. It is the child of his ignorance — the offspring of evil education, of jealousy, envy, malice, and all uncharitableness. The proof that it is foreign to man's nature is, that it makes him unhappy. Our benevolent Creator has implanted nothing in our nature but *that* which, with due culture, would produce fruit conducive to well-being.

Of other artists established in London, when Allston visited that city, he thus speaks: — "Of Sir Joshua Reynolds, whose lectures I imported and read before I went to Europe, I have always had a very high opinion. There is a fascination about his pictures which makes it almost ungrateful to think of their defects. They never produced in me anything like *hesitation,*

from the first moment I saw them. His taste was exquisite. —
Had he been a learned designer, his Infant Hercules, and his
Puck, or Robin Goodfellow, show what he might have done
in history. I scarcely know, in the whole compass of art, two
purer examples of poetic invention.

"It is very remarkable, that the three men whose works may
be said to have laid the foundation for a new era in art, or,
at least, to have revived a good one, should, though contemporaries, have had little or no intercourse with each other; I
mean, Sir Joshua, Wilson, and Gainsborough: they were
scarcely acquainted, and never companions; yet they seem to
have emerged, as by consent, with the same power and purpose, from an age of lead.

"The following characteristic anecdote of Wilson was told
me by Mr. West. Before the Royal Academy was formed,
the Society of Painters (as I think they were then called), held
their annual exhibition in Spring Gardens. On a certain
year Mr. West and Mr. Wilson happened to be appointed joint
hangers. It was a memorable year for the crudeness of the
performances; in consequence, I suppose, of the unusual
number of new adventurers. When the pictures were all up,
Wilson, with an expressive grin, began to rub his eyes, as if
to clear them of something painful. 'I'll tell you what, West,'
said he, after a while, 'this will never do, we shall lose the little
credit we have; the public can never stand such a shower of
chalk and brickbats.' 'Well, what's to be done? We can't
reject any pictures now.' 'Since that's the case, then, we must
mend their manners.' 'What do you mean?' 'You shall see,'
said Wilson, after a pause — 'what Indian ink and Spanish
liquorice can do.' He accordingly despatched the porter to
the color man and druggist for these *reformers;* and, dissolving
them in water, actually washed nearly half the pictures in the
exhibition with this original glaze. 'There,' said he, ' 'tis as
good as asphaltum; with this advantage, that if the artists
don't like it they can wash it off when they get the pictures
home.' And Mr. West acknowledged that, 'they were all the
better for it.' "

In one of his letters he has said, "I arrived in London about the middle of June, 1801, near the close of the annual exhibition. The next year, 1802, was the first of my adventuring before the public, when I exhibited three pictures at Somerset House. The principal one, a French soldier telling a story (a comic attempt), — a Rocky Coast (half length), with banditti; and a landscape, with horsemen, which I had painted at college, as before alluded to. I received two applications for the French soldier; which I sold to Mr. Wilson, of the European Museum; for whom I afterwards painted a companion to it, also comic — The Poet's Ordinary, where the lean fare was enriched by an incidental arrest.

"Malbone returned to America after a short stay — I believe five months — on account of his engagements in Charleston. — I little thought, when we parted, that it was for the last time: he died before my return.

"Amongst the artists we called upon was Fuseli, to whom we introduced ourselves as Americans. He received us with great courtesy, and invited us into his painting room. Upon my regretting that we had arrived too late to see his Milton Gallery (it had closed but a few months before), he inquired if I was an artist. I answered, 'Not yet; but that I had come to London with the hope of becoming one.' He then asked, 'In what branch of the art?' I replied, 'History.' 'Then,' said he, 'you have come *a great way* to starve, sir. There,' he added, 'is the Milton Gallery,' pointing to some rolls of canvas, that reached from the floor nearly to the ceiling. There were three or four, however, belonging to the series still on their stretching frames, which he showed us, and he seemed gratified that we were pleased. But he would not suffer us to like everything; for when I stopped before one, and expressed the pleasure I felt (and it was sincere), he said abruptly, 'No, sir, you don't like that — you can't like it — 'tis bad.' As he found, from my quoting Milton, that I was not unacquainted, at least with the subjects of his gallery, he good-naturedly presented me with one of his catalogues. I do not remember the strain in which I talked to Fuseli, but if at all in accordance with the enthusiasm that I felt, I think he could not have been displeased with our visit. I then thought Fuseli the greatest painter living. I am still his admirer, but in a more qualified degree."

Fuseli found a purchaser for a part of the Milton Gallery in Mr. Angerstein. On another occasion, and in another letter, Mr. Allston gives the following opinion of Fuseli. "It was, a few years ago, with many criticizing people (not critics, except those can be called so *who make their own ignorance the measure of excellence*) the habit to laugh at Fuseli. But Fuseli, even when most extravagant, was not a man to be laughed at; for his very extravagancies (even when we felt them as such) had *that* in them which carried us along with them. All he asked of the spectator was but a *particle* of *imagination*, and his wildest freaks would then defy the reason. Only a true genius can do this. But he was far from being always extravagant: he was often sublime, and has left no equal in the *visionary;* his spectres and witches were born and died with him. As a critic on the art, I know no one so *inspiring*. Having, as you know, no gallery of the old masters to visit here, I often refresh my memory of them with some of his articles in Pilkington's Dictionary; and he brings them before me in a way that no other man's *words* could: he even gives me a distinct apprehension of the style and color of some whose works I have never seen. I often read one or two of his articles before I go into my painting room; they form indeed almost a regular course at breakfast.

"Before I leave Fuseli I must tell you a whimsical anecdote, which I had from Stuart. He was one day at Raphael Smith's, the engraver, when Fuseli, to whom Stuart was then unknown, came in; who having some private business, was taken into another room. 'I know that you are a great physiognomist, Mr. Fuseli,' said Smith. 'Well, what if I am?' 'Pray did you observe the gentleman I was talking with just now?' 'I saw the man. What then?' 'Why I wish to know if you think he can paint.' 'Umph! — I don't know but he might — *he has a coot leg.*' Poor Stuart! that same leg — which I well remember to have been a finely formed one, became the subject of a characteristic joke with him but a few weeks before he died. I asked 'how he was?' He was then very much emaciated. 'Ah!' said he, 'you can judge'; and he drew up his pantaloons. 'You see how much I am out of drawing.'

"Now I have got into anecdote, I will relate another, though not at all relevant to this communication, of Sir Wm. Beechey. A young artist one day brought a picture, for the benefit of Sir William's criticism. 'Very well, C.' said Beechey; — 'very well indeed. You have improved, C. But C. why did you make the coat and the background of the same color?' 'For harmony, sir.' 'Oh, no! C. that's not harmony, that's monotony.' I have often thought this anecdote would have *told* for the latter in Lord Byron's perverse controversy with Mr. Bowles.

"I will add another, as little to my purpose, of Fuseli, after he became keeper to the Royal Academy. 'Well, Sam,' said Fuseli to Strouzer, the academy porter, 'what do you think of this picture?' 'Law! Mr. Fuseli, I don't know anything of pictures.' 'But you know a horse, Sam; you have been in the Guards, you can tell if that is like a horse.' 'Yes, sir.' 'Well?' 'Why it seems to me, then, Mr. Fuseli, that—that five men could ride on him.' 'Then you think his back too long.' 'A bit, sir.'"

After three years' residence in England, Mr. Allston passed over to France in company with Mr. John Vanderlyn, of New York, who was then pursuing the same coy mistress, and encouraged by her smiles. In the year 1804 Mr. Allston first saw the glories of the Louvre. The Louvre gallery was at that time in its full splendor. The great robber of Europe, who loved the fine arts as he loved the liberty and happiness of mankind, had collected in Paris the treasures of art which were scattered over the continent, as one means by which to dazzle France, and gratify his inordinate selfishness. The artist profited by the success of the spoiler's labor, and had an opportunity of studying without the expense of money, time, and labor in travelling, the *chefs d'œuvre* of every school and of every master, from the north of Germany to the south of Italy.

Mr. Allston, in the letter before mentioned, thus expresses

his feelings on visiting this splendid accumulation of plunder: "Titian, Tintoret, and Paul Veronese, absolutely enchanted me, for they took away all sense of subject. When I stood before the 'Peter Martyr,' the 'Miracle of the Slave,' and the 'Marriage of Cana,' I thought of nothing but of the *gorgeous concert of colors*, or rather of the indefinite forms (I cannot call them sensations) of pleasure with which they filled the imagination. It was the poetry of color which I felt; procreative in its nature, giving birth to a thousand things which the eye cannot see, and distinct from their cause. I did not, however stop to analyze my feelings — perhaps at that time I could not have done it. I was content with my pleasure without seeking the cause. But I now understand it, and *think* I understand *why* so many great colorists, especially Tintoret and Paul Veronese gave so little heed to the ostensible *stories* of their compositions. In some of them, the 'Marriage of Cana' for instance, there is not the slightest clue given by which the spectator can guess at the subject. They addressed themselves not to the senses merely, as some have supposed, but rather through them to that region (if I may so speak) of the imagination which is supposed to be under the exclusive dominion of music, and which, by similar excitement, they caused to teem with visions that 'lap the soul in Elysium.' In other words, they leave the subject to be made by the spectator, provided he possesses the imaginative faculty — otherwise they will have little more meaning to him than a calico counterpane."

The reader will perceive that Mr. Allston is far from being devoid of the imaginative faculty which he here speaks of, and that he saw objects with a poet's as well as a painter's eye — indeed they are the same. His own pictures are replete with this magic of color, at the same time that he is strictly attentive to the story in all its parts, character, actions, and costume. It certainly is not fair to leave the spectator to make out the story of a picture, and to be puzzled by finding Pope Gregory alongside of Saint Peter, and both dressed in costume as far from truth as they were from similarity of opinion. All the charm of color may be attained without sacrificing truth.

In pursuing the subject, Allston says, "I am by nature, as it respects the arts, a *wide liker*. I cannot honestly turn up my nose even at a piece of still life, since, if well done, it gives me pleasure. This remark will account for otherwise strange transitions. I will mention here a picture of a totally different kind, which then took great hold of me, by Lodovico Carracci. I do not remember the title, but the subject was the body of the virgin borne for interment by four apostles. The figures are colossal; the tone dark, and of tremendous depth of color. It seemed as I looked at it as if the ground shook under their tread, and the air was darkened by their grief."

How delighted would the spirit of Carracci have been, if, hovering near this work, he had heard a kindred spirit uttering such words, or evincing such feelings. This picture, with many others, the spoil of nations, has been restored to its home. "Even-handed justice" "here, even here upon this bank and shoal of time," brought the poisoned chalice to the inventor's lips, and made him drink the potion to the very dregs. So be it with all who usurp the rights of their fellow men! The work of Lodovico Carracci, which had so powerful an effect upon his brother painter, has been carried back to Italy: in what place it is deposited I do not know; but if any American traveller, after reading the above passage, should stand before the picture, how will his pleasure be enhanced by recollecting these words of Allston. The painter-poet goes on thus: "I may here notice a false notion which is current among artists, in the interpretation they put on the axiom that 'something should always be left to the imagination,' viz.: that some parts of a picture should be left *unfinished*. The very statement betrays its unsoundness: for that which is unfinished must necessarily be *imperfect;* so that according to this rule *imperfection* is made essential to *perfection*. The error lies in the phrase, 'left to the imagination,' and it has filled modern art with random flourishes of no meaning. If the axiom be intended to prevent the impertinent obtrusion of subordinate objects (the fault certainly of a mean practice), I may observe that the remedy is no remedy, but rather a less fault substituted for a greater. Works of a high order, aspiring to the poetical, cannot make good their pretensions, unless they *do affect* the imagination; and *this* should be the test — that they set to work, not to finish what is less incomplete, but to awaken images *congenial* to the compositions, but not *in* them expressed; an effect that never was yet realized by misrepresenting anything. If the objects introduced into a picture *keep their several places* as well in the deepest shadow as in light, the general effect will suffer nothing by their truth; but to give the *whole* truth in the midnight as well as the daylight, belongs to a master."

It may be added that it will gain — as is indeed implied by the words of Mr. Allston. Such remarks from such a painter, and such a thinker, are invaluable to the student. May it not be added that this eulogium on necessity for truth in painting, is a proof of the value of that quality, in all the relations and transactions of life. Falsehood causes deformity in the moral picture; and when mystery is called in to hide it, the scumbling causes a blot, and creates suspicion of even greater faults than those it was intended to veil.

CHAPTER XX.

ALLSTON — *Continued.*

MR. ALLSTON remained but a few months in Paris, at the time of his visit in 1804: long enough, however, to paint four original pictures, and make a copy from Rubens, in the Luxemburg gallery. He then proceeded to Italy, passing leisurely through Switzerland, crossing the lake of the Four Cantons, and then over St. Gothard to Belanzona, on the Italian side of the Alps. The traveller in one of his letters, says, "the impressions left by the sublime scenery of Switzerland, are still fresh to this day. A new world had been opened to me — nor have I met with anything like it since. The scenery of the Apennines is quite of a different character. By the bye, I was particularly struck in this journey with the truth of Turner's Swiss scenes — the poetic truth — which none before or since have given; with the exception of my friend Brockendon's magnificent work, on the passes of the Alps.* I passed at night and saw the sun rise on the Lake Maggiore. Such a sunrise! The giant Alps seemed literally to rise from their purple beds, and putting on their crowns of gold, to send up a hallelujah almost audible."

He remained in Italy about four years; the principal part of that time in Rome. Among his fellow students at a private academy, or association, were Mr. Vanderlyn of New York; since known so well as an artist, and the Danish sculptor

---

* The great success of Mr. Turner is mentioned in an English journal, of the year 1833, as being beyond that of any other. "It is said that he has realized upwards of a hundred thousand pounds, by his pencil." They speak of his industry as "astonishing," and his prices great. — "The stores of prints from his works in the finest possible state, which will some day or other deluge the print market, will be beyond all precedent." They tell us an anecdote of a ragged, dirty-looking lad, "bidding at a guinea a bid at an auction sale, for one of this artist's pictures, to the astonishment of all competitors; and when it was knocked down to him, he proved an agent of Mr. Turner's, who, after retouching, sold it for three times the amount." Thus we see united great talents and a just appreciation of the good gifts of fortune.

Thorwalsden,[1] whose fame has spread over the civilized world —
the only modern who has yet seized the spirit of ancient
sculptors, and associated himself with the sculptors of Greece.

Of the effects produced by the great masters of the bygone
days of Italy, on such a mind as Allston's, some idea may be
formed from the following effusion of his pen. "It is needless
to say how I was affected by Raffaele, the greatest master of
the affections in our art. In beauty he has often been surpassed,
but in grace — the native grace of character — in the expression of intellect, and above all, sanctity, he has no equal.
What particularly struck me in his works was, the *genuine* life
(if I may so call it) that seemed, without impairing the dis-
tinctive character, to pervade them all; for even his humblest
figures have a *something* either in look, air, or gesture, akin
to the *venustas* of his own nature, as if like living beings under
the influence of a master-spirit, they had partaken, in spite of
themselves, a portion of the charm which swayed them. This
power of infusing one's *own life*, as it were, into that which is
feigned, appears to me the sole prerogative of genius. In a
work of art, this is what a man may well call *his own;* for it
cannot be borrowed or imitated. Of Michaelangelo, I know
not how to speak in adequate terms of reverence. With all
his faults (but who is without them) even Raffaele bows before
him. As I stood beneath his colossal prophets and sybils, still
more colossal in spirit — I felt as if in the presence of messen-
gers from the other world, with the destiny of man in their
breath, in repose even terrible. I cannot agree with Sir Joshua
that the 'Vision of Ezekiel,' of Raffaele, or the ' Moses ' of Parmegiano, have anything in common with Michaelangelo.
Their admiration of Michaelangelo may have elevated their
forms into a more dignified and majestic race; but still left
them *men*, whose feet had never trod other than this earth.
The supernatural was beyond the reach of both. But no one
would mistake the prophets of Michaelangelo for inhabitants
of our world; yet they are true to the imagination, as the
beings about us are to the senses. I am not undervaluing these
great artists, when I deny them a kindred genius with Michael-

1   For Thorwalsden read Thorwaldsen

angelo; they had both a genius of their own, and high qualities which nature had denied the other."

The studies of Allston when in Italy, were not confined to drawing and painting. He made modelling in clay, a separate branch of study, and devoted much time to it. He has said of this study, in after life, "I would recommend modelling to all young painters as one of the best means of acquiring an accurate knowledge of the joints: I have occasionally practised it ever since."

Another acquisition was made by the painter in Rome. He there became acquainted with Mr. Coleridge. It is only his own words that can do justice to his estimation of this gentleman. In one of his letters, after mentioning a friend, he proceeds, "I have had occasion in former letters more than once to mention the name of another most valued friend, of whom I would gladly say more, did I not feel that it is not for me to do justice to his extraordinary powers. I would observe, however, that to no other man whom I have known, do I owe so much *intellectually*, as to Mr. Coleridge, with whom I became acquainted in Rome, and who has honored me with his friendship for more than five and twenty years. He used to call Rome the *silent* city; but I never could think of it as such, while with him; for, meet him when, or where I would, the fountain of his mind was never dry, but like the far-reaching aqueducts that once supplied this mistress of the world, its living stream seemed specially to flow for every classic ruin over which we wandered. And when I recall some of our walks under the pines of the Villa Borghese, I am almost tempted to dream that I had once listened to Plato, in the groves of the Academy. It was there he taught me this golden rule: *never to judge of any work of art by its defects;* a rule as wise as benevolent; and one that while it has spared me much pain, has widened my sphere of pleasure."

Mr. Allston returned to America in 1809. When Robert W. Weir, Esq. of New York, was studying his profession in Rome, many years after Allston left it, the artists of Rome asked him after an American painter, for whom they had no other name than the American Titian. When Weir mentioned the name of Allston, they exclaimed "that's the man!" Sully and others say that Mr. Allston's coloring is more like Titian than that of any modern artist. He remained in his native country three years, in the early part of which time he married Miss Channing, the sister of the celebrated writer and divine, the reverend Dr. Channing, the ornament of American literature. In 1811 he returned to England, taking with him his wife, and as a pupil Samuel Finley Breese Morse, confided to his care by his father, the Reverend Dr. Jedediah Morse, celebrated for his works on geography.

The first labor in which Mr. Allston engaged on his return to England, was his great picture of the "Dead man revived by touching Elisha's bones." He says to his correspondent, "My first work after returning to London — with the exception of two small pictures (if they can be called exceptions, which were carried on at the same time with the larger one), was the 'Dead man revived by Elisha's bones,' which is now in Philadelphia.[1] My progress in this picture was interrupted by a dangerous illness, which after some months of great suffering, compelled me to remove to Clifton, near Bristol. My recovery, for which I was indebted under Providence, to one of the best friends, and most skilful of the faculty, was slow and painful, leaving me still an invalid when I returned to London — and indeed as my medical friend predicted, in some degree so to this day.* The 'Dead man,' was first exhibited at the British Institution, commonly called the British Gallery — an institution patronized by the principal nobility and gentry — the Prince Regent then president: it there obtained the

* The medical friend here mentioned, was Mr. King, of Clifton, a surgeon who was introduced to Mr. Allston by Mr. Southey. Mr. King is married to a sister of the celebrated Miss Edgeworth, whose novels and tales have mended more hearts, and guided more minds, than all the professed moral writers of England. With these friends, and Coleridge and Southey, aided by the delights which nature and art have bestowed upon Clifton, and around Bristol, when looking down from the terraces of Clifton upon the city below, in company with such congenial minds, though slow, the recovery of the American painter must have been made certain, by the physical and intellectual enjoyments that surrounded him.

[1] The "Dead man revived by Elisha's Bones" was purchased by the Pennsylvania Academy of Fine Arts in Philadelphia in 1816 for $3500.

first prize of two hundred guineas. As I returned to London, chiefly to finish this picture, that done, I went back to Bristol where I painted and left a number of pictures; among these were half-length portraits of my friend Mr. Coleridge, and my medical friend Mr. King, of Clifton. I have painted but few portraits, and these I think are my best. My second journey to London was followed by a calamity of which I cannot speak — the death of my wife — leaving me nothing but my art — which then seemed to me as nothing. But of my domestic concerns I shall avoid speaking, as I do not consider them proper subjects for *living* biography."

The propriety of a man's avoiding a detail of his own domestic concerns, as subjects for his biography while he is living, cannot be questioned; but that which restrains him does not bear upon the ordinary biographer. When a man has made himself a conspicuous object before the world, either as a poet, a painter, a sculptor, an architect, an engraver or an actor, the world has a right to inquire into everything respecting him. If an author we have a desire to know if his conduct squares with the lessons he teaches; if an artist, we wish to know how art has affected his character, and whether the contemplation of the sublime productions of human genius has raised and purified mind, or the contrary. The good artist who is not a good man, is a traitor to the arts, and an enemy to society; and it is the duty of his biographer to expose him in his true colors as a warning to others. If the biography of the living is useful, and that it is (of every person who appears before the public voluntarily and attracts admiration), few can doubt, then it follows that the biographer shall truly point out the causes of his celebrity; and if he fails or falters in his high career, the cause of such deterioration. The artist's happiness, as well as that of other men, depends upon his domestic concerns. He is supported in the paths of virtue, and encouraged to strenuous exertions for the benefit of mankind by the beloved ones around him — or if disappointed in his hopes, he may sink in character, or fail in his efforts of art — or, if living for himself alone, become a cynic, a miser or a misanthrope.

If a man is worth the world's attention, let the world know the truth of him, and as far as possible the true cause of his actions.

While happy in his domestic concerns and surrounded by literary friends, or when recovering from a dangerous and painful illness by the aid of such society, Mr. Allston composed, it may be presumed, those poems, which he gave to the world in the year 1813, for in that year was published in London a duodecimo volume of poetry from his pen.

A critic has observed on this work, "Poetry and painting are kindred arts. A refined sensibility to beauty and deformity, a voluptuous relish for the luxury of nature, and an exquisite perception of the shades of character and sentiment, are essential to the attainment of excellence in either. The same fervor of fancy is requisite to both.

"The resemblance between the professions, holds, too, in another point, — mere enthusiasm is incompetent to portray its own conceptions, however vivid, — a great painter and a great poet must alike be formed by study and instruction. The elementary course of their education is parallel. Expansion is given to the same powers of mind; — the same models are held up to their admiration; — similar passions are to be delineated by each, and both are intent to catch the living features. It is only in the application of principles to practice, that their paths diverge. Versification and coloring, plot and perspective, are the mechanical branches which constitute the difference of their arts." This is true, and these qualities, with study and instruction, were united in the subject of this memoir.

Mr. Allston has only said of his return to London after his second sojourn with his friends at Clifton, "My second journey to London was followed," etc. This was not merely a "journey to London," but an attempt for the first time to establish himself in the independent character of a housekeeper. On this return to London he had, for the first time, taken a house and furnished it. He might, with the confidence which happily attends upon his fellow mortals, look forward to the comforts of a domestic establishment with the chosen friend who had accompanied him from his native home, and attended him in a foreign land through pain and sickness. During the first week of their residence in Tinney Street, Mrs. Allston fell sick, and in less than a week died. The shock produced a temporary derangement or prostration of the artist's intellect.[1] He took refuge with his friends Morse and Leslie, at their abode. They had been with him through the dreadful trial, and now superintended the last sad offices required by humanity. The only persons present at the funeral of the wife of Allston and sister of Channing were, Samuel F. B. Morse, Charles R. Leslie, and John Howard Payne, three of her countrymen.

If the biographer may not record the events which influenced a man in the days of his gladness or those of his mourning, he may record effects, but is denied the privilege of tracing them to their causes, perhaps the most essential part of his work.

It has been well said, "say nothing of the living but what is true," and most stupidly, "say nothing of the dead but what is good." "Biography of living persons has some exceptions to it. It has the air of adulation when you praise, and of envy or malice when you condemn." Truth is the object of this book, and good or evil shall be recorded of dead or living, as truth shall dictate.

While Mr. Allston was engaged in painting the great picture of the "Dead man touching the bones of the prophet," he likewise painted "The Mother and Child," and a landscape. The three are in this country. To Mr. James McMurtrie, of Philadelphia, America owes the possession of the great picture first mentioned. That gentleman being in London persuaded Mr. Allston to put the painting in his charge to convey to Philadelphia, feeling assured that the Pennsylvania Academy of Fine Arts would purchase it. Mr. Allston had entrusted the sale of the picture to Messrs. Sully & McMurtrie, and the first intimation he had of the transaction was through a Boston correspondent, who informed him that "The Dead man" was

[1] Dunlap is in error in stating that Allston's intellect was in any way affected by the death of Mrs. Allston.

sold to the Pennsylvania Academy for the sum of $3500. A price very inadequate, but probably as much as that institution could afford to give.

In a letter from London, dated 13th June, 1816, to James McMurtrie, Esquire, of Philadelphia, Mr. Allston writes: "When you first made me the generous offer of taking out my picture, you may remember with what implicit confidence I submitted the entire management and disposal of it to yourself and Mr. Sully. I would not have done this if I had not been fully assured that, whatever might be the event, I should have every reason to be grateful, for even if it had wholly failed of profit, I should still have felt myself indebted for every exertion that kindness and liberality would make. If such would have been my feelings in the event of a total failure (an event too, which I had suffered myself almost to anticipate) you may well judge what I now feel at the account of this most agreeable and unexpected result. I beg you both to accept my warmest and most grateful acknowledgments. The sale is in every respect highly gratifying, both as affording a very seasonable pecuniary supply, and on account of the flattering circumstances attending it. As necessary and acceptable as the money is to me, I assure you I think more of the honor conferred by the Academy becoming purchasers of my work."

We here see that the highest mental powers, united to the keenest physical perceptions of the good and the beautiful, are consistent with, and perhaps produce the most delicate sensibility, diffidence in self, and confidence in the acts and opinions of others. How different from that irritable, and at the same time dogmatical character who considers all the praises bestowed upon others, or the gifts of fortune not falling to himself, as so many injuries inflicted on him. Such an one is as blind to his own defects as to the merits of others, and in self-confidence pronounces by words, or acts, or both, his own superiority. This conduct sometimes succeeds for a time, for the world will take a man's word for his worth rather than take the trouble to inquire into a subject that does not immediately touch their interests. But the truth will appear; and the pretender is generally the victim of disappointment and morbid irritability — shunned by those who can best appreciate his worth, and finally sinking into private imbecility and public contempt. A contrast between such a character (and such characters exist) and that of the subject of this biographical sketch, is as complete as the imagination can conceive.

It appears that Mr. Allston had conceived the design, and partly executed it, of a great picture on the subject of Christ's healing in the temple. In the letter above quoted from, written in 1816 to Mr. McMurtrie, is the following passage: "If I am constrained, from various circumstances, to disappoint you as to your proposal respecting a picture from my sketch of 'Christ healing,' I yet trust you will believe me not insensible to the kindness that dictated it; and also hope that the proposal which I in my turn make will be as agreeable to you, as if it had been in my power to comply with the first. Upon reconsidering the sketch some months since, though still pleased with the general arrangement, I found the principal incident so faulty and inefficient, and myself so unable to suggest a better, that I was forced to the resolution of relinquishing the subject altogether — or lay it by for some future period, in the hopes that my imagination might then supply a more suitable incident. It is of the first importance to a large work that the principal incident should be striking and obvious; leaving no doubt on any one of its meaning. Now in the incident alluded to, I have attempted to express the miracle of *restored health* to a sick man, and that I have failed in it is certain: because not one who has seen it has been able to guess my intention. I could easily express disease in any stage of languor or emaciation; there would then be no incident but only a sick man waiting to be healed, which is but repeating what West has already done, and very finely done. My object was not to treat the subject thus, but in a very different way; that is, to show both the *operation* and the *effect* of a miracle. The blind boy, or rather the boy that *was* blind (which you may recollect on the sketch), is, I think, a very happy incident; for the miracle there is obvious, and clearly explains itself: but it is a miracle that has been *already* wrought, and therefore forms a subordinate part of the picture. Had I been equally successful in the principal object, who is supposed to be under the *immediate influence* of the Saviour's word, I should not only be satisfied with the composition, but have reason to think I had achieved something *great*. I still like all the rest of the sketch; but this great and radical defect in it has long since compelled me to give it up. But were I even perfectly satisfied with it, I do not think it would be in my power to paint it on a large scale (as it would employ me full eighteen months or two years) for less than nine hundred or a thousand guineas without loss; for, in addition to my present expenses, I should be obliged to hire another large room. But though it is not in my power, for the reasons above stated, to engage in a large picture from this sketch, I should be most happy to undertake another subject for you, of five or six figures, size of life; which would make a picture about the dimensions of the ' St. Peter in prison' (the St. Peter, by the bye, employed me more than six months after you left London, instead of two, as I had calculated); — and this I would do for the sum you mentioned, say five hundred guineas. Such a picture I could paint in my present room, and could finish, I should hope, in somewhat less than a year. Should this be agreeable to you, you will please to say what kind of a subject you would prefer: I think Scripture subjects, as being most known and interesting to the world, are the best. Should this proposal meet your views, you have the best reasons for depending on my very best efforts. Perhaps some splendid subject, uniting brilliancy of coloring with character and expression." In another letter, dated October 25, 1816, he says, on the subject of the "Christ healing," — "I may here observe that the universal failure of all painters, ancient and modern, in their attempts to give even a tolerable idea of the Savior, has now determined me never to attempt it. Besides, I think his character too holy and sacred to be attempted by the pencil."

To go back to the letter of June, the whole is so interesting and instructive to students and artists, that not to continue it here would be injustice to them. "Whenever you send the portfolio of drawings, I will with pleasure attend to your wishes respecting them. Mr. West, who is, as I believe, one of the most learned in Europe in these matters, will, I doubt not, be happy to assist me in assigning to them the names of their proper authors. I know that he has a great esteem for you. Since you still encourage me with the hope of selling the landscape, I will send it out in the course of the summer. I think I gave you a memorandum of the price: I do not recollect whether it was 200 or 150 guineas. If it is worth anything it is worth 200, having cost me four months' hard labor. At the same time I shall send you the little picture of the Virgin and Child, which, as I know it is a great favorite with you, I beg you to accept, as a small testimony of my esteem. I have lately improved it very much; having repainted the mother's head, and the whole of the infant, as well as retouched the background."

It is probable that these are the two small pictures which he painted while the great picture of the "Dead man" was in progress. In October he wrote, "I have shipped and addressed to you the two pictures mentioned to you in my letter of June last, viz. the Landscape and the Mother and Child. — I wish you not to consider it now as the "Virgin and Child," but simply as a mother watching her sleeping offspring. A Madonna should be *youthful;* but my mother is a matron. Besides, there are other reasons, which I have not room to state, that would fix the propriety of the change not made in the title. The first, the Landscape, to be exhibited and disposed of in any way that shall seem best to you: of the other I beg your acceptance, as a small testimony of my esteem and gratitude. I have a double pleasure in offering this little present, inasmuch as, since the retouching, I think it one of my best works; and as I know it will be possessed by one who can *truly* appreciate whatever merit it may have. It does not always happen that the possessors of pictures are also possessed of taste; and therefore it is a source of no small gratification to an artist to know that his works are cherished by those who

will neither mistake nor overlook their excellencies, however
subordinate." *

* The great picture of the "Dead Man restored to Life, by touching the Bones of
the Prophet Elisha," was put up in the Pennsylvania Academy of Fine Arts in April,
1816, in a good light and situation for its display, and has been a source of delight and
instruction to the public and to artists. The size of this picture is 13 feet by 11. The
passage on which this composition is founded is as follows: — "And the bands of the
Moabites invaded the land at the coming in of the year. And it came to pass as they
were burying a man, that, behold, they spied a band of men, and they cast the man
into the sepulchre of Elisha; and when the man was let down, and touched the bones of
Elisha, he revived." 2d Kings, chap. xiii. ver. 20, 21.

The following description is taken from the pen of Mr. Allston: —

"The sepulchre of Elisha is supposed to be in a cavern among the mountains, such
places, in those early ages, being used for the interment of the dead. In the foreground is the man at the moment of re-animation; in which the artist has attempted,
both in the action and color, to express the gradual recoiling of life upon death. Behind
him, in a dark recess, are the bones of the Prophet, the skull of which is *peculiarized* by
a preternatural light. At his head and feet are two slaves, bearers of the body; the
ropes still in their hands, by which they have let it down, indicating the act that
moment performed: the emotion attempted in the figure at the feet is that of astonishment and fear, modified by doubt, as if still requiring further confirmation of the
miracle before him; while, in the figure at the head, is that of unqualified, immovable
terror. In the most prominent group above is a soldier, in the act of rushing from the
scene. The violent and terrified action of this figure was chosen to illustrate the miracle,
by the contrast which it exhibits to that habitual firmness supposed to belong to the
military character, showing his emotion to proceed from no *mortal* cause. The figure
grasping the soldier's arm, and pressing forward to look at the body, is expressive of
terror, overcome by curiosity. The group on the left, or rather behind the soldier, is
composed of two men of different ages, earnestly listening to the explanation of a priest,
who is directing their thoughts to heaven, as the source of the miraculous change: the
boy clinging to the old man is too young to comprehend the nature of the miracle, but,
like children of his age, unconsciously partakes of the general impulse. The group on
the right forms an episode, consisting of the wife and daughter of the reviving man.
The wife, unable to withstand the conflicting emotions of the past and the present, has
fainted; and whatever joy and astonishment may have been excited in the daughter
by the sudden revival of her father, they are wholly absorbed in distress and solicitude
for her mother. The young man, with outstretched arms, actuated by impulse *not
motive*, announces to the wife, by a sudden exclamation the revival of her husband;
the other youth of a mild and devotional character is still in the attitude of one conversing — the conversation being abruptly broken off by his impetuous companion.
The sentinels in the distance at the entrance of the cavern mark the depth of the
picture and indicate the alarm which had occasioned this tumultuary burial."

CHAPTER XXI.

Allston — *Concluded.*

In the year 1817 Mr. Allston visited Paris, in company with his friend C. R. Leslie. The same year he writes from London, acknowledging the receipt of the first instalment for his picture of the "Dead man"; and then goes on to say, "I am now engaged on 'Jacob's Dream,' a subject I have long had in contemplation. It has been often painted before, but I have treated it in a very different way from any picture I have ever seen; for, instead of two or three angels I have introduced a vast multitude: and instead of a ladder, or narrow steps, I have endeavored to give the idea of unmeasurable flights of steps, with platform above platform, rising and extending into space immeasurable. Whether this conception will please the matter of fact critics I doubt; nay I am certain that men without imagination will call it stuff! But if I succeed at all, it will be with those whom it will be an honor to please. The picture is of the same size with the landscape I sent out." Mr. Allston's prize picture, "Uriel in the Sun," is in England, in the collection of the Marquis of Stafford.

In a letter from Martin to the editor of the " London Athenæum," I find an account of his first introduction to Leslie and Allston, and an acknowledgment, that to a conversation with Allston, who told him that he intended to paint "Belshazzar's Feast," he owes the suggestion of the subject which he shortly after painted and engraved — with a great deal of perspective and architectural effect, much poetic imagination and more false drawing, outré attitude, and exaggerated or unnatural expression. I publish one extract, as connected with my subject, in the year 1814:

"My next painting, 'Clytie,' 1814, was sent to Mr. West, the president, for his inspection; and it was on this occasion that I first met Leslie, now so deservedly celebrated.

"I shall never forget the urbane manner with which West introduced us, saying, 'that we must become acquainted, as young artists, who, he prophesied, would reflect honor on their respective countries.' Leslie immediately informed Allston, who resided in the same house with him, that he had met me. Allston requested to be introduced, as he had felt a strong desire to know me, from the time he had seen my 'Sadak'; but a sort of reserve had prevented his introducing himself, although he had several times taken up his pen to do so. Thus, twenty years ago, commenced a friendship which caused me deeply to regret Allston's departure for his native country; for I have rarely met a man whose cultivated and refined taste, combined with a mild yet enthusiastic temper, and honorable mind, more excited my admiration and esteem.

"It is somewhat singular, that my picture of 'Belshazzar's Feast,' originated in an argument with Allston. He was himself going to paint the subject, and was explaining his ideas, which appeared to me altogether wrong, and I gave him my conception. He then told me, that there was a prize poem at Cambridge, written by T. S. Hughes, which exactly tallied with my notions, and advised me to read it. I did so, and determined on painting the picture. I was strongly dissuaded from this by many; among others, Leslie, who so entirely differed from my notions of the treatment, that he called on purpose, and spent part of a morning, in the vain endeavor of preventing my committing myself, and so injuring the reputation I was obtaining. This opposition only confirmed my intentions, and in 1821 I exhibited my picture. Allston has never seen it; but he sent from America to say, 'that he would not mind a walk of ten miles, over a quickset hedge, before breakfast, to see it.' This is something from a bad walker and a worse riser. His own 'Belshazzar' was not completed for many years, not till very lately, I think." Of that more will be said hereafter.

The reader has seen, that this distinguished American artist was in England during the last war between America and Great Britain. He went thither in 1811; when insult, oppro-

bium, and injury were heaped upon his country by the government and the writers of the United Kingdoms; and he remained until the character of the United States had been
vindicated, and the pride of England mortified, both on the
land and sea. He was among men who felt irritated by the
defeat of their vessels of war (hitherto triumphant in every
encounter) by the despised Yankee seamen, and of their in-
vincible soldiers before the militia of America; yet he was
beloved and his talents appreciated as though he were a native
of Britain. The poet painter became "homesick," as he says,
and, on the return of peace, when his engagements permitted,
he left his English friends.

He thus speaks of the land of his forefathers, that glorious
land, whose brightest ornaments we claim as belonging to us
as much as to our transatlantic brethren — men from whose
example and instruction we derive our greatest blessings.

"Next to my own country," says Allston, "I love England,
the land of my ancestors. I should indeed be ungrateful if I
did not love a country from which I have never received
other than kindness: in which, even during the late war, I
was never made to feel that I was a foreigner. By the English
artists, among whom I number some of my most valued friends,
I was uniformly treated with openness and liberality. Out of
the art too I found many fast and generous friends. — And
here — though I record a compliment to myself, I cannot deny
myself the satisfaction of repeating the kind words of Lord
Egremont, a few weeks before I left England. 'I hear you are
going to America,' he said. 'I am sorry for it. — Well, if you
do not meet with the encouragement which you deserve, in
your own country, we shall all be very glad to see you back
again.' This munificent nobleman had done me the honor
to introduce himself to me, and is the possessor of one of my
best pictures, 'Jacob's Dream.'

"I have ventured to allow myself this piece of egotism, for
the sake of my countrymen, who, I hope, will never let any
deserving British artist, who should come among us, feel that
he is not welcome. England has never made any distinction

between our artists and her own — never may America. In reference to Lord E.'s kind speech, I must stop here to say, that I have received from my countrymen the kindest treatment and the most liberal encouragement — far indeed from what I ever expected, for which I cannot be too grateful."

Thus it is that the good and the grateful spirit, united to talent and intelligence, finds friends everywhere; and while this great artist felt himself indebted to Lord Egremont, that enlightened nobleman felt himself proud of, and honored by the society of the man of genius, and rich in the possession of the emanations of his mind, as displayed upon the glowing canvas.

"Among the many persons," says Allston, "from whom I received attentions, during my residence in London, I must not omit Col. Trumbull, who always treated me with the utmost courtesy. Among my English friends it is no disparagement to any to place at their head Sir George Beaumont. It is pleasant to think of my obligations to such a man — *a gentleman in his very nature*. Gentle, brilliant, generous — I was going to attempt his character, but I will not; it was so peculiar and finely textured, that I know but one man who could draw it, and that's Coleridge, who knew him well — to know whom was to honor."

After thus expressing himself respecting his English friends, Mr. Allston continues. "A homesickness which (in spite of some of the best and kindest friends, and every encouragement that I could wish as an artist) I could not overcome, brought me back to my own country in 1818. We made Boston Harbor on a clear evening in October. It was an evening to remember! The wind fell and left our ship almost stationary on a long low swell, as smooth as glass and undulating under one of our gorgeous autumnal skies like a prairie of amber. The moon looked down upon us like a living thing, as if to bid us welcome, and the fanciful thought is still in my memory that she broke her image on the water to make partners for a dance of fireflies — and they *did* dance, if I ever saw dancing. Another thought recurs: that I had returned

to a mighty empire — that I was in the very waters, which
the gallant ' Constitution ' had first broken, whose building I
saw when at college, and whose 'slaughter-breaking brass,' to
use a quotation from worthy Cotton Mather's ' Magnalia,' *but
now* 'grew hot and spoke' *her name* among the nations! This
patriotic feeling is not a thing for which any credit is claimed,
it would only have been discreditable to have been without it."

Let knaves and fools laugh at patriotism; it is only knaves
and fools who can make jest of the most holy feelings of man's
breast! The American returning from Europe who does not
feel the glow of patriotism at the recollections of the free institutions of his country, the unparalleled diffusion of enjoyment
among the *people*, and the improvement of every kind flowing
from the establishment of a Democracy — is a wretch to pity
or abhor. "The public virtue," says Gibbon, "which among
the ancients was denominated patriotism, is derived from a
strong sense of our own interest in the preservation and
prosperity of the free government of which we are members."
The slaves of their own vices and the vices of a corrupt government will always mock at patriotism.

It was in this year, 1818, that Mr. Allston was elected an
associate of the Royal Academy of England. On this subject,
he has said in a letter of recent date, "my friends wrote me
that I should have been made an academician some years ago
had I been in London, on the occurrence of a certain vacancy;
but by the original laws of the Academy (for which the present
members are not accountable) no one is eligible as an academician who is not a resident of the United Kingdom. This law
is peculiar to the English Academy, and I cannot but think it
a narrow one."

On the 17th of November, 1818, Mr. Allston writes to his
friend McMurtrie, from Boston: "As I propose to remain
here during the winter, I must beg you to remit the balance
due me, of which you speak, to this place, directed for me to
care of Timothy Williams, Esquire, Boston. With respect to
the interest due from the Pennsylvania Academy, I beg you
to state to them that the delay of the payment of the purchase

money not having occasioned me any inconvenience, I with
pleasure relinquish it. I am sufficiently rewarded both by the
honor they have done me in the purchase of the picture and
in the sum paid. The success I have lately met with in England
left me but one finished picture to bring with me, 'Elijah in
the Wilderness,' and which, had I remained a few weeks longer,
I had the prospect of transferring to another proprietor.* I
have brought, however, several others *on the stocks*, some of
which are considerably advanced, particularly 'Belshazzar's
Feast, or the Handwriting on the Wall,' sixteen by twelve in
size, which, I believe, is by several feet larger than the 'Raising
of the Dead Man.' I purpose finishing it here. All the laborious
part is over, but there still remains about six or eight months'
more work to do to it. As I get on with it and other smaller
works, which I may probably proceed with at the same time,
I will take the liberty occasionally to drop you a line. In the
spring or summer I may not unlikely pay you a visit. I have a
great desire to see your city, and the state of the arts there.
Though I have not the pleasure of a personal acquaintance
with Mr. Sully, I yet so well know him through his friends and
the friendly services he in conjunction with yourselves has
rendered me, that I must, in a particular manner, beg you to
present him my respects. I left Leslie well. He intends embarking for America in the spring. He has lately finished a
beautiful little picture of Anne Page inviting Master Slender in
to dinner, from the 'Merry Wives of Windsor.' It is finely
composed and (here the letter is torn) I thought it his happiest"
(torn again).

From the above we see that the great work, not yet finished
in 1834, was considered by the painter as only wanting six
or eight months' labor to be completed in 1818, fifteen years
ago. "All the labor is over." How little do we know of our-

---

* This picture was soon after purchased by an English traveller and sent to England.
Titian and other Venetians are supposed to have painted their skies and other distances
in distemper, and then having varnished them with strong size, finished their pictures
in oil colors. Allston painted his "Elijah in the wilderness" with colors ground in milk,
and having perfected the work as far as he could in this manner, he varnished with
copal, and finished or retouched it in oil colors.

selves, our works, or our futurity! This great picture was valued at $10,000, and divided into ten shares, some of which, it is understood, was paid in advance. Of the circumstances which have delayed the finishing Mr. Allston has spoken in a letter to be laid before the reader. Allston once said to Sully, "Oh, do not undertake anything that cannot be accomplished by your own means." Sully before had had the burnt child's experience on that score in his picture of "Crossing the Delaware."

May 27, 1831, Mr. Allston writes thus to Mr. McMurtrie: "I have but a few weeks since been established in my new painting room, which I have built in this place (Cambridgeport, near Boston). 'Belshazzar' has been rolled up and reposing in a packing case for more than three years, in consequence of my former large room in Boston passing into the hands of a new owner, who has converted it into a livery stable; since which I have been compelled to work in a small chamber, where I have been employed altogether on small pictures. ' Belshazzar ' will still remain some time in his case — some embarrassing debts and my immediate necessities being the cause. I must be free in mind before I venture to finish it. I trust, however, that the time will not be very long. Your room which you mention must be a noble one. I wish there were such a one in each of our large cities. It is a great desideratum with me, as I mean hereafter, that is, when I once more become *free*, and should Providence grant me life, to confine myself chiefly to large works. I suppose that you know that I have become a benedict.* I have been married about a year, and this village is now my home. It is but two miles from Boston, where I can be at any time, by means of an hourly stage, in twenty minutes. I am in better health, and certainly in better spirits, than I have been these ten years."

In a letter to a friend, Mr. Allston had said that it was not his wish to give a catalogue of all his pictures. He was afterward prevailed upon to give the following brief notice of a part of his works. "I will mention only a few of the principal

* He married in 1830, a relative of his first wife.

which I painted during my first visit to England, viz: ' The
Dead man restored to Life by the Bones of Elisha.' The
'Angel liberating St. Peter from Prison.' This picture was
painted for Sir George Beaumont (the figures larger than
life), and is now in a church at Ashby de la Zouch. 'Jacob's
Dream,' in the possession of the Earl of Egremont. There are
many figures in this picture, which I have always considered
one of my happiest efforts. 'Elijah in the Desert.' This I
brought to America, but it has gone back, having been purchased here by Mr. Labouchere, M. P. The 'Angel Uriel in
the Sun,' in possession of the Marquis of Stafford. This is a
colossal foreshortened figure, that, if standing *upright* would
be fourteen feet high, but being foreshortened, occupies a
space but of nine feet. The directors of the British gallery
presented me with a hundred and fifty guineas, as a token of
their approbation of ' Uriel.'* Since my return to America, I
have painted a number of pictures, but chiefly small ones.
These pictures being pretty well known here, I shall mention
only a few of the larger ones, viz: 'Jeremiah dictating his
prophecy to Baruch, the scribe'; the figures as large as life.
'Saul and the Witch of Endor,' and 'Spalatro's vision of the
bloody hand.' This last is a small picture, but I mention it
because it is perhaps more extensively known, and because,
too, I consider it one of my best. The others which I have
omitted are landscapes, and, with three or four exceptions,
small figures. Although my large picture, " Belshazzar's Feast "
is still unfinished, yet I ought perhaps to say something about
it, as many inquiries have been made respecting my progress
in it, and the probable time of its being completed. In assigning this reason for speaking of it in this place, I do not mean
to admit any *right* in the public to be made acquainted with
it; for so far, it is wholly a matter between the subscribers
and myself. Still I am not disposed to withhold all information from a very natural curiosity. On some accounts I cannot but feel gratified with the general interest that has been

---

* They had before presented him with 200 guineas as the first prize for "The Dead
Man revived."

manifested in relation to it. All, however, that I can now say, is, that so soon as it is in my power to apply myself without interruption to the completion of the picture, I shall do it with the utmost alacrity; and that when circumstances will admit of this, it will not take a long time to finish it. If the subscribers to it have been anxious for its completion, many and many-fold greater has been my desire to see it done: and great indeed would be the relief to my mind. I could long ago have finished this and other pictures as large, had my mind been free: for indeed I have *already* bestowed upon it as much mental and manual labor as, under another state of mind, would have completed several such pictures. But to go into the subject of all the obstacles, and the hindrances upon my spirit, would hardly be consistent with delicacy and self-respect. Nor could I be far enough understood if I should do it, to answer by it any essential purpose. Those feelings which are most intimately blended with one's nature, and which most powerfully and continuously influence us, are the very feelings which it is most difficult to give any distinct apprehension of to another. For this reason then, as well as for the others assigned by me, I will be silent respecting them. I may add, however, in conclusion, that I have the prospect of a time, not very far distant, when I expect to be in a condition to complete this picture; an event which it is not possible for any one to desire more than myself."

Mr. Allston says, "I had a delightful visit from Morse. Its only fault was being too short. The same from my old friend Fraser." Samuel F. B. Morse, president of the National Academy of Design, the worthy pupil of Allston, after returning from this visit, exclaimed, "I go to Allston as a comet goes to the sun, not to add to his material, but to imbibe light from him." After having passed some years in Italy and France, surrounded by, and studying the masters of Europe, Mr. Morse finds his former instructor even greater than before. He has a large painting room, built under his direction, at Cambridgeport, but still the great picture is in prison. He expressed his strong desire to work on it; but by this building he is involved in debt, which prevents his mind (as he expresses) from being free. This is, however, on the point of being removed. It was thus that Benjamin West, being under the necessity of building his house and galleries in Newman Street, was, although constantly employed, obliged to live with rigid economy that he might pay the debt contracted, and support those appearances required in the associate of men overwhelmed with wealth, and after a life, a long life of virtue, frugality, and extreme industry, leave to his children less than a merchant would consider a fair gain upon a cargo of cotton. Mr. Allston's prospects are brightened — he soon will give to the world his great picture, the size of which has been so great an obstacle to its accomplishment, and in the meantime several pictures on a smaller scale are partly finished, which his pupil thinks will rank him by the side of Raffaele; among them is "Gabriel setting the guard of the Heavenly Host." Retired from the world, and engrossed by his delightful studies and assiduous labors, there can be no doubt that Mr. Allston will be free to realize his wishes by devoting himself to that grand style, both in size and composition, which has placed him at the head of living artists. As in West, so in Allston, the choice of subject for his pictures, indicates the character of the man. Does not the warmth or coldness of a painter's coloring depend upon his character likewise? — and perhaps the freedom of his handling. Can a warm hearted, benevolent man paint cold, purply, hard pictures habitually? Be this as it may, the choice of subject is a sure indication of the mind of the artist. When Mr. Allston was consulted on the subject of painting for the government, and was asked whether he would undertake to fill the vacant panels in the rotunda, if it was determined by Congress so to do, his reply was, "I will undertake one only, and I choose my own subject. No battle piece."

It has been said of Mr. Allston that when, in London, he had by a great picture produced a great effect, he did not follow it up. The public heard no more of him for years. That the time he threw away in smoking his cigar, and delighting his friends with conversation and delightful stories, of which he was a most prolific inventor and unrivaled *teller*, should have been employed in keeping up, by a succession of efforts, the name he had obtained. But the robust and untiring man can make no allowance for the man of more delicate frame, and for the lassitude and disease which follow in some men the extraordinary exertion of mind and body. I would not be the excuser of late hours at night even with temperance, and the waste of heaven's light by appropriating the day to sleep; but I can feel for a mind and frame like Allston's, and though I regret that much of his time has been spent without the pencil in hand, I do not believe that time wasted which appeared to be spent in idleness — such minds are never idle.

Washington Irving tells me that he first met Allston in Rome. That under his guidance he visited the works of art, and was taught by him to profit by a visit to a picture gallery: "Select two or three pictures and look at no others until you come again, then take two or three more, and your mind will be free from the confusion caused by the multiplicity of objects; you may study those you select and make yourself master of their merits and defects." Delighted with the society of Allston, and having all his love for art renewed and increased, Irving says that he was at one time resolved to study the art, encouraged by Allston. If so what might we not have gained? What must we not have lost![1]

[1] By request of Dunlap, Washington Allston contributed some interesting material for the sketch of his life. When the book appeared Allston was much disturbed by its statements and inferences touching his personal habits. In a copy of Dunlap's work presented to Allston by the author, there was found this portion of the copy of a letter written to Dunlap by Allston under date of March 20, 1835. "At present I will only point out one — the only important one — which is contained in the last paragraph but one, which contains but only two grains of truth; namely, that I smoked and sat up late; the rest, that is, what is supposed to have been connected with these habits, is not true. You must not think that I am here wincing at the mention of my faults. I know that I have faults enough and to spare, and what is more, I have long learned to bear the mention of them. But the fault imputed to me by inference, in this paragraph, is really not mine. The passage which I allude to as giving a false impression of me is this: 'that the time he threw away in smoking his cigar, and delighting his friends with conversation and delightful stories, should have been employed in keeping up by a succession of efforts the name he had obtained.' Now, the inference drawn from this is, that I was an idler, wasting my time in company continuously. I cannot take that to myself. I was then, and am still, a very different man. Next to what is vicious, there is no character more offensive to me, or one that I would most strenuously avoid realizing in my own person, than a company-loving idler. So far from wast-

ing time in company, my friends both in England and here have often complained that I did not go into it enough. I would not be an excuser of late hours. My late hours were spent not in company, but in solitary study: in reading, often in sketching, or in other studies connected with my art. As to general company, it always was and is to this day irksome to me. And though I take great pleasure in the society of my friends, my visits among them have always been rare, and from choice. Nay, it is the very rareness of these visits that sometimes makes them so pleasant — bringing out what is most pleasant in myself. Strangers who have seen me with my friends, and observed the zest with which I enjoyed conversation, have probably been misled by it, and set me down as one who needs prefer it to labor. You, indeed, have judged me truly when you say that such 'minds are never idle.' Without assuming the compliment implied, I may say that mine is so constituted that I could not be idle for six months and continue sane. Either that or my hands are always at work. But much as I love the interchange of mind, both the literary and intellectual, still more do I love my art. I have never found the labor in it irksome, though often plied in misery and abortive: for when I have been most wretched, and consequently working to no purpose, it has still been to me an unchangeable friend. Although it is not natural for any man to desire the exposure of his faults, yet I am not one who would gainsay what is true, though it be against me."

CHAPTER XXII.

ALEXANDER WILSON.

I SHALL give the biography of this extraordinary man principally by making an abstract from Ord's life of him, published in Philadelphia by Hall.

* Alexander Wilson was born in the town of Paisley, Scotland, on the 6th of July 1766. The rudiments of literature were attained in his native place before the age of thirteen; and he was bound apprentice to a weaver, in whose service he continued until eighteen years of age, and acquired the nickname of the "lazy weaver," from his love of reading in preference to the labors of the loom. He derived from his mother a taste for music, and showed a decided preference to weaving verses rather than cloth.

Freed from his bonds, he indulged his propensity for rural scenery and rambling, by shouldering a pack and commencing trade as a pedlar; but aspiring to the immortality of a poet,

---

* It seems proper that earlier students of the natural history of our country, who had some title to be called artists, should not be passed over; and first, Mark Catesby, F. R. S., who was born in England in 1679, and visited America in 1712. He remained seven years studying the botany of the country. He then returned home; but, being encouraged by the friends of science, made a second visit to the colonies, and took up his headquarters at Charleston, S. C., from which place he made excursions to the interior, through Georgia and Florida. An Indian was generally his companion, who carried his materials for drawing and painting, and such specimens of natural history as he collected. He returned to England in 1726, and studied the art of etching, that he might engrave the plates of his intended publication, which he did from his own paintings. His work is entitled "The Natural History of Carolina, Florida, and the Bahama Islands; containing the Figures of Birds, Beasts, Fishes," etc., "in English and French." This estimable and ingenious man died in 1749, aged seventy, leaving a widow and two children dependent upon the profits of his work. Kalm, the Swede, whose name was given to one of our most beautiful flower-bearing shrubs, the Kalmia or laurel, was, I believe, no artist, but Wangenheim, whose book on our forest trees was published in Germany after his return, designed the pictures himself, if I recollect aright, for it is many years since I read the work. He was an officer in the Hessian army of our Revolutionary War. William Bartram designed, and is mentioned in Wilson's memoirs. Dr. Barton drew subjects of natural history correctly, and very neatly.

he unfortunately published his poems, and endeavored to unite the pedlar and the poet, his pack and his poems, to the disadvantage of both. Though disappointed, he still continued his love for literature, and shared the poverty which such an attachment generally causes. He returned to Paisley and to weaving, but the revolutionary spirit of America and France having spread among the weavers, he of course joined the democracy, and took the liberty to publish a satire upon a wealthy knave of the aristocracy; but though published anonymously, it was traced to Wilson, and he was sentenced "to a short imprisonment, and to burn, with his own hands, the poem at the public cross of Paisley." The shouts and applauses of the weavers accompanied him; he was looked upon as a martyr to truth, but the circumstance weighed upon his spirit, and was a cause of his determination to migrate to America.

To raise funds for this purpose he became industrious and economical, living for less than a shilling a week, and hoarding the proceeds of his labor. He had read the advertisement of a shipmaster who was to sail from Belfast; and on foot he left Paisley, embarked at Port Patrick, and reached the desired ship: but her complement of passengers was filled, and Wilson, with a companion who left Paisley in company, consented to sleep upon the deck. With such accommodations the hardy poet crossed the Atlantic, and landed at Newcastle, Delaware, on the 14th of July, 1794, in the 28th year of his age.

He was now in a strange land, with not a shilling in his pocket. To enable him to reach Philadelphia, he borrowed a small sum from a fellow passenger of the name of Oliver, and feeling that he was free, shouldered his fowling piece, and walked, light as air, thirty-three miles to the capital of Pennsylvania. His love for American ornithology was kindled by a redheaded woodpecker, the first bird he saw in the western world.

After working as a copperplate printer, and at his old trade of weaving in Philadelphia, he tried Shepherdstown in Virginia; but only finding employment as a weaver, he returned, and in 1795 travelled through the north part of New Jersey as a pedlar, keeping a journal, full of interesting observations, and not only increasing his knowledge but his cash. He now opened a school, and for several years followed the honorable profession of a teacher, assiduously studying those branches of learning in which he was deficient; and making himself a mathematician, to the business of a teacher he was enabled to add that of a surveyor.

The companion of his journey of emigration was his nephew, William Duncan, whose mother had been compelled by poverty to follow her son, bringing with her a family of small children. To find an asylum for these, Wilson combined with Duncan, and, by the aid of a loan, purchased a farm in Ovid, Cayuga County, New York, where the son resided with his widowed parent.

After changing his place of residence several times, Wilson's good fortune placed him in a schoolhouse on the banks of the beautiful Schuylkill, and but a short distance from the residence of the philosopher, philanthropist, and naturalist, William Bartram, and within four miles of Philadelphia.

At a former period of my life, when the study of botany filled a portion of my time, I made a delightful pedestrian excursion from Philadelphia to Bartram's botanic garden, in company with Doctor Elihu H. Smith, my fellow student in the science, and Charles Brockden Brown, now so well known as a novelist. Although this has no connection with Wilson, the reader may forgive the feeling which dictates it. We found the botanist in his garden, dressed, as an European would say, like a peasant, and spade in hand; but we found the simplicity of a lover of nature and the courtesy of a gentleman under the homely garb. Such was the man into whose vicinity, and within the sphere of whose instruction, Wilson was now thrown. Bartram was pleased to find in Wilson a lover of nature, and an observer of the manners of birds, a subject dear to himself, and they soon became intimate and ardent friends.

Mr. Alexander Lawson told me that he often accompanied Wilson in his visits to Bartram, but the drudgery of a school, the confinement and the poverty that still haunted Wilson, rendered him melancholy, and instead of the exercise which might have cheered his mind, he played the flute and wrote verses, only tending to increase the evil by dwelling on it. He sometimes, in conversation, dwelt on his fruitless efforts and disappointed hopes, and hinted at suicide. Lawson suggested drawing to him — he thought it impossible — "if he could only draw as well as Bartram, he should be delighted." "You shall draw better, if you will follow my advice." Bartram had not devoted much time, or shown much talent for delineating the objects he loved to study and cultivate. Wilson consented to try drawing; but on endeavoring to copy some small human figures, he saw the imperfection of his work, and was confirmed in his opinion that he could never draw. His friend suggested flowers as subjects for his imitation: this was approaching the goal at which he was destined to arrive. He was encouraged, and persevered. He then tried to draw a bird, from nature — delighted himself and surprised his friend. He now approached his home — his resting-place. Reeves's colors were brought, and he painted, from nature, a bird he had shot. Thus was he, as far as a man can be at this time of day in civilized society, self-taught.

The study of ornithology went hand in hand with his progress in the art of designing the objects most interesting him. He read, and was dissatisfied — he sought the meadows, the rivers, and the woods, and found all he wished — he described — he painted — and found himself a draughtsman and an ornithologist. Then arose the desire to communicate to others. He formed the plan of publishing, and communicated with Bartram, who cautiously discouraged an undertaking that might involve him in difficulties; but his mind had received its impulse, and he had an answer for every objection.

Lawson approved of Wilson's scheme of making a collection of all the birds of the Middle States, or even of the Union, but saw more difficulties in bringing such a work to perfection, and before the public, than the schemer did. However, Wilson went on; and the time he had devoted, when not employed in teaching, to flute playing, verse making, solitude, and despondency, was now employed in increasing his collection of birds, of drawings, and knowledge of the nature, manners, and history of the subjects.

Wilson's letters to Bartram exhibit him in a most amiable point of light, and show that his studies at the schoolhouse had not failed to improve his style: these letters are before the public. Hoping that by some literary effort he might relieve himself from the confinement and the drudgery of a school, he sent some essays to my friend Charles Brockden Brown, who then wrote for and conducted "The Literary Magazine" for the proprietor, Conrad; and he contributed to Denny's "Portfolio," but these efforts produced no change in his situation.

In the month of October, 1804, Wilson, with two companions, made a pedestrian tour to the falls of Niagara. This produced on his return "The Foresters," published in the "Portfolio." In 1805, Wilson was, like an honest man, inflicting privations on himself to pay his debt to his friend: "I associate with nobody, spend my leisure hours in drawing, wandering through the woods, or playing on the violin." He was now seriously employed in making a collection of all the birds of Pennsylvania, and with all the ardor of genius conceived that he might etch them himself, and then color them. Lawson instructed him in etching, but he soon found not only that much time must elapse before he could etch, but that the graver must finish the work. Full of his project of publication, he wished Lawson to join with him in it; but he saw objections which Wilson could not, and declined. "I will proceed alone then in the publication, if it costs me my life!"

The enthusiastic Wilson conceived hopes of visiting the Mississippi under the auspices of Mr. Jefferson, but was disappointed; but as a literary man he had better fortune in 1806, being engaged at a liberal salary by Mr. Samuel F. Bradford as assistant editor. Mr. Bradford, six years after, not only released Charles R. Leslie from the bonds of apprenticeship, but actively promoted that subscription which wafted

him to Europe, being himself a liberal subscriber, and thus
smoothed the path by which a truly virtuous man has attained
the highest rank in the arts. Mr. Bradford thus opened the
way for Wilson to prosecute his favorite object, and shortly
after agreed to become the publisher of Wilson's Ornithology,
and furnish the requisite funds. Lawson was engaged as the
engraver, and admirably he acquitted himself.

In the month of September 1808, the first volume of the
"American Ornithology" made its appearance; and although
the prospectus had been before the public for two years, the
surprise and delight was as great as if it had never been announced; for no one could conceive that America could produce a splendid work on science that vied with the proudest
productions of the old world.

The author now set out on a journey to the eastward, in
search of subscribers. He went as far as Maine, and returned
through Vermont to Albany and Philadelphia, better freighted
with compliments than subscriptions. Almost immediately on
his return, he commenced a journey on the same errand to the
South, through Virginia, the Carolinas, and Georgia. When at
Charleston he had obtained a hundred and twenty-five subscribers; at Savannah they had amounted to two hundred and
fifty, he says, "obtained at a price worth five times their
amount."

The second volume of the Ornithology was published in
January 1810, and in February the artist and author proceeded
to Pittsburg, and thence alone in a skiff down the Ohio. His
letters to Alexander Lawson, his friend and the engraver of his
birds, have been repeatedly published, and can alone give a
true idea of the man. He visited the numerous towns which
had even then sprung up in the wilderness, and every object
of interest he could hear of and approach. Near Louisville he
sold his skiff, and performed the journey to Natchez partly
on foot and partly on horseback. In his diary he says, "This
journey, four hundred and seventy-eight miles from Nashville,
I have performed alone, through difficulties which those who
never have passed the road could not have a conception of."

He proceeded to New Orleans, and thence to New York and Philadelphia.

Seven volumes of the Ornithology were published by the extreme exertion of Wilson, the unremunerated expenditures of S. F. Bradford, and the friendly labors of Lawson. The United States were proud that such a work should originate and be thus far perfected in the country — Philadelphia, still more delighted, claimed the honor of being its birthplace, yet among all her learned and rich, the literati, the men of benevolence, and the men of wealth — among her thousands of high-minded men, and well-minded men, only seventy became subscribers for Wilson's Ornithology, "more than half of whom," says his biographer, "were persons of the middle class of society."

In 1812, Wilson was chosen a member of the "Society of artists of the United States." In 1813, Mr. West sent him a proof impression of his "Death of Nelson." The same year he completed the letterpress of his eighth volume; but before the plates were ready, on the 23d of August, 1813, a dysentery put a period to his days, in the forty-seventh year of his age.

The admirable trait in Wilson's character is his undeviating adherence to, and innate love of truth. He was strictly honorable in his dealings, and in all trials through life rigidly a virtuous man. His fault, and I learn but of one, was irritability; which perhaps counteracted, in some measure, the good effect which his high moral character produced.

In person he was of the middle size, of a thin habit, his features coarse, and a "dash of vulgarity in his physiognomy," which was forgotten when the intelligence of his eye was called forth, or the charms of his intellect displayed in conversation.

Of his poetical and other essays I shall not speak; and I hope my readers are too well acquainted with the merit of his composition, in his descriptions of the subjects of his study and his work, to need my eulogium.

His remains are deposited in the cemetery of the Swedish Church, Southwark, Philadelphia.

The following is from a Scotch paper: "July 13, 1833,

Wilson's anniversary. On Monday night the anniversary of this celebrated ornithologist and poet was honored by a number of his townsmen at Paisley. Thomas Crichton in the chair, Robert Lang, croupier." Crichton was the intimate friend and correspondent of Wilson. The memory of the deceased American ornithologist was "drank in solemn silence" after a speech from the chair. It is gratifying to record this testimony paid to the worth of a man of virtue and talent by his townsmen twenty years after his death.

My readers will be gratified by the perusal of a letter from my friend Dr. Francis, just received, which (as well as other matters relative to the arts) has so much original information respecting Wilson, as to make it a most valuable appendix to the foregoing memoir.

"Newport, September 8, 1834.

"Dear Sir, — You will perceive that I breathe a new atmosphere, and I now purpose enjoying myself for some three or four days at Newport, renowned for its salutiferous air — as the birthplace of Stuart and of Malbone, and the scene of some of the most active and laudable operations of the celebrated Bishop of Cloyne. I have again visited Mrs. W ——, where we had the gratification of seeing once more the 'Hours,' that exquisite work of genius and art by Malbone, which commands unmeasured praise from untold visitors at this place, who seek the opportunity of admiring this production of the pencil, not surpassed, in all probability, by the work of any foreign artist. We were also shown a number of unfinished heads, in miniature, by the same extraordinary master; a portrait of Mr. W. in crayons, done by Malbone, and his own portrait, a superior performance, kit-cat, in oil colors. From this an indifferent copy was taken by Gimbrede and subsequently engraved. There are other works of value by the same great artist to be seen in a distant part of the country; among them one entitled 'Devotion,' and another 'The Birth of Shakespeare,' of peculiar merits, *in umbra*. Malbone's life, though short, was sufficiently long to secure to him a permanent reputation. Miss Hall seems to me the only artist who has

made a close approximation to his best efforts. His 'Hours'
has awakened the powers of many a worthy poet. Among
others, his personal friend, the late Dr. Farmer, wrote some
clever verses on it; tinged, however, rather too deeply with
his own sombre associations as well as with deep grief at the
premature death of the painter.

"We rode to the house where the Bishop of Cloyne once
resided. Somewhat more than a century has elapsed since
he occupied it; it was once a substantial wooden frame farmhouse of two stories, and the room which we considered as
the bishop's library, still retains its old Holland ornaments
of earthen figures round the mantel and fire-jambs. It is contemplated soon to take down this venerated building, in which
case I have made an engagement to be supplied with a relic
to make two or three snuff boxes, one of which shall certainly
be reserved for you. And why not as well have a box of the
residence of the good bishop, as of the tree so famous for the
Indian treaty by Penn? The memorable line of the poet for
Berkeley, will apply with like verity to both these exalted
characters. At no great distance from the bishop's house are
the Paradise Rocks, seen projecting near the margin of the
sea; they are called by the people the Bishop's study. Here
he used to retire and write, and few places are more romantic,
or better calculated for health and inspiration. With your
present bodily ailings, you would do well to come hither for
a short time and finish your projected volumes. We shall have
fine green tea and flapjacks for your breakfast, water of the
spring of Dr. Franklin's temperature as your *medicina mentis*,
and coppices of verdant beauty for your eyes to gaze upon,
equal to any Humphrey Repton ever formed. It is affirmed,
as you probably will recollect, that the bishop wrote his
' Minute Philosopher' in America; and this sequestered spot,
with its Paradise Rocks before us, is fitted for the contemplation
of the most ardent votary of Plato.

"If it were not too professional I might also dwell upon
the fact, that Newport is known in our medical annals as the
first place on the American continent where a public course

of anatomical lectures was given. They were delivered by Dr. William Hunter so early as 1754. Dr. Hunter was by birth a Scotchman, born in 1729, and like many others, engaged in the cause of the pretender in 1745. After the fight of Culloden he repaired to this country and settled at Newport, where he died in 1777. He had received the earlier part of his education under the elder Monro, and acted as surgeon's mate in the contest just stated, his principal being Middleton; that Middleton who was afterwards the eminent professor of medicine in King's College, New York. There is an admirable portrait of Hunter in the family mansion, done by Cosmo Alexander in 1769; and also one by the same artist, of rather inferior merits, of Mrs. Hunter and her daughter. The curious who visit Newport sometimes carry away with them some fragment of the renowned ship 'Endeavor'; a portion of whose hull is still to be seen at Wilkham's wharf. This vessel is associated with the discoveries of Captain Cook, who, with Banks and Solander, made in her their first circumnavigation round the world, about, I believe, 1769. I possibly may err a little in the date, but I am too far off to consult the Redwood Library. The 'Endeavor' was afterwards purchased as a whaler, and used some time in that capacity, but being pronounced not seaworthy, has been suffered to lie here and decay.

"I cannot, however, permit the present opportunity to pass without addressing you a few lines relative to your 'History of the Arts of Design in America.' Your laborious and minute researches will probably leave little to be gleaned by your successors, in those inquiries in which you have so long been employed. The subject is of deep interest to all who feel a becoming pride in the talents which our native artists have so amply displayed, and on the reflection that Stuart, West, and Trumbull; Allston and Newton are of American origin. It seems to me that *Wilson*, the ornithologist, will have claims to your notice, and if he falls within the scope of your work, you will probably find it in conformity to your plan to precede your account of him by some slight sketch of his predecessor, in our natural history, the celebrated Catesby. Like Wilson,

Catesby was an artist; his zeal and industry were scarcely surpassed by Wilson, and his honesty and integrity in preserving faithful memorials of the objects of his attention, have been such as to secure the strongest approbation of experienced and qualified observers. A copy of his natural history may be seen in the library of the Rev. Dr. Hawks; it is in two volumes, large folio; the edition by Edwards. The figures of this work were originally etched by himself, and the colors were done either by him or under his inspection. As the reputation of this amiable, unassuming and excellent man has been somewhat impugned by Gordon and others, I hope you will allow me to give you the testimony of one of the best judges now living, on his merits. Wilson often refers to Catesby with suitable consideration, and with the ardor of a true worshipper. We are to remember that Catesby's plates do not afford specific distinctions of all he saw; it was not his object; his delineations of the various parts of a flower are imperfect, but for the best of reasons; botanical science among us had not yet received the aids of the Linnæan classification, though Colden, on the banks of the Hudson, about that period, took up with increased delight his investigation of plants, excited by new feelings the inspiration of his Swedish master. According then to the testimony of the best judges and most eminent naturalists, no delineator of the works of the Creator has excelled in merits Catesby, considering the time when he published, and the circumstances in which he was placed. Audubon, in speaking of him, remarked to me distinctly that the utmost confidence might be placed in all his statements. 'I have examined, him,' he added, 'with the closest severity, and I have scarcely seen in his descriptions, so far as they go, a single error. I confide in all he says. Others since his time have enlarged upon certain parts of him with the additional advantages of modern and more precise science.' After the triumphant declaration of Audubon let us no longer hear it asserted that Catesby defaced nature, and that his magnificent volumes cannot be consulted without regret and indignation.

"It was my happiness to be personally acquainted with

Alexander Wilson. The first time I saw him was in the latter part of October, 1808: he had just completed the first volume of his Ornithology, and had come to New York to solicit subscribers. The slender countenance he received to aid him in his vast undertaking, was somewhat depressing to his feelings. He stated briefly the great efforts he had made, the better to justify his application for subscriptions. 'I determined,' said he, 'to let the public see a perfect specimen of my work, before I sought their pecuniary support, and I carry my volume with me. I shall not abandon my design, however lukewarm it may be looked upon: but cherish the hope that there is in this widely extended and affluent country, a number of the admirers of nature sufficient to sustain me in my enterprise. What pains me,' he further remarked, 'is the indifference with which works in natural history are often regarded, by men of cultivated understanding and rank in life. I have just returned to your city, after a visit to Staten Island, to submit my volume to your governor. He turned over a few pages, looked at a picture or two; asked me my price; and while in the act of closing the book, added, "I would not give a hundred dollars for all the birds you intend to describe, even had I them alive." Occurrences such as these distress me; but I shall not lack ardor in my efforts.' — This little incident I confess to you it was sufficiently mortifying to hear. Moreover, the governor of the State of New York is always presumed to be an enlightened character: by charter he is a member of the board of regents, a body constitutionally created, who direct and control the intellectual pursuits of an empire state.

" Wilson on his subsequent visits to New York, seemed to be in better spirits, both on account of the patronage he had received, and the progress he had made in his work. He seized moments of leisure he had, in closely examining books in natural science, in different libraries to which he could obtain a ready access. The American Museum, which had now been well fitted up, was, however, his most gratifying resort. Scudder, the founder of this institution was indeed a rough diamond; but few could surpass his enthusiasm in studying the volume of nature, as he termed every subject in natural history. Wilson was loud in his praises of the *preservative* talents of this *artiste*, of materials in natural science: but at that day we had not the experience and results of Waterton before us. Few greetings could be more joyous, than that of these men; great as was the disparity in their scientific knowledge and intellectual culture. Scudder remarked, 'I have many curiosities here, Mr. Wilson, but I myself am the greatest one in the collection!' Scudder continued, and stated the trials he had passed amidst rocks and glens, referred to the time when he carried his museum on his back, and exulted at the success which thus far crowned him. He believed that a taste for nature's works was more diffused: he said he had travelled thousands of miles, in order to bring various objects of natural science together, worthy of study. All this was listened to by Wilson with feelings of great gratification: but when the museum-man added, 'Yet, notwithstanding all, and my success so far, I still find that the Witch of Endor, and Potiphar's wife, bring me ten dollars where my natural history does one'; the ornithological biographer, filled with emotion and changing countenance, gave utterance to a vehement expression on the listlessness of man in contemplating the harmony of nature; and while recounting his pedestrian excursions through our extensive country, gave vent in a philippic against closet naturalists and sedentary travellers. He seemed to have as great dislike to this last-named class of beings, as ever our old friend Dr. Williamson cherished.

"It was during one of these, his later excursions to the city, that Wilson waited upon our mutual friend Dr. Mitchill, whose fame had now extended far beyond the 'Grampian Hills, or the chalky cliffs of Dover.' Wilson found the doctor in his study: he had about this time commenced his investigations of the qualities and numbers of the fishes of the waters of New York. Surrounded by his cabinets of conchology and mineralogy, and with his room still further enriched with collections of Indian tomahawks and antiquities, and the dresses of the inhabitants of the South Seas, the doctor poured out of the

immense treasures of his prompt memory, and gave ingenious
illustrations on divers topics for the mental gratification of
Wilson. The meeting was highly satisfactory to both: the
ornithologist found the amiable and benevolent philosopher
the most accessible of mortals, expert in disquisition, whatever
the subject, — a monad or the Niagara; and no less ready at
the composition of songs for the nursery, than in expounding
his beautiful theory of the heavens. 'You have wandered
largely through our country, Mr. Wilson' (says Dr. Mitchill),
— 'I no longer travel — travellers come to me.' The result of
this interview was a promise on the part of the doctor to furnish Wilson with the history of the pennated grouse of Long
Island, in relation to which such a mass of foreign ignorance
has been displayed. How well he complied therewith, is known
to all who have read his admirable letter in the Ornithology.

"We have strong reasons to infer, that Wilson was greatly
disappointed at the state of society, and the condition of
literature in America, so far at least as they might be associated
with the encouragement of his designs. He had abruptly left his
own country, the victim of indiscretion if not of persecution.
He was tinctured with the political excitements of the times of
1790-4, and sought abroad what he deemed not within his
reach at home. His whole life from its early dawn, to its unexpected close, was a perpetual struggle. Bradford was indeed
his friend, and the venerable horticulturist near Philadelphia,
William Bartram, delighted to speak of him to the passing
traveller. His firmest resolves were often suddenly abandoned,
and as often re-resolved. He was of the *genus irritabile*, and
suffered at times from what is occasionally termed a constitu-
tional morbidness. But this itself, doubtless, added to the
intensity of his devotion to his sublime pursuits. When men
of power and place were indifferent to his glorious plans of
natural science, he sometimes betrayed a consciousness of
the supremacy of his studies, and of his own mental superiority.
Hence, republican as he was, he could not brook the frigid
apathy of our republican governor.

"An instructive parallel might be drawn between Wilson

and Michaux the younger. All who knew the latter, remember
with admiration his personal intrepidity and hardihood. Like
Wilson he had in reality abided the pelting of the pitiless
storm. Nothing but unintermitting efforts, under the most
discouraging circumstances, enabled him to complete his
'History of American Forest Trees.' Michaux, like Wilson,
sustained himself under every social privation, and became
a tenant of the woods; scarcely for weeks, months, nay, seasons, participating of the shelter of the domestic roof and the
comforts of the culinary fire. He was, moreover, often so outré
in his appearance, from necessity and habit, as rarely perhaps
to command the civilities of refined life: the metamorphoses of
Naso, were at times almost outdone by the peculiarities of his
outward attire. But the materials of his Sylva having at length
been brought together, from every quarter of our widely
spread country, he repaired with them to Paris, and there,
under the patronage of the savants of that metropolis, gave to
the world his elegant volumes. He still lives near the Sorbonne,
blessed with the remnant of a good constitution, at comfortable
ease, enjoying the national bounty willingly granted him for
his services; and the students of nature greet him as one of
their choicest associates. All who visit the Jardin des Plantes,
will learn how much he has enriched it, and behold the Platanus
and the Bignonia associated as neighbors, though of distant
climes, in amicable rivalry with the lordly Adansonia. — He
has effectively benefited the arts and rural affairs; he points
to the furniture around his dwelling, as examples of the beautiful adaptation of the products of our native woods, to the
elegancies of the dining room and the boudoir. He loves
America — it was the theatre of his reputation — and her
forests yield the loveliest and the loftiest trees. Poor Wilson
on the contrary, with all his high and ennobling aspirations,
was ever subjected to the caprices of indigence and want.
With the contemplative eye of philosophy, he enjoyed the
luxury of interrogating nature, in the most attractive of her
forms of animated existence; and he saw in prospective, the
accomplishment of his disinterested designs. But sickness

invades him with his unfinished labors before him, and in his
premature death, we have a striking illustration of the uncertainty of all human things.

"Exalted as all will pronounce the contributions of Michaux
the younger, I think that you should view the subject in another
bearing, when considering the relative merits of the author of
the 'Forest Trees,' and of the 'American Ornithology.' —
Michaux cannot fairly be looked upon as a pioneer in his voca-
tion. Not a few eminent arboriculturists had long ago given
some account of the riches of our forests. Since the time of the
Swede, Kalm, Wangenheim had penetrated into various parts
of our country, the better to understand aright the capabilities
of the North American tree, for transplanting and propagation
in Germany, and had dedicated to his sovereign, the king of
Prussia, his large folio with numerous plates. His drawings, I
understand, were made by himself; and when we consider the
professional capacity to which he was restricted during our
Revolutionary War, it is almost marvellous what he effected.
The ingenious Masson and the unfortunate Dombey, had also
touched our shores, and Michaux the father having explored
the North American regions for a period of more than twelve
years, had illustrated in folio, in a manner corresponding to his
subject, the oaks of North America. These then with John
and William Bartram and others had somewhat opened the
field for subsequent and better qualified observers, and Michaux has deservedly secured the triumph.

How different is the fact as regards that department in
which Wilson excelled: excluding the labors of Catesby, in a
limited district, with the exception of a casual notice here and
there, and the imperfect catalogue of birds by Mr. Jefferson,
hardly a correct observation in ornithology is to be found,
prior to the appearance of Wilson. The most improved works
in our natural history abounded in narratives of the incanta-
tions of the serpent, the *sub-terrene* hybernation of the swallow,
and a thousand other absurd stories touching the economy of
animals, which, from the plausibility with which they were
sustained, caused philosophy itself to be debased by its cred-

ence in such asinine hypotheses. Our birds were songless and without plumage, and the forbodings of the raven was our only melody. In this state of doubt and ignorance, like the dauntless mariner on unknown seas, without chart or compass, Wilson appears. With the force of genius he becomes an original explorer of untrodden wilds of vast extent and peril; shade and sunshine are alike to him; his pursuit is his happiness: with a diligence surpassing commendation, he enlarges the boundaries of human knowledge, and with the simplicity of truth, elevates "American Ornithology" to the certainty of a science, and worthy the cultivation of the highest intellect.

"You will pardon me, if, before I conclude, I record one or two circumstances concerning Wilson's reputation abroad. I allude to the popular and exalted renown he attained almost immediately after the completion of the Ornithology, by Mr. Ord his estimable friend who published his biography. The work of Wilson had indeed received from the American press, a few literary notices during the progress of its publication. Governor Clinton had written one or two friendly critics, with his wonted earnestness for the promotion of the science, and Wilson was gratified that he enjoyed the consideration of a character so conspicuous. But with his transatlantic countrymen, his memory became an object of deep interest. Paisley, his birthplace, had long known him as the author of 'Watty and Meg,' a popular ballad, which I recollect in my earliest schoolboy days, to have been echoed in our streets. I believe he was also the writer of some pathetic verses on the loss of a lovely boy by drowning, entitled, 'Pale wanderer of the silent night,' a production not alluded to in any notice of his muse that I have seen. Within a year or two after his work was finished, his countrymen at Paisley were urgent in their inquiries of American travellers concerning him and his great production. 'You must allow, after all,' said they, 'that you are indebted to a Scotchman for the true account of the birds of America. He was our townsman, and it gratifies us to learn any particulars of him. Near this place, he was once a faithful weaver among us; and "Watty and Meg" please us e'en now.' Perhaps these expressions of popular feeling struck me with the greater force, inasmuch as an occurrence of a somewhat different complexion took place a day or two before. Encountering a highland lad, who was discoursing sweet music to a song of Burns, I expressed my pleasure by remarking, we had no such poetry by American bards. 'You have not produced Burns,' replied he, 'but you have produced a greater man than all Scotland has, — Doctor Franklin, — he taught the way to make money.'

"When the Dukes John and Charles of Austria attended a *converzatione* at Sir Joseph Banks in 1816, the royal visitors expressed a desire to examine the library and vast collections in natural science of the venerable president of the Royal Society. 'I have nothing worthy of your special examination,' said Sir Joseph, 'except the "American Ornithology" of Wilson': and further inquiries were dropped upon the inspection of this extraordinary work. 'Our Radcliff Library is deficient,' observed Dr. Williams, the Regius Professor of Botany: 'we have had no opportunity of procuring the "American Ornithology" by Wilson: we learn the work is terminated; and it is remarkable that no "Edinburgh" or "Quarterly" has taken notice of it: in what way can we soonest obtain a copy from your country?'

"Thus the sod has scarcely covered the grave of the lamented Wilson, ere his matchless efforts as nature's historian, were the theme of popular and scientific admirers in regions far remote and distant from each other. While therefore his earthly remains have commingled with their kindred dust, like the delightful solo of that chief * of song among the feathered tribe, whose vocal powers amidst the fragrant magnolia, he has so eloquently described as unrivalled, his own surpassing labors will ever command the admiration of the disciples of nature in every part of the habitable globe.

"But I am fearful of enlarging this epistle, and hasten to assure you of my sincere esteem and regard.

"JOHN W. FRANCIS.

"WM. DUNLAP, Esq."

*The mocking bird.

CHAPTER XXIII.

PARADISE — WALDO — CATTON — KEARNEY — FROTHINGHAM — DICKINSON — PETER MAVERICK.

JOHN PARADISE.

THIS very worthy citizen and pious man was born in Hunterdon County, New Jersey, October 24th, 1783. His ancestors were English, his grandfather having emigrated to Maryland. The father of the artist was a saddler in Pennington village; and John, after a country school education, was taken by him into the workshop. He, however, preferred printing to saddle making; but, on trial, was not found strong enough, and returned to his father's. He had a taste for music, and learned to practise both on the flute and violin; but his great delight was in attempts at drawing, and after copying from prints, he even attempted faces from the life. As usual, there were admirers to encourage, and at the age of eighteen he took himself to portrait painting. He soon after became acquainted with Elizabeth Stout, and in a short time after married her. To this circumstance my informant attributes the future good of his life. He became a pious as well as a moral man, and pursued his chosen avocation with additional industry and perseverance. He went to Philadelphia, and for a very short time put himself under the tuition of Volozan; and in 1803 he commenced professionally as an artist. In 1810 he removed to New York, and was actively engaged in his profession for many years: but his health declined, and he had affections of the head, which at times rendered him incapable of business.

The sect to which Mr. Paradise was attached contributed to his success and employment as a portrait painter. Most of the engravings in the "Methodist Magazine" are from paintings by him. He died as he had lived, relying upon the mercy of his

God. According to his wish, he had been removed to the house
of his brother-in-law, Philemon Dickinson, near Springfield,
New Jersey, that he might die in presence of his sister. His
decease took place on the 26th of November, 1833.

Samuel L. Waldo.[1]

This gentleman was born in the town of Windham, Connecticut. His father was repeatedly elected, by his townsmen,
to represent them in the State Legislature; but, being of that
honorable class of citizens, yeomen cultivating their own
soil, young Waldo was early accustomed to habits of laborious
industry. His education was that of a good country school, but
had a circumstance connected with it worthy of notice — his
first teacher was afterwards the well-known General Eaton.

The usual fate of writing books belonging to boys, who as
men become painters, attended those of Waldo; and the desire
to become an artist induced him, at the age of sixteen, to
request his father to place him with a portrait painter of Hartford; assuring him, that if he would pay for his tuition, he
would never ask another dollar from him. His father indulged
him, and paid one hundred dollars to a Mr. Stewart, whose
skill and knowledge were not worth as many cents.

Waldo made the best of such instruction; and at the age of
twenty, with (as he has said) fifteen dollars in his pocket,
the price paid by a British commodore for the first portrait
the young painter attempted from the life, he took a painting
room, and set up his easel in the city of Hartford. Success
did not attend his efforts, and even his moderate expenses
exceeded his income. Happily he boarded at the same table
with a young lawyer, who, although just starting in life's race
himself, could feel for one who appeared to be lagging and
heavily laden. This was Thomas Day, Esq. since secretary
of state for Connecticut. Mr. Day advised Waldo to try
Litchfield, and gave him a letter to a friend in that place. —
He did more — he furnished credit for a new suit of clothes, to
make a suitable appearance among strangers. Theodore

[1] Samuel L. Waldo was born in 1783 and died February 16, 1861.

Dwight, Esq. gave him a letter likewise to a person of wealth and official rank. The persons to whom these letters were addressed had both invited the young painter to visit Litchfield and promised him employment.

On arriving at Litchfield, with little else in his pockets but these letters, he, with fluttering heart, proceeded to deliver them. One of the patrons by promises was very glad to see him, but extremely sorry that the friend whose portrait he wanted was sick and could not sit. He called on the other, who bowed him out with assurances that he should at all times be exceedingly happy to see him at his house. But there are friends as well as patrons in the world, and Mr. Waldo's conduct through life entitled him to expect friendship — and he found it. It so happened that a gentleman of Litchfield, at the time unknown to him, witnessed the cold reception and formal bow with which he had been received, or rather, dismissed; and being a warm-hearted man, benevolence dictated measures which he immediately put in practice, to counteract the effects of politeness. As he took leave of the last patron with heavy heart, and was proceeding to his inn, a gentleman followed him, and calling him by name, said, "My name is Gould — I saw your pictures at Hartford — I am happy to see you in Litchfield. Will you go with me to my house? it is but a few steps." The invitation was accepted; and the young artist introduced to Mr. Gould's family, and persuaded to stay and take dinner. Before dinner was ready Waldo observed a man entering the courtyard of the house, with his baggage and professional apparatus; which, by order of Mr. Gould, was carried upstairs into a spacious and well-furnished room, to which he led the painter, saying, "This is your chamber, and my house is your home: you may commence painting my wife's portrait as soon as you please, and then my face is at your service." There certainly are two kinds of people in this world of ours.

What a sudden revolution must have taken place in the feelings of a youth, who the moment before had in a strange place seen all his hopes blasted, and had not money enough to carry him back — and now found himself surrounded by friends — the employment he sought, offered spontaneously — free quarters provided for him, and a bright prospect for futurity opened before him. Day started him — Gould sped him on, and from that moment, though sometimes among shoals and shallows, he has sailed with the flood-tide to the haven he has found.

Mr. Gould introduced him to his friends — portraits were engaged — and the empty pocket was filled with $160. At Litchfield, Mr. Waldo met the Hon. John Rutledge, of South Carolina, who employed his pencil and invited him to accompany him to Charleston. The offer was accepted, and having discharged debts and visited his parents, the young artist sailed before the wind to the South.

At Charleston he was employed constantly; but feeling as he advanced in his profession the want of instruction, he, after a visit to Connecticut, and a second voyage to Charleston, by aid of the warm sons of the South, was enabled to visit London with letters of West and Copley. In 1806, he was received with friendship by Mr. West, and civility by Mr. Copley — and Charles B. King arriving about the same time, they took a room jointly in Titchfield Street. Mr. Copley introduced Waldo to the Royal Academy, the advantages of which he enjoyed for more than two years. Among those who had induced Mr. Waldo to visit London, some had done it by promises, and he found himself more than once placed in embarrassing circumstances. Mr. Elihu White of New York, and Mr. Charles W. Green, of Boston, relieved him by loans which he has repaid by cash and gratitude.

Mr. Waldo painted a few portraits at five guineas each, in London, but had not employment enough to pay expenses. — Robert Fulton was in London, and did him essential service by his advice. After passing nearly three years in England, Mr. Waldo returned home, and landed in New York on the 24th of January, 1809 (as he has said), "With two guineas in my pocket, and indebted to my friends six or seven hundred dollars." In addition to this burden (for all debt is a burden to an honest man), he had made the dangerous experiment of bringing a wife from her native country, and had an increasing family depending upon his exertions. It is to his honor, that by industry and economy this gentleman has discharged all pecuniary obligations, and remains to this time (1834), a prosperous and popular portrait painter, who can talk of his bank shares and stock like a merchant, while his children are a joy to his increasing years.

About the year 1812, William Jewett came to him for instruction, and was to give his services for three years, but in the second, he proved so useful as to induce his teacher to give him a salary in addition to his board and lodging; and in a short time to take him into a partnership, which continues to this day with increasing friendship. They paint jointly as Waldo and Jewett, and most of their pictures have the labor of both on them.

Mr. Waldo being a director of the American Academy of Fine Arts, proposed opening a subscription for employing Lawrence to paint a full length of West, as he has said, "That artists might see what constituted a work of art in that branch of painting." To this scheme the president and directors assented, and Waldo beginning the subscription with $100, *most* present followed the example. The list was filled up promptly by citizens of New York, and the $2000 raised and paid in due time to Lawrence by Mr. Rush, then our ambassador at London. On seeing this picture, George the Fourth ordered a copy of it. This is the full length of West, which Williams and Cunningham, the biographers of Lawrence, say that he presented to the American Academy on being elected an honorary member, and one of these historians tells us, that in consequence of Lawrence's generosity, and in hope to share it, an Italian Academy sent him notice of like honors.

It may be seen by this sketch, that industry and perseverance can raise a prudent man from poverty and debt to independence in fortune; and from a very middling standing, as an artist (even after his return from England), to a decided degree of merit and popularity.

Charles Catton.

This intelligent and pleasant old gentleman (for he was old when I knew him, in 1813) was the son of Charles Catton, R.A. of London; a celebrated painter of heraldry, and Elizabeth his wife: the younger Charles was born in London on the 30th of December, 1756. Having become a widower, and being possessed of property which he supposed would render him independent in the New World, the republican institutions of which were congenial to him, he emigrated in 1804, bringing with him, to New York, two daughters and a son.

To one of these daughters (Mrs. Gill, of New York), I am indebted for particulars relative to her father, which appear to me highly interesting, and eminently worthy of being rescued from that oblivion which must soon have enveloped them with impenetrable darkness.

The father of our subject had, in the pursuit of his art of blazonry, studied animal painting assiduously, and rendered the monsters of ancient heraldry beautiful and picturesque representations of nature, as far as the absurdities of the mystery would permit. He published a volume, with plates, on his favorite study. He died in 1798, having enjoyed the well-earned reputation of being the first artist in his branch of painting in Great Britain. Herald painters were in his time, ranked with artists in other departments of painting; and Mr. Catton's skill in animal painting, and knowledge of the human figure, gained him the rank of Royal Academician. Such was the instructor of young Charles; who, under so able a teacher, imbibed a love for his father's branch of art, and derived from him his intimate knowledge of animal painting — strengthened and confirmed by his own studies. He was a pupil likewise of the Royal Academy.

His father and grandfather having been victims to the gout, and Charles fearing the same inexorable tyrant, he was told that the only probable means of escape was travel. He accordingly visited most parts of England and Scotland, making drawings; from which, on his return home, he selected those he most approved, and painted them in oil. Many of these

views are engraved and published, and some of the prints may
be found in this country.

On the very respectable authority of Mr. Catton's daughter,
Mrs. Gill, I give the following anecdote: — Mr. Catton, her
father, was intimate with Mr. Beechey, since known as Sir Wm.
Beechey. Mr. Beechey was a favorite painter with George
the Third, and the king gave him an order for his portrait on
horseback. Beechey proceeded to execute his majesty's order,
and had frequent sittings of the king, with opportunities of
studying the horse intended to be commemorated. He, however, felt that he was not sufficiently *au fait* with the larger
animal of the two, and applied to his friend Catton for assistance. Catton undertook to paint the living throne of the king
but expressly stipulated that the affair should be kept secret,
and of course that no one should see him when at work. He
had proceeded with his usual skill and knowledge in this branch
of painting, nearly to a close; when one day some one entered
the apartment while he was at work, and thinking it was
Beechey, he went on painting, and the intruder took his stand
well behind him, and looked on, as his friend frequently did. —
" Well," said Catton, "how do you like your horse?" And looking up as he spoke, he was astonished to see the king; who
answered, "Very well — very well indeed — I like my horse
very well — sit still, sir — don't put down your palette —
I will look on a little while — go on — go on — go on — you
are doing very well, sir — go on."

The painter went on, and the monarch entered into conversation with him in his usual rapid and peculiar manner, asking
questions particularly respecting horses; which Catton readily
and promptly answered, much to the king's satisfaction. —
Beechey came in, and found that the secret was discovered —
the doors had opened of themselves on the approach of royalty
— every precaution had been in vain. The king laughed at
his painter, and expressed his satisfaction with Catton. Several
other interviews took place between the king and the painter
of his horse, during which the amiable monarch became very
much pleased with Catton's conversation, as well as skill:

and while sitting to Beechey, he expressed his approbation of his friend in very strong terms; concluding with, "I like him very much, Beechey — Beechey, I'll knight him — I'll knight him — tell him so."

This is the cheap way in which monarchs can pay debts and confer favors; and by a nickname and a piece of ribbon tickle the vanity of the silly creatures who support them by their labor.

Beechey of course communicated "his majesty's gracious intention" to the astonished Catton; who (probably after laughing at the proposal) begged his friend to make the proper apologies to the king, and decline the favor. Accordingly, when the portrait painter had the next sitting, he made excuses for his friend Catton, and announced his having declined the title and the intended honor. George took it all in good part; but, as he determined to get rid of a portion of his knight-making power, he said, "Well, well, well, Beechey — if he will not be knighted I will knight you, Beechey — you must not refuse — ha? I will knight you." Such is my informant's version of the story of Sir William Beechey's knighthood.

Mr. Catton, on his arrival in this country, purchased a farm up the Hudson, in Ulster County, and resided there many years, occasionally painting landscapes and animals. In 1813 he visited New York, and I became acquainted with him. He painted a drop scene for a theatre my friend John Joseph Holland opened in Anthony Street; and he represented all the prominent characters of Shakespeare in appropriate costume, with good expression, and well managed throughout. I was at this time taking up the pencil for oil painting, after an interval of twenty years; and the old gentleman frequently called upon me and encouraged me. "You shall be the portrait painter and I will be the historical painter," he has frequently said: but I never saw any historical composition from his pencil, or any grouping of human figures, except the Shakspeare characters, and two pictures mentioned below. My friend Elias Hicks, Esq., has a landscape of Mr. Catton's painting, with animals introduced.

The last picture he painted was "Noah's Ark," and the animals entering and congregated for the purpose. This is in the possession of Colonel Bomford; and a copy of it was shown to me by Charles W. Peale, painted for his Ark in Philadelphia. Mr. Catton died on the 24th of April, 1819, aged 63.

Some time after his death two pictures were shown in New York, said to be painted by Hogarth, and brought to this country by Mr. Catton. It is said they were sent to this city for sale by Mr. Catton's son, and were in the possession of Mr. Samuel Maverick, the son of Peter R. Maverick, one of the earliest engravers. I had no hesitation in saying, that one of them had no mark of Hogarth's pencil upon it, or of his genius in the design: the other (a Recruiting Sergeant enlisting a Clown), was so good, and reminded me so forcibly of "The March of the Guards to Finchley," that I said, — "this may be Hogarth's, though I doubt it." The drummer sitting at his porter potations was particularly good. A friend of mine asked Mrs. Gill if she knew anything of two pictures by Hogarth, brought to this country by her father, and in his possession to the time of his death. She replied, that she had never heard of his having any picture by that master in his possession at any time. My friend described the recruiting scene; when the lady stepped to one of her father's portfolios and produced the original colored drawing; saying, she remembered perfectly the time he painted it, and all the circumstances attending it; particularly her delight, as a child, when she saw the monkey in the corner of the picture.

FRANCIS KEARNEY[1]

This gentleman was born in the city of Perth Amboy, New Jersey, about the year 1780. His father, at one time a merchant in New York, was likewise a native of Perth, and his grandfather, an eminent lawyer, long resided there, if not a native. The mother of Francis Kearney was the daughter of Judge Lawrence, of Burlington, New Jersey, and sister of the gallant Captain Lawrence, of the United States navy, whose flag he graced with one of its many victories, and after-

---

1 For Kearney read Kearny

wards fell uttering the well-known cry of "Don't give up the ship."

At the age of eighteen Francis, having a predilection for drawing and engraving, was placed with Peter R. Maverick, the best engraver, at that time, in New York, but miserably deficient, as he had no education in the art, and owed all his attainment to his own persevering industry.

Maverick demanded and received $250 for the instruction of this youth for three years, besides the advantage of his ingenuity and labor. The attention of young Kearney[1] was principally directed to the human figure, and to such compositions as raise engraving from the mechanical arts to the arts of design. His first plate of any account was done for an Encyclopedia, published by Mr. John Law, of New York.

Drawing he studied under Mr. Archibald Robertson and his brother Alexander. Line engraving, etching, aquatinto, stippling and soft ground etching were all studied by the young engraver, principally by the aid of books.

At the end of the term agreed for, he commenced business as an engraver for himself, with the usual discouraging circumstances which attend the unknown; but some time after Mr. Collins, a publisher, commenced a quarto Bible with plates, which was considered at the time as a great undertaking. Leney, an engraver of merit, who arrived in this country about 1808 or 9, Peter Maverick, the son of Peter R., Scoles, Anderson, and Kearney, engravers of New York, with Tiebout, and Boyd of Philadelphia, were engaged on the plates for this work.

Philadelphia was at this time far before New York in the business of publishing books, reprints of English works, and the decorations of such works gave the principal employment to our engravers. In 1810 Mr. Kearney removed to the capital of Pennsylvania, and immediately found himself in full and constant employment, which continued for twenty-one years that he resided there.

In 1820 he entered into a partnership under the firm of "Tanner, Vallance, Kearney & Co.," for the term of three years. The object was bank-note and other engraving. This proved an unfortunate connection for him, and, as I am informed, at the end of three years he lost the amount of his labor for the whole time. Mr. Henry S. Tanner managed the financial concerns. The publication of the large North American Atlas was commenced; and at the winding up of the business, the financier took the plates, as the other partners complain, and, by finishing them, realized a great profit. However this may be, Mr. Kearney[1] lost the labor of three years of his life.

Since this unsuccessful copartnership Mr. Kearney has been employed on various works for souvenirs and other publications, principally religious subjects, and in 1830 commenced engraving a large plate of the " Last Supper " of da Vinci, from Raphael Morghen's celebrated plate. This has been successful, and added to his reputation as an artist. During the progress of this work he returned to his native place, on business relative to his father's estate, but continued his application to his great work of the " Last Supper."

In June 1833 he returned to New York, and there finished this plate, which he sold to Mr. Carpenter, who has already disposed of 1500 impressions at $5 each, and the demand continues.

JAMES FROTHINGHAM.

Mr. Frothingham, at this time (1834) one of our best portrait painters, commenced the working business of life as a builder of chaise bodies, the trade his father followed and intended for him. He was born in Charlestown, Massachusetts, near Boston, in the year 1786. James early commenced attempts at drawing, and as he succeeded, to the admiration of his schoolmates, applause excited ambition. In due time he gained the art and mystery of chaise building under his father's tuition; but his attempts at drawing having led him to dabble in colors, his first step towards the painting art was to color the chaise bodies made by himself and his father. This was, at the time, one of those mysteries only imparted by masters to their apprentices under seal of secrecy, and the youth had

---

1 For Kearney read Kearny

to devise means by which to compel the colors to adhere to
the wood, and make one layer of paint keep its place over
another. Many unsuccessful experiments did not discourage
him, and he finally, notwithstanding the extreme closeness of
the coach and chaise painters in the neighborhood, obtained
the art.

In the meantime his experiments in drawing had been in
progress; and from copying a print from a child's book, line
by line, he had attained to the representation of a bowl, a hat,
and other objects technically called still life, with an encouraging degree of truth. At this period of his progress, towards
his destined profession, some one suggested that portraits
might be made with black and white chalk on grey paper.
He tried with charcoal and chalk, and prevailed upon a relation to sit to him. This was pronounced a monstrous likeness.
He next sat to himself, and produced a portrait in Indian ink.
The portrait of his grandfather, in oil colors, was the next
experiment. He had never seen a painter's palette but contrived a machine for himself, such as he thought proper for the
purpose — it was a piece of board, in which he made holes to
receive as many *thimbles* as he had colors, which diluted with
oil, were thus disposed of, every color to its thimble and every
thimble to its hole in the board, ready to receive the brush.
Of tints or mingling of colors he knew nothing. With this original apparatus and without instruction, he commenced portrait
painting, while yet applying himself to the discovery of some
mode by which to accomplish chaise painting, at the same time
working at his trade. His mode of making out a likeness was
as unusual as his palette was original. He painted first the
forehead and finished it, then one eye and afterwards the other,
finishing each as he went, and so feature by feature to the
chin. The hair was then put on, the drapery followed, and last
a background. Even thus working in the dark, he made such
pictures as called forth the applause of his father's neighbors
and his own associates.

That the lad should have been in the neighborhood of
Boston all his life and striving to paint from childhood, and

yet have remained in total ignorance of the mode of operation adopted by others, is a curious fact. Of the fact I am assured by Mr. Frothingham himself. It marks a degree of seclusion from that portion of society to which all these matters are familiar, which at first sight appears very strange; but perhaps we should find in the occupation of the father, and the associates of the young man, a sufficient explanation. So far Frothingham had been almost self-taught.

Having been sent on business to Lancaster, Massachusetts, he there first met with a portrait painter. Mr. Whiting was the son of General Whiting, an old Revolutionary soldier. This gentleman did not continue long in the profession, but entered the army of the United States. At this time, however, he had the power and the will to show young Frothingham what kind of an instrument a painter's palette is, and how painters use it. Mr. Whiting had sought and received instruction from Stuart. He communicated freely what he had freely received, and Frothingham was told with what colors the great painter set his palette, how he mingled his tints, and in some measure how he used them.

The youth returned home elated with his acquired knowledge, and eager to put in practice the lessons he had received. He procured a palette — dismissed his thimbles, procured colors and oils as directed, and began a portrait in the usual manner as he had been instructed by Whiting. About this time likewise, he obtained the privilege of reading Reynolds' "Discourses" — the first book he had seen on the subject of painting. This again marks the seclusion to which a young man may be confined, although within the precincts of a dense and enlightened population.

His success in the mode of painting now adopted by him was so great, that at the age of twenty he found sufficient employment as a portrait painter at low prices, to induce him to abandon the painting of carriages, just as he had mastered the mystery by his own efforts. He was likewise induced to marry, while yet he had to obtain a profession or property to support a family.

Stuart, as we have seen, took up his residence in Boston in 1805, and his name had previously reached Frothingham; but although desiring above all things to see the great painter, and obtain his instruction, it was far from his thought that such good was attainable. He had found that coach painters had secrets, which could only be obtained by a long service as an apprentice, and he concluded that a great portrait painter would require still longer servitude or payment of money far beyond his means, before communication of his higher mysteries. At length, after Stuart had removed to Roxbury, and was surrounded by his family, after much debate the young man determined to approach the awful presence of the first portrait painter in the country. There was at this time, an ingenious painter of signs and ornaments in Boston of the name of Penniman. This man had talents which had attracted the notice of Stuart. Penniman accidentally saw the portrait of a Mr. Foster, painted by Frothingham, and advised him to see Mr. Stuart. The young man with great trepidation walked to Roxbury, determined to gain admittance within the lion's den. He thought he would present himself as one wanting his picture painted, and make inquiry respecting Mr. Stuart's prices. He was admitted without difficulty, but Stuart was not at home. His son Charles received him, answered his questions, and showed him the works of his father.

Encouraged by Penniman, he soon after determined to show one of his own heads to Stuart, and again walked from Charlestown, through Boston and over the neck to Roxbury; this time carrying the portrait of Foster. He knocked and Mrs. Stuart opened the door. He presented himself without showing in the first instance that he had brought a picture, — leaving it out of sight of whoever might come to the door. "Your name, sir, and I will announce you." This appeared as an awful ceremony to the young painter — but he must go on. He gave his name, and was ushered into the old gentleman's painting room. He mustered courage to communicate his business. "I will tell you anything I know — have you brought any specimen of your present skill?" "I have brought

a portrait, sir — it is out o' doors." "Bring it in, sir, we don't
turn pictures out of doors here — bring it in."

On the great painter's easel was a portrait of Judge Jones,
thought by Mr. Frothingham, one of his best. Stuart placed
the young man's work by the side of it. He asked him what
his present business was. "Coach painting, sir." "Stick to it.
You had better be a tea-waterman's horse in New York, than
a portrait painter anywhere."

Notwithstanding this damper, Frothingham saw and heard
enough to encourage him; and he obtained permission to come
again. On his next visit he did not see the painter, who was
engaged with a sitter, but his son Charles told him that his
father had said, "That young man's coloring reminds one of
Titian's." This was fixing Frothingham in the pursuit fated
for him. He from this time forward carried his portraits to
Roxbury, and never went without receiving a lesson of importance. The sixth picture he carried for criticism, he was
amply repaid for his long and fatiguing walk by the remark,
after due examination, "You do not know how well you have
done this."

In the year 1810, Stuart said to his pupil, for such Frothingham must now be called, after looking at a recently painted
portrait, "There is no man in Boston, but myself, can paint
so good a head." And not long after, went further by saying,
"Except myself, there is no man in the United States can
paint a better head than that," pointing to the last his pupil
had brought to him.

Mr. Frothingham removed from Charlestown to Salem, —
it was there I first saw him. He was full of employment, but
I remember nothing in his rooms at that time that would
justify the high eulogium above given, or that could compare
with portraits from his pencil since painted in New York. He
was induced to remove to Boston, but Chester Harding had
gained the public favor, and even Stuart was left unemployed!
In 1826, Mr. Frothingham removed to New York, where he
remains painting heads with great truth, freedom and excellence, but not with that undeviating employment which popular

painters of far inferior talents at the same time find. He has, as he says, been made to remember Stuart's first characteristic advice and remark, "Stick to coach painting. You had better be a tea-waterman's horse in New York, than a portrait painter anywhere."

But this is not a fair estimate of the profession. It will be found by every candid examiner of the disappointments and vexations attending upon the portrait painter, that like all other troubles which befall man, much is owing to himself. It is hard to bear the supercilious conduct of the rich and ignorant who assume the patronizing tone, but it is best to smile in the confidence of superior knowledge. It is hard to have appointments broken which have caused hours of preparation; but it is best to receive a sitter so as to give token of the injury done you, but without ill humor. When a well-informed person engages a portrait, the engagement is held sacred, but with the vulgar a contract of that nature is not thought binding, although one for a hogshead of tobacco or pipe of rum, would be considered as not to be violated. The painter is injured in his feelings, and through the preparations he makes, and the reliance he places on the faithless individual — but he has no redress, and had better smile than scold. I have heard of painters, who if a sitter came a few minutes beyond the time appointed, would turn him or her away — this is churlish and injures his practice.[1]

ANSON DICKINSON

Was born at Litchfield, Connecticut, in 1780. He was apprenticed to a silversmith, and worked as such. He commenced miniature painting in 1804, or before. I first saw him at Albany in 1805, and his painting was then indicative of talent. He became a very good colorist. He was a very handsome, promising young man, but the promise of his youth has not been realized. In 1811 he was the best miniature

[1] Frothingham painted portraits in Boston, Salem, Mass., and New York City, and died in Brooklyn, N. Y., in 1864.

painter in New York. He has led a wandering, irregular life, without credit to himself or his profession.[01]

PETER MAVERICK.[2]

The son of Peter R. Maverick above noticed. Taught by his father, but far excelling him as an artist, Mr. Maverick was, for a time, in most prosperous circumstances, his emoluments principally accruing from bank-note engraving. Some misfortunes connected with a partnership business, left him late in life to commence anew, with a very large family to support. A. B. Durand was his pupil, and in him the arts owe to Mr. Maverick unbounded gratitude — for however great the talents of the pupil, much is due to the master. Mr. Maverick died when still in the prime of life at New York, the place of his birth.

01 In 1818 he went to Canada and in 1840 settled in New Haven, then removing to Hartford, Conn., where he died in 1852. He worked for a time in Boston.

2 Peter Maverick was born in New York City October 22, 1780, and died there on June 7, 1831. He was a prolific engraver and the proprietor of a copperplate engraving and printing establishment in the same city.

CHAPTER XXIV.

COGDELL — HOVEY — FÜRST — MILLS.

JOHN STEPHANO COGDELL.

THIS gentleman was born in the city of Charleston, South Carolina, on the 19th of September, 1778; and at about seventeen years of age left the Charleston College, and was placed in the office of a distinguished member of the bar; this gentleman, Judge Johnson, being promoted to the State judiciary, Mr. Cogdell, having charge in part of the business he left, found his health so much injured by application to it, that he seized the opportunity of a friend's visiting the Mediterranean and its shores, embarked with him in June 1800, and visited Gibraltar, Leghorn, Pisa, Florence, Sienna, and Rome. Previous to this he had felt no great passion for the arts, and only amused himself with water-colored copies from prints; but the pictures of Italy and a visit to Canova called forth latent powers and excited ardent aspirations, which were counteracted by continued ill health. With little bodily amendment, he returned home in about eight months and resumed his professional labors.

The desire to become an artist, however, increased, and he solaced himself for the hours devoted to legal duties by procuring materials and attempting painting in oil, and at the same time imported casts and applied himself to drawing from the round: from the plaster he advanced to the living head for his study, and painted many of his friends' likenesses as presents.

His preceptor, Judge Johnson, having been removed to the federal court, invited him to visit Washington City, which he did in 1806. On his return he received from Mr. Jefferson, then president, an appointment as consul at Rome, no doubt with a view to gratify his taste, and facilitate his study of the

371

arts of design; but Mr. Cogdell could not avail himself of this kind intention, as his circumstances were not equal to the expense of the visit, and the appointment conveyed no emoluments.

After a happy marriage with Miss Gilchrist, Mr. Cogdell's business as a lawyer increased; and although his study of art was diminished, he found time to paint a Crucifixion as a present to his former instructor at college, the Rev. Simon Flex Gallagher, which was placed as an altarpiece in his church. He likewise painted a picture for the Orphan House, and many others, heads and landscapes, as presents to his friends.

Mr. Cogdell made frequent visits to the cities of the North, and found pleasure, encouragement, and instruction from his intimacy with their artists. In the year 1825, Mr. Cogdell visited Boston for the second time, and met his friend and fellow townsman Washington Allston, whom he had not seen for twenty years. Mr. Allston strenuously advised him to model in clay, and he promised that he would make the attempt.

In 1826, Mr. Cogdell very wisely applied himself to the study of anatomy, and on one occasion mentioned to the professor, the promise he had made to his friend Allston: this led to an agreement with the professor, by which he submitted his head for a study, and Cogdell, although only verbally instructed in the use of clay, modelled his first bust. This year he again visited Boston, and was encouraged by Allston to proceed, and the result was, on his return home, a bust of General Moultrie, a cast of which was presented to Congress, placed in their library, and occasioned very flattering compliments on the floor of the House of Representatives.

While pursuing his profession with industry, Mr. Cogdell found time to design and model not only busts, but figures. But he had one favorite object in view, which was to visit England, France, and Italy, and taking with him a wife, whose attachment and congenial taste would aid and encourage him to devote himself to the arts in the latter country. Steadily pursuing this object, he had accumulated a capital nearly amounting to what might support him in Italy, by its interest, when circumstances threw in his way a citizen of New York —

a member of the bar — a former president, and then solicitor and director of a bank in that city. By the recommendation of this gentleman, he was induced to sell out stocks in Charleston, and send the proceeds subject to his proffered friendly investment.

In a letter before me, communicated by the friend of Mr. Cogdell, from whom I derive my knowledge of the above particulars relating to him, he says, "My fancy had almost numbered the months in which I should be enabled to plume my wings, and revel in the works of art in England, France, and again in Italy; but in the spring of 1828 I received in about ten lines from the gentleman, a picture of my ruin in the bank's failure, in which he had invested my funds." He says in another passage: "I have never heard since from the gentleman."

Thus were his liberal and favorite hopes blasted. Happily he had a profession, and held an office under the general government in the customs, and summoning philosophy to his aid, he pursued his studies in art in unison, with attention to his immediate occupation as a man of business.

Mr. Cogdell has served in the legislature of his native State, and has held the office of comptroller general. In 1821 he was appointed by President Monroe, naval officer of the customs of Charleston, reappointed by John Q. Adams, and afterwards by Andrew Jackson. From this situation he was taken in July 1832, to superintend the business and interests of the bank of South Carolina, as president.

Mr. Cogdell has distinguished himself as a painter, and without having even seen any one model, he has modelled busts, figures, and groups, and without seeing any one chisel in marble, has executed several works in that material, particularly a tablet with three figures, which forms part of a monument erected in St. Phillip's Church by himself and brothers, to the memory of his mother.

Thus happily situated (notwithstanding his disappointment), with ample competency, honored and intrusted by his country, Mr. Cogdell enjoys the blessings attendant upon a virtuous and industrious life.[0]

0 Faithful to Charleston, Cogdell died there the 25th of February, 1847.

Otis Hovey.

It is questionable whether this name should be entered as that of an artist, or of one who furthered the progress of the arts of design in America; but as his pictures, though merely copies, were, as such, extraordinary for one in his circumstances, here he is. He was born in Massachusetts in 1788, and his father removing to Oxford, State of New York, the boy's genius (as we call it) was first discovered there as usual, by his attempts to draw familiar objects. Samuel Miles Hopkins, Esq., of the city of New York, saw the boy's attempts,. and wishing to aid talent, invited him to the city in 1805, and supported him there. At this period he made several copies in oil, which are with Mr. Hopkins, and possess merit as such; and as the productions of an ignorant youth, much merit. An attempt was made by Mr. Hopkins to interest our rich merchants in the lad's fate, so far as to raise money to send him to Europe, but the plan failed— the money was not forthcoming. In the meantime, Hovey showed a vulgar disposition for vulgar enjoyment, and his friend was obliged to send him home. He there painted portraits of the neighbors for a time, and then sunk to oblivion.

Moritz Fürst.

This gentleman is a die sinker, well instructed in his art, which is in many respects so distinct from the other arts of design, that I hoped to give a sketch of its history, and an account of the process by which such beautiful works are produced. I had promises given me by Mr. Moore, the Director of the mint of the United States, and by a practical die sinker of New York, but they have proved — promises.

Mr. Fürst, in answer to my inquiries respecting himself, says that he was born at Bösing, near the well-known city of Presburg, in Slavonia, a province of Hungary, in the month of March, 1782. His principal instructor was Mr. Würt, die sinker in the mint of Vienna. Under this gentleman, Mr. Fürst was taught the art of sinking dies for coins and medallions. He had a second instructor in Mr. Megole, at Manche-

neries, who had pursued his profession at Vienna in his youth, but was afterwards superintendent of the mint of Lombardy.

In the year 1807 Mr. Fürst was engaged by the American consul at Leghorn to be die sinker to the mint of the United States, and arrived in America in September of that year. Mr. Fürst says, "I was installed in that capacity by Joseph Clay, Esq. in the spring of 1808."

I have heard from others that Mr. Fürst has experienced injustice. That he is a good artist I know. He resided in New York many years ago, and in 1816 executed some work under my direction for the swords presented by the State to military and naval officers who had distinguished themselves.

Mr. Fürst has again resided in New York for the last four years, but I fear his emoluments from his profession have not been equal to his skill or deserts.

ROBERT MILLS.

This gentleman is a native of Charleston, South Carolina, and was educated at the college of that city under the charge of Bishop Smith and Dr. Gallagher.

In the year 1800, Mr. Mills was sent by his father to the city of Washington, and placed in the office of James Hoban, Esq. architect of the public buildings then erecting in that city. Here he prosecuted his studies about two years, when he made a professional visit to all the principal cities and towns in the United States; and on his return to Washington was introduced to Mr. Jefferson, president of the United States, under whose patronage Mr. Mills resumed his studies, being furnished from Mr. Jefferson's library with such architectural works as he had (principally Palladio's). Mr. Jefferson was a great admirer of architecture, and was highly pleased to find an American directing his attention to the acquisition of this useful branch of science with a view to pursue it as a profession, and therefore gave Mr. Mills every encouragement to persevere. The president was then erecting a mansion at Monticello, which he afterwards occupied, and engaged Mr. Mills to make out the drawings of the general plan and elevation of the building; the drawings of the details Mr. Jefferson reserved to himself; and it is surprising with what minuteness he entered into these, every moulding was designated, and its dimensions, in figures, noted, so that nothing was left for the workmen to conjecture. He introduced every order of architecture in the finish of the various rooms, all true to the rules of Palladio. Mr. Jefferson was altogether Roman in his taste in architecture, and continued so to the day of his death, as may be seen on examining the University buildings in Virginia, designed by him, and carried into execution under his supervision.

Mr. Mills soon after visited his native city, and while there, designed the Congregational church of that place, a building of a novel form, a complete circle internally, ninety feet in diameter, and covered with a dome of equal span, the first attempt in this country to execute such an immense spread of roof without any intermediate support. He also laid before the governor of that State designs for a penitentiary institution, accompanied by an examination of its principles. He shared, sometime before this, in the premium given by the legislature of South Carolina for the best design for the new college, since built at the seat of government of that State (Columbia).

On his return to Washington, Mr. Mills was introduced by the president to Mr. Latrobe, then recently appointed architect of the capitol, and advised to enter as a pupil into that gentleman's office, which he did. His studies were now directed to engineering, and he was soon transferred to the seat of operation, in the State of Delaware, where the work of examination and location of the canal between the two bays began, of which Mr. Latrobe had been appointed engineer. This important survey was completed, and the work begun, when it had to be abandoned for want of funds. Mr. Mills removed to Philadelphia, where he was employed in designing and executing several buildings; among which was the Bank of Philadelphia, a Gothic structure (the first attempt of this style of architecture in the United States), a work of the most intricate and difficult character to execute, from the curious forms of the vaultings, and great span of the centre arch, all of which were built of solid masonry.

He likewise designed and executed the Washington Hall, afterwards destroyed by fire in consequence of omitting that part of the plan which recommended making the first story fireproof. He designed, also, the Baptist Church in Sansom Street, a building planned and constructed upon acoustic principles, expressly to insure a good hearing and speaking room capable of containing four thousand persons. The result proved the correctness of the principles advocated by Mr. Mills: it is, perhaps, the most perfect speaking and hearing room, for its size, in the United States.

The fireproof wings of the State House in Philadelphia, for the public records, were also designed and executed under Mr. Mills's superintendence. The bridge near the Waterworks, Philadelphia, which spans with a single arch the Schuylkill River, and which has the largest chord of arch in the world, is the design of Mr. Mills.

The company had fortunately engaged in its service a man well skilled in the business of bridge building, and who had both enterprise and nerve to carry the plan proposed for a single arch into execution, and he effected it greatly to the honor and advantage of the bridge company, creditable to the builder, Mr. Lewis Wernwag, and gratifying to the architect; it was besides an achievement in the arts which the city of Philadelphia may justly be proud of. The chord line of this bridge exceeds 340 feet.

All the timbers are sawed through the heart, and no two pieces touch each other, being separated by iron plates, securing by this means the works from the attack of the dry rot. It is upwards of twenty years since its erection, and it is now as firm and sound in its main timbers as when first raised.

Mr. Mills was one of the first promoters of the Society of Artists in Philadelphia, and acted as the secretary of that institution while he remained there.

The court house at Richmond was designed by Mr. Mills, as well as several private buildings in that city.

The Burlington County prison, New Jersey, constructed upon the fireproof plan, was also designed by Mr. Mills.

After the close of the late war a premium of $500 was offered for the most approved design of a monument to Washington, to be erected in the city of Baltimore, which was adjudged to Mr. Mills; being an important work, he was invited to remove to that city and take the charge of its execution, which he accepted, and accordingly in 1817 took up his residence in Baltimore, and prosecuted this great work to its present state. He was soon after appointed president and engineer to the water company of Baltimore, and projected and executed many works of improvement connected with that city.

Among the public buildings designed and executed by him in Baltimore are the Baptist Church, a circular building, eighty feet in diameter, surmounted by a dome, also the St. John's Church. Mr. Mills, while a resident of Baltimore, presented designs for the State House, then about to be erected at Harrisburg, Pennsylvania, and obtained one of the premiums. During the pecuniary pressure of 1819, when property was at a low stand in Baltimore, and there was a great falling off in the trade of the West, which was diverted down the Mississippi to New Orleans, Mr. Mills published a work on the internal improvements of Maryland, urging upon its citizens the importance of opening a permanent intercourse and trade with the western country, by means of a continuous canal from Baltimore to Ohio River, with a branch to the Susquehanna. While this subject was under examination he was invited to his native State to enter into her service, in prosecuting a system of internal improvement there. Operations being suspended for the present on the Washington monument, he was at liberty to accept the invitation, and in 1820 removed to South Carolina, and was appointed one of the acting commissioners of the board of public works, and engineer and architect of the State. Here he designed, and had executed a number of public buildings for court houses, prisons, record offices, etc., all upon the fireproof plan. He designed also the lunatic asylum at Columbia, a very spacious and costly building, constructed entirely fireproof. During this period a premium was offered of $500 by the legislature of Louisiana, for the best plan of a penitentiary, to be built at New Orleans, and Mr. Mills' design was approved of. The principle upon which this design was founded has been adopted in other penitentiaries, since erected. Aware of the importance of a more efficient system of internal improvement than was pursued by his native State, Mr. Mills published a work on the practicability and advantages of a continuous canal from Columbia to Charleston, to render effective what had been done, pointing out, at the same time, the all-important object of opening an intercourse as speedily as possible with the western country, to secure the rich boon here freely offered, and to secure which, all the great Atlantic cities were striving. Mr. Mills sent a copy of this work to Mr. Jefferson, and received a very flattering reply.

He also called the attention of the citizens of South Carolina, to the improvement of their rich swamp lands, the mines of the State, as promising not only wealth, but health to the people of that State.

Among the buildings designed by Mr. Mills in Charleston, are the fireproof offices, for the public records; a fireproof magazine, upon a new plan of dividing the powder among several buildings (so that in the event of any accident happening to one, the other might be safe from explosion), and a fireproof prison wing. The Baptist Church in that city, was designed also by Mr. Mills. While in South Carolina, he undertook and completed a great work, " The Atlas of the State of South Carolina, from actual survey," embracing twenty-eight copper engraved maps of the districts of the State, on a scale of two miles to the inch: he also published as an appendix to the atlas, the statistics of the State, a voluminous work.

During the visit of General Lafayette to South Carolina Mr. Mills assisted as architect, to lay the cornerstone of the monument dedicated to De Kalb, erected in the city of Camden, near the Presbyterian church (which was also designed by him).

During a visit which Mr. Mills made to Baltimore, about
this period, he published a series of papers addressed to the
citizens of that city, upon the importance of securing and
facilitating the trade with the Susquehanna River, by the construction of a railroad between Baltimore and York Haven,
which is now in considerable progress; and would have been
long since completed, but that a charter had not yet been
granted by the State of Pennsylvania, to take it through its
territory. On his return to South Carolina, he drew the attention of the citizens of that State, and particularly of Charleston,
to the propriety and expediency of making a railroad from
that city, to Hamburg and Columbia, which has resulted in
the accomplishment of the work, at least to Hamburg, much
to the advantage of commerce and the travelling.

The Bunker Hill monument committee, having invited
plans to be offered for the monument, Mr. Mills forwarded
drawings of an obelisk design for their approval, and it is now
under execution, differing only from his design, by the omission
of some decorations which he considered essential to the beauty
and utility of the structure. In one of Mr. Jefferson's letters
to Mr. Mills, who had mentioned the character of the design
he had made for this monument, Mr. Jefferson remarks,
"Your idea of the obelisk monument is a very fine one. I
think small temples would also furnish good monumental
designs, and would admit of great variety; on a particular occasion, I recommended for General Washington that, commonly
called the lantern of Demosthenes, of which you once sent me
a drawing handsomely done by yourself."

Great complaints being made, from time to time, by the
members of Congress, of the difficulty of hearing and speaking in the Hall of Representatives; and no satisfactory plan
being settled upon, to remedy the defect, Mr. Mills took an
opportunity, when on a visit to Washington, to lay before the
House a plan of alteration and improvement of this hall,
which would remedy, in a great degree, the evil complained of.
He went into a scientific examination, at the same time, of
the causes of the existing difficulties, grounded upon well-

established principles in acoustics; and showed what the effect would be were these causes removed. The subject being referred to a select committee they reported in favor of the plan proposed by Mr. Mills, and recommended an appropriation to be made to carry it into execution; which has since been effected under his supervision; and the present Congress are now deriving the advantages of the alterations made, which have not disappointed public expectation, being acknowledged to be a decided improvement. Mr. M. is now engaged in the service of the general government, and resides at Washington.[0]

[0] Robert Mills was Architect of Public Buildings from 1836 to 1851. Four years later, on the 3rd of March, he died.

CHAPTER XXV.

BECK — DEARBORN — BOURDON — WEST — LENEY — OTIS —
MASON — EICHOLTZ — METCALF — CRAWLEY — THOMP-
SON — KRIMMEL — TILYARD.

BECK — DEARBORN — BOURDON — WM. WEST.[p]

MR. BECK is, as far as I am informed, only entitled to notice as the first painter who penetrated beyond the Alleghanies.

Mr. Lambdin says, in a letter to me, "Beck may be justly considered the pioneer of art in the West. His landscapes are scattered over the entire Union. He was for many years engaged in teaching a seminary of young ladies in Lexington, Kentucky, and died in 1814. His widow survived until 1833, and painted many clever pictures from his sketches."

The same obliging correspondent says, "Dearborn is the first portrait painter of whom I can gain any knowledge as having practised in the West. There are several of his portraits in Pittsburgh, painted from 1807 to 1810."

"About the same time," says Mr. Lambdin, "appeared at Pittsburgh a French refugee, who painted small portraits in an indifferent style. He figured in the triple capacity of painter, musician, and dancing master." His name was Bourdon.

[p]

WM. S. LENEY.

An English engraver, and born in London.[1] He served his time with Tomkins, of London, and before he emigrated had established a reputation in stipple engraving by several plates of magnitude. I remember particularly that from Rubens's "Descent from the Cross." He entered into a partnership with Mr. Rollinson of New York, in bank-note engraving.

---

1 January 16, 1769. Stauffer states that he was of Scotch descent, and that he died at Longue Pointe, near Montreal, Canada, November 26, 1831. He came to this country about 1805, practising the art of engraving with success in New York, and later in Montreal.

Leney was a prudent man, made money and kept it. His manners were remarkably simple, and yet the cockney was thoroughly impressed upon them. He retired from business and purchased a farm on the river St. Lawrence, a little below Montreal; where I passed a day with him, and went out on the river with him in pursuit of plover. His eldest son was the farmer; and he, having renounced his occupation to enjoy life — died.

Bass Otis.[1]

Mr. Otis was born in the New England States, and apprenticed to a maker of scythes. As a portrait painter he appeared in New York about the year 1808. He removed to Philadelphia, and exhibited portraits at the Academy in 1812. He painted a view of his master the scythe-maker's shop, and presented it to the Pennsylvania Academy. His painting began, as I am informed, by working with a coach painter.

Mr. Otis, as a portrait painter, has strong natural talents, and a good perception of character. Many of his heads are well colored. At one period he painted many portraits in Philadelphia, but they were all of one class; if not so originally, he made them so.

Mr. Otis has occasionally returned to New York and set up his easel with temporary success.

Wm. Mason.

This gentleman, one of our early engravers on wood, was born in Connecticut in the year 1804. He was apprenticed to Abner Reed, copperplate engraver, of Hartford; who, at the same time, painted signs, and occasionally executed a wood cut, in what his apprentice calls "the old type metal style." The beautiful effects produced in wood, by Doctor Anderson of New York, excited the admiration and ambition of Mr. Mason; and in 1808 he made his first essays in wood engraving on ornaments for toy books. Want of proper tools

---

[1] Bass Otis, painter, engraver and early experimenter in lithography, was born in Bridgewater, Mass., in 1784, the son of Dr. Joseph and Suzanna Orr Otis. He died in Philadelphia November 3, 1861.

and want of experience impeded his efforts, and stimulated his ingenuity to supply deficiencies in both. His success determined him to persist in wood engraving. Learning that there was no engraver on wood in Philadelphia, he proceeded thither as soon as out of his apprenticeship (1810), and was well received and amply employed.

During the last war with Great Britain Mr. Mason entered into other employments, and relinquished his wood engraving to his pupil, Mr. George Gilbert.

JACOB EICHOLTZ.[1]

I cannot do better than to let this gentleman tell his own story.

"I was born in the town of Lancaster, Penn., in the year 1776, an eventful year it was to Americans, and I often bless my stars that I was born some time after the Declaration of Independence, not wishing to have been a British subject, this smacks of democracy you will say, but so it is, I can't help it, I took in the fresh air of independence; but I digress — my parents were both descendants of Germans, and reared a large family of children, — I must digress again, and state that my father and three brothers, all carried arms in our struggle for independence. My parents being in moderate circumstances, could ill afford to give their children more than a plain English education. The first impulse I remember to have felt for drawing, was when a child not more than seven years of age, generally confining myself in the garret, when I should have been at school, to delineating objects that struck my fancy, on the wall with red chalk. My father not knowing the full value of the arts, felt little inclined to foster my first rude efforts. 'Tis true, a common sign painter was at length called in to give me the first rudiments of drawing. This painter being a man of strong passions, in a fit of unrequited love, committed suicide by shooting himself. I shall ever remember the pang I felt on first hearing of the destruction of my teacher, I considered myself forever cut off from a favorite pursuit. The instruction I received from this source was little better than

[1] Jacob Eicholtz died in Lancaster, Penn., May 11, 1842.

nothing, yet the seeds were sown. At the proper time I was put apprentice to a coppersmith (a wretched contrast with a picture maker), when still my predilection for drawing showed itself in the rude sketches of my fellow apprentices pictured on the walls of the shop with a charcoal. After the expiration of my apprenticeship, I commenced the coppersmith business on my own account, with pretty good luck; still the more agreeable love of painting continually haunted me. Chance about this time threw a painter into the town of my residence. This in a moment decided my fate as to the arts. Previous to the arrival of this painter, I had made some rude efforts with tolerable success, having nothing more than a bootjack for a palette, and anything in the shape of a brush, for at that time brushes were not to be had, not even in Philadelphia. At length I was fortunate enough to get a few half-worn brushes from Mr. Sully, being on the eve of his departure for England, this was a great feast to me, and enabled me to go on until others were to be had (1809). About this time I had a family with three or four children, and yet had not courage to relinquish the coppersmith and become painter. To support my family as a painter, was out of the question. I divided my attention between both. Part of the day I wrought as coppersmith, the other part as painter. It was not unusual to be called out of the shop, and see a fair lady who wanted her picture painted. The coppersmith was instantly transferred to the face painter. The encouragement I received finally induced me to relinquish the copper business entirely. About this time a Mr. Barton, whose memory I will ever gratefully cherish, strongly urged me to visit the celebrated Stuart at Boston. I went, and was fortunate enough to meet with a handsome reception from that gentleman, through the cooperation of the late Alexander J. Dallas and his son George, who were at Boston at the time, and who felt a lively interest in my success. Previous to visiting Boston, I had painted a portrait of Mr. Nicholas Biddle, President of the United States Bank, and as it required, in visiting Stuart, that I should have a specimen of skill with me, in order to know whether I was an impostor or not, Mr. Biddle very politely offered me the picture I had painted for him, and which was well received by the great artist. Here I had a fiery trial to undergo. My picture was placed alongside the best of his hand, and that lesson I considered the best I had ever received: the comparison was, I thought, enough, and if I had vanity before I went, it left me all before my return. I must do Stuart the justice to say that he gave me sound lectures and hope. I did not fail to profit by them. My native place being too small for giving scope to a painter, I removed to Philadelphia, where by an incessant practice of ten years, and constant employment, I have been enabled again to remove to my native place, with a decent competence, and a mind still urging on for further improvement, having but now, at this period of my life, just conceptions of the great difficulty of reaching the summit of the fine arts. I look forward with more zeal than ever. — It is a fire that will never quench; and I hazard nothing in saying that I fully believe that the freedom and happiness of the citizens of this free country will one day produce painters as great, if not greater than any that have embellished the palaces of Europe."

I copy from a letter of Sully's, his account of his first meeting with Mr. Eicholtz:

"When Governor Snyder was elected, I was employed by Mr. Binns to go on to Lancaster, and paint a portrait of the new chief magistrate of the State. Eicholtz was then employing all his leisure hours, stolen from the manufacturing of tin kettles and copper pans, in painting: his attempts were hideous. He kindly offered me the use of his painting room, which I readily accepted, and gave him during my stay in Lancaster, all the professional information I could impart. When I saw his portraits a few years afterwards (in the interim he had visited and copied Stuart), I was much surprised and gratified. I have no doubt that Eicholtz would have made a first-rate painter had he begun early in life with the usual advantages." *

* In my intercourse with Mr. Eicholtz, I have admired in him a man of frank, simple, unpretending manners, whose conversation marked his good sense, and whose

ELIAB METCALF.

One of the many of our artists who sprung from the true nobility of America, the yeomanry of the land. He through life displayed the virtues which are derived from good early education — an education in the bosom of a family where order, morality and religion were the practice and joy of the inmates.

Eliab Metcalf was born in the town of Franklin and State of Massachusetts, on the 5th of February, 1785. His ancestors, from the time of the landing of the Pilgrims at Plymouth had, in successive generations, occupied the same farm, and tilled it, prosperously serving their country, and ever bearing the character which led to the flight from European oppression. Eliab's father bore the same high character. His name was James. The mother of the painter was Abigail Harding, a near relative of Chester Harding, now one of our first portrait painters. Eliab was the third son of his parents, and was intended to succeed his father as an agriculturist; but it was written otherwise in the book of that law by which the universe is governed and is advancing to its perfection.

After a common school education, the youth was occupied in the labors of the farm, until the age of eighteen, when a cold affected his lungs and disabled him for the employment. This *cold* was the foundation of the disease which pursued him through life. At this time, 1807, he became acquainted with a youth of the name of Loviel, a native of Guadaloupe, who was receiving his education in the United States, and accepted his invitation to pass the winter with him in his native island, as a means of restoring his health. This visit to Guadaloupe influenced his movements in after life. In the spring Metcalf returned home, but on the passage renewed *his cold*, and was confined under the care of my early friend Dr. Wright Post, for many weeks at New York. To his care and skill Mr. Met-

conduct evinced that propriety which has led to his success and ultimate independence. Mr. T. B. Freeman informs me, that in 1821 he saw at Harrisburgh a portrait by Eicholtz, which excited his curiosity; and going to Lancaster, he called upon him, and invited him to Philadelphia, where the first portrait he painted was Freeman's, and soon afterwards Commodore Gale's.

calf attributed his recovery from this attack. Less fitted than
ever for agricultural labors, Metcalf, always partial to drawing,
thought of painting as a profession better suited to his impaired health and debilitated frame. His friends opposed this
wish, and by their advice he passed the succeeding winter
in mercantile pursuits in the West Indies. He was unsuccessful
in commerce, but returned home in the spring with renewed
health, and his books filled with attempts at drawing. Fully
determined to pursue painting as a profession, his father
reluctantly consented, for the worthy yeoman could see no
prospect of fortune in an occupation which appeared to him
trifling. Young Metcalf now commenced painter of miniatures,
without any knowledge of drawing, like a great many before
and since. He was confined to his father's house under care of
a physician, but improved himself in painting by copying
pictures. Being sufficiently recovered, he travelled as a miniature painter for several years in the Eastern States, Canada and
Nova Scotia. Feeling his deficiencies, he came to New York,
and in that city, a perfect stranger, established himself as a
painter, and studied drawing under John Rubens Smith,
whose instructions have forwarded many artists, although he
never could paint decently himself.

In September, 1814, Mr. Metcalf married Ann Benton, the
daughter of Captain Selah Benton, an officer of the Revolution.
In 1815, Metcalf made his first effort in oil painting, under the
kind instruction of Messrs. Waldo & Jewett, who resided in his
neighborhood. They lent him pictures to copy, and directed
his efforts. Business slowly but gradually increased with his
increasing skill; but his health, which had been gradually failing, had, in 1819, become so poor that his physician recommended a journey to the South. He could not well take with
him a wife and two children, and to leave them and his friends,
and his increasing employment, was a hard trial to a man
devoted to domestic quiet and the happiness of a husband and
father. But even for the sake of those dear to him, the effort
must be made; and with letters to influential persons in New
Orleans, he, in the autumn of 1819, arrived at that city. He

was the only portrait painter in the place, and found abundant employment. His health improved. He gained many friends prominent among whom was the late Rev. Mr. Larned, who introduced him to men of taste and literature, that could appreciate the artist and the man. Mr. Metcalf remained three years in New Orleans, with the exception of one visit to New York, travelling, by advice, on horseback through the Western States. In the autumn of 1822, he visited the island of St. Thomas. His success, and the high estimation in which he was held there, have been mentioned to me by my young friend the Rev. Mr. Labagh, who is settled in that island, a native of New York, and son to our worthy alderman of that name.

At the islands of St. Thomas and St. Croix Mr. Metcalf remained four years, fully employed in his profession. He painted the governors, and many of the principal men of both islands. Being invited by the men in authority at Porto Rico to paint the governor of that island for a stipulated sum, he consented to go thither for that purpose, and a government vessel was sent for him. He was treated with the greatest possible respect, and remained six months on the island fully employed.

Mr. Metcalf improved constantly in his profession, and the pictures he sent home and exhibited at Clinton Hall placed him on a permanent stand of high elevation among our portrait painters. After remaining four years among these islands, the artist thought his health sufficiently re-established to allow the indulgence of passing a winter with his beloved family, and perhaps to remain with them. The experiment failed — he was confined to his house most of the winter — his cough grew alarmingly worse, and in the autumn of 1824 he again took leave of his wife and children, now four in number and sailed for the Havana. The Spaniards received him coldly, but for two years he found ample employment from Americans; his health improved, and for six more years he found a more general employment. During these eight years, he visited his family every summer. When the jealousy of the Spaniards was overcome, he had friends and employers of the first grade. The bishop, the governor, and other inhabitants of distinction, treated him with marked kindness; and his family particularly point out among his friends Wm. Picard, Esq. and Mr. Cleveland, the American vice-consul.

In April, 1833, the cholera raged in Havana. Mr. Metcalf was seized with this disease, but recovered so far as to be pronounced out of danger. But he never touched pencil more. The pictures begun were left unfinished, yet such was the esteem in which their author was held, that in that State they were sought for, received, and at full price paid for.

The invalid recovered so far as to return to his family in June, but no effort could restore his wasted frame. Hope that the warm clime of the West Indies might yet restore him, led him to return to Havana accompanied by his second son, and his faithful servant Francis, who for the last eight years had scarcely left him for a moment, and to whose kindness and care the artist was indebted for a great portion of the comfort his feeble health had permitted him to enjoy.

The voyage was short, tempestuous, and cold. The sufferer was received with open arms by kind friends — lingered in growing debility until the 15th of January, 1834, and then closed his eyes in death as in sleep.

Mr. Metcalf was among the many amiable men I have known, and I always highly esteemed him. Those who were intimately acquainted with his virtues, speak of him as a model of purity, charity, and exalted piety. His moral character was never tarnished by a single stain, nor has calumny ever dared to affix a blot upon his fair fame.

JOHN CRAWLEY.

The father of Mr. Crawley was an Englishman, who emigrated to New York and married a lady of the name of Van Zandt. He was successful as a merchant, and returned to his native country, where John was born in 1784. His parents, however, after a very few years, returned to America, bringing him with them when very young, and settled at Newark, New Jersey. John's love of painting, and desire to become a painter, was excited by the portraits of Sharples; and after an education at a country school, he was sent to New York for instruction in painting. He was placed with Savage soon after John Wesley Jarvis left him, and had as a fellow student Charles B. King. From Mr. Archibald Robertson he obtained more than from Savage, and learned those rudiments of drawing, and the management of water colors, which have enabled him to be useful as a drawing master.

Mr. Crawley painted portraits in Philadelphia, and exhibited at the first opening of the Pennsylvania Academy of Fine Arts. After marrying, he took up his abode at Norfolk, in Virginia, where he has continued to this time.

Previous to marriage, Mr. Crawley had made arrangements to go to London, and had visited the brother of Benjamin West on the old Springfield farm, and obtained a letter from him to the painter. He was stopped by the embargo which preceded our last war with England. Mr. Crawley has a son (likewise John Crawley) now in New York, who has devoted himself to lithographic drawing, and is eminently successful.

THOMPSON.

A person of this name painted poor portraits in Norfolk, but managed to procure employment and make money enough to buy a farm in his native village "down east" and retire, independent of all but mother earth, and the rain and sunshine which fertilize her bosom and ripen her products.

JOHN LEWIS KRIMMEL. [0]

This very extraordinary young man appears to me to have possessed a combination of talents with integrity, wit with kind feelings, genius with prudence, imagination with industry, that must have given him a distinguished station in society, if he had lived to the ordinary bounds of man's earthly sojourn, notwithstanding the impediments which the state of society in our country a few years back presented in the path of the man who devoted himself to the Muses rather than to the powers who preside over dollars and cents. I do not recollect any

0 John Lewis Krimmel died July 15, 1821. He had been made President of the Association of American Artists early in the same year.

foreigner, who has visited America, who had superior claims to admiration as an artist, and esteem as a man, to Mr. Krimmel.

J. L. Krimmel was born in the town of Edingen, in the duchy or principality of Würtemberg, Germany, in the year 1787, and came to this country in company with his countryman Rider, in 1810. He had been well instructed in drawing and the management of colors. The brother of the young painter had preceded him in emigration, and having been some time in Philadelphia as a merchant, sent for the subject of our memoir to come over to him, his intention being to connect him with himself in commerce, but the young man preferred the pencil; and finding this difference of opinion made his situation onerous, he renounced trade and threw himself upon the resources of his own skill and genius.

He at first painted portraits, and those of the master and mistress of his boarding house, and the boarders who were its inmates introduced others, until he found himself independent, or only dependent on his own exertions. I have reason to believe that these portraits were miniatures in oil, somewhat in size like those with which Mr. Trumbull commenced his career. He soon showed that the style in which Wilkie excelled, and the humor which had inspired the pencil of Hogarth, were his own; such scenes were his delight, and to display them on the canvas his sport. The first effort of this kind which attracted public attention to the young stranger was his "Pepperpot Woman." Pepper-pot is an article of food known nowhere else in the United States but in Philadelphia — I presume introduced from the West Indies; and though it is, year after year, and day after day, cried in the streets, it is never seen at the house of a citizen by a stranger. The pepper-pot woman is an animal only known in the streets of Philadelphia.

About this time the print of Wilkie's "Blind Fiddler" came out, and Krimmel was so delighted with a composition congenial to his taste and feeling, that he made a picture in oil colors from it, of the same size, and in every respect truly admirable. His "Blind-man's-buff," an original picture of the same size, soon followed; this was likewise in oil and of great merit, but the sketch in water colors has even more. These were followed by the "Cut Finger," and others in the same style, which all elicited admiration. In 1811, the year after his arrival, he exhibited the "Pepper-pot Woman"; "Celadon and Amelia," "Aurora," and "Raspherry girls of the Alps of Würtemberg," all marked in the catalogue *for sale*.

Small was his remuneration for these extraordinary efforts; and he, with his friend Rider, likewise an artist, became teachers of drawing. Such was Krimmel's strict economy, that at the end of a few years he found himself enabled to revisit his dear *faderland*. He took passage for and landed in France, travelled to Vienna, visited other parts of Germany, particularly his native town of Edingen — the steeple of whose church appeared much lower to him than when he had looked back upon it from Philadelphia, and probably many other things had diminished in the same proportion; and after seeing many good pictures and good people, he appears to have been content to return to America as the land of his choice. The store of gold with which he left Pennsylvania was not great, yet, with honest pride, he threw a portion of it on his friend's table at his return, as a proof of his prudence, temperance and economy.

On returning to Philadelphia, Krimmel resumed his occupation of teacher of drawing. The principal portion of the emolument resulting from this source proceeded from a great boarding school for young ladies. Krimmel, like an honest and conscientious man, was in the habit of teaching the girls what to do, how to do, and then leaving them to do it, under instruction. The consequence was, that his pupils did not produce, in a given time, such pretty pictures as were presented to their parents by the young ladies of a rival establishment, where the cunning and complaisant teacher put his lessons in practice by finishing the work his pupils were utterly incompetent to the production of, and thus cheating papas and mamas, and increasing the reputation of the school. Krimmel was told by the proprietor of the establishment that he must not only teach her scholars to draw and paint, but must draw and paint for them, or give up the school. The unbending Würtemberger did not choose to be an agent in deceit, and chose the latter part of the conditions. Honesty, poverty, a clear conscience and independence were preferable, in his mind, to money, servility and falsehood.

My valued correspondent, John Neagle, Esq., says of Krimmel: "He confessed to me that he could not paint in a manner broad, and at the same time delicate enough to please himself. He could not paint hair well, arising perhaps, from his having too perfect a vision, which conveyed every minute particular. He could stand at a great distance and count the different courses of bricks in a building without a glimmer before the eyes. He was candid and honest to everyone, very blunt to those who asked his opinion, but too kind of feeling to wish to wound. He was free to communicate anything he knew, he had no secrets to sell. His acuteness of vision led him to the use of very small brushes, some no thicker than a common pin. After his death I purchased, at a sale of his effects, all his brushes, many were so small as to be useless to me, and I gave them to his friend Rider, who works with the same kind of tools."

In 1812 Mr. Krimmel exhibited in the Pennsylvania Academy of Fine Arts, a picture representing a crowd in the Centre Square, Philadelphia, which is said to rival Hogarth in truth, nature, and humor.

Notwithstanding his extraordinary talents, Krimmel received no commissions, and had little to do. He did not seek to paint portraits, and works of the species he delighted in were not sought after by the wealthy patrons of art. He wanted little — he called upon no one for aid or employment — he enjoyed the friendship of his brother artists — he studied, sketched, and occasionally painted.

The last work he finished is a great composition of several hundred figures in miniature oil, executed with a taste, truth, and feeling, both of pathos and humor, that rivals, in many respects, the best works of this description in either hemisphere. This picture I have seen. It is a Philadelphia election scene, in Chestnut Street, in front of the State House. It is filled with miniature portraits of the well-known electioneering politicians of the day. It has a portrait of the venerable building within whose walls the independence of America was declared. The composition is masterly, the coloring good, every part of the picture carefully finished, and the figures, near or distant, beautifully drawn. This picture was either painted for, or purchased by, Mr. Alexander Lawson, who began to engrave it, but, for some reason to me incomprehensible, has been discouraged from proceeding with the work, after bestowing much time and labor on it. Surely the citizens of Philadelphia alone would amply remunerate him.

Mr. Lawson advised Krimmel to paint his favorite subjects without waiting for commissions, and take his chance for the sale. The advice was good, and one would suppose the employment would have been pleasant to him; but he was adverse to the plan, and continued to study and sketch. At length he was engaged to paint a picture of Penn's treaty with the Indians. But while preparing for this arduous task, he went to visit a friend in Germantown; and going with the children of the family to bathe in a neighboring mill pond, he strayed from his young companions, and they having finished their sport, waited for him a long time to accompany them home — as he did not return they sought him, but found only his corpse. In the prime of life, with increasing skill and accumulating knowledge, brilliant genius, and immovable in love of the good and the true, this fine young man was lost to the world, probably owing to the circumstance of choosing a solitary spot to bathe unobserved by his young companions, who might perhaps, when the cramp seized him, have afforded the necessary succor.

The moral character of Krimmel was faultless. His love of truth exemplary. His simplicity of manners endeared him to his friends, and his shrewd remarks made him at all times an entertaining companion. There was a downright bluntness in his conversation which, although justly appreciated by those intimate with him, did not serve to smooth his path in life, perhaps even retarded his progress.

My friend Francis B. Winthrop possesses several of Krimmel's pictures. He had corresponded with the artist, but had not seen him. One day a man entered and announced himself in a manner partly characteristic, and partly the effect of foreign education, "I am Krimmel." Mr. Winthrop was soon much pleased with his guest.

There is a pleasing mode of behavior, evincing a wish to accommodate one's self to the wishes of others, which is serviceable to a man by gaining good will, even if it is only the product of education, and the habit formed in early good society; but when suavity of manner and the wish to oblige is perceived to be the result of a feeling, and a true sense of man's duty to man, it is irresistible in its effects, and attaches all hearts to its happy possessor. Such manners are the result of good feeling, united to an extensive knowledge of human nature, a cheerful disposition, and a true sense of our duty. Such manners are therefore rare.

TILYARD.

An honest and unfortunate man of genius. He was born at Baltimore in 1787; and was taught the rudiments of art as a sign painter, which was his original occupation. He committed a fault in buying a lottery ticket, and was grievously punished by drawing a prize of $220,000. The possession of this wealth induced him to enter into commerce, and in a short time he broke — failing for more than he was worth. His sense of justice and propriety was so outraged, that he never recovered from the shock. He resumed his original business of sign painting. My friend Sully says of Mr. Tilyard, in 1810 "his attempts at portrait are admirable: he made great efforts to get on as a portrait painter, and I helped him all I could. Peter Hoffman told me that Tilyard, after his failure, visited him. He did not know him, as his business as a merchant had been transacted by his partner. Tilyard reminded Hoffman of the loss his failure had occasioned him, and said the object of

his visit was to request Mr. Hoffman to permit him to paint
portraits for him to the amount of the debt. He thus relieved
his mind and made a friend of Hoffman, who employed him,
and *paid him*. A few years before his death (which occurred in
1827, at the age of forty) he lost his reason." The worldling
will say he was always mad.

My friend Robert Gilmor, Esq., of Baltimore, says of Tilyard, "He had a true genius, and taught himself to paint
excellent portraits. He died mad. Had he been well educated, he would have been a distinguished artist." In another
letter Mr. Gilmor says, "He attained considerable excellence
as a portrait painter, but died poor and insane; from dwelling
too much on his situation, and the difficulty of supporting his
family by his pencil."

APPENDIX.

NOTE A (page 232).

This extract from a letter written by Mr. Latrobe to Wm. Jones, Esq. then secretary of the navy, on the occasion of his resigning his situation of superintendent of the works at the Navy Yard, admirably illustrates many parts of Mr. Latrobe's character, and shows the difficulties that he was obliged to contend with. It is a satisfactory vindication too against the charge that was so often made against him of extravagance; and in every particular does equal credit to his head and his heart.

"I take this opportunity of asking you to devote a few moments of your valuable time to an explanation respecting myself, which is called for only by a wish that you should in all respects think well of me.

"There is, perhaps, among all the persons holding employment under government, not one so unpopular as myself. That I should be so, is a thing quite of course. It results from the habits of my early life, which I cannot change by any effort that I can make. Having acquired the knowledge, and been for some years in the practice of my profession in Europe, I believe I have the despotism of manner, which belongs to all artists, and appears to be inseparable from some degree of public reputation. My efforts to lay aside a haughtiness of deportment, which I am accused of, while treating of professional subjects, are awkward, because *studied*, and unnatural; and they cannot of course be consistent. Employed in procuring convenience to the course of legislative proceedings, and often personal accommodation to the members of the legislature, I have been justly accused of going on my own course, without consulting the wishes, or even informing the curiosity of those who are most interested in what I was doing; of sacrificing everything to the interests of my reputation hereafter; of keeping aloof from the members of Congress in private association, and in general of acting as if in the performance of my public duties, I did not acknowledge, in any degree, the right of the legislature to direct my operations according to their humor, even if contrary to my wishes and judgment.

"That this should be my character before the public, is as much a necessary result, even of my unbending honesty (and of *honesty* I may boast, without, I hope, forfeiting my claim to modesty), as it might be of an irrational pride. My time has been fully employed. I have had no assistance in the most laborious parts of my operations. My family has been my greatest and almost my only scene of short relaxation and of enjoyment. I could only have devoted my evenings to the members of Congress, scattered through an extent of four miles in length, had I the talent or inclination to visit or entertain them. But in truth, I neither felt the wish nor the propriety of *appearing* to consult any one on my designs, or the mode of my operations, while I felt myself competent to perform my duty without any assistance; and still less could I bend to solicit votes for the passage of laws, as if I had a personal interest in the appropriations required, which the public good did not point out as necessary.

"My unpopularity, therefore, has arisen from circumstances belonging to the invariable effect of personal character on public measures, rather than from the charge which is in everybody's mouth, and which is the only *acknowledged* charge against me, that of *extravagance*. Of want of skill, or want of the very humble virtue, pecuniary integrity, my bitterest enemies have never accused me. But I am extravagant. And yet these very men erected the north wing of the capitol at the expense of $330,000, a building half finished only, of lath and plaster, and rotten wood internally paying

398

four and a half dollars for stone per ton and five to six dollars per thousand, for bricks, while the south wing, in quantity and quality, of materials of three times the value, vaulted throughout, sculptured and painted, stone costing from six to ten dollars per ton; bricks from seven to eight dollars per thousand — was built by me for $274,000. The fact would be proved on investigation both here and in Philadelphia, that my works are the *cheapest* yet erected in the United States. Their appearance is against them. They have a more magnificent *look*, of course a more expensive *look* than others.

"There is another subject which I do not touch upon without regret, I mean the positive instructions of Mr. Jefferson in respect to design, and to *calls for money*, which he afterwards, when censure ensued, did not *publicly* justify, leaving me to bear the blame of extravagance and of inadequate estimates. Of this kind were his positive orders that I should introduce Corinthian columns into the House of Representatives, and put one hundred lights of plate glass into the ceiling, contrary to my declared judgment, and earnest entreaties and representations. In other respects, however, the honor which the friendship of that great man has done me, obliterates all feeling of dissatisfaction on account of these errors of a vitiated taste, and of an imperfect attention to the *practical* effects of his architectural projects. I will mention only one other cause of my unpopularity.

"When I was appointed surveyor to the public buildings, all the persons formerly employed had been dismissed. My system was totally in opposition to that formerly established. Every step I have taken for ten years past has been watched and reported, and the members of Congress have been besieged in detail with complaints of my arbitrary extravagance. The federal newspapers have been filled with abuse of me. I have been too proud and too innocent to defend myself. By little and little that which is often repeated becomes established as a truth.

"But my works speak for themselves. They will live after me, and my children will have no reason to be ashamed of their father. As to my personal character, those who know me intimately may judge of it. Knowing too much of my difficult art to believe myself a *great* man in it; looking up to many others with a deference to their abilities and acquirements which precludes a hope of equalling them; more sensible of my inferiority, and of the humbleness of my attainments than those who calumniate me, I still have learned by the success of twenty-five years' active service of the public, that I am not too ignorant to be very useful. That I have been *useful*, and that I have brought others to be so, is my *legitimate* pride. Nor shall I disgrace myself at my age by forfeiting my right to be thus proud.

"In a few months I shall be no longer in the service of the United States. In this letter I have no further object to answer but to retire from it, with the hope that nothing you may hear against me will deprive me of your confidence and of your kindness. I shall, I confess, leave the service of the department, of which you are the head, with regret; but I shall feel a patriotic joy, that your station is filled, not only by honor and moral worth, but by talents improved and perfected to an extent adequate to the exigencies of our country."

Note B (page 233).

Copy of a letter from Mr. Latrobe to Mr. Jefferson, on resuming his office of superintendent, at Washington, after the destruction of the public buildings by the British.

"Permit me now to assure you that the confidence you are pleased to express in me as to the future conduct of the public works, from your experience of my former services, is to me, by far a more gratifying reward than I could possibly have received from any emolument or any other commendation. It is not only because you are certainly the best judge of the merits of an artist, in the United States, but because you certainly know me better as an artist, and as a man, than any other, that your good opinion is valuable to me. And why should I say so to you, who have forever retired from the seat from which honors are to be dispensed, and to whom adulation would be an insult, if I were not most sincere in what I express on the subject. You will remember, that if I committed an error in executing the trust you reposed in me; it was not by blindly yielding my professional opinions to yours, or in executing, without even remonstrance sometimes, what was suggested, in order to win your favor. My thanks therefore for the kindness with which you express your approbation of what I have formerly done, are offered with sentiments of the sincerest attachment.

"Some details respecting the state of the ruins of the buildings may perhaps be new, and not unpleasant to be received by you; and may perhaps find you at leisure to read them, as your library is no longer around you.

"The south wing of the capitol was set on fire with great difficulty. Of the lower story nothing could be burned but the sashes and frames, and the shutters and dressings, and the doors and doorcases. As all these were detached from one another, some time and labor were necessary to get through the work. The first thing done was to empty into buckets a quantity of the composition used in the rockets. A man with an axe chopped the woodwork, another followed, and brushed on some of the composition, and on retiring from each room, the third put fire to it. Many of the rooms, however, were thus only partially burned, and there is not one in which some wood does not remain. In the clerk's office, the desks and furniture, and the records supplied a more considerable mass of combustible materials than there was elsewhere, and the fire burned so fiercely that they were obliged to retreat and leave all the rooms on the west side entirely untouched, and they are now as clean and perfect as ever. Two other committee rooms have escaped, and the gallery stairs have none of their wooden dressings injured. Above stairs, the committee room of Ways and Means, and Accounts, in uninjured, and the whole of the entrance, with all the sculptured capitals of the columns, has fortunately suffered no injury but in the plastering, and that from the wet and frost of the winter. In the House of Representatives the devastation has been dreadful. There was here no want of materials for conflagration, for when the number of members of Congress was increased, the old platform was left in its place, and another raised over it, giving an additional quantity of dry and loose timber. All the stages and seats of the galleries were of timber and yellow pine. The mahogany furniture, desks, tables and chairs, were in their places. At first they fired rockets through the roof, but they did not set fire to it. They sent men on to it, but it was covered with sheet iron. At last they made a great pile in the centre of the room of the furniture, and retiring set fire to a great quantity of rocket-stuff in the middle. The whole was soon in a blaze, and so intense was the flame, that the glass of the lights was melted, and I have now lumps, weighing many pounds of glass, run into mass. The stone is, like most free stone, unable to resist the force of flame, but I believe no known material would have been able to resist the effects of so sudden and intense a heat. The exterior of the columns and entablature, therefore, expanded far beyond the dimensions of the interior, scaled off, and not a vestige of fluting or sculpture remained around. The appearance of the ruin was awfully grand when I first saw it, and indeed it was terrific, for it threatened immediately to fall, so slender were the remains of the columns that carried the massy entablature. If the colonnade had fallen, the vaulting of the room below might have been beaten down, but fortunately there is not a single arch in the whole building which requires to be taken down. In the north wing, the beautiful doric columns which surrounded the Supreme Court room, have shared the fate of the Corinthian columns of the Hall of Representatives, and in the Senate Chamber, the marble polished columns of fourteen feet shaft, in one block, are burnt to lime, and have fallen down. All but the vault is destroyed. They stand a most magnificent ruin. The west end containing the library, which was never vaulted, burned very fiercely, and by the fall of its heavy timbers, great injury has been done to the adjoining walls and arches, and I fear that the free stone is so much injured on the outside, that part of the outer wall must be taken down; otherwise the exterior stands firm and sound, especially of the south wing; but of about twenty windows and doors, through which the flames found vent the architraves, and other dressings are so injured, that they must be replaced. All the parapet is gone.

"The most difficult work to be performed was to take down the ruins of the Hall of Representatives. Our workmen all hesitated to touch it; to have erected a scaffold, and to have risked striking the ruins with the heavy poles necessary to be used, was not to be thought of; an unlucky blow against one of the columns might have brought down one hundred ton of the entablature, and of the heavy brick vault which rested upon it. It therefore occurred to me, to fill up the whole with fascines to the soffit of the architraves: if anything gave way then, it would not fall down; the columns would be confined to their places, and the fascines would furnish the scaffold. The commissioners approved the scheme, but as time would be required to cut the fascines from the commons, Mr. Ringold most fortunately recommended the use of cord wood which has been adopted, and most successfully. Four-fifths of the work is done, and the remainder is supported, and will be all down in ten days. The cord wood will sell for its cost. It required five hundred cord to go half round; it was then shifted to the other side. I have already nearly completed the vaults of two stories, on the west side of the north wing, according to the plan submitted by you, with the report to Congress in 1807. I need not, I hope, apologize to you for this long detail. An alteration is proposed and adopted by the president, in the Hall of Representatives. I will send you a copy of my report, as soon as time will permit."

NOTE C

Extracts from a letter of Mr. Latrobe, after visiting Mount Vernon, in 1797.

"On the 6th of July I set off, having a letter to the president from his nephew, my particular friend, Bushrod Washington, Esquire. Having alighted at Mount Vernon, I sent in my letter of introduction, and walked into the portico, west of the river. In about ten minutes the president came to me. He wore a plain blue coat; his hair dressed and powdered. There was a reserve, but no hauteur in his manner. He shook me by the hand, said he was glad to see a friend of his nephew's, drew a chair, and desired me to sit down. Having inquired after the family I had left, the conversation turned upon Bath, to which they were going. There was no moroseness in his observations; they seemed the well expressed remarks of a man who has seen and knows the world. The conversation then turned upon the rivers of Virginia. He gave me a very minute account of all their directions, their natural advantages, and what he considered might be done for their improvement by art. He then inquired whether I had seen the Dismal Swamp, and seemed particularly desirous of being informed upon the subject of the canal going forward there. He gave me a detailed account of the old Dismal Swamp Company, and of their operations — of the injury they had received from the effects of the war, and the still greater which their inattention to their own concerns had done to them.

"After many attempts on his part to procure a meeting of directors (the number of which the law provided should be six, in order to do business), all of which proved fruitless; he gave up his hopes of anything being done for their interests and sold out his shares in the property, at a price very inadequate to their real value. Since then his attention has been so much drawn to public affairs, that he had scarcely made any inquiry into the proceedings either of the Swamp or of the Canal Company. I was much flattered by his attention to my observations, and his taking the pains, either to object to my deductions, where he thought them ill founded, or to confirm them by very strong remarks of his own, made while he was visiting the swamp.

"This conversation lasted above an hour, and as he had at first told me, that he was endeavoring to finish some letters to go by post, upon a variety of business, 'which, notwithstanding his distance from government, still pressed upon him in his retirement,' I got up to take my leave, but he desired me, in a manner very much like Dr. Johnson's, to 'keep my chair'; and then continued to talk to me about the great works going on in England, and my own objects in this country. I found him well acquainted with my mother's family in Pennsylvania. After much conversation upon the coal mines, on James' River, I told him of the silver mine at Rochester. He laughed most heartily at the very mention of the thing. I explained to him the nature of the expectations formed of its productiveness, and satisfied him of the probability that one might exist there. He made several minute inquiries concerning it, and then said, 'it would give him real uneasiness, should any silver or gold mine be discovered that would tempt considerable capitals into the prosecution of that object, and that he heartily wished for his country, that it might contain no mines but such as the plough could reach, excepting only coal and iron.'

"After conversing with me for more than two hours, he got up and said that, 'we should meet again at dinner.' I then strolled about the lawn, and took a few sketches of the house, etc. Upon my return I found Mrs. Washington and her granddaughter, Miss Custis, in the hall. I introduced myself to Mrs. Washington, as the friend of her nephew, and she immediately entered into conversation upon the prospect from the lawn, and presently gave 'ne an account of her family, in a good-humored free manner, that was extremely pleasing and flattering. She retains strong remains of considerable beauty, and seems to enjoy good health and as good humor. She has no affectation of superiority, but acts completely in the character of the mistress of the house of a respectable and opulent country gentleman. His granddaughter, Miss Eleanor Custis, has more perfection of form, of expression, of color, of softness, and of firmness of mind, than I have ever seen before.

"Young Lafayette, with his tutor, came down some time before dinner. He is a young man of seventeen years of age, of a mild, pleasant countenance, making a favorable impression at first sight.

"Dinner was served up about half-past three. It had been postponed half an hour in hopes of Mr. Lear's arrival from Alexandria. The president came into the portico a short time before three, and talked freely upon common topics with the family. At dinner he placed me at the left hand of Mrs Washington, Miss Custis sat at her right, and himself next to her. There was very little conversation at dinner. A few jokes passed between the president and young Lafayette, whom he treated more as a child than as a guest. I felt a little embarrassed at the silent reserved air that prevailed. As I drink no wine, and the president drank but three glasses, the party before long returned to the portico. Mr. Lear, Mr. Dandridge, and Mr. Lear's three boys soon after arrived, and helped out the conversation. The president retired in about three quarters of an hour. As much as I wished to stay, I thought it a point of delicacy to take up as little time of the president as possible, and I therefore ordered my horses to the door. I waited a few minutes till the president returned. He asked me whether I had any very pressing business to prevent my lengthening my visit. I told him I had not, but that as I considered it an intrusion upon his more important engagements, I thought I could reach Colchester that evening by daylight. 'Sir,' said he, 'you see I take my own way. If you can be content to take yours at my house, I shall be glad to see you here longer.'

"Coffee was brought about six o'clock; when it was removed, the president addressed himself to me, inquiring as to the state of the crops about Richmond. I told him all I knew. A long conversation upon farming ensued, during which it grew dark, and he then proposed going into the hall. He made me sit down by him, and continued the conversation for above an hour. During that time he gave me a very minute account of the Hessian fly, and its progress from Long Island, where it first appeared, through New York, Rhode Island, Connecticut, Delaware, part of Pennsylvania, and Maryland. It has not yet appeared in Virginia, but is daily dreaded. The cultivation of Indian corn next came up. He dwelt upon all the advantages attending this most useful crop, and then said, that the manner in which the land was exhausted by it, the constant attention it required during the whole year, and the superior value of the produce of land in other crops, would induce him to leave off entirely the cultivation of it, provided he could depend upon any market for a supply elsewhere.

"He then entered into the different merits of a variety of ploughs, and gave the preference to the heavy Botheram plough, from a full experience of its merits. The Berkshire iron plough he held next in estimation. He had found it impossible to get the iron work of his Botheram plough replaced in a proper manner, otherwise he should never have discontinued its use. I promised to send him one of Mr. Richardson's ploughs, of Tuckahoe, which he accepted with pleasure.

"Mrs. Washington and Miss Custis had left us early, and the president left the company about eight o'clock. We soon after retired to bed.

"I rose with the sun, and walked over the grounds; I also took a view of the house. The president came to the sitting room, about half-past seven o'clock; here all the latest newspapers were laid out. He talked with Mr. Lear about the progress of the works at the great falls, and in the city of Washington. Breakfast was served up in the usual Virginian style — tea and coffee, cold and broiled meat. It was very soon over, and for an hour afterwards, he stood upon the steps of the west door, talking to the company who were collected around him. The subject was chiefly the establishment of the university at the Federal city. He mentioned the offer he had made of giving to it all the interests he had in the city, on condition that it should go on in a given time; and complained, that though magnificent offers had been made by many speculators, for the same purpose, there seemed to be no inclination to carry them into effect. He spoke as if he felt a little hurt upon the subject. About ten o'clock he made a motion to retire, and I requested a servant to bring my horses to the door. He then returned, and as soon as my servant came up with them, he went to him and asked him if he had breakfasted. He then shook me by the hand, desired me to call if I came again into the neighborhood, and wished me a good morning.

"Washington has something uncommonly majestic and commanding in his walk, his address, his figure, and his countenance. His face is however characterized more by intense and powerful thought, than by quick and powerful conception. There is a mildness about its expression, and an air of reserve in his manner which lowers its tone still more. He is sixty-four, but appears some years younger, and has sufficient vigor to last many years yet. He was frequently entirely silent for many minutes, during which time an awkward silence seemed to prevail in the circle. His answers were often short, and sometimes approached to moroseness. He did not at any time speak with remarkable fluency; perhaps the extreme correctness of his language, which almost seemed studied, prevented that effect. He appeared to enjoy a humorous observation, and made several himself. He laughed heartily several times, and in a very good humored manner. On the morning of my departure, he treated me as if I had lived for years in his house, with ease and attention; but in general, I thought there was an air about him as if something had vexed him."

POSTLIMINY OF TEXT
OMITTED FROM THE 1918 EDITION

PAGE 3

The Doric, Ionic, and Corinthian are acknowledged the universal standard of taste in the art.*

> ** A few technical terms.*
> A module is the lower diameter of a column ; when divided into 60 parts, is the architectonic scale.
> The facade is the front of a building, generally ornamented with a projecting portico, surmounted by a pediment.
> A pediment consists of a tympanum and a cornice. The first is the interior area, usually ornamented.
> Intercolumniations are the spaces between the pillars, which spaces are from one module and a half in width to four modules.
> The entablature and column are the distinguishing features of an order. The first consists of cornice, frieze and architrave ; the second, of capital, shaft and base.
> The architrave (epistyle) is the part which rests on the columns, and represents the main beam of primitive temples.
> The frieze is the centre division, and rests on the architrave, and the cornice crowns the whole and supports the roof.
> The capital, shaft and base of a column are too well known to need explanation.

PAGE 26

"He then," continues his amanuensis, "returned to Lebanon, (to the object of his first love, he said,) and afterward went to Boston to profit by studying the works of Copley and others, where he remained until 1779, occupying the room which had been built by Smybert, in which remained many of his works.*

> * I am sorry to see in a work written by Mr. Trumbull, and published in 1832, such assertions as the following respecting the motives which induced him to study painting. "Ardently anticipating the vast consequences of the revolution, and the future greatness of his country ; and having a natural taste for drawing, in which he had already made some progress, Colonel Trumbull resolved to cultivate that talent, with the hope of thus binding his name to the great events of the time, by becoming the graphic historiographer of them and of his early comrades. With this view he devoted himself to the study of the art of painting, first in America, and afterwards in Europe."

404

PAGE 42

It might appear, from this statement of Mr. Trumbull, that he was appointed by the government of the United States, as well as Mr. Gore and Mr. Pinkney, but it was not so; the appointment was by some agreement between the British and American commissioners conferred upon him.*

* In the letter of Mr. Trumbull to Mr. Wilde, speaking of this commission, he says, "The commission was composed of five members, Mr. Gore and Mr. Pinkney on the part of the United States; Dr. Nichols and Dr. Swabey, (two of the most eminent civilians) on the part of Great Britain; and I was the fifth commissioner, representing both nations." And he says, "all questions where the commissioners appointed by England and the United States did not agree, were decided by the fifth commissioner."

PAGE 91

Those who truly admire the great event which established the liberty of this country, and who wish to see the blessing cherished by all who may be heirs to it, will need no exhortation to contribute their reasonable aid to a work which is so well calculated to blend with the glory of the present, a lesson to future generations.

Among the means employed by the wisest and most virtuous people for nourishing and perpetuating the spirit of freedom and patriotism, monumental representations are known to be amongst the most ancient, and perhaps, not the least influential. And as it is the happiness of this country to enjoy an occasion, more glorious and more auspicious to it, than has been the lot of any other, there ought to be felt a pride, as well as satisfaction, in commemorating it, by a spectacle as unrivalled as the occasion itself. Should the plan, now offered, be successful, this object will be fully attained; for it may, without hazard, be affirmed, that no similar work of equal magnitude and merit, can be boasted by the nations most distinguished for their munificent zeal in rendering the fine arts auxiliaries to the cause of liberty.

Although it was deemed proper to provide for an eventual assumption of the monument and the expense by the government of the United States; yet it was necessary, both as an immediate and a certain resource, to appeal to the patriotic liberality of individuals. In one view it may be particularly desirable that the monument should be founded on voluntary and diffusive contributions. The event to which it is dedicated, the emblems of which it is composed, and the effect which it is meant to produce, have all an intimate relation to the rights and happiness of the people. Let it be commenced then, not through the organ of the government as a political act, but in a mode which will best testify the sentiments which spontaneously glow in the breasts of republican citizens.

The artist contemplated for the work is Mr. Ceracchi, of Rome; who, influenced by admiration for the revolution, and by a desire of distinguishing himself as the instrument of erecting a monument worthy of so great a subject, came to the city of Philadelphia in 1791, with a design to prosecute the undertaking, if sufficient means could be found. Since that period he has prepared the model, of which the description is annexed. The model of itself evinces the capacity, genius and taste of the author, and concurs with other proofs of his distinguished qualifications, to inspire a wish that he could be enabled to execute his plan. The material of the monument is to be statuary marble; its height one hundred feet; its circumference three hundred feet; the height of the principal figure fifteen feet, and the others of various proportional dimensions. It is computed that ten years will be required to complete it.

A hope is entertained that the public spirit of the citizens of the United States, seconded by a taste for the fine arts, will induce them not to suffer to escape so fair an opportunity of raising a lasting monument to the glory of their country ; and that a sufficient number will be found ready to furnish, by subscriptions, the necessary sums. The confidence which is placed in your personal disposition to forward the commendable design, has pointed you out, among a few others, for soliciting and receiving the subscriptions, and is the apology for imposing the task upon you.

A description of the monument consecrated to liberty:

The goddess of liberty is represented descending in a car drawn by four horses, darting through a volume of clouds, which conceals the summit of a rainbow. Her form is at once expressive of dignity and grace. In her right hand she brandishes a flaming dart, which, by dispelling the mists of Error, illuminates the universe; her left is extended in the attitude of calling upon the people of America to listen to her voice. A simple *pileus* covers her head ; her hair plays unconfined over her shoulders; her bent brow expresses the energy of her character; her lips appear partly open, whilst her awful voice echoes through the vault of heaven, in favour of the rights of man. Her drapery is simple ; she is attired in an ancient *chlamys*, one end of which is confined under her zone, the rest floats carelessly in the wind ; the *cothurnus* covers her feet.

Saturn is her .charioteer, emblematical of the return of the golden age ; he has just checked the horses, upon his arrival on the American shore. Immediately as the car lights upon the summit of a lofty rock, various groups are seen issuing from compartments at its base, to hail the descent of the goddess, by whose beneficent influence they are at once animated into exertion.

The first compartment is consecrated to poetry and history. Apollo, attired in the characteristic dress of that deity, is seated with his lyre in his hand, and his countenance glowing with the sublimity of his song. Clio is employed in recording the hymns with which Apollo salutes the arrival of the goddess of freedom; while the INDEPENDENT STATES, which are blessed by their influence, appear upon a globe which is placed beside her.

In the second compartment, Philosophy, without whose assistance liberty would soon be obscured by ignorance, is represented as presiding at this memorable epoch. He appears in the character of a venerable sage, with a grave and majestic aspect. On his head he wears the *modius*, an ornament given to Jupiter by the Egyptians, as a symbol of perfect wisdom. The fasces are in his hand. He is seated, dressed in the consular habit, and leaning upon the altar of Justice. As the inflexible friend of Truth, he is seen tearing off from a female figure, who stands near him in the character of Policy, the false veil which has so long concealed the science of government. Anxiety appears painted on the countenance of Policy; her head is shaded by a small pair of wings ; her right arm supports a roll of geographical charts; and a robe of exquisite thinness, gives an additional appearance of velocity to her motion. The gigantic figure below (designed to represent National Valor) rises at the voice of Liberty to combat the oppressors of his country. He eagerly seizes on his arms, which lie near him, and prepares to abandon the tranquil occupations of agriculture for the hazards and tumults of war. His form is muscular and robust ; his mantle is thrown carelessly over him ; the disorder of his hair, and the fierceness of his countenance inspire Despotism with terror.

The adjoining group represents Neptune seated between two rivers ; he appears exhorting Mercury (who stands near him) to take American commerce under his protection, and to increase the glory of the American flag.

At the powerful voice of liberty NATURE, whose simplicity had been forced to give way to the introduction of the meretricious refinements of *art*, appears starting to life, burst from the bosom of the earth, and seems about to resume her ancient dignity. A dewy mantle, studded with stars, is supported by her right hand ; with her left she is employed in expressing streams of water from her flowing ringlets, allegorically emblematic of the source of rivers.

The last group represents Minerva, the patroness of the arts and sciences. In order to designate the country to which they owe their origin, she is seated on a fragment of an Egyption obelisk, and holds the *papyrus* in her left hand. Near her stands Genius, with a flambeau in one hand, and a butterfly, the emblem of immortality, in the other—expressive of the grand principles of fire and animation.

His countenance is fixed in an attitude of silent attention, whilst the goddess commands him to inspire, with his divine influence, the bosom of the children of Freedom. Behind, is a figure designed to represent Fame, with her appropriate emblem. A pair of ample pinions shades her shoulders; she holds her trumpet in her left hand; and, with her right, points to the Declaration of Independence, which is inscribed upon a massy column.

Articles of subscription towards erecting a monument to the American revolution.

I. Thirty dollars to be the amount of subscription for one year.

II. Each person, at discretion, to subscribe for one year, or for any greater number of years, not exceeding ten.

III Where the subscription of any person shall be for one year, the whole sum to be immediately paid; where it shall be for more than one year, the amount of one year's subscription to be immediately paid; and an equal sum on the first Monday in January in each succeeding year, during the term for which the subscription shall be made; unless the subscriber shall prefer to make greater or earlier payments.

IV. The monies subscribed and paid shall be deposited in the Bank of the United States, to the credit of "The subscribers towards erecting a .nonument to the American revolution," and shall be subject to the disposition of the secretaries of state, of the treasury, and of war, the attorney-general, and the treasurer of the United States, for the time being; who, or any three of whom, being met together, are hereby empowered, by majority of voices of those met, to apply the said monies to the purpose of erecting the said monument, in such manner as shall appear to them proper.

V. The work shall not be begun until the sum of thirty thousand dollars shall have been subscribed and paid; and in case it should happen that the said sum should not be subscribed in one year from the date thereof, the monies which shall have been subscribed and paid shall revert to the subscribers, whom the said managers shall cause to be reimbursed.

VI. Subscriptions may be received by and paid to any person who may have a copy of this paper, certified by the managers and persons named in the fourth article.

VII. The United States may, at any time within six calendar months after the monument shall be completed, become proprietors thereof, or, at any time sooner, may become proprietors of so much thereof as shall have been executed by making effectual provision for reimbursing the subscribers, or their lawful representatives, the sums which shall have been advanced by them, towards carrying on the work.

VIII. The monument shall be erected or placed at the permanent seat of the government of the United States.

IX. The said managers, if they shall judge it necessary, may convene the subscribers, (giving six months notice of the time and place of meeting, in one or more gazettes or newspapers,) who may convene in person, or by proxy, or attorney, and shall be entitled each to one vote for each yearly subscription, which he or she shall have subscribed and paid.

X. Those whose names are subscribed hereto, severally engage to pay, according to the tenor of the third article hereof, thirty dollars for each year of the number of years set against their respective names.

Dated, this fourteenth day of February, in the year one thousand seven hundred and ninety-five.

With great consideration we are, sir, your very obedient servants.

Philadelphia, February 14, 1795

PAGE 137

PRACTICAL DIRECTIONS FOR MINIATURE PAINTING,

BY T. S. CUMMINGS, ESQ.

MINIATURE painting is governed by the same principles as any other branch of the art, and works in miniature should possess the same beauty of composition, correctness of drawing, breadth of light and shade, brilliancy, truth of colour, and firmness of touch, as works executed on a larger scale ; and the artist who paints in miniature, should possess as much theoretic knowledge and the same enlarged views of his art, as if he painted in any other style.

It may be asked, what is the proper preparatory course of study for a miniature painter ? We should unquestionably answer, the same as for any other branch of the art. It is in the mechanical part only that it differs.

Miniatures, as they are at present painted, are usually executed on ivory,* and in transparent (water) colours,† and according as the mode of application of the colours to the ivory partakes of the line, the dot or smooth surface, is the style,* technically termed hatch, stipple or wash. In the first named, the colour is laid on in lines, crossing each other in various directions, leaving spaces equal to the width of the line between each, and finally producing an evenly-lined surface. The second is similarly commenced, and when advanced to the state we have described in the line, is finished by dots placed in the interstices of the lines, until the whole has the appearance of having been stippled from the commencement. The third is an even wash of colour, without partaking of either the line or dot, and when properly managed, should present a uniform flat tint. Artists vary much in their style of execution, and even in the degree of smoothness they bestow on their pictures, some preferring a *broad*, others a minute style ; though the first is decidedly the most masterly. It must, however, be governed, in a great measure, by the size of your picture and your subject.

In the mode of obtaining the desired result, and in the colours to be used for producing it, there is also a great difference of opinion. This is unessential to the student.

The following process I have found to possess many advantages, and I believe as free from errors as any that has fallen under my experience.

Having your colours and ivory prepared, and your subject

selected, your next step is to procure a correct outline. If it be a head from the life, (which will perhaps best illustrate my meaning,) you will carefully examine it in all its views; both as to attitude, and light and shadow; and having selected that position which in your judgment possesses most of the likeness and character of the individual, you will proceed to outline it.† Your outline carefully drawn on your ivory, you will next lay in the dark shadows with a light and warm neutral tint,* sharp, firm, and of the right shape. Having carefully placed these, both with regard to individual form and relative, bearing to each other, you may proceed with the lighter shadows or middle tints.† They should also be laid in very lightly, colder in colour than the shadow tone, but still definite in form, however light. These effects correctly obtained, and as much depth given as you think necessary for the proper rounding of your subject, you strengthen your dark shadows, altering their forms if necessary. All being justly situated, you then lay in the general colour of the complexion,‡ and having produced the requisite depth, you will, with a sharp lancet,§ scrape off the shining lights on the face, such as the high light on the forehead, nose, &c., and again compare with your original, particularly as to general effect; this proving correct, you proceed with each feature, giving its individual parts more attention, still keeping the whole effect in view, and the work broad; endeavouring to preserve the general effect in conjunction with the completion of the detail. Having gone over all the features, corrected their drawing and colour, you next examine if the drapery and hair of your sitter suit you; if so, copy them, if not, leave them for another and more happy arrangement of forms, and then complete them, at least as to general form. Your picture then is sufficiently advanced to put in your background.

It is commenced with a round-pointed pencil‖ and faint colour, in broad lines, crossing each other at an acute angle, gradually increasing in fineness as you approach the completion; and then still further finish by stippling, constantly bearing in mind that its beauty is more dependent on preserving the masses even, and the grain open, than on the smallness of the dot, or line, which, however minute, will never produce effect, unless the general massing be attended to. Your back ground so far advanced, it is time to insert your drapery. If light, you proceed much the same as with the face; if dark, it is treated with opaque colours. The outline previously obtained, you with a full pencil float on a quantity of the colour* you wish to produce, always giving it body by the addition of white, and smoothness by laying the picture horizontally during the operation; this will allow the colour to become perfectly flat from its fluidity. When dry, it is ready to receive the lights and shadows, as indicated by your model. Your picture equally advanced to this stage, it becomes impossible to lay down rules for its further progress; it must depend altogether upon circumstances arising from the proper performance of the foregoing, as to what additions the picture may require. Generally you will find the flesh-colour deficient, and the shadows weak; these you strengthen and improve, in accordance with the original, adding such colour as in your judgment you think will render it more like the nature before you; and lastly, give brilliancy and transparency by the addition of gum† with your colours, in the dark parts, or wherever else you may deem transparency desirable.

In this we have given directions for the management of a head only; it is however easily adapted to any subject, as the leading principles must of necessity be the same.

Your success in this, as in any other mode of painting, will depend upon your knowledge of the principles of the art, combined with the study of well selected models by masters eminent in the department of art you wish to pursue.

These, with a careful study of nature, judiciously examined by a mind previously accustomed to a careful study of the antique, are the only means calculated to give promise of future excellence in this, or any other class of the arts of design.

The above is from the pen of T. S. Cummings, Esq. from whom, if I can persuade him, the public may receive a more ample treatise on the theory and practice of this beautiful branch of the art of painting.

---

* Ivory for miniature painters' use may be purchased at most of the ivory turners or fancy stores, sawed in thin sheets. It should be selected for the closeness of its grain, mellowness of colour, transparency and freeness from changeable streaks. It is then prepared for use, by first scraping out the marks of the saw, if any appear, and afterwards grinding it with finely pulverized pumice and water on a glass slab until all *polish* is removed; it is then washed with clean water, perfectly free from the pumice, and left to drain itself dry; when dry it is attached to white card paper, by dots of gum on the corners, and is then ready for use.

† Colours are now manufactured in cakes ready for use, only requiring to be diluted with more water, though some miniature painters regrind them. Those manufactured by Newman, of London, are generally considered the best, and I believe, if genuine, are fine enough for all purposes. Fineness of texture and permanency are the great requisites. It is however necessary that the student understand the qualities of the pigments made use of, both as to the tints they form when mixed with one another, and their transparency, or opacity; for on this must depend their fitness for different parts of the work, even when the

same tint is procured. They may be classed under three heads, transparent, semi-transparent, and opaque, though it is by no means my intention to enumerate all the varieties of colour, those generally used will be sufficient.

Opaque colours.	Semi-transparent.	Transparent.
Constant white,	Burnt ter. de sienna,	Gall stone,
Flake white,	Indian yellow,	Brown pink,
Vermilion,	Ultramarine,	Lake,
Indian red,	Cobalt,	Carmine—burnt do.
Yellow ochre,		Vandyke brown.
Burnt umber,		Sepia,
Lamp black.		Indigo,
		Pr. blue,
		Ivory black,
		Burnt madder.

To prepare a palette for a miniature painter it is only necessary to rub the colours, with the addition of water, on a glass, china or ivory palette, in spots agreeable to the requisition of the artist.

* The style or manner of execution is decided by the taste of the artist, and is after all of little consequence. There is no manner in nature. That style which gives the best imitation of nature, and conceals most the means used to obtain it, must undoubtedly be considered the best.

† It may be well if the student's hand be not firmly fixed in drawing, to make an outline on paper of the required size, and afterward transfer it, by placing the ivory over it. Its transparency will enable you to trace it very distinctly. There are many advantages in this method. You insure a clean outline on your ivory, the head of the proper size, and in the proper place in your picture, which will not always be the case if you outline directly upon the ivory.

* A good neutral tint may be made with Indian red and a little blue, which will form a reddish pearl colour.

† Middle tints may be composed of the colour you use for your shadows, with the addition of a little more blue.

‡ In washing in the general colour of the face you will reverse the picture, commencing at the chin; by this means you will obtain the gradation of colour requisite for your head; the brush becoming exhausted, will naturally make the forehead the lightest part. This is of course presuming the head to be painted in the ordinary light used by painters.

§ The lancet is a very useful instrument in the hands of a skillful practitioner in augmenting the high lights; it must, however, be sparingly used by the student, and should never be considered as an eraser.

‖ Pencils used for miniature painting are the sables. They should be elastic, and drawn to a firm point when wet; if they open, they are not fit for use. The size must be governed by the kind of work, or degree of finish you want them for. Generally young miniature painters are too fond of a sharp pointed pencil; it gives dryness and hardness to their work, and will in no way contribute to the finish they vainly hope to attain by such means.

* The mode of mixing this opaque colour, is by grinding such colour as you desire for your use, and adding to it white, to produce the requisite opacity. Blue cloth may be obtained by mixing indigo, indian red, and white. Black cloth, by ivory black, indian red, and perhaps blue. The red is necessary to give the warmth observable in a cloth texture. In silks it is omitted, and blue substituted in greater quantities, according as the silk partakes of the blue tone. It is, however, impossible to make rules for the imitation of colour—the artist's eye is the best guide.

† Gum is used with the colours in finishing your picture. It is the ordinary gum arabic, dissolved in water.

PAGE 142

He writes further : " I have not painted many pictures since I left Charleston ; I am painting one now which I shall bring with me. It is ' the Hours ; the past, present, and the coming.' "*

* The following verses were addressed to the artist by an unknown hand, through the New-York press; and they serve to show the impression made upon his countrymen by this specimen of his study while abroad.

> Whoe'er beheld thy rosy Hours,
> And could unfelt their beauties see,
> The mind is his where darkness lowers,
> And his the heart that mine should flee.
>
> May memory to thy mind present
> The past with gentle, placid mien,
> When hope, prophetic spirit sent,
> Waving her golden hair was seen.
>
> And may thy present hours be bright
> As the fair angel smiling there ;
> Without a cloud to dim their light—
> Without a thought that sets in care.
>
> But for the future—Oh! may they
> Be crown'd with bliss, and wealth, and fame!
> And may this little humble lay
> Be lost 'midst songs that sound thy name.

PAGE 155

But truth and virtue were his guides ; and all testimony agrees that he was a good man, and a great artist.*

---

* Having received the following letter unexpectedly, I subjoin it to the previous notice.

" Newport, Sept. 9th. 1834.

" Dear Sir—I am happy to learn, through Dr. Francis, that my letter of the 20th of March was satisfactory. He has expressed a wish to know where the finest specimens of my brother's paintings are to be seen. Upon looking over some of his papers I find the following memorandum, dated April 6, 1807, a month only before his death.

' Presented to Mr. Robert Mackay, of Savannah, Georgia, a Miniature Picture representing Devotion, as a present for Mrs. Mackay, (who was then in England to Mr. Mackay, a miniature of a Scotch Lady.'

" Mrs. Mackay has also in her possession either two or three female heads, of the most exquisite finishing— some of the finest of his productions ; and a small picture of the Birth of Shakespeare, done in umber. These pictures were loaned to take out to London ; and, from some unfortunate circumstances, were never returned.

" There is a fine Miniature of Colonel Scolbay, of Boston, in possession of his daughters ; they told me that Stuart used to come, at least once a year, to see it, desiring them to take great care of it, as it was decidedly the finest miniature in the world.

" Agreeably to Dr. Francis' request, I subjoin a list of some of the paintings done in Charleston, S. C. in 1803 and 1804 ; the memorandum for 1805 and 1806, &c. not being at hand.

" Dr. Bruilesford ; Mr. R. A. Fraser ; Mrs, Cockran ; Mrs. Ball ; Mrs. Thomas Pinckney ; Mr. Sam. Sawbere ; Mrs. F. Rutledge ; Mrs. F. Haywood ; Mr. Vaughan ; Mrs. Sinkler ; Mrs. Trappere ; Miss Huger ; Mrs. Edward Rutledge ; Mrs. Loundes ; Major Wrag ; Mr. Manigault ; Mrs. Poincet ; General Pinckney ; Major Hamilton ; Dr. W. Allston ; Mrs. Middleton ; Mr. Izard's three daughters ; Col. Chesnut ; Mr. Bowman ; Mrs. Calhoun ; Miss Sarah Loadson ; Miss Fenwick ; Mrs Gadson ; Dr. Poinsett ; Miss Poinsett ; Dr. Drayton ; Mr. Ratcliff. He also painted a picture of Col. Trumbull, and a number of others, in New-York."

PAGE 161

" During the second year of his residence at Rome, he painted his celebrated picture of ' Marius amid the ruins of Carthage,' which met the general approbation of the artists assembled there, and gave him reputation.*

---

* Mrs. Child has published the following beautiful lines on Mr. Vanderlyn's Marius:

Pillars are fallen at thy feet,
  Fanes quiver in the air,
A prostrate city is thy seat—
  And thou alone art there.

No change comes o'er thy noble brow,
  Though ruin is around thee ;
Thy eye-beam burns as proudly now
  As when the laurel crown'd thee.

It cannot bend thy lofty soul,
  Though friends and fame depart ;
The car of Fate may o'er thee roll,
  Nor crush thy Roman heart.

And genius hath electric power,
  Which earth can never tame;
Bright suns may scorch, and dark clouds lower,
  Its flash is all the same.

The dreams we loved in early life,
  May melt like mist away;
High thoughts may seem 'midst passion's strife,
  Like Carthage in decay.

And proud hopes in the human heart,
  May be to ruin hurl'd,
Like mouldering monuments of art,
  Heap'd on a sleeping world.

Yet there is something will not die,
  Where life hath once been fair ;
Some towering thoughts still rear on high,
  Some Roman lingers there.

PAGE 182

While Mr. Peale was in London he published a memoir on the Mammoth, which is honourably mentioned and quoted by Cuvier.*

* In the year 1802 the skeleton of the Mammoth having been completed by the ingenuity of Charles Wilson Peale, it was determined that Rembrandt should take the monster to England, and the following advertisement was issued from the press: "AMERICAN MIRACLE.—The skeleton, with which it is Mr. Rembrandt Peale's intention shortly to visit Europe, was yesterday so far put together, that previous to taking it to pieces for the purpose of packing it up, HE AND TWELVE other gentlemen partook of a collation WITHIN THE BREAST of the animal, all comfortably seated round a small table, and one of Mr. Hawkins's patent portable pianos; after which the following toasts were drank accompanied by music." I omit the toasts.

PAGE 225

But of Jarvis's stories it is very difficult to give an idea.— He introduced them well and pointed them happily. Beside that his hearers were generally, if not excited by wine, or whiskey punch, at least divested of all worldly care for the moment, and ready for frolic and fun. Few *readers* are in this state. However, I shall endeavour to tell two or three of those stories in sober black and white, which have amused the companions of the painter at the board, or the auditors of Mathews in the theatre; for the comedian derived some of his best extravaganzas from the Yankee painter. Mathews told the following to the writer in private company, and he repeated it to Hacket at Utica, before he made the stage his profession. Hacket has since dramatized it, with what success I know not; but as the incident is very simple, I should think it was not sufficiently dramatic for the theatre.

"An old French gentleman, who resided at Charleston, as a place of refuge from the horrors of the Parisian revolution and massacres, anxiously awaited a letter from his only child, a daughter, left in Paris. This gentleman's name was *Mallet*, which, as my readers know, is by the French pronounced *Mallai*. The interest, or the humour of the story of Monsieur Mallet, rests altogether on the different modes of pronouncing the name by French or Englishmen. The emigrant is supposed to be a man of rank, with the courteous manners of a noble of the old school, and all the national vivacity, with the irritability of the pampered aristocracy of the monarchical regime. He goes to the post-office, with the anxious feelings of a parent, who had been obliged to leave his child exposed to dangers from which he had fled; and he knocks at the window where inquiries for letters are made. The clerk opens the little door which supplies the place of a pane of glass, and presents his face as ready to answer questions. "Sair, if you please, sair, have you any lettaire for Monsieur Mallai?"— The clerk looks among the M's, and then answers respectfully, "None, sir." "Mon Dieu! is it possible? It is ver strange, sair. It is now more dan six mont dat I hear noting from my shilde, my daughter, sair." "None, sir;" and the little door is shut. Monsieur Mallet bows and walks away. Again and again Monsieur Mallet appears, and knocks, and asks for a letter for Monsieur Mallai, and receives the same answer, "None, sir." At length, having received the usual answer, he makes request for search, with the utmost politeness. "I pray you, sair, be so good look again; perhaps it is mislaid: it is now more dan six monts since I hear noting of my daughter, who is in Paris, and exposed, sair, for my sake, for de sake of her fader, to all de ferocity of de Jacobin regicide faction, and de fury ——" "I have looked—there is no letter for you." "Oh! mon Dieu! she must have been sacrificed! My dear sair!——" The door is shut. The poor old gentleman walks sorrowfully away. This goes on, with every variation that the good teller of good stories can invent.

At length when Monsieur Mallet is sitting at the café and reading the newspapers, he sees a long list of letters advertised by the post-office, as uncalled for. Eagerly, though hopelessly, he looks over the columns, and to his astonishment he sees a letter noticed for Monsieur Mallet, as one that had not been asked for. His blood both natural and aristocratical boils with rage. He seizes the newspaper and hastens to the post-office, determined to convict the postmaster or clerk. He has the evidence of their guilt and falsehood in his pocket. He knocks as usual, and assumes a look of more than usual courtesy. The clerk appears, with no very pleasant aspect. "So, sair, I suppose dare is no lettaire for Monsieur Mallai—ha?" "There is no arrival since you were here this morning." "And dare is noting for Monsieur Mallai—ha?" "Nothing." "No lettaire?" "I tell you none." "A ha! None!" His rage breaking out by degrees. "None! You will please to look again, sair!" "I have looked again and again, and I tell you there is none." "Stop sair, don't you shut dat leetle door in my face!—Dare is no lettaire for Monsieur Mallai? 'Now sair," producing the newspaper, "for vat you tell me mont after mont dat dare is *none! none!* I will show you, sair, look at dis paper, sair; is dis from your post-offeece?" "To be sure it is." "Aha! It is; den look

dare, dare is a lettaire for Monsieur Mallai ! dare sair, dare !"
striking the paper with his finger and trembling with rage.
" It may be *there*, but there is none *here*." " Vat sair, you
deny your own advertisement ? Look dare sair, look dare !"
and he gives the paper and points to the name.   " O, for Mr.
Mallet ; yes, here has been a letter for Mr. Mallet this three
months, it has never been inquired for, there it is."   The
enraged noble takes the letter.   " Mon Dieu ! tree mont, and
I suffaire, you scoundrel ! you dam post-offeece ! I come every
day and ask for it dis tree, four mont."   " You *never* asked
for it !"

An altercation takes place ; the enraged father forgets what
it is that he holds in his hand ; the insult to his dignity by
the denial of his assertion, drives from his mind all other images—the daughter—the precious letter is not thought of, and
as he raves he tears the document, which he had so long
yearned for, into pieces, and scatters the fragments, when
reduced to the smallest size, in every direction to the winds.
He is brought to his senses by a demand for the postage. He
looks for the letter—he feels his pocket—he is soon convinced
that the intelligence from his daughter, so long and anxiously
sought, has been irretrievably lost by the indulgence of rage
at its detention.   If there is any moral to the tale it is, that
the indulgence of passion inevitably leads to misery and
repentance.

This post-office story suggests another, which I will tell,
though not one of Jarvis's.   An English merchant, whose
name was unfortunately adapted to the addition of that aspi-
rate which causes such murder of the king of England's language, for in that country the language is the king's, although
they may have imported him from Germany or Holland,
where he never heard it spoken.   Thus the cockney who
talks of *hatmospheric hair* is said to murder the king's English.   So our English trader, whose name was Ogton, always
called himself by the degrading appellation of Hogtown,
following the London practice of adding an *h* in speaking,
when it was necessarily omitted in writing.

In the earlier times of his residence in America, and before
the clerks of the post-office knew his person or he had clerks
to send for his despatches, he called day after day to inquire
if there were " any letters for John Hogtown ?" and the invariable reply was, " None, sir." " Very strange," said he, and
he began to feel as uneasy about his goods and bills of exchange as Monsieur Mallet about his daughter.   One day

after the usual question of " Any letters for John Hogtown ?"
His eye followed the clerk and he observed that he was looking among the letters beginning with *H.* " Olloh!" cried
honest John, "what are you doing there ? I said John Hogtown." · " I know it sir, and I am looking for John Hogtown.
There is nothing for you sir." " Nay, nay !" shouted John,
" don't look among the *haitches*, look among the *hoes.*" And
among the *O*'s, John Ogton's letters had been accumulating
for months. We can scarcely conceive a more. efficacious
lesson to mend a merchant's cacophony.

Another story, which Mathews dressed up for John Bull,
originated with Jarvis. From a friend I have what I suppose
to be the original scene. My friend was passing the painter's
room, when he suddenly threw up the windows and called him
in, saying, " I have something for your criticism, that you
will be pleased with." He entered, expecting to see a picture,
or some other specimen of the fine arts, but nothing of the
kind was produced—he was, however, introduced with a great
deal of ceremony as Monsieur B—, " celebrated for his
accurate knowledge of the English language, and intimate
critical acquaintance with its poetry—particularly Shakspeare." Mr. A—, as I shall call my friend, began to
understand Jarvis's object in calling him in.—After a little
preliminary conversation, Jarvis said, " I hope, Monsieur
B—, you still retain your love of the drama ?" " O certainly, sir, wid my life I renounce it." " Mr. A—, did
you ever hear Monsieur recite ?" " Never." " Your recitations from Racine, Monsieur—will you oblige us ?"

The polite and vain Frenchman was easily prevailed upon
to roll out several long speeches, from Racine and Corneille
with much gesticulation and many a well-rounded *R.* This
was only to introduce the main subject of entertainment.
" Monsieur B— is not only remarkable, as you hear,
for his very extraordinary recitations from the poets of his
native land, but for his perfect conquest over the difficulties of
the English language, in the most difficult of all our poets—
Shakspeare. He has studied Hamlet and Macbeth thorough—
and if he would oblige us—do Monsieur B—, do give us
' To be, or not to be.' " " Sur, the language is too difficult—
I make great efforts to be sure, but still the foreigner is to be
detected." This gentleman's peculiarities were in extreme
precision and double efforts with the *th* and the other shibbo-
leths of English. The unsuspecting and vain man is soon induced to give Hamlet's soliloquy, the *th* forced out as from a

pop-gun, and some of the words irrisistibly comic. " But, Monsieur B—, you are particularly great in Macbeth— *that* ' if it were done, when it is done,' and, ' peep through the blanket,'—come, let us have Macbeth." Then followed Macbeth's soliloquies in the same style. All this was ludicrous enough, but upon this foundation Jarvis raised a superstructure, which he carried as high as the zest with which it was received by his companions, his own feelings, or other circumstances prompted or warranted. The unfortunate Monsieur B— was imitated and caricatured with most laugh-provoking effect; but to add to the treat, he was made not only to recite, but to comment and criticize. " If it were done," " peep through the blanket," and, " catch with the sursease, success," gave a rich field for the imaginary critic's commentaries—then he would expose, and overthrow Voltaire's criticisms, and give as examples of the true sublime in tragedy, the scene of the witches in Macbeth.

" Huen shall we ththree meet aggen ?" but, " mounched, and mounched, and mounched," was a delicious feast for the critic—and " rrump fed rronion," gave an opportunity to show that the English witch was a true John Bull, and fed upon the " rrump of the beef," " thither in a sieve I'll sail and like a rat without a tail, I'll do—I'll do—I'll do," being recited in burlesque imitation, gives an opportunity for comment and criticism, something in this manner. " You see not only how true to nature, but to the science of navigation all this is. If the rat had a tail, he could steer the sieve as the sailor steer his ship by the rudder ; but if he have no tail, he cannot command the navigation, that is the course of the sieve ; and it will run round—and round—and round—that is what the witch say—' I'll do—I'll do—I'll do !' "—But how can the humour of the story-teller be represented by the writer— or how can I dispose my reader to receive a story dressed in cold black and white—in formal type—with the same hilarity which attends upon the table, and the warm and warming rosy wine ? The reader has perceived the want of these magical auxiliaries in the above. But all Jarvis's stories did not want the aid of the bottle to give them zest. I remember meeting him when soberly walking in the Mall, at Boston, and he gave as a travelling incident connected with his journey from New-York, the following narrative, which if I mistake not, does not require the powers of the goblet to support it.

" We had for companions in the stage four travellers like ourselves, and two of them luckily proved characters. General Q—, who is a most dignified personage, and so self-important as to be unapproachable, and a sprightly little French gentleman who had no hesitation in approaching any one. He had seen enough of the world to know how to make himself agreeable, and he had all the 'dispositions in the world' to do so. The foreign gentleman soon addressed the American general with 'Wer fine weddair, sair!' The great man drew himself to his greatest height—not less than six feet two—and answered by something like a sound you may have heard from a pig-pen, a kind of 'humph.' By and by the French gentleman took out his snuff box, gave it a lively tap, and presented this link in the social system to the military hero, who drew back without even deigning a bow of thanks. The box was handed round, and Henry and I took each a pinch and entered into conversation with the owner; who, as if he was determined not to be repulsed by the ill-breeding of the self-sufficient yankee general, (who, by the by, came from south of the Delaware, again with great suavity of manner took the opportunity which a jolt gave, to remark on the state of the roads; but he only received a still more repulsive 'humph.' The Frenchman then turned his back upon the warrior, and without appearing to notice his insolence, entered again into familiar chat with less dignified companions of the voyage, but from that time he began to show marked contempt for the general.

"At the end of the day's journey, we were all shown into the room appropriated to travellers who journey by the stage; but the general, as if his dignity had been offended by such democratic treatment, after a minute or two of surly silence, called loudly for the waiter. Instantly the Frenchmen echoed him—'Vaitaire?' The general looked at the little man and seated himself. The little man looked at the great general, and took his seat also. The waiter, an Irishman, entered and stood between the incipient belligerents, looking unutterable mis-intelligence. 'Bring me a pair of slippers!' said the man of insulted dignity. 'Bring a me *two* pair sleepaire!' shouted Monsieur. The general looked ten thousand contempts. Pat stood like Francis between fat Jack and lean Hal. 'Give me a candle, sir!' said the *militaire*. 'Bring a me, sair, *two* candaile!' shouted the foreigner. Pat was immovable—an image of confusion worse confounded. 'Quick, sir,' said the general, 'show me to a bed.' 'Queek, sair,' was the echo, 'show me to *two* beds.'

"The general kept up his dignity by retiring from the contest, and the next day proceeded in a private carriage.

"'Now if I know the maining of this, I'll be bothered!'

said Pat." It means that common courtesy when travelling smooths the road better than macadamizing.

I dramatized this story in a farce called "A trip to Niagara," and with effect. I will attempt one more of Jarvis's stories; which, as I did not hear it from him, the reader may imagine to be in Jarvis's language or in mine, as seems most agreeable to his notions of verisimilitude.

"Some years ago, when it fell out that in the fall of the year the yellow fever visited New-York before the 'yellow leaf' appeared in the country, I took refuge at a farmer's house on Long Island, where I saved *my* bacon and eat *his*. He had an empty building about half a mile off, which I hired for my painting room, and thither conveyed my unfinished pictures, my paints, brushes, oils, and varnishes, and took my seat, palette, and maul-stick in hand by my esel. No one came to see me, for I had nothing to eat or drink at this place, and the only living creature that patronized me was a cat. I thought at first that she was one of the farmer's family; but soon found that puss was a fixture in my painting establishment, and never moved any distance from the door, that is, not out of doors, generally sleeping near my esel, (as soon as she found that I was a quiet, inoffensive creature like herself,) and every day, about a certain hour, walked lazily up stairs to the garret. I say lazily, for she was too fat to move otherwise. The plump and sleek condition of this cat, caused a con*cate*nation of conjectures to pass through my mind with the force of projectiles from a *cat*apult—in short, my thoughts were like a *cat*aclysm, and overwhelmed me like a *cat*aract: to give you a *cat*alogue of them is impossible. The question was, 'how could this *cat*-creature keep up fat and flesh in a place where there was nothing to eat?' This worried me thin. I could not paint for thinking of this fat cat. It was a secret worth the philosopher's stone. It was the *cat*holicon. If a man could live, and live fat, without eating, he might laugh at fortune and defy death. I could not make it out; and it was in vain to *cat*echize the cat. Her answers, though not *cat*echistical, were as far from the purpose as if they were. To *catch* the cat napping was no difficulty, for except when she took her walk up stairs, she was as stationary as a *cat*head. 'The mystery must be in the garret, and I'll dog the cat but I'll find who *cat*ers for her.' So thought I.

"Accordingly, the next time puss stretched herself after the usual nap, I put down palette, pencils, and maul stick, and prepared not only to follow the cat but the *cat*enation, (if I could but discover it) until the *cat*astrophe should be established *cat*egorically. Up went puss and up went I, as silent as *cat*gut dissevered from horse hair. I took off my new boots, for they squeaked like *cat*calls. I tried to avoid being seen. I kept out of the line of direct vision, and there was nothing that could discover me *catoptrically*.

I saw puss very deliberately sit down and lick the bottom of her feet. "If that's necessary," thinks I, "I can't do it."—Puss having performed this leading operation with as much gout as if the soles of her feet were *cat*es, or as a gourmand would lick his lips when sauced with *cat*sup, she got up and traversed the centre of the room, backwards and forwards, as if confined within a circle. Looking sharply at the spot on the floor which seemed to confine her, as a *cat*erpillar would be if surrounded by a ring of molasses, I saw that it was covered with small seed. This I knew would, with the saliva, form a *cat*aplasm. My curiosity was now intense. The cat, having satisfied herself that all was ready for the next step, approached a window, always open, because broken half out, and making one spring, vanished. There was no light, as you perceive, thrown upon the subject by the window; but I would not lose sight of my *cat*er-cousin and prospect of immortality thus. I came from the hole, as dark as a *cat*acomb, where I had been ensconced, and on tiptoe went to another broken window, all the time expecting to hear a *cat*erwauling on the house-top—but no, all was silent as *Cat*aline. I looked out and saw puss in the gutter—on her back—her legs stiff and fixed upright as if she had been struck by *cat*alepsis. In short, my teacher of a way to live forever, appeared dead and stark as a fried *cat*fish. I was not long at my window before a little chipping-bird alighted on the roof, and came hopping towards puss. The little rogue shyed for a while, then started, and was winging its flight over the cat's feet, when seeing the seed, he wheeled round, closed his wings, and descended on her forepaw. No sooner did his beak touch the bait, but the trap closed on his head—he struggled—gave a faint stream—and I saw in the *cat*astrophe a *cat*egorical answer to all my doubts, and an end to my vision of life without eating.

"Thus you see she contrived to *cat*er for herself by becoming a *cat*-erect though on her back, and every bird she made a shift to *cat*ch was an addition to the string of *cat*astrophes on which she feasted. I found that all the difference between puss's way of living and mine, was that she killed and dressed her own tid-bits – she 'killed her own mutton.'

" My only consolation for this overthrow of all my hopes of
being a second St. Leon, was to sit down and draw up a
statement of this case, which I entitled *Catology*. This document is deposited among the archives of the New-York Philosophical Society ; and ensures me one kind of immortality,
though I have been disappointed in that which I confess is
more to my way of thinking."

PAGE 317

This is true, and these qualities, with study and
instruction, were united in the subject of this memoir.*

* The reader of this unpoetical book shall be indulged with a description of
autumn, from " The Sylphs of the Seasons."

And now, in accents deep and low,
Like voice of fondly-cherish'd wo,
   The Sylph of Autumn said :
Though I may not of raptures sing,
That grac'd the gentle song of Spring,
Like Summer, playful pleasures bring,
   Thy youthful heart to glad ;

Yet still may I in hope aspire
Thy heart to touch with chaster fire,
   And purifying love :
For I with vision high and holy,
And spell of quick'ning melancholy,
Thy soul from sublunary folly
   First rais'd to worlds above.

What though be mine the treasures fair
Of purple grape and yellow pear,
   And fruits of various hue,
And harvests rich of golden grain,
That dance in waves along the plain
To merry song of reaping swain,
   Beneath the welkin blue ;

With these I may not urge my suit,
Of Summer's patient toil the fruit,
   For mortal purpose given :
Nor may it fit my sober mood
To sing of sweetly murmuring flood,
Or dies of many-colour'd wood,
   That mock the bow of heaven.

But know, 'twas mine the secret power
That wak'd thee at the midnight hour,
   In bleak November's reign :
'Twas I the spell around thee cast,
When thou didst hear the hollow blast
In murmurs tell of pleasures past,
   That ne'er would come again :

And led thee, when the storm was o'er,
To hear the sullen ocean roar,

By dreadful calm opprest;
Which still, though not a breeze was there,
Its mountain-billows heav'd in air,
As if a living thing it were,
      That strove in vain for rest.

'Twas I; when thou, subdu'd by wo,
Didst watch the leaves descending slow,
      To each a moral gave;
And as they mov'd in mournful train,
With rustling sound, along the plain,
Taught them to sing a seraph's strain
      Of peace within the grave.

And then uprais'd thy streaming eye,
I met thee in the western sky
      In pomp of evening cloud;
That, while with varying from it roll'd,
Some wizard's castle seem'd of gold,
And now a crimson'd knight of old,
      Or king in purple proud.

And last, as sunk the setting sun,
And Evening with her shadows dun,
      The gorgeous pageant past,
'Twas then of life a mimic show,
Of human grandeur here below,
Which thus beneath the fatal blow
      Of Death must fall at last.

Oh, then with what aspiring gaze
Didst thou thy tranced vision raise
      To yonder orbs on high,
And think how wondrous, how sublime
'Twere upwards to their spheres to climb,
And live, beyond the reach of Time,
      Child of Eternity!

And as the "Paint King" belongs to our subject, the reader may, if he pleases be amused with this playful balled in imitation, and in burlesque of Scott's "Fire King," Lewis's "Cloud King," and other sportive effusions much read at that time.

Fair Ellen was long the delight of the young,
      No damsel could with her compare;
Her charms were the theme of the heart and the tongue,
And bards without number in ecstasies sung,
      The beauties of Ellen the fair.

Yet cold was the maid; and though legions advanc'd
      All drill'd by Ovidean art,
And languish'd, and ogled, protested and danced,
Like shadows they came, and like shadows they glanced
      From the hard polish'd ice of her heart.

Yet still did the heart of fair Ellen implore
      A something that could not be found;
Like a sailor she seem'd on a desolate shore,
With nor house, nor a tree, nor a sound but the roar
      Of breakers high dashing around.

From object to object still, still would she veer,
      Though nothing, alas, could she find;

Like the moon, without atmosphere, brilliant and clear,
Yet doom'd, like the moon, with no being to cheer
 The bright barren waste of her mind.

But rather than sit like a statue so still
 When the rain made. her mansion a *pound,*

Up and down would she go, like the sails of a mill,
And pat every stair, like a woodpecker's bill,
 From the tiles of the roof to the ground.

One morn, as the maid from her casement inclin'd,
 Pass'd a youth, with a frame in his hand.
The casement she clos'd—not the eye of her mind ;
For, do all she could, no, she could not be blind ;
 Still before her she saw the youth stand.

" Ah, what can he do," said the languishing maid,
 " Ah, what with that frame can he do ?"
And she knelt to the Goddess of Secrets, and prayed,
When the youth pass'd again, and again he displayed
 The frame and a picture to view.

" Oh, beautiful picture !" the fair Ellen cried,
 " I must see thee again or I die."
Then under her white chin her bonnet she tied,
And after the youth and the picture she hied,
 When the youth, looking back, met her eye.

" Fair damsel," said he, (and he chuckled the while)
 " This picture I see you admire :
Then take it, I pray you, perhaps 'twill beguile
Some moments of sorrow ; (nay, pardon my smile)
 Or, at least, keep you home by the fire."

Then Ellen the gift with delight and surprise
 From the cunning young stripling receiv'd
But she knew not the poison that enter'd her eyes,
When sparkling with rapture they gaz'd on her prize—
 Thus, alas, are fair maidens deceiv'd !

'Twas a youth o'er the form of a statue inclined,
 And the sculptor he seem'd of the stone ;
Yet he languish'd as though for its beauty he pined
And gaz'd as the eyes of the statue so blind
 Reflected the beams of his own.

'Twas the tale of the sculptor Pygmalion of old ;
 Fair Ellen remember'd and sigh'd;
" Ah, couldst thou but lift from that marble so cold,
Thine eyes too imploring, thy arms should enfold,
 And press me this day as thy bride."

She said : when, behold, from the canvas arose
 The youth, and he stepped from the frame ;
With a furious transport his arms did enclose
The love-plighted Ellen : and, clasping, he froze
 The blood of the maid with his flame !

She turn'd and beheld on each shoulder a wing,
 " Oh, heaven !" cried she, " who art thou ?"
From the roof to the ground did his fierce answer ring,
As frowning, he thunder'd " I am the PAINT-KING !
 " And mine, lovely maid, thou art now !"

Then high from the ground did the grim monster lift
    The loud-screaming maid like a blast;
And he sped through the air like a meteor swift,
While the clouds, wand'ring by him, did fearfully drift
    To the right and the left as he pass'd.

Now suddenly sloping his hurricane flight,
    With an eddying whirl he descends;
The air all below him becomes black as night,
And the ground where he treads, as if moved with affright
    Like the surge of the Caspian bends.

"I am here!" said the Fiend, and he thundering knock'd
    At the gates of a mountainous cave;
The gates open flew, as by magic unlock'd,
While the peaks of the mount, reeling to and fro, rock'd
    Like an island of ice on the wave.

"Oh, mercy!" cried Ellen, and swoon'd in his arms,
    But the Paint-King, he scoff'd at her pain.
"Prithee, love," said the monster, "what mean these alarms?"
She hears not, she sees not the terrible charms,
    That work her to horror again.

She opens her lids, but no longer her eyes
    Behold the fair youth she would woo;
Now appears the Paint-King in his natural guise:
His face, like a palette of villanous dies,
    Black and white, red and yellow, and blue.

On the skull of a Titan, that Heaven defied,
    Sat the fiend, like the grim giant Gog,
While aloft to his mouth a large pipe he applied,
Twice as big as the Eddystone Lighthouse, descried
    As it looms through an easterly fog.

And anon. as he puff'd the vast volumes, were seen
    In horrid festoons an the wall,
Legs and arms, heads and bodies emerging between,
Like the drawing-room grim of the Scotch Sawney Beane,
    By the Devil dress'd out for a ball.

"Ah me!" cried the damsel, and fell at his feet
    "Must I hang on these walls to be dried?"
"Oh, no!" said the fiend, while he sprung from his seat,
"A far nobler fortune thy person shall meet;
    Into paint will I grind thee, my bride!"

Then, seizing the maid by her dark auburn hair,
    An oil jug he plung'd her within.
Seven days, seven nights, with the shrieks of despair,
Did Ellen in torment convulse the dun air,
    All cover'd with oil to the chin.

On the morn of the eighth on a huge sable stone
    Then Ellen, all reeking, he laid;
With a rock for his muller he crush'd every bone,
But, though ground to jelly, still, still did she groan;
    For life had forsook not the maid.

Now reaching his palette, with masterly care
    Each tint on its surface he spread;
The blue of her eyes, and the brown of her hair,

And the pearl and the white of her forehead so fair,
    And her lips' and her cheeks' rosy red.

Then, stamping his foot, did the monster exclaim,
    " Now I brave, cruel Fairy thy scorn !"
When lo ! from a chasm wide-yawning there came
A light tiny chariot of rose-colour'd flame,
    By a team of ten glow-worms upborne.

Enthron'd in the midst of an emerald bright,
    Fair Geraldine sat without peer ;
Her robe was a gleam of the first blush of light,
And her mantle the fleece of a noon-cloud white,
    And a beam of the moon was her spear.

In an accent that stole on the still charmed air
    Like the first gentle language of Eve,
Thus spake from her chariot the Fairy so fair :
" I come at thy call, but, Oh Paint-King, beware,
    Beware if again you deceive.'

' 'Tis true," said the monster, "thou queen of my heart,
    Thy portrait I oft have essay'd ;
Yet ne'er to the canvas could I with my art
The least of thy wonderful beauties impart ;
    And my failure with scorn you repaid.

" Now I swear by the light of the Comet-King's tail !"
    And he tower'd with pride as he spoke,
"If again with these magical colours I fail,
The crater of Etna shall hence be my jail,
    And my food shall be sulphur and smoke.

" But if I succeed, then, oh, fair Geraldine !
    Thy promise with justice I claim,
And thou, queen of Fairies, shall ever be mine,
The bride of my bed ; and thy portrait divine
    Shall fill all the earth with my fame."

He spake ; when, behold, the fair Geraldine's form
    On the canvas enchantingly glowed ;
His touches—they flew like the leaves in a storm
And the pure pearly white and the carnation warm
    Contending in harmony flow'd.

And now did the portrait a twin-sister seem
    To the figure of Geraldine fair :
With the same sweet expression did faithfully teem
Each muscle, each feature ; in short not a gleam
    Was lost of her beautiful hair.

'Twas the Fairy herself ! but, alas, her blue eyes
    Still a pupil did ruefully lack ;
And who shall describe the terrific surprise
That seiz'd the Paint-King, when, behold, he descries
    Not a speck on his palette of black !

"I am lost !" said the Fiend, and he shook like a leaf ;
    When, casting his eyes to the ground,
He saw the lost pupils of Ellen with grief
In the jaws of a mouse, and the sly little thief
    Whisk away from his sight with a bound.

"I am lost !" said the Fiend, and he fell like a stone ;
    Then rising the Fairy in ire,

With a touch of her finger she loosen'd her zone,
(While the limbs on the wall gave a terrible groan,)
   And she swelled to a column of fire.

Her spear now a thunder-bolt flash'd in the air,
   And sulphur the vault fill'd around :
She smote the grim monster ; and now by the hair
High-lifting, she hurl'd him in speechless despair
   Down the depths of the chasm profound.

Then over the picture thrice waving her spear,
   "Come forth!" said the good Geraldine ;
When, behold, from the canvas descending appear
Fair Ellen, in person more lovely than e'er,
   With grace more than ever divine !

PAGE 382

" About the same time," says Mr. Lambdin, " appeared at Pittsburgh a French refugee, who painted small portraits in an indifferent style. He figured in the triple capacity of painter, musician, and dancing-master." His name was Bourdon.

My friend, R. Gilmor, Esq. of Baltimore, says, that " Wm. West was the son of the rector of St. Paul's, Baltimore ; and showing, by attempts at painting, that he had incipient talent, was sent, in 1789 or 90 to England, to his name-sake, Benj. West, and studied under his instruction." I am led to believe that this gentleman, after returning home, married and settled in Lexington, Kentucky, and became the father of W.E.West, who will occupy another page of this work.